LEONARD WOOD

JACK McCALLUM

LEONARD WOOD

Rough Rider, Surgeon,
Architect of American Imperialism

New York University Press • *New York and London*

NEW YORK UNIVERSITY PRESS
New York and London
www.nyupress.org

Library of Congress Cataloging-in-Publication Data
McCallum, Jack Edward, 1945–
Leonard Wood : rough rider, surgeon, architect
of American imperialism / Jack McCallum.
p. cm.
Includes bibliographical references and index.
ISBN–13: 978–0–8147–5699–7 (cloth : alk. paper)
ISBN–10: 0–8147–5699–9 (cloth : alk. paper)
1. Wood, Leonard, 1860–1927.   2. Generals—United States—
Biography.   3. United States. Army Biography.   4. United States.
Army—Surgeons—Biography.   5. Spanish–American War,
1898—Biography.   6. Military governors—Cuba—Biography.
7. Presidential candidates—United States—Biography.
8. Governors general—Philippines—Biography.   9. Philippines—
Politics and government—1898–1935.   10. United States—
Territorial expansion.   11. United States—History, Military.   I. Title.
E181.W856M33   2005
973.91'092—dc22   2005013002

New York University Press books are printed on acid-free paper,
and their binding materials are chosen for strength and durability.

Manufactured in the United States of America
10 9 8 7 6 5 4 3 2 1

To Dana, Katie, Jen, and Merrin

Contents

All illustrations appear as a group following p. 198.

Acknowledgments

This book would not have been possible without the help and encouragement of a number of people. The help of the research staff of the manuscript division of the Library of Congress and the research staff at the Southwestern branch of the National Archives were invaluable. My agent Kristin Nelson helped me organize the manuscript into a more accessible form and my editor Debbie Gershenowitz made it a better book than it might have been. Dr. Peter Janetta first introduced me to Leonard Wood and told me the story of his operations. Special thanks are due to Spencer Tucker, who shepherded me through my graduate training in history and gave unstintingly of his time in reviewing and correcting this manuscript. Of course, any errors of fact or interpretation are mine alone.

I

Boston, 1927

AT 9:30 in the morning on August 6, 1927, an orderly wheeled sixty-seven-year-old Leonard Wood into the neurosurgical operating room at Boston's Peter Bent Brigham Hospital. The general's brain tumor, operated twice in the previous twenty-two years, had recurred and rendered him paralyzed on the left side and nearly blind. Wood had been a physician, an Indian fighter, a Rough Rider, chief of staff of the army, governor of Cuba and the Philippines, and very nearly president of the United States. This day he was a patient with his life in another man's hands.

That man was Harvey Cushing, the legendary chairman of the Brigham's surgery service. Wood's tumor was large, bloody, and in a singularly dangerous part of the brain; the chief warned his team they were in for a "desperate procedure."[1] Cushing had been in the midst of a European tour, celebrating his extraordinary scientific and surgical achievements, when Dr. Alexander Lambert of New York urgently wired that the general had just returned from the Philippines in shocking condition and needed immediate surgery.[2]

Cushing was taken aback at Wood's deterioration and awed by his courage. He found the general "bloated in body and face . . . crumpled up on a couch with face distorted, eyes almost closed, a grotesque, pitiful figure, yet talking as though there were nothing particular the matter with him at all."[3] Wood had to be led about, dressed, and all but fed by his Chinese nurse but still insisted that Cushing operate immediately so he could get back to eradicating leprosy in the Philippines. The next morning Cushing took Wood and his wife up to Boston and checked his old friend into the hospital.

That night Wood ate a light dinner and shampooed before retiring. The next morning, the general was awakened early so Cushing's barber could shave his head, already scored with deep horseshoe-shaped scars from the previous procedures. The general's bare scalp was washed again and wrapped in a towel before he was brought into the operating room and transferred to a white enamel table. Cushing's team, composed of an anesthetist, surgical nurses, assistant surgeons, and an assortment of residents, congregated around the table like white-robed priests, heads covered and faces masked.

Stiff pillows and hard sand bags would hold the general still in the hours ahead. His head was wrapped in antiseptic soaked cheese cloth held in place by a black rubber band that doubled as a tourniquet. A blood pressure cuff—Cushing's innovation—was placed on Wood's arm, and, at 8:00 A.M., his scalp was injected with novocaine and adrenaline. Wood's first two operations had been done under ether, but Cushing decided late in his career that operating on awake patients forced the surgeon to be more delicate and was safer. While the local anesthetic was injected, the general talked and joked with the surgical team.[4]

Cushing cut through the cheesecloth along the old scar and peeled the skin off the skull with little trouble. Up to that point, the tourniquet and the adrenaline had done their job, but in the next few minutes things got difficult. He drilled a series of "keyholes," sawed around the edges of the old opening, and loosened the bone from the fibrous dural membrane that separated the brain from the skull. The tumor originated from that membrane and there were innumerable tenacious, bloody attachments between the skull, the dura, the tumor, and the brain. As he pried off the bone, Cushing faced his first serious hemorrhage.

Hundreds of arteries erupted in life-threatening jets. Mechanical suckers hissed and gurgled as Cushing's assistants tried to clear the field so he could see to operate. Blood poured out of the head, soaked the sheets, and pooled on the floor. Cushing spent the next four hours in "constant combat" trying to control the hemorrhage while Wood calmly chatted with the operating team. For hours the general tried to lie perfectly still, apologizing when he became restless and moved about. Then Wood's blood pressure dropped, came back, and dropped again. By 1:00 in the afternoon, Cushing was exhausted and wanted to abandon the procedure even though he had only opened the skull and had not yet started to remove the tumor. Wood, still awake and unwilling to have his wife sit through a second operation, insisted that Cushing press on.

A medical student donated 500 cc of blood, and the general's blood pressure stabilized. Cushing began to core out the center of the tumor and, as he did so, the lesion's outer rind pushed out of Wood's head.

They were past a point of no return; if the entire tumor was not removed, it would be impossible to close the wound. Over the next two hours, Cushing removed all but a nub of tumor near the top of the head. The last bit invaded the brain's large midline vein, but the spot where the tumor pierced the vein was out of sight beyond the edge of the bone opening. When Cushing pulled the last of the tumor from under the bone, the great vein tore and the hemorrhage was uncontrollable. Cushing first stuck his finger in the hole and then filled it with cotton balls. The bleeding seemed to stop and he closed the wound over the cotton and waited.[5]

For the next hour, the general lay quietly in the operating room while Cushing paced and chain smoked. Wood's pulse was stable but his blood pressure fell, and Cushing tried another transfusion. At 5:30 in the evening—nine hours into the surgery—Wood's blood pressure plummeted, he became unconscious, and Cushing was forced to reopen the wound. This time he thought he had found the main bleeder when he trapped a pumping vessel in a silver clip. Wood regained consciousness and, for the second time, Cushing packed and closed the wound and waited. Two hours later—it was now 8:20 in the evening—the general's pulse and respiration spiked; within minutes, he became unresponsive, and, at 1:50 in the morning, he died. At autopsy Wood was found to have extensive bleeding in ventricular cavities deep inside the brain; the hemorrhage had never really been controlled.[6]

Cushing was distraught. He closed his operative note with an uncharacteristic apology: "So ended the life of a gallant man through the failure on a surgeon's part to exercise good judgement regarding the proper time in the course of a critical procedure to postpone its completion for a second stage."[7] For weeks he did not operate and lay awake at night going over each detail of the procedure.[8]

That "gallant man's" professional life began in 1880, when the United States was just a generation away from the adolescent growth spurt that culminated with the Civil War. In that year, older Americans still recalled the Mexican War and their sons had fought in the war precipitated by the territorial acquisitions after that war. In the forty years that followed, the nation blossomed into the world's premier scientific, economic, political, and military power, and Wood's career touched every aspect of that evolution.

The 1880s were the decade in which American medicine transformed itself from a cult to a science, and Harvard Medical School, where Wood trained as a physician, was the nexus of that revolution. From the likes of Henry Bigelow and Oliver Wendell Holmes, he learned to apply the experimental method in understanding disease.

Wood enlisted as a military surgeon, helped capture Geronimo, and won the Medal of Honor just as Frederick Jackson Turner declared the American frontier closed. In the years that followed, he married the adopted niece of a Supreme Court justice and was Georgia Tech's first football coach before moving to Washington, where he acquired William McKinley's hypochondriacal wife as a patient and McKinley's flamboyant assistant secretary of the navy, Theodore Roosevelt, as a lifelong friend.

Having fulfilled their manifest destiny and having watched the Europeans carve up Africa and Asia, Americans cast covetous eyes on Spain's decaying empire. When Joseph Pulitzer, William Randolph Hearst, and a coterie of jingoist industrialists and politicians dragged McKinley into the Spanish War, Wood and Roosevelt browbeat him into letting them recruit a "cowboy regiment." The Rough Riders, collected from Wood's western contacts and Roosevelt's assortment of Ivy League ex-athletes, were the basis of one man's personal legend and the other's transformation from medic to professional soldier.

When eastern Cuba fell after a pair of nondescript land battles and a naval rout, the United States Army had its first taste of winning a short war and finding itself responsible for creating a government. Santiago City's abysmal sanitation threatened both Cuban inhabitants and American troops and administration of the city fell by default to the young doctor who, alone among the generals, had skills appropriate to the problem. Wood proved to be a natural administrator and a zealous autocrat. He combined his medical training with his force of personality to mobilize the city's population and turned an infamous cesspit into a livable city. He applied his prodigious capacity for work and his boundless self-confidence to disarming the Cuban insurgents, creating a bureaucracy, and restoring the economy to self-sufficiency. Within a year, he was governor general of the entire island.

Wood turned insurgents into a Rural Guard that restored order with virtually no help from the American military. He kept the existing body of Spanish law but fired corrupt judges and insisted on open, fair, documented court proceedings. He either sanitized or closed prisons, asylums, and orphanages, and he created a public education system where none had previously existed. Perhaps his crowning achievement was funding and taking responsibility for Walter Reed's yellow fever experiments and authorizing William Gorgas to use the findings to virtually eradicate yellow fever and malaria from the island. After three years, Wood turned Cuba back to the Cubans, orderly, clean, and solvent if not exactly prosperous. That what should have been a triumph and the beginning of a long and fruitful relation between Cuba and the United States was not speaks to both Wood's failings and those of his government.

In the Philippines, America did not fare as well. Unlike the Cuban insurgents, the Filipinos refused to disarm, forcing the American army into a protracted battle to control the archipelago. The worst of the fighting was against Moslem rebels, who had contested Spanish rule for centuries and had no inclination to replace masters from Madrid with new ones from Washington. Wood went to Mindanao as military commander and imposed a tenuous peace at a frightful cost in lost lives and lost trust and never accepted the idea of Philippine independence.

By the end of the new century's first decade, the United States was a world economic power with a colonial empire, but the miniscule American army remained scattered among a patchwork of western forts, suited only for fighting Indians long since confined to reservations. Wood became a passionate advocate of military reform, and, when he became chief of staff, he attacked the fossilized system of deskbound bureau chiefs that crippled American military efficiency. As the Great War approached, Wood railed against American military weakness and organized a series of privately funded summer camps that trained students and businessmen as a ready corps of reserve officers. In the process, he infuriated Woodrow Wilson and destroyed his chance for combat command.

Wood spent the war training divisions in Kansas but emerged with the reputation and popularity of one victimized by authority. Roosevelt had told his supporters that he wanted Wood to run for the Republican presidential nomination in 1920 if, for any reason, he was unable to run himself. When the old Bullmoose died in 1919, Wood collected a group of Roosevelt supporters, militarists, and wealthy industrialists and ran the most expensive presidential campaign in American history. He came to the Republican convention solidly in the lead but was defeated by a combination of political manipulation and last minute bribery.

After the election, President Warren G. Harding denied Wood a seat in the cabinet and exiled him half a world away as governor general of the Philippines to play his last part in America's maturation from international backwater to the world's lone superpower.

2

Pocasset, 1860–1880

LEONARD WOOD was born October 9, 1860, in the largest, and by all accounts the ugliest, house in Pocasset, Massachusetts, to Caroline Wood. Her husband, Dr. Charles Jewett Wood, was a dour New England Congregationalist who proudly traced his ancestry to the *Mayflower*.

Charles had taken an apprenticeship with a local physician before enrolling in the Massachusetts Medical School (later Harvard) on North Grove Street in Boston. The school was a proprietary operation where luminaries like George Shattuck, Henry Bigelow, and Oliver Wendell Holmes delivered fee-based lectures to an assortment of erratically prepared and variably attentive students. After a single winter of classes, Wood judged his prospects sufficient to consider marriage and won the hand of Caroline Hagar, an admittedly plain twenty-three-year-old from nearby Weston. The Hagars, also *Mayflower* descendants, were unenthusiastic about the impecunious student physician, but age had brought Caroline to the brink of spinsterhood. The two married in the winter of 1856, and Wood almost immediately deposited his new wife with her family and went up to Dartmouth to continue his studies. He spent that winter in New Hampshire, took a few more classes at North Grove Street the following summer, and ran out of money.

Forced to make a living, Wood took a job in Manchester, New Hampshire, painting window blinds for $25 a week. He rented a one-room apartment above a tailor shop, furnished it from a second-hand store, and brought Caroline from Massachusetts in April 1860. On October 9, they had their first child whom they named Leonard after Charles's deceased father. Painting window blinds was brutal work with no future, so Charles, without actually attending any more classes, cadged a degree from the Eclectic Medical College of Pennsylvania, an odd institution run by botanically oriented fringe practitioners, akin to Homeopaths, whom most of the orthodox medical establishment dismissed as untrained frauds.

Wood returned to Massachusetts where a successful practice proved elusive, so, after the Union's second defeat at Bull Run in August 1862, he volunteered for the army. He was, however, in for yet another humiliation. Traditionally trained physicians controlled the army's medical boards and they had no use for Homeopaths, Thomsonians, or Eclectics. Wood entered the army as a lowly hospital steward for the Forty-second Massachusetts Volunteers. Bitterly disappointed, he moved Caroline and Len back into her father's house and set off to war.

Wood returned from an eleven-month tour in Louisiana weakened by malaria and spent the next seven years wandering among various Massachusetts towns trying to find a place suitable to his fragile health and limited medical talent. When Len was four, the Woods had another son, Jacob, followed by a daughter, Barbara, three years later. Ultimately, the family settled in Pocasset on the rocky hill overlooking Buzzard's Bay into which their Pilgrim ancestors had sailed two centuries earlier.

Len grew into adolescence as taciturn and withdrawn as his father. He had few friends, a quick temper, and a reputation for getting in— and winning—fights. Schooling on the south Cape was difficult. Pocasset was small, remote, and cold, and teachers seldom lasted even one term before seeking more comfortable surroundings. In 1876, Charles, who chaired the school board, hired Miss Jesse Haskell of Hallowell, Maine, as the Pocasset School's sole teacher. Like the rest, she lasted only a few months, but, when she quit, Charles brought her to live with his family and privately tutor Len in French, Latin, mathematics, literature, history, religion, and philosophy. In the summer of 1878, Wood enrolled as a day student in Pierce Academy at Middleboro, where he studied Greek, Latin, mathematics, chemistry, and physics, all taught by a young Brown graduate who doubled as the school's headmaster. Wood was an adequate but not an inspired student with a quick temper and more interest in football and fighting than academics.

After a year at Pierce, Wood tried for an appointment to the United States Naval Academy but was turned down by President Rutherford B. Hayes. He toyed with trying for West Point but, having no great interest in the army, dismissed the idea. He was nineteen years old, unemployed, mostly friendless, and without discernable plans for the future. In an effort to expand their son's limited horizons, the Woods forced Len to take dancing lessons, but the girls found the white-blond young man too stocky to be graceful and too freckled to be attractive. He considered signing up for a voyage to the Arctic, backed out at the last minute, and narrowly missed an icy death when the ship vanished without leaving a trace. His mother suggested he might sign onto a mackerel boat, but he never got around to it. The boy was drifting aimlessly.

In 1880, Len's life abruptly changed when his sister unexpectedly became ill and died. If anything ever stirred Charles Wood's phlegmatic soul, it was his daughter, and, a few days after Barbara's demise, he died as well, leaving nothing but an ungainly, expensive house and a sheaf of uncollectible bills. Caroline and Jake could just get by by taking in boarders, but Len had to fend for himself.[1]

3

Boston, 1880–1885

He wants to go to college more than any boy I ever knew, but I can't afford to send him and do justice to the other children, so he must be content with something else.[1]

THANKS TO JESSE HASKELL, Len had a bent toward learning, a tendency hampered by his father's endemic lack of funds. After Charles Wood died, Elijah Perry, his mother's stepfather, introduced Len to H. H. Hunnewell, a Wellesley businessman who had underwritten the education of other deserving men, and Hunnewell agreed to help. Although the philanthropist typically made loans rather than outright grants, he later said that, of all the men he had helped, only Wood ever made any attempt to pay him back. Exactly how much Wood received is not recorded, but it was enough to let him enroll in Harvard Medical School in 1880.[2]

Medicine through the first three-quarters of the nineteenth century was more vocation than profession and often more cult than either; aspiring physicians rarely held baccalaureates, and a medical degree was the meager cousin to the Bachelor of Arts. Courses were generally taught by a faculty of practicing physicians who collected fees from the students and divided the proceeds. The curriculum was taught by lecture with only a few lucky students getting apprenticeships that afforded exposure to actual patients; most simply got practical experience on the job after graduation. A scattering of the better schools like Harvard were loosely affiliated with actual institutions of higher education, but, even in these, academic and financial control remained the jealously guarded province of the medical faculty.[3]

Reform in American medical education began in earnest when Charles Eliot was named Harvard president in 1869. A Boston Brahmin trained in chemistry, Eliot made improvement of Harvard's professional schools his pet project, and, in spite of vigorous opposition led by the curmudgeonly surgical icon Henry Bigelow, Eliot brought the medical school's finances under university control and put its professors on salary. He increased the academic year from four to nine months and the total course from two to three years. Students, once required to pass only a majority of their courses, had to pass them all. Laboratory experience in physiology, chemistry, and pathological anatomy were added to the didactic schedule. Charles Jewett Wood learned medicine by apprenticeship and anecdote; his son would come to the profession in the vanguard of medical scientists.[4]

Wood arrived in Boston at 11 A.M. on October 1 and went directly to the medical school's industrial brick building on North Grove Street for a physiology lecture he dismissed as "rather dry."[5] From that inauspicious beginning, he proceeded across the Commons to Dr. Reginald Fitz's Back Bay office to purchase his matriculation card before he rented an attic room on Charles Street in Beacon Hill. His room was a short block from the Massachusetts General Hospital, was in sight of the Charles, and, to his relief, cost only $5.50 a week including board. By 1:00, Len was back at North Grove Street for an anatomy lecture by "Dr. Homes." Witty, erudite Oliver Wendell Holmes was a perennial student favorite and Wood "liked his appearance very much."[6]

Within the month Wood began "the dreary season of perpetual lectures, from morning till night, to large classes of more or less turbulent students."[7] Harvard medical students were subjected to five or six consecutive hours of lectures beginning at 7:00 A.M. and running through the lunch hour. The last class of the day was reserved for "Homes," the only faculty member entertaining enough to hold the students' attention late in the day. Holmes brought three things to his students that influenced Wood's future. First, he was an early proponent of the germ theory of disease. His 1843 article "Contagiousness of Puerperal Fever" preceded Ignascz Semmelweiss's classic description of the role of contamination by physicians' hands in childbed fever by several years. Second, Holmes brought a microscope back from Paris and made it part of American medical education. Finally, he was one of the earliest opponents of the "heroic" American pharmacopeia with its purgatives, emetics, and poisonous mercurials, wryly informing his colleagues that, with few exceptions, their entire list of drugs could be thrown into the sea to the ultimate benefit of their patients and the detriment of the fish.[8]

Wood was exposed to a pantheon of medical educators who straddled the chasm between classical American medicine and science. Henry Jacob Bigelow was a giant of American surgery, who had been present when William Morton first used ether at Massachusetts General Hospital in 1846, and became one of general anesthesia's most insistent advocates. Paradoxically, he was also an arch traditionalist and one of the staunchest opponents of Eliot's reforms. On the other side of the reform battles stood Henry Pickering Bowditch, grandson of the great mathematician and navigator and the first member of the medical school faculty hired solely as an investigator without clinical responsibilities. Bowditch, like Holmes, was an early proponent of the theory that bacteria caused disease and was a vociferous advocate of animal experimentation. Reginald Fitz was one of the first advocates of Rudolf Virchow's cellular pathology and had been Eliot's major ally in expanding the medical school course to three years, giving written exams, and requiring that students pass all their courses instead of just the majority.[9] The last requirement was nearly Wood's downfall. With a passing grade of 50, Wood did reasonably well in Medical Chemistry (88),[10] Holmes's Anatomy (86), and Bigelow's General Surgery (82), but he came close to disaster in Obstetrics (59), Theory and Practice (56), and Clinical Medicine (55).[11]

Eliot's reforms had shrunk the medical school class from two or three hundred to a little over sixty when Wood enrolled, but, even in the smaller group, he was a country boy in a city hard and cold as bricks in winter. Wood took to loitering around the railroad station when the train from Cape Cod was due in hopes of seeing a familiar Pocasset face. The other students formed eating clubs, but Wood, bashful and poor, remained aloof until his final year when he at last summoned the courage and funds to join the Cardiac Club, hosted a bibulous inaugural dinner at Taft's Restaurant, and, uncharacteristically, had to be carried home by a Princeton football player, a Harvard oarsman, and a New England boxing champion.[12]

Wood occasionally played tennis, rowed on the Charles, and (after being knocked out in a fight with a classmate) took boxing lessons, generally finding it easier to compete than to socialize. But a penchant for grinding effort eventually served him well; his class ranking improved each year and, at the beginning of his second year, he proudly informed Jessie Haskell, "I worked pretty hard last year, but think I was pretty well paid for it, for aside from the satisfaction of knowing that I had not wasted my time, I recd a scholarship."[13]

After three years at North Grove Street, Wood applied for an internship at Boston City Hospital, a relative newcomer in the Harvard medical system. Massachusetts General, where the students received most of their clinical exposure, was founded in 1821, but ground was not broken for Boston City until 1861, when South Boston businessman and philanthropist Elisha Goodnow left a bequest of $26,000 with the stipulation that the new hospital be built in his home wards well south of the city center. The only available site was 6.7 acres of foul landfill, crossed by an open canal carrying sewerage from Roxbury to the bay. The original four-building facility comprised an awkward Greek revival administration building, two industrial-looking brick patient pavilions, and a boiler house. The only operating room (the "ether dome") was in the attic of the administration building where light from the glass ceiling illuminated patients' various creases and crevasses. By the time Wood started his internship, an isolation building (the "foul wards"), a new medical building, a surgical building, two single story wards, and a kitchen had been added.[14]

When Wood started his internship, Boston City's resident staff had three services with a senior member, a junior member, a man assigned to the outpatient services, and an "ophthalmic extern" who did eye exams in the hospital's peripheral clinics. The usual term of service was eighteen months during which house officers lived in rooms off the patient wards that afforded only sporadic access to showers and privies and no privacy. Interns were fed hospital food and were expected to be in assigned dining hall seats at precisely defined times. Wood, unused to regimentation and constitutionally resistant to authority, was repeatedly disciplined for arriving late and landing in the wrong seat.

The hospital proper admitted over 4,800 patients and, along with its clinics downtown and in East Boston, saw nearly 12,000 outpatients a year. Of the clinics, Wood told Jessie Haskell:

> For the last 4 mo., I have been doing a good deal of dispensary work down in the rough parts of the city, having made about 2000 visits. I thought I knew something of crime and poverty before but I found that I had not even an idea of the true state of affairs. It is an experience which teaches many things, among others not to complain at trifles.

Truly one with as light a pocket as usual, and that's saying a good deal,
could go home and rejoice that he had enough to eat and a bed to sleep
on. Dickens' wildest flights are but too true. At first one distrusts
everyone, but not long. I have no finer friends in the world than
among some of the worst people in the city. I sometimes think, indeed
I know, that it must have been circumstances, not disposition, which
made them what they are. It rather shakes up a fellow's settled ideas,
though.[15]

Interns were left to their own devices in the clinics, but, at the hospital, they were expected to learn by standing back and watching senior "visiting" physicians at work. When Wood was an intern, Boston
City housed about 480 patients, many of whom were the subjects of surgical clinics held every Friday in the ether dome by the legendary David
Cheever, E. H. Bradford, and C. D. Homans. Patients were brought on
hand-powered, pulley-driven elevators that creaked up four floors
from the basement. The dome held a semicircle of observer benches rising above a cloud of carbolic acid atomized from hand pumps operated
by a relay of junior assistants. The instruments were soaked in carbolic
as well, and the surgeons washed their hands in the astringent chemi-
cal that left an acrid pungency permeating every flat surface and bit of
cloth in the room.

Anesthesia was by "open drop" ether; the liquid was dripped onto
gauze covering the patient's face, usually by a junior house officer striv-
ing mightily to strike a balance between a patient awake and fighting
and one too comatose to breathe. Respiratory rate could be counted but
was not actually recorded, and blood pressure would not be measured
for decades to come. Wood suggested rectal anesthesia in operations on
the face and head where the open drop technique was not feasible, but
senior surgeons dismissed the idea: "Rectal etherization was used . . .
with indifferent success."[16]

The house staff was allowed to function independently inside the
hospital on only the rarest of circumstances. Interns were expected to
change dressings and answer after hours calls, but they were forbidden
to operate alone without the express permission of the superintendent.
Interns were allowed to manage dire emergencies in the dark of night,
so Wood took to stretching the definition of emergency and doing more
and more on his own. In August 1884, the board of trustees put him on
probation for operating without proper supervision. Wood ignored the

warning and, a month later, after harvesting skin from a healthy child to cover another child's open wound, he was fired.

If one accepts Wood's letters to his friends and family, there is no doubt that, had he finished his internship, he would have spent his life quietly practicing medicine in Massachusetts. His training was good and he had enough contacts that he could have made a comfortable living. Without hospital privileges, his prospects suddenly went from bright to bleak. Wood was twenty-five years old, out of a job and out of money. The financial outlook for a new physician without hospital affiliation was dismal; as late as 1904, the American Medical Association estimated an average private physician's annual income to be only $750, and it was not at all unusual for a beginning practitioner to realize only $10 to $15 a month before expenses.

One of Wood's former classmates had started a practice in a downtown tenement row on Staniford Street, near North Grove. The practice had not done well, and the young doctor had taken a job with the Southern Pacific Railway so Wood took over the struggling office. He made a little money fixing broken heads referred to him by his Irish policeman landlord and tried his surgical skills on cataracts in old Gaelic women. A few of his Boston City patients followed him, but neither they nor his Staniford neighbors could often afford to pay. Business was slow and income was even slower. He covered the rent by tutoring medical students, but, by February 1885, it was obvious he needed a better way to make a living.[17]

Wood decided to try the examinations for the army medical corps in March, although he was not at all confident he could pass and was not altogether sure he wanted to be in the army if he did. Besides, he worried that if he joined the army he would never be able to come back into private practice. On the other hand, he wrote Jesse Haskell, "It means money at once and you know I am not *very* rich." A commission as army doctor came with a rank of first lieutenant and promotion came relatively quickly in the medical corps.[18] Starting pay was $25 a week ($16 in cash and the rest in lodging, food, and other allowances), far more than the average beginning private physician could earn.[19]

The examinations were difficult, lasting five hours a day for six days, and the general exams were, to Wood's mind, even more difficult than the professional ones. They included Latin, mathematics, ancient and modern history, English and American literature, chemistry, and physics. He wrote Miss Haskell, "You have no idea how severe they are." Wood had been studying for nearly a year but was taken aback by questions such as the "Blood claims of many to the English crown; chief events in Europe during the reign of James I . . . works of Chaucer, Sidney, Bacon; time of publication and in whose reign; dates at which U.S. purchased Alaska, Louisiana, etc. and sums paid, etc. This with an hour or so at the board constituting all sorts of amazing optical instruments, solving problems, served to while away the hours and show one just how little a man could know and live."[20] The general examination was followed by three days of written, oral, and practical examinations on professional subjects. With all his scores above 90, he had the second highest score of the fifty-nine who took the exams. But there was only one commission available.

Unable to make him an officer, the army offered a twelve-month contract at $100 a month if Wood was willing to go to Arizona, where Apache renegade Geronimo had just escaped the reservation and a company was being formed to chase him. The contract lacked the prestige of a commission, but there was at least the possibility of converting the contract if a spot became available. Wood signed up on June 13, 1885, and left for Arizona ten days later.

4

Fort Huachuca, 1885–1887

WOOD SIGNED his contract as acting assistant surgeon to the United States Army one month after Geronimo broke out of the White Mountain Reservation and ran for the Mexican mountains. Terrified Arizona and New Mexico settlers wanted the Apaches chased down and returned to the reservation; that required troops, and troops needed doctors. For a young surgeon who had never been out of New England, the rolling plains and oceans of wheat and corn were unfamiliar, but the open sky and expansive horizon were reminiscent of the ocean and a welcome respite from Boston's urban claustrophobia.[1]

When the first settler came from the East, the Chiricahuas had been friendly; Cochise, allowed the Butterfield Stage Company to cross his land unmolested until 1861, when Lt. John Bascom wrongly accused the Apache chief of stealing horses and kidnapping a local white boy. Cochise came to Bascom under a flag of truce only to be imprisoned by the inexperienced officer who hanged three of his relatives. The chief escaped, gathered a force of young warriors, and retreated to Arizona's Dragoon Mountains and then south to the remote safety of Mexico's Sierra Madres, where the Apaches survived for ten years by stealing cattle and killing the ranchers who tried to stop them.

In 1871, the Commissioner of Indian Affairs decided to bring the renegades to heel. The government offered a treaty that would confine the Apaches to a reservation, but Cochise, remembering his relatives hanging from United States Army gibbets, refused to negotiate.[2] Besides, the Chiricahuas had no desire to leave their upland pine forests for the sand flats of the Arizona desert.[3] That year, President Ulysses Grant sent General George Crook to Arizona with specific instructions to get the Apaches out of the hills, off the warpath, and onto a reservation.[4]

In the end, Cochise, exhausted by years of hiding in the mountains, let Crook bring him to the San Carlos Reservation, although he candidly admitted that neither he nor his tribe had any intention of giving up raiding ranches, at least on the Mexican side of the border. The situation was complicated by the fact that the San Carlos Reservation was a jumble of different Apache bands and tribes, each with a long history of rivalries and hatreds but none with experience living together.[5]

Crook barely managed to keep the Chiricahuas under control until Cochise died in 1874. Taza succeeded his father as chief, but the young man, lacking the old chief's charisma, could not hold the tribe together, and the Chiricahuas dissolved into small bands, drifted off into the mountains of Sonora, and went back to raiding ranches.[6]

Just when his maturity and judgment were most needed, Crook was transferred to the Department of the Platte to deal with a Plains Indian uprising, leaving John Clum, a sympathetic, honest Bureau of Indian Affairs agent, in charge of San Carlos. By 1875, Clum had installed an Apache police force and native-run courts on the reservation, but, just as things looked like they might stabilize even without Crook, Clum received orders to remove the Chiricahuas from San Carlos to a 2.5 million-acre reservation at White Mountain. Half the Chiricahuas agreed to the transfer, but the other half, including a band led by a forty-six-year-old Bedonkhe Apache named Goyathlay (Geronimo), broke away and melted into the Sierra Madres.[7] Geronimo's small group survived by stealing horses and cattle from Mexicans and bringing them across the border to be sold for cash or traded for rifles, hats, boots, and whiskey. While he raided in Mexico, Geronimo sometimes left his women and children camped near the Ojo Caliente agency in Arizona, a reservation occupied by his relatives the Mimbres Apaches. In March 1877, Clum was ordered to move the Mimbres tribe to White Mountain and to arrest Geronimo and any other renegades living around the agency.[8]

Geronimo was captured at Ojo Caliente and imprisoned for four months before being moved to White Mountain. The renegades tolerated the reservation until September 1881, when the cavalry, with the disingenuous justification that White Mountain held an uncontrollable number of the most recalcitrant Apaches, added several companies to their garrison. Geronimo responded by taking Cochise's son Naiche and seventy braves, women, and children and slipping back into Mexico.[9] As Wood started his second year at Harvard, Geronimo embarked on the last Indian war.

In September 1882, the army, worried that the Apaches would resume raiding in Arizona and New Mexico, thought better of Crook's reassignment and brought him back from the northern plains to Whipple Barracks in southern Arizona. Years fighting Indians had turned the general into a reluctant admirer of his adversaries, convinced that the only solution to the Indian problem was to establish the Apaches as self-governing subsistence farmers. He bought their excess hay, barley, and corn and reestablished Clum's police and court systems.

While Crook's White Mountain Indians worked toward self-sufficiency, Geronimo continued to prey on Sonora, Arizona, and New Mexico, forcing the United States and Mexico to reluctantly agree that either nation's army could cross the border in pursuit of the Apaches. In March 1883, Crook sent fifty soldiers and two hundred Apache mercenaries into the Sierra Madres to find Geronimo. The cavalry, commanded by Captain Emmet Crawford, found the Apaches' mountain camp while the men were off raiding and captured the Indian women and children. Disconsolate, Geronimo agreed to surrender so he could rejoin his family. Crook let the Apaches keep their rifles and side arms provided they would return to San Carlos and farm for a living. In May 1872, 251 Chiricahua women and children and 123 warriors started for Arizona leaving Geronimo and a handful of men behind to collect the last stray braves. Crook feared Geronimo would stay in Mexico and resume raiding, but, to his amazement, the renegade and his stragglers appeared at White Mountain eight months later. Unfortunately, they also brought along a herd of stolen Mexican cattle that the general felt bound to commandeer and sell. To Geronimo's lasting disgust, Crook gave the $1760 profit back to the Mexicans.

For a little more than a year Crook could brag that there was not a single hostile Apache in his department. Crook's combination of sympathy for indigenous opponents who followed his rules and implacable opposition to those who did not would make a lasting impression on young Leonard Wood. A second Crook strategy that Wood later employed in both Cuba and the Philippines was using natives to control natives. Crook's long-time adjutant said his boss learned that ploy from British colonial administrators, and that "General Crook is the only officer of our army who has fully recognized the incalculable value of a native contingent, and in all his campaigns of the past thirty-five years has drawn about him as soon as possible a force of Indians."[10] Wood alone among Crook's officers took that lesson to heart.

On the night of May 14, 1885, Crook's short peace ended. Geronimo and his braves spent the evening drinking tiswin (a coarse beer made from partially fermented corn), a transgression that, along with wife beating, Crook had expressly forbidden. The following morning, Lt. Britton Davis, who of all Crook's lieutenants was the most sympathetic toward the Apaches, confronted the offenders. The old warrior Nana baited the young officer: "Tell Nantan Enchau (Fat Chief) that he can't advise me how to treat my women. He is only a boy. I killed men before he was born." The brave went on to brag that every man in the tribe had spent the night drinking and he challenged Davis to try to jail them all.[11]

The lieutenant wired his immediate superior, Captain Francis Pierce, for instructions, but the captain, new to Arizona Territory, ignored the message and failed to tell Crook. On the afternoon of May 18, friendly Indians informed Davis that Geronimo, Nana, Chihuahua, Naiche, and an unknown number of Chiricahua and Warm Springs Apaches had left the reservation. Crook later claimed that, had he known of Davis's telegram, the subsequent trouble would never have occurred, but, by the time he found out, it was too late.[12]

Geronimo, forty-two men, and ninety women and children rested in the hills overlooking San Carlos that night before setting out on a 120-mile forced march south during which they neither stopped to rest nor even to feed the children. Crook mobilized 2,000 Apache mercenaries and regular troops to pursue the hostiles, but they were hopelessly behind. Geronimo's Apaches split into bands of eight or ten, pushed their horses until they broke down, and then stole fresh mounts and food. After taking what they needed, the Apaches slaughtered the ranchers and their families. By stealing food rather than carrying it and by riding their horses to exhaustion, the Chiricahuas covered up to seventy-five miles a day, a distance the cavalry could not possibly match. Newspapers filled their front pages with Indian sightings and lurid tales of ranchers and miners tortured and killed by the hostiles fleeing toward Mexico.[13]

Crook sent four troops of the 4th Cavalry under Captain Henry W. Lawton from Fort Huachuca along with parts of the 10th and 6th Cavalry to occupy every mountain pass and water hole along the border in hopes of preventing the Apaches' return once they finally crossed the Rio Grande. He put units of the 10th Cavalry behind Lawton's line to catch any Apaches that might slip through and additional units along the railroad for quick transport to wherever there might be trouble. Finally, he kept reserves at Forts Thomas, Grant, Bayard, and at Ash Springs and in the Mogollon Mountains—all to catch forty-two braves and their women and children. Such was the situation when Leonard Wood came to Arizona.[14]

Within a month it was obvious even to Crook that the Chiricahuas had made good their escape, and the general was under intense political fire. Early reports put the renegade numbers as high as four hundred, and Geronimo, Nana, Naiche, and Chihuahua were notorious all the way back to Washington. Crook's superiors offered to send reinforcements, but, insisting he could handle the situation, the general declined.[15] His cordon around the border crossings and water holes was dismissed as "a miserably managed business"; thirty soldiers for every Indian had failed to kill a single brave and had captured exactly two squaws.[16]

Wood arrived at Fort Whipple on June 29, 1885. He rode into one of the few remaining stockade forts in the Southwest, an enclosed square of rough-cut pine logs with barracks, officers' quarters, stables, and storage facilities inside walls around the parade ground. Outside the walls was a scattering of outbuildings and pine trees framed by distant mountains. Inside the walls, the main topic of conversation was the Apache break-out.

When he got to Whipple, Wood found a telegram ordering him to report to Crook at Fort Bowie before taking a permanent post at Fort Huachuca near the Mexican border. He wrote his brother that everyone he talked to thought his assignment was extraordinarily fortunate:

> The largest and pleasantest post in the department. . . . It is in the Indian country near the Apaches and I shall prob. get a good deal of active service as about 400 of them are out on the warpath. I think and so does everyone that I am lucky. . . . Think I shall have an immense time.[17]

Two parallel rail lines crossed Arizona Territory; the Atlantic and Pacific which ran north of Fort Whipple on which Wood had come to Flagstaff, and the Southern Pacific two hundred miles to the south that passed Fort Bowie. Wood took a stagecoach south over the mountains to Maricopa where he could catch the eastbound Southern Pacific. The trip took two days and a night and involved five changes of horses and drivers through "perfectly wild" country. At night they stopped in "dirty holes" passing as hotels. The ride was hot and dry and relieved only by a few watermelons shared among Wood and his fellow passengers.

When he got to Maricopa, the young medical officer found orders directing him straight to the Apache wars.[18] He arrived at Huachuca at 6:30 P.M., July 4, 1885, and was on patrol at 7:00 the next morning.

Troop B of the 4th Cavalry was commanded by Captain Henry Lawton, a forty-two-year-old bear of a man who began his career as a Union volunteer in the Civil War. Lawton stood six feet five, weighed close to 300 pounds, had a florid face and an exuberant moustache and, in a superfluous augmentation of his considerable size, sported a towering top hat. He was outgoing, quick tempered, fearless, and inordinately fond of whiskey—a failing prone to getting him into scrapes from which his subordinates regularly rescued him.

On July 6, Wood wrote his brother from "2 miles north of Mexican border." Troop B had left Huachuca and gone over a trail "which I do not believe you would think a horse could crawl" to take position at the head of a canyon the Apaches were known to use in crossing between Mexico and the United States. The trail wound and switched back through mountains rising almost 9,000 feet where a slip might lead to a five-hundred-foot rolling fall. Lawton, testing his fresh eastern doctor, "whooped her up a little in some tough places." It was unnerving for a New Englander whose previous equestrian experience had been confined to riding an antiquated Cape Cod mare, but Wood was buoyed by the novelty and enormously proud of meeting the challenge.[19]

Since Wood was often the only officer besides Lawton up to the demands of Troop B, the acting assistant surgeon (yet to receive his commission), had a chance to get into action by default. It was exactly what he wanted. In those first days, Wood and his captain formed a friendship that lasted until Lawton's death a decade and a half later.

Wood spent that summer on and off the post at Fort Huachuca. The men saw an occasional Apache—usually friendly and at a distance—but spent most of their time futilely chasing renegades who raided ranches, stole stock, and killed civilians almost at will. The young post surgeon became an adequate rider inured to sixteen or eighteen hours in the saddle covering forty, fifty, or sixty miles a day. He wrote Jake, "Nothing to eat since 9:30 A.M., when had raw bacon and ham with water out of a cow puddle, awful. You would not drink it for $1 a drop —no idea how it tastes. . . . I am near starved. Bread and bacon and so on."[20] The bacon was a particularly sore subject. In the heat of the Arizona summer, the fat melted leaving only a desiccated leathery mass stuck to the bottom of a government-issue can.

At Fort Huachuca, an acting assistant surgeon dwelt in an uneasy official limbo, neither soldier nor civilian. Although the medical men were listed with the officers on post returns, they were appended to the end of the list—each officer with a carefully numbered line and the doctors lumped as an afterthought at the bottom of the roster. Socially, it was the same. The medical officers were included in the parties, dances, and poker games, but mostly as a matter of courtesy. Wood, with boundless enthusiasm for long rides and a compulsive interest in hunting and exploring, was particularly annoying. The officers passed their time drinking and gambling and soldiered only when forced. Wood worked, hunted, and, when there was time left over, read medicine and tried to learn Spanish.

The freedom to come and go as he wished was curtailed at the end of the summer. Fort Huachuca's post commander, Colonel William Royall, had been on sick leave since before Wood's arrival. When the superannuated martinet—whose career began in the Mexican War and ultimately ended with retirement for nervous instability—returned, he found a hyperactive young surgeon who grated on his fragile nerves. Royall ultimately reached a truce with his medical officer when both agreed that, as long as Wood more or less abided by the rules, he could spend as much time as he liked away from the fort.

Wood attended a few social events, but the post's ladies found him homely and socially inept. He had shed the long sideburns of his Boston days, but his white-blond hair, bandy legs, broad chest, and oversized head were not deemed especially attractive. He did spend some time riding with Royall's daughter, an association he carefully nurtured in an attempt to soften the edges of the testy relationship with his commanding officer, but, on the whole, he was happier alone in the desert.

Months before Wood's arrival, Crook had assigned three of his best junior officers to supervise the reservations. Second Lieutenant Britton Davis was put in charge of scouts hired from the San Carlos Agency; First Lieutenant Charles Gatewood had the scouts from White Mountain Reservation; Captain Emmet Crawford had overall control of the reservation and reported directly to Crook. Each of the three had extensive experience with the Apaches and they, with Crook, shared a mutual respect with their sometime allies and sometime enemies. Each was also committed to Crook's dual policies of making the Indians self-supporting on their reservations and using Apache mercenaries to chase down recalcitrant escapees.

Crawford was an intensely serious man just over six feet tall with an imposing glare and steel-gray eyes. He took every opportunity to forward his subordinates' careers, a practice that endeared him to his men and was anything but routine in the late nineteenth-century cavalry. Crook, frustrated at his inability to stop the Chiricahua renegades raiding on the United States side of the border, sent Crawford into the Sierra Madres to get them.

In December 1885, Crawford took one hundred Apache scouts and crossed the line into Old Mexico. On the evening of January 9, after traversing fifty miles of impossibly difficult mountainous terrain, Crawford's scouts found Geronimo's main camp. During the night, Crawford and his men quietly surrounded the hostiles, and, when the sun rose, they attacked. Virtually all Geronimo's horses and supplies were taken along with a number of the women, but his men slipped into the rocks and escaped.[21]

Geronimo later said that he knew there were upward of 2,000 American and Mexican troops and irregulars searching the Sierra Madres for him and that he had to come to an agreement with one government or the other. The following morning, the hostiles sent a delegation of women to Crawford to inquire about surrender. Geronimo knew he would fare better on an Arizona reservation than with the Mexicans.

On the morning of January 11, Crawford's camp was attacked by Mexican troops who had also been chasing Geronimo. Crawford's Spanish-speaking lieutenant, Marion Maus, tried to get the Mexicans to stop firing as Crawford, waving a white cloth, climbed on a rock between the attackers and his Apache scouts. When Maus turned he saw Crawford lying on the rocks in a pool of blood and brains. The captain died after five days in coma. Maus and his Apaches attacked the Mexicans, killing their commander, their second in command, and fifteen soldiers before they withdrew. Geronimo and his men sat by as mildly amused spectators.

Maus resumed negotiations with Geronimo after the Mexicans were driven off, but the chief would only speak with Crook. Meeting at Cañon de Los Embudos (Canyon of the Deceivers), Crook told Geronimo he had only two choices: surrender or go back on the warpath, in which case he would be pursued until the last Apache was killed. Chihuahua, Nana, and the bulk of the band agreed to Crook's terms.[22]

FORT HUACHUCA, 1885–1887   25

Unfortunately, Bob Tribolett, an American bootlegger acting on behalf of Tucson merchants whose prosperity depended on prolonging the hostilities and the attendant military contracts, gave Geronimo and Naiche a generous supply of whiskey. Geronimo later claimed he had heard that Crook had been ordered to either imprison or kill him and it was fear rather than whiskey that made him run.[23] Whatever the reason, filled with liquor and distrust, he took twenty men, thirteen women, and six children back into the mountains.[24]

The loss of Geronimo effectively ended Crook's career. He was relieved of his command on April 2 and Brigadier General Nelson Miles took over the Department of Arizona on April 28, 1886. His time under Crook taught Wood three invaluable lessons in guerilla warfare: unrelenting pursuit, use of mercenaries to fight their own countrymen, and the importance of offering an acceptable peace. Miles, on the other hand, taught Wood the importance of politics and influence.

Nelson Appleton Miles, like Wood, came from a Massachusetts family of limited means. He started his career as a clerk in a Boston crockery store while taking commercial courses at night. When the Civil War started, he took his limited savings, borrowed $2500 from his uncle, and raised a regiment of volunteers from Roxbury, the Boston neighborhood adjacent to Boston City Hospital, but his captain's commission was voided on the basis that, at twenty-two, Miles was too young to command a regiment. The appointment went to a man with more political influence teaching him that, if one were to advance in the world, influential friends were a necessity.[25] That was the main lesson he passed on to Wood.

Miles entered the army as a lieutenant of volunteers, fought in almost every one of the Army of the Potomac's major battles, was wounded four times, and won the Medal of Honor. When the war ended, Miles, still only twenty-six, was a major general in the volunteer army. While waiting for a permanent commission, he was made jailer to captured Confederate President Jefferson Davis. Secretary of War Edwin Stanton and General Ulysses Grant chose Miles specifically because he was not from the line of West Point–trained professionals who might treat the former officer with military courtesy.

Miles was commissioned colonel in the regular army and given a regiment in October 1866. His fortunes took a turn for the better when he met and courted Mary Hoyt Sherman, niece of General William Tecumseh Sherman and his brother John, a powerful Ohio senator.

Miles and Mary Sherman were married in June 1868 shortly before his transfer to the northern plains to fight Indians. The general gained national attention and promotion to brigadier general for his relentless pursuit and capture of Chief Joseph and his Nez Perce followers as they tried to escape into Canada. Miles's career stalled for the next six years as he waited for one of the army's three major generals to die or retire so he could get his second star. His chance finally came when Crook lost Geronimo. When Miles replaced Crook, he inherited a force of just under 5,000 out of a total United States army of less than 27,000. Miles's force, like the rest of the army, was disproportionately weighted to cavalry, although most of the men fought dismounted and only used their horses as transportation.[26]

Miles left Crook's orders to guard border ranches and watering holes in effect, but he changed virtually everything else. Crook had used Apache scouts to track fellow tribesmen, intending to coerce the renegades back to the reservations to become farmers and herders. Miles meant to replace the scouts with soldiers ordered to capture or kill Geronimo's band or, at the very least, force an unconditional surrender. He divided the territory into districts each with enough troops to "keep them clear of hostiles." He posted units of cavalry lightly enough equipped that half the men could ride while the other half went on foot to save the horses.

Miles meant to fight the Chiricahuas on their own terms. It was accepted by soldiers and Indians alike that no white man could keep pace with an Apache either on horseback or—especially—on foot. The new commanding general meant to prove that assumption wrong; he wanted the fittest men in his command to physically outperform the Apaches on their own terrain. He was determined to "ascertain if the best athletes in our service could not equal in activity and endurance the Apache warriors." To that end he selected "one hundred of the strongest and best soldiers that could be found" from his command.[27]

Although he relied on regular army troops, Miles recognized that his soldiers needed a few Indians who knew the Mexican mountains and could follow Indian trails. After dismissing Crook's Apache scouts, Miles personally went to the reservation to pick his mercenaries. Like the soldiers, the scouts had to be in first-rate condition. "Only the best physical specimens were to be selected, men who were rugged and healthy."[28]

Miles orders were harsh and specific: "Where a troop or squadron commander is near the hostile Indians he will be justified in dismounting one-half of his command and selecting the lightest and best riders to make pursuit by the most vigorous forced marches until the strength of all the animals of his command shall have been exhausted."[29] That was sweet music to Wood, who had devoted the previous year to building his stamina and honing his riding skills. He went out of his way to be at Fort Bowie within days of Miles's arrival so he could inform the general of his personal conviction that the "right sort of white man could eventually break these Indians up and compel them to surrender."[30]

Henry Lawton, with his "brilliant war record and splendid physique,"[31] precisely fit Miles's idea of an Indian fighter, and the general gave him the unit meant to operate in Mexico until the last of the Chiricahuas was captured. Miles agreed to send Wood with Lawton, though in a medical rather than a military capacity. Miles told the doctor, "You are probably in as good physical condition as anyone to endure what they endure. I want you to go with Lawton and to take every opportunity that is given you to study the Indians. If they are better men physically than the white men, I want you to find out what makes them better."[32]

On May 5, 1886, Lawton left Fort Huachuca with one company of infantry, thirty-five cavalry troopers, twenty Apache scouts, thirty packers, and 100 mules. Wood wrote his brother:

> I leave this Post tomorrow for a three month's scout in Mexico. . . . We are expecting a very hard time and it is Gen. Miles' great effort to do what Gen. Crook failed to do. . . . We are going way down into the hot lands of northern Mexico and into the rough unknown Sierra Madre Mts.[33]

It would be a remarkable four-month campaign in which Lawton, Wood, and the few men who managed to stay with them covered 3,041 miles, largely on foot, over some of the most difficult terrain on earth.

The climate of the Arizona, New Mexico, Sonora, and Chihuahua borderlands is a function of altitude rather than latitude. In the upper elevations, the air is cool in the day and cold enough, even on a midsummer night, to freeze water at the same time the rocky lowland plains are unbearably hot. The mountains are steep and ascending paths hug five-hundred-foot drops. Horses were nearly useless on the narrow tracks, and even normally sure-footed mules had to be pushed against the mountain sides to prevent their stumbling to death on the rocks below. At the lower elevations the terrain was unrelievedly sere. Water in the desert only reached the surface in rare depressions of sand and rock. In the best of times, it accumulated in four- or five-inch-deep pools contaminated with mud, green slime, and feces. As the pools evaporated, they shrank into algal slurry, thickened to mud, and disappeared. The Apaches had lived in the desert for generations and knew every water hole, but even they did not know whether the hole would be wet or dry. The men often marched for a day without water only to find that their night's water had vanished. It was common to go thirty-six hours without a drink. Bathing and washing clothes were great rarities, and lice were a perennial problem, best solved by stripping, piling the filthy clothes on a red ant mound, and kicking the hill so the agitated insects would attack the clothes and eat the vermin. Then uniforms and cotton underwear were shaken out, dirty, but uninfested.

There was no such easy solution to the dust that covered every inch of the skin until it became an integral part of the natural pigment. Horses scuffed the trails raising a fine powder—yellow in the sand, red in the rocks, and gray-white in the alkali flats—that coated the skin and invaded the lungs of man and beast alike. Men stopped talking and used their energy just staying upright. Sun heated their canteens until the water was too hot to drink and baked rifle barrels until they were too hot to touch. For miles the only vegetation was mesquite with three-inch thorns that ripped men's clothes and horses' skin. Where there was an open sore, blow flies dropped eggs and, in a matter of hours, the wounds were alive with maggots. Over time, clothes wore out and the men left one rag after another lying beside the trail. Toward the end of the campaign, Wood wore only a pair of cotton drawers, a torn shirt, and the tattered brim of a campaign hat whose crown had long ago been lost.

Although they were occasionally resupplied by pack trains from Arizona, their food ranged from monotonous to inedible. Except for the occasional beef bought from a Mexican rancher or venison shot along the trail, the diet was hardtack and bacon from which the sun had long since rendered the last ounce of fat—meager nutrition for marching forty miles a day.

Lawton and Miles's hand-picked "athletes" left Fort Huachuca on a bright morning in late spring. The men had spent weeks attending to the myriad details of "a long scout" and were anxious to get started. Even the Apaches, most of whom were either relatives or former companions of Geronimo and his band, were "excited and happy over the prospect of going out on another campaign."[34]

They spent their first day riding across rolling plains before camping next to the Sonora and Arizona Railroad, "thankful that the bother of getting started was over."[35] Wood trailed the main group, having stopped to visit a patient recovering from a compound leg fracture, a gratifying result in an era when most physicians, fearing infection, simply amputated such limbs. Although wanting to be a soldier, Leonard Wood remained a competent if unenthusiastic physician.

Miles's instructions to Lawton were to find the Indians' trail and maintain an unrelenting pursuit. Specifically, he was not to allow the hostiles time to establish camps in the Sierra Madres where they could rest and from which they could steal cattle and horses. The pursuers would not rest and were to be resupplied on the move by mule trains from Arizona. Miles's men were primed and ready to test their strength and endurance against Geronimo's Chiricahuas.

The second morning out, Lawton's cavalry, the Apache scouts, and an infantry company under Lieutenant Henry Benson moved southwest along the railway toward Nogales. They passed the forlorn remains of Camp Crittenden, an antebellum outpost whose overgrown cemetery held the forgotten remains of soldiers killed in the previous generation's Apache wars. They followed the railroad west for another day before turning toward the border. Lawton's cavalry crossed into Mexico on May 8 heading toward the Pinito Mountains in Sonora where, six days earlier, Captain T. C. Lebo and his African-American Tenth Cavalry "Buffalo Soldiers" had skirmished with the Apaches, losing one man killed and another wounded.[36] Hearing of Lebo's fight, Benson and the infantry pushed ahead into Mexico, but the inexperienced lieutenant exhausted his men, leaving them so tired they simply dropped in the desert, unable even to walk back to camp.

On May 10, after collecting Benson's exhausted men and seeing to food and water for the troops and livestock, Lawton took Wood and two other officers, sixty soldiers and Indian scouts, and a small mule train to look for Geronimo's trail. Tracking was almost impossible because a group of Mexican irregulars, also chasing the Indians, had hopelessly muddled the trail, and, if that were not enough, the fleeing Apaches set fires behind them to further confound the pursuit. That night the soldiers camped in a canyon surrounded by fire so intense they had to light backfires to keep from being engulfed. They coughed, sweated, and ate hardtack and bacon and drank the foul water seeping through the rocks. The heat and smoke from the fire, swarms of insects, and thin blankets on flinty rock made sleep impossible, even for men who had marched eighty miles in hundred degree temperatures in seventy-two hours. Wood was learning firsthand why Apaches had been able to survive while the "right sort of white men" retired to their forts.

The next morning the soldiers started south into the Mexican mountains. As they climbed into the foothills, ranks of high ridges rose on the horizon. Climbing into the mountains, they passed bloated carcasses of used up Apache horses. They crossed the spine of the Las Pinas range and down a steep descent on the south side past the baking corpses of two miners, each killed with a single bullet to the head which, Wood wryly noted, "spoke well for the shooting qualities of the Indians."

A railroad spur ran from the Southern Pacific through Nogales and down to the Sonoran town of Imuris, where the United States Army maintained a telegraph station. On May 14, Wood took the train to town to buy food and forage and, that night, shared an undersized bunk with the burly, inebriated Irishman the army had detailed to run the telegraph. Wood, tired enough to overlook the snoring and the aroma of sweat and Irish whiskey, slept soundly.

Lawton's men spent the next two weeks thrashing about the Sonoran desert in a fruitless search for the hostile Indians. Geronimo split his band into small units and left the Americans thoroughly frustrated. They found horses abandoned by the Indians, butchered remains of stolen cattle, and camps so fresh that the fires still had meat smoldering on them. They found ranches and small towns with people massacred only hours earlier, but they never saw a single Chiricahua.

They had only gone about twenty miles into Mexico when the trail doubled back north toward the Arizona railroad town of Calabasas. Miles came out to meet Lawton and discuss what to do next, and Wood, happy to be out of the desert where it had been 107 degrees in the shade, went into town with his captain to sleep on the hotel veranda. Even for just one night, it was good to be under a roof and to sleep on boards instead of rocks.

Miles and Lawton correctly assumed the Indians had sent their women and children south into the Sierra Madres while the men went north as a diversion. While they were in Calabasas, word came that Geronimo's braves had killed a rancher near Pantano, seventy miles north of where they were and thirty miles east of Tucson. Miles used the railroad to move his men north to resume the chase. When they got to Pantano, Wood and Lawton learned that Geronimo had, as they had expected, started back toward the border. They had lost him again.

Lawton had no idea what to do next. He needed someone to ride back to the Pantano telegraph station to wire Miles for orders, but the locals, knowing Apaches had been in the area, refused to ride cross country at night. Lawton needed instructions immediately, so Wood volunteered to take one other man ("an old soldier, about used up") and carry the message himself. The two set out at 4:00 in the afternoon after having marched all day. Wood's companion, mounted on a mule as tired as its rider, gave out two-thirds of the way to Pantano, so Wood pushed on alone. He reached the telegraph station after dark, got instructions from Miles—follow the Indians' trail as best they could wherever it led—had his horse reshod, and started back for Lawton's camp at 2:00 in the morning. Wood, lighting matches to follow the trail, repeatedly got lost and had to back track. When he got back to camp at 7:30 the next morning, he had ridden over seventy miles.

Lawton, determined to follow Miles's orders as expeditiously as possible, wanted an early start. Wood's horse was exhausted, and there were only two other mounts in camp, one for Lawton and one for the infantry lieutenant, so Wood had "the pleasure of a days march" on foot after his all night ride. That day he added thirty hot, waterless miles to the ninety of the day before (counting both the regular day's march and the ride to Pantano). On June 1, Wood wrote Jake that, since leaving on their "long scout," he had traveled over five hundred miles—nearly four hundred of it on foot—but noted proudly that he was "in first rate health" and could "run with the Indian scouts all day and be fresh as ever in the morning."[37]

But the day after the ride to Pantano was almost too much. The last seven miles were at a dog trot (alternately running and walking) and, for the last six miles, it was all he could do to blindly throw one foot in front of the other. When Wood made camp, he was so exhausted that he dropped his blanket, collapsed on top of an ant hill, and was thoroughly chewed.[38] (Miles cited that miserable two days in Wood's Medal of Honor citation.) Since arriving in Arizona, Wood had walked and ridden a total of over 4,000 miles and kept a pace none of the regular soldiers could match.

By June 1, Lawton and his men were back at Calabasas preparing to cross the line into Sonora. Wood took a brief trip back to Fort Huachuca to restock his medical supplies, taking the opportunity to sleep in his own bed and have dinner with Colonel Royall and his daughter and Colonel William Shafter and his wife and daughter, whom he met for the first time. When Wood got back to Calabasas, Lawton had already left for Mexico, leaving his supply train behind. Lieutenant Benson, the original commander of the pack train, had been sent to Fort Huachuca to "settle some money matters," and Lawton's only other lieutenant was under arrest for habitual drunkenness, so Wood, the sole remaining officer, took command of the mule train. Soon Wood and Lawton would be the only officers left.

The trail into Sonora crossed a rugged divide in the Sierra Azul Mountains, the highest in northern Sonora, and led along canyon walls traversed by narrow paths covered with leaves and pine needles so slick that even mules slipped and somersaulted down the mountain. By night, Wood's men and animals were spent, but, aware that the Apaches would kill for the ammunition and supplies they carried, the troops spent a restless night listening for noises in the dark. Three long days and nights and 160 miles later, they caught up with Lawton. Wood, in his first command, brought four troopers, eight packers, seventy animals, and Lawton's supplies home having lost one mule and no men.

After Wood rejoined Lawton, the pursuit into the Sierra Madres began in earnest. Unlike their first foray into Mexico, Lawton's cavalry were well south of the border and chasing the Apaches straight into their ancestral hiding places. The Americans were reliant on a pack mule supply chain that stretched hundreds of miles across hostile country, supplemented only by what they could forage, and they had no idea how long they would be out.

For two weeks after Wood rejoined him, Lawton fruitlessly combed the trails and canyons between the Magdalena and Sonora Rivers. Back in Arizona, the papers complained that Geronimo could

> run like a deer, jumping from side to side while you are trying to shoot
> at him. He can drop down on all fours and slapping his rump ridicule
> your attempt to shoot him, while he runs away spider fashion.

He could

> live on snakes, ants or any creeping thing, even to those that inhabit his
> own head. Our soldiers must have ham and eggs. . . . He can lope off
> over the country at a dog-trot for a hundred miles without sleeping.

In contrast, they ridiculed Lawton's men, who whether "mounted, on foot, or with cannon" were no match for the Indians.[39] To make the situation even more irritating, the Sonoran prefect, wanting to catch Geronimo for himself, demanded the Americans not go any further into his country, an order Wood dismissed as ridiculous.[40]

Afternoon temperatures reached 127 degrees so Wood and the soldiers got up two hours before sunrise and marched until midmorning before taking whatever shade they could find until evening. Sometimes there would be a water hole, sometimes a bit of shade under a mesquite or behind a greasewood, and sometimes just rock too hot to touch. At dusk they got up and marched until midnight hoping to find a stream or water hole where they could camp. On the worst days, they were reduced to a desolate "dry camp."

Early in July, Wood, Lieutenant Robert Brown, and a few Apache scouts moved south toward the Moctezuma River. Lawton and the main force followed the existing road while Wood and Brown headed out across a patch of mountainous desert where the Mexican locals had seen Indians. In the mountains, the Americans finally found water. Deer were plentiful as pine forests replaced barren rock in the upper elevations, but midday temperatures in the lower elevations still exceeded 120 degrees. On the brighter side, Lawton's scouts found fresh Apache tracks, raising hopes that they would at last get to fight the Chiricahuas.

On July 2, Lawton, running out of officers, gave Wood command of the infantry that had come out from Huachuca and put Brown, his only lieutenant, in command of the Indian scouts. In addition to commanding the infantry company, Wood remained a doctor. He cared for the soldiers and treated the locals, many of whom had not seen a physician for years. Wood wrote his brother that "when we strike a town, all the lame, halt and blind turn out to see an Army surgeon."[41] Over a hundred people came out to be treated from one village. Wood even enlisted Lawton's help to operate on a crossed eye in a Mexican officer's daughter.[42] On July 11, Wood got his own medical trouble when a tarantula bite on his leg became infected and so swollen that he was repeatedly forced to lance his own wound.

Still they chased about the mountains pursuing reports of Indians they never saw. Lawton wanted his Apache scouts to locate the Chiricahua camp so his soldiers could sneak up at night and surprise Geronimo before his people could escape into the mountains. On July 13, they got their opportunity; scouts sent word that they had found the Chiricahuas in a canyon only eight miles away. The Indians' tents were on level ground bounded by cliffs on one side and the Yaqui River's muddy rapids on the other. It looked like they could only escape up or down the river bank. The scouts were sent to take the up-river trail, leaving the down-river approach to Lawton, Wood, and the troops. Since the river was too deep for the Chiricahuas to swim, they were surely trapped. Lawton and Wood took every man they thought capable of climbing the ridge separating them from the Indian camp. The day was so hot the men, unable to hold the metal chisels needed to open their ammunition boxes, broke them on the rocks and filled their pockets with shells before starting the climb.

Peeking over the ridge, the soldiers could see Geronimo's camp next to the river. For the first time since they left Fort Huachuca two months earlier, Wood and his men actually saw Indians—men, women, and children milling about the camp. Brown and his scouts had been sent up-river and Lawton, Wood, and their men began working their way along the trail on the down-river side into the camp, but, when they rushed the camp, they found only Brown. One of Geronimo's braves had seen the scouts, sneaked back into the camp, collected the Chiricahua band, slipped around Brown's Apaches, and escaped. The Indians lost their supplies and livestock, but got cleanly away.

Swallowing his bitter disappointment, Lawton resumed the chase. Meanwhile, Wood's spider bite had gotten worse and he was able to march his fourteen remaining exhausted, shoeless men only five miles before he collapsed. Lawton, convinced his only remaining officer was near death, made camp. The next morning Wood tried to march again, but every few yards he became dizzy and fell. The troopers put him on a mule, but he managed less than a mile before passing out and tumbling to the ground. Lawton had no choice but to rig a travois and send his last remaining officer to a nearby ranch. He wrote his wife:

I am almost broken up at this misfortune. It not only leaves the command without a medical officer, but no one to look after him, and he has always been my warmest friend and supporter. I don't know what I shall do without him.[43]

Luckily, Wood's fever broke the next morning and the swelling in his leg receded enough that his men could prop him back on the mule and return to camp. The following day they were back on Geronimo's trail. The change of season brought rain accompanied by clouds of biting insects, but, as miserable as they were, Wood, Lawton, and the dwindling force were nearing the end of their expedition.

Geronimo had lost his horses and food in the Yaqui River raid. He later said that his band, chased by both Mexicans and Lawton's men, had not had a good night's sleep in six months; the Apaches were tired and discouraged. They moved north toward the Mexican town of Fronteras, where Geronimo dispatched two of his women to approach Mexican officials about surrendering. Geronimo later claimed he reached an agreement with the Mexicans that he would, in return for safe passage, cross back into the United States, but, given his previous experience with the Mexicans (and they with him), it is likely he was only delaying until he could work out a better arrangement with the Americans.[44]

On the other side of the border, Miles was running out of time. He had heard rumors of the overtures from Geronimo to the Fronteras prefect and rightly assumed that losing the renegade to the Mexicans would effectively end his own career. Moreover, the territorial press was overtly hostile. The Prescott papers grudgingly allowed that, if Miles could promptly see Geronimo and his men deported to Florida or (preferably) hung, he might deserve their thanks, although the skeptical editors believed General Crook would have been better suited to the job.[45] President Cleveland and General Philip Sheridan were also getting impatient, and Miles was well aware of what befell his predecessor when the powers in Washington had last gotten nervous about the Apaches.

If pressure from Washington and the Arizona settlers was not enough, relations between the United States and Mexico abruptly deteriorated. E. K. Cutting, publisher of the *El Paso Herald* which circulated on both sides of the border, had written a series of articles sharply critical of President Porfirio Díaz. When Cutting foolishly visited the Mexican side of the border, Díaz had him arrested. Texans demanded immediate military action, and the governor preemptively mobilized the National Guard. On August 11, Arizona newspapers reported that Mexico had retaliated by taking Lawton and his entire command captive. Miles had begun assembling a troop to rescue Lawton when he learned the news reports were false, but Lawton's safety two hundred miles south of the Rio Grande was unquestionably tenuous.

While inspecting Fort Apache on July 1, Miles met Ki-e-ta, a Chokonen Apache who had recently left Geronimo. Ki-e-ta told the general Geronimo's warriors were tired of fighting and would surrender if approached by people they trusted. Using Apaches to negotiate with Apaches smacked of Crook's policies, but Miles, pressured from every direction, swallowed his pride, and, in addition to Ki-e-ta, enlisted Martine, a Nedni Apache influential on the reservation, to deal with Geronimo. Miles also needed an army representative that the Chiricahuas trusted. Of Crook's three former lieutenants, Crawford was dead, and Britton Davis had left the army to become a rancher. That left Charles Gatewood who was stationed at Fort Stanton, New Mexico.

Miles brought Gatewood back and charged him with negotiating Geronimo's surrender. Gatewood was a remarkable individual whom Davis described as "cool, quiet, courageous; firm when convinced of right, but intolerant of wrong; with a thorough knowledge of Apache character and conversant with the causes leading to the outbreak."[46] He was tall, rail thin, and sported a nose other soldiers charitably called Romanesque. The Apaches called him Chief Big Nose or, in reference to an equally prominent attribute, Big Foot. Nicknames notwithstanding, the Chiricahuas knew the lieutenant and trusted him.

Gatewood assembled a small group comprising himself, Ki-e-ta and Martine, interpreter George Wratten, packer Frank Huston, and courier "Old Tex" Whaley. Miles, anticipating the public outrage he would suffer if Gatewood were captured or killed, ordered the lieutenant to take an additional twenty-five troopers and to never meet the Indians without his entire escort.[47] Gatewood, realizing that Geronimo would not let him close with an entourage that large, made only a superficial effort to get the additional men before slipping off to Mexico with his original five. Just across the border, he met Lieutenant James Parker and a unit of the Fourth Cavalry who escorted him into the mountains where Lawton's men were frantically looking for Geronimo.

On August 3, Lieutenant Parker brought Gatewood into the American camp on the Arras River. It was not exactly clear how Gatewood officially related to Lawton. The captain correctly understood that the mission from Arizona was a direct comment on his failure to find the hostiles, and a resentful Lawton wrote his wife that his support for Gatewood would only extend to doing his utmost to capture or kill Geronimo, thereby saving the interloper the trouble of a negotiation. Wood brusquely noted that Gatewood "reported to Lawton for duty."[48] In truth, Gatewood carried a set of orders from Miles instructing any American officer he encountered to help him complete his mission. Lawton was, in effect, working for Gatewood.[49]

About the time Gatewood arrived, Lawton received word that Geronimo had been sighted two hundred miles north, near Fronteras. He took Gatewood and what was left of his command on a rush for the border. As Lawton marched north he heard rumors of Apache attacks on Mexican ranches and supply trains, and word came that Geronimo planned to cross the border into the United States. Lawton frantically dispatched messengers to Miles and the border detachments warning them of the danger. One courier actually encountered Geronimo and Naiche who told him they were on the way to Fronteras to negotiate with the Mexicans. They told the courier they "did not wish to harm Mexicans any more, but wished to secure a home then to raid in New Mexico and Arizona."[50] Given the mutual hatred between Geronimo and the Mexicans, it is likely that the Indians were only using the threat of surrender to improve their chances of successfully negotiating with the Americans, but Lawton did not know that.

On August 18, Martine and Ki-e-ta, who had gone ahead of the main party, returned with confirmation that Geronimo was talking with the prefect at Fronteras. According to Wood, Gatewood, acutely ill with a bladder infection, had been begging to be sent back to Arizona. Wood also said Lawton had to order Gatewood to Fronteras and threatened to replace him when he delayed his departure.[51] Britton Davis, Gatewood's friend and supporter, never mentioned that, emphasizing Gatewood's desire to establish immediate contact with the Indians. The lines were drawn in what became a decades-long battle over credit for Geronimo's surrender.

Gatewood rode seventy miles that night, and, when he got to Fronteras the next day, he learned that the renegades had, indeed, sent two women into town to discuss surrender. Mexican officials held the women, so Gatewood and his party stayed in Fronteras as well. When Lawton and Wood (now joined by Lieutenant Thomas Clay of the 10th Infantry who had come with a supply train) arrived in the Mexican town, Lawton was furious that Gatewood had not left to search out Geronimo. Wood took it upon himself to order Gatewood to "take his Indians and immediately go out on the trail."[52]

The prefect, urged by the Americans to release the Indian women, sent them back to Geronimo loaded with food and mescal. The Mexican hoped to keep the Apaches drunk and stationary while he collected enough soldiers to kill the men and capture the women and children.[53] That night Gatewood, pressured by Lawton who feared he would lose Geronimo to the Mexicans, slipped out of Fronteras and found the Chiricahua women's trail. With two Apache scouts, Huston, Wratten, and ten of Lawton's soldiers, he followed the hostiles for three days, carrying a white flour sack in front of him as a flag of truce the entire time. On August 24, Gatewood sent his two scouts ahead, and, to everyone's surprise, Ki-e-ta and Martine were allowed into the Chiricahua camp. Geronimo told the mercenaries he was ready to surrender and, the next morning, Gatewood himself came into the camp. For the first time since the May break out, an American officer actually met the renegades face to face.

Geronimo first wanted to eat and then announced that, after three days drinking Mexican mescal, he was a little shaky and would benefit from some decent whiskey. The undersupplied Gatewood was unable to oblige, so the parched Apaches reluctantly agreed to talk about surrender. The lieutenant offered only two choices: give up and be deported to Florida or be hunted and killed. Geronimo demanded return to his Arizona reservation, but Gatewood told him that all the Warm Springs and Chiricahua Apaches, including Naiche's and Geronimo's families, were either already in Florida or about to be sent east; none of his tribe was to live in Arizona ever again. The Chiricahuas, unaware of the deportations, were crestfallen, but Geronimo was out of options. He asked what sort of man Miles was. Could he be trusted? What did Gatewood think they should do? When Gatewood's only suggestion was unconditional surrender, the Apaches sadly adjourned for the night.

Meanwhile, Lawton had moved four miles from the Indian camp to await the outcome of Gatewood's conference, leaving Wood behind to bring in the unit's mule train and supplies. The next morning Geronimo and his party returned to Gatewood's camp. The Chiricahuas agreed to surrender if they could do so to Miles in person and in Arizona. They wanted to keep their arms until their formal surrender and to be protected from the Mexicans until they crossed the border. Geronimo agreed to come in voluntarily and in company with the soldiers, but not as a prisoner. If all went well and Miles abided by Gatewood's terms, the war was over.

Geronimo came to Lawton's camp and, when he arrived later that day, Wood met the Apache renegade for the first time. Wood's account of what happened differs from Gatewood, the Apaches who were present, and even his unfailingly complimentary biographer, Hermann Hagedorn, who simply ignored Wood's description of the events.

Wood says he arrived at Lawton's camp early on the morning of August 27 and learned that "Some of Geronimo's Indians were in camp yesterday,"[54] leaving the clear implication that nothing much had happened. Wood continued that, on the day he arrived, Geronimo came to Lawton's camp and, "Had a long talk, during which all arrangements for surrendering to us and going with us to Skeleton Cañon were gone over and agreed to." He went on, "There were no definite terms offered the Indians at this time. They were told that General Miles sent word that he would use every possible effort to send them promptly out of Arizona to save their lives."[55] In the light of subsequent events, it seems likely that Wood added this to cover Miles's difficulties in arranging the final surrender. Wood made no mention of Gatewood having met with the Indians to finalize the surrender terms before bringing them to meet Lawton. Wood was not above retrospectively editing his diary and, on this occasion, he maximized his own and Lawton's role and minimized Gatewood's.

Newspaper and official accounts are equally contradictory. The Arizona papers, quoting an "officer just from Lawton's command" reported that "Geronimo and fourteen bucks came into Lawton's camp, threw down their arms and asked permission to surrender."[56] At the other extreme, Crook wrote Sheridan in his résumé of the Geronimo campaign, "It is difficult to arrive at the true conditions accepted by the Indians in the surrender . . . however, it is certain the efforts of the troops in the field had little or nothing to do with it."[57] Without question, Gatewood and not Lawton first negotiated with Geronimo. Just as unquestionably, the surrender would never have taken place had not Lawton, Wood, and their troopers chased Geronimo with more determination and stamina than either their countrymen or the Apaches thought possible. Gatewood and his two scouts deserve credit for entering the Chiricahua camp alone, but Lawton and Wood had persevered in their pursuit for the previous fifteen months. They had chased down an enemy that "traveled with lightning speed, never stopped to battle, and were . . . as hard to find as last year's moccasin track on a granite boulder."[58] In 476 days on the warpath, Geronimo and his small band had killed over 400 civilians and led a chase of over 3,000 miles. His surrender made Wood, Lawton, and Miles (but never Gatewood) heroes.

As soon as Geronimo agreed to surrender, Lawton started for the border. The Indians and the soldiers marched in separate columns, seldom closer than two miles from each other. At Geronimo's request, Gatewood and Wratten were the only white men riding with the Chiricahuas. Wratten later wrote, "We weren't accompanied home by any of the Army, but went along by ourselves, out of sight most of the time of any troops. We hadn't gone out with any of the Army, and we didn't need any of them."[59] The rivalry between Gatewood, a Crook man, and Lawton and his men was bitter from the time Miles replaced Crook and remained so years after the end of the Apache Campaign.

The two columns started up the San Bernardino River valley toward Skeleton Canyon in southern Arizona where Miles had agreed to meet Geronimo. Almost immediately there was a crisis that threatened to destroy the peace before it had really begun; a column of 180 Mexican irregulars under the prefect of Arispe was sighted approaching from the south. The prefect was furious that the Indians had surrendered to the Americans and was intent on taking and killing them himself. He closed first on Lawton's army group and the captain ordered Lieutenant Abiel Smith, the scout Tom Horn, and Wood—the only three in his command with horses saddled and ready to ride—to intercept the Mexicans before they panicked the Indians and caused them to flee back into the mountains. Meanwhile, Lawton's mule drivers piled their packs and what stones they could find into makeshift breastworks and the Apache scouts stripped naked in preparation for battle. Some of the packers had been on Crawford's expedition when he was murdered by a similar column of Mexicans and were "on the whole rather hoping there would be a fight."[60] Geronimo's Apaches heard about the approaching column and turned back to join Lawton, hopeful for one last chance to kill a few Mexicans.

Again there is disagreement between Wood and other participants as to how the confrontation between the soldiers and the prefect actually unfolded. Wood said he got to the Mexicans first and "had a long talk with them and told them if they came on there would be a fight."[61] A more plausible version has Smith, the senior member and only line officer in the group, conducting the conversation with the prefect. At any rate, they sent for Lawton who informed the Mexicans that, if they attacked, the Apaches and the soldiers would fight them together. The prefect agreed to withdraw if he were allowed to meet personally with Geronimo and satisfy himself that the Chiricahua had actually surrendered. Lawton arranged the meeting, although that, too, was nearly a disaster.

When the Mexican and the Indian were face to face, the prefect nervously pulled his holster around from his side so he could more easily draw his gun. Geronimo then half drew his own weapon and, according to Wood's account, "Lawton, Clay, and myself jumped between the two parties."[62] Hagedorn says the three were joined by Gatewood in separating Geronimo and the Mexican. Gatewood said that, when Geronimo threatened the prefect, the latter put his hands behind him and backed down.[63] Although Wood amplified his and Lawton's roles at Gatewood's expense, the prefect did agree to take his men back south and let the Americans and Chiricahuas proceed unmolested.

As they neared the border the Indians became more nervous. They did not trust Lieutenant Smith who had assumed command while Lawton went ahead to send a heliographic message to Miles. The Apaches overheard Smith discussing plans to guard against any attempted escape, so they began preparations to do just that. Gatewood and Smith were at odds, and an anxious Wood took it upon himself to send a courier begging Lawton to return post haste. Lawton complied and reestablished peace between Smith and Gatewood, reassured Geronimo, and resumed the march to Skeleton Canyon.

Lawton, however, had a more serious problem. The Arizona settlers and the newspapers had been insisting that the "Apache cutthroats" be treated as common criminals and brought to trial with every intention of hanging them.[64] This was a direct contradiction of Lawton's promise that the Chiricahuas would be protected as prisoners of war. Miles was getting pressure from the chain of command all the way to the White House to hold the Indians for civil trial, although the president had authorized Lawton to negotiate more lenient terms. Miles's solution was to avoid coming to Skeleton Canyon for the final surrender. This left Lawton with a band of armed hostiles who were not really prisoners but who, if he lost them, would certainly be his responsibility. As they neared the rendezvous, Wood noted that there was "a perfect epidemic of couriers" between Lawton and Fort Huachuca, but no sign of Miles.[65]

Lawton wired his commander, "Earnestly wish the General would himself come and conduct affairs in person. If they do not surrender I feel they will raid again in the States, and it will be again as terrible as they can make it, as they will be desperate."[66] By September 2, Lawton was desperate himself. He begged Miles for help. "I am aware now that I assumed a great responsibility when I allowed them to come to my camp and promised them safety until they could see you, and have regretted a thousand times that Lt. Gatewood ever found my command, but I sincerely believed and do yet they wished to surrender, and that I was furthering your plans. I have followed them four months and know how hard it is to surprise them, and believe that they should not now be driven out again."[67] Miles's first response was a thinly veiled suggestion that Lawton lure Geronimo into his camp and kill him. Lawton indirectly refused by commenting that it would be much too difficult to surprise the Indians.

Finally, on September 3, Miles appeared and, after a day's negotiation, accepted Geronimo's surrender. According to Geronimo, Miles promised, "I will take you under Government protection, I will build you a house; I will fence you much land; I will give you cattle, horses, mules, and farming implements. You will be furnished with men to work the farm, for you yourself will not have to work. In the fall I will send you blankets and clothing so that you will not suffer from cold in the winter time."[68] The president and the Arizona citizens thought they were going to see the Apaches hung. Miles finally—reluctantly—did the honorable thing, honored Lawton's agreement, and took the Indians as prisoners of war. He took Geronimo and Naiche with him by ambulance wagon to Fort Bowie in a quick one-day ride while Lawton, Wood, and the rest of the band came along in a more leisurely three-day march.

What happened when they arrived at Fort Bowie was certainly not what Geronimo expected and was not what Lawton negotiated. The entire band (including Martine and Ki-e-ta, who had risked their lives to make the surrender possible) was marched to the rail station at Bowie and put aboard cars for transport to Florida. Meanwhile, Miles had been surreptitiously increasing the number of soldiers in and around Fort Apache. On September 5, he summoned the Warm Springs and

Chiricahua leaders to a conference at which he informed them that they were all—men, women, and children—to go to Washington for a conference with the "Great Father." The Indians at Fort Apache had, for several years, been peacefully farming and selling their excess grain and hay to the army. Some were well on the way to self-sufficiency and were reasonably content with their surroundings, but Miles was convinced that the only way to prevent future outbreaks was to move the entire tribe out of Arizona Territory. In fairness to the general, he preferred a more hospitable location than Florida, and he had written his superiors that the mountain-dwelling Apaches, unlikely to survive in the southern swamps, should be sent to Oklahoma's Indian Territory. Moreover, the commander at Fort Marion had informed the War Department that he could accommodate no more than seventy-five additional Indian prisoners with his current facilities, although he could, at a cost of about $200 per person, build tent housing for more. The decision was made. President Cleveland, relishing a $200 bargain, instructed Miles to treat the entire tribe as prisoners and transport them to Fort Marion forthwith.

On the morning of September 7, the soldiers marched the remaining 434 members of the two tribes the hundred miles from Fort Apache to the rail station at Holbrook. The column, composed of the Indians, their portable belongings, 1,200 horses, and over 3,000 dogs, stretched two miles across the desert with two companies of infantry in front and behind and cavalry along the flanks. Miles was taking no chance that the men might change their minds and return to the warpath. The tribes got to Holbrook on September 12 and were loaded onto eighteen "tourist cars" the following morning. Most of the Indians had never been on a train until the soldiers physically threw the frightened women and children into the cars. The men, concerned for their families, followed voluntarily. The horses were rounded up by members of the Tenth Cavalry and eventually sold at auction. When the train pulled out, the Apache's dogs followed the cars for miles. Some were shot by the soldiers for sport, and some dropped from exhaustion after running twenty miles down the tracks. The Indians' belongings were simply left where they lay.[69]

Lawton, Wood, and Geronimo's renegades got to Fort Bowie on September 7, allowed the Indians to rest for one night, and had the captives on the train for Florida by 1:30 the next afternoon. As they were boarding the train, William Thompson, Miles's acting assistant adjutant general, emboldened by a morning of celebratory imbibing, sidled up to Wood and whispered, "I have got something here which would stop this movement, but I am not going to let the old man see it until you are gone, then I will report it to him."[70] What Thompson had were orders from Washington to keep Geronimo and his men prisoners in Arizona, a course that would have violated Miles's and Lawton's promises and would almost certainly have resulted in the Indians being hanged. Although Thompson was protecting his general, Miles knew full well that he was violating the president's wishes by moving the hostiles out of Arizona. He had received specific instructions from Sheridan on September 7 and from Adjutant General of the Army Hugh Drum on September 8 to hold Geronimo and his men at Fort Bowie until further orders.[71]

Instead the train, accompanied by Miles, Lawton, Wood, and a group of soldiers headed east. Miles left the train at Deming, but Lawton and Wood stayed on to San Antonio. Although the soldiers were putatively assigned to prevent the Apaches' escape, they were equally necessary to protect their prisoners from civilians along the route. Photographers, newsmen, and hostile crowds plagued the Apaches at every stop until they arrived in San Antonio on September 10. Wood expected to go on to Fort Marion, but the commander at San Antonio had been ordered to hold the Indians and to question Geronimo as to exactly what Miles had promised, so Wood took the train back to Albuquerque on September 13.

Geronimo and his men were detained in San Antonio for over a month before being transferred to Fort Pickens near Pensacola. There they were held out of contact with their families for nearly two years before being reunited on a southern Alabama reservation. As Miles had predicted, the Indians did poorly in the wet southeastern climate where they spent the next five years. Most of the Apache children were taken from their parents and sent to the Indian School at Carlisle, Pennsylvania, while adults who were not bedridden with recurrent fevers were kept at hard labor. Finally, after years of effort by Crook, Hugh Scott, and John Clum, the remaining Chiricahua and Warm Springs survivors were transferred to Fort Sill, Oklahoma in 1894. There Geronimo lived and farmed with his family until he died in 1909.

Wood went back to Fort Huachuca where he spent a few days finishing paper work before returning to Albuquerque to take an honored part in a "general celebration . . . over the windup of the Apache Campaign," featuring appearances by the governors of both the New Mexico and Arizona Territories.[72] Wood spent September 27 at a party in the morning, a dance in the evening, and horse racing at a special territorial fair after the dance, and that was only the beginning. After a full week of social activities, he wrote his mother that he had not had a night's rest for days and that the locals were coming close to killing him with kindness.

Moreover, Wood stood to benefit from Miles's promise of career advancement for the men who had supported him. Wood told his brother that the general "seems inclined to do all he can for those of us who did the hard work and as things look now I am pretty sure he will at some time."[73] Miles proved every bit as good as the young surgeon's expectations; Wood remained Miles's favored protégé for the balance of the latter's career. Miles's influence not only brought Wood unique professional opportunities, but it also ultimately resulted in his being awarded the Medal of Honor for his part in the Geronimo Campaign. Miles and Lawton, both of whom had the highest military medal, spearheaded the drive that led to Wood's finally receiving the honor in 1898. The citation accompanying the medal read:

> Throughout the campaign against the hostile Apaches in the summer of 1886, this officer, serving as Medical Officer with Captain Lawton's expedition, rendered specifically courageous and able services involving extreme peril and display of most conspicuous gallantry under conditions of great danger, hardships and privations. He volunteered to carry dispatches through a region infested with hostile Indians, making a journey of seventy miles in one night and then marched thirty miles on foot the next day. For several weeks, while in close pursuit of Geronimo's band and constantly expecting an encounter, Assistant Surgeon Wood exercised the command of a detachment of Infantry to which he requested assignment and that was without an officer.[74]

It is certainly true that Wood performed his regular duties without a hint of complaint and then volunteered to do more and that his strength and endurance matched that of the Apaches and exceeded that of every other man in his unit. With no prior command experience, he took an undisciplined, demoralized infantry company, won their respect, and turned them into an effective unit. Whether he actually met the medal's requirement of being a serving army officer and whether he actually saw combat were other matters altogether. His status as contract surgeon clearly does not meet the standard for the Medal of Honor, and chasing the Chiricahuas across northern Mexico was, no matter how arduous, hardly combat. Both shortcomings were glaringly obvious to regular army officers, especially "Crook's men," who saw Wood as a self-promoting parvenu. None of Miles's other officers, mostly West Point graduates who had spent their entire careers in the Southwest, received similar honors, and their bitterness dogged the rest of Wood's career.

Nevertheless, the Geronimo Campaign was of immeasurable benefit to Leonard Wood. He emerged confident of his own physical and mental strength, he had a heady taste of command, he fought his first guerilla war, he acquired his first influential mentor, and he laid the foundation of a military reputation while helping close the American frontier. It was a year and a half well spent.

5

The Army, 1887–1898

AFTER GERONIMO'S SURRENDER, Miles sent Wood back into Mexico to retrieve a handful of Apaches that had not come in with Geronimo and returned to Los Angeles. In January 1887, the general ordered Wood to California on the thin pretext that his assigned surgeon had arthritis and was useless. The War Department lacked Miles's enthusiasm for an extra surgeon in Santa Monica and, in May 1887, summarily ordered Wood back to Fort Huachuca. Wood's exile to Arizona ended in September when Miles overturned a carriage and broke both bones in his lower leg. The local surgeon, recognizing the fracture as one notoriously difficult to heal, recommended amputation, but Miles refused the operation until Wood could personally examine the injury. Wood came, and, through a combination of patience and luck, got the break to mend. Still, after a few weeks in California and over Miles's vehement objections, Wood was again ordered back to Arizona.

Miles kept pestering Washington to get "his" surgeon back until the exasperated secretary of war stepped in personally and shipped Wood to Fort McDowell outside Phoenix. Wood glumly pronounced it "the hottest place in the world where white troops are stationed." Ground temperatures reached 170 degrees during the day and even buried water pipes got so hot that baths had to be drawn a day early to allow the water to cool.[1] But Wood got by; he renovated the hospital, doctored, and—when the heat permitted—hunted, fished, and played tennis.

Finally, in June 1889, Wood was transferred to the Presidio, the ancient pink adobe headquarters of the Division of the Pacific. Miles took his men on maneuvers on the Monterey peninsula that summer. What the enlisted men called the Monkey War of Jackrabbit Flat was run by Wood's old Arizona acquaintance, 350-pound Colonel William Shafter who billeted the officers in the luxurious Hotel Del Monte. During those maneuvers Wood met James Runcie. Runcie, who had graduated near the top of the West Point Class of 1879, was asthenic, witty, and personable, and the two became inseparable. Wood also took responsibility for the troops' physical conditioning, organizing a marathon around the Seventeen-Mile Drive which he finished well ahead of the troops.

Monterey was an unquestionable improvement over Fort McDowell, and things got even better with the arrival of Judge Stephen Field and his entourage. Field, brother of millionaire Chicago inventor Cyrus Field, was an associate justice of the United States Supreme Court at a time when the justices divided their time between Washington and the various federal circuits. When Field rode the Pacific circuit, he divided his time between San Francisco and the Hotel Del Monte. Although he had no children of his own, the judge had taken responsibility for Louise and Alice Condit-Smith. The girls' father had served as a colonel on General William Tecumseh Sherman's staff and as quartermaster general of the Army of Tennessee. His first wife had died when the girls were young and he had married Field's sister-in-law. When Colonel Condit-Smith died, Field brought the girls and their mother to Washington where he established them in the house next to his and became the girls' legal guardian.

The socially inept Wood was stricken by Louise. Suddenly he found that he "enjoyed life at the hotel very much" walking, riding, and lunching with "Miss Louise C.S." virtually every day.[2] His persistence finally forced the judge to ask Miles about this young doctor chasing his favorite "niece." When Field summoned him for an interview, Wood had "a deuce of a time" but survived.[3]

Back in San Francisco, Wood spent almost every evening with Louise until she and Field returned to Washington in the fall. In the spring Wood went to Washington. The judge decided the young doctor would do, and Wood's engagement to Louise was announced during the visit. In June he went back to San Francisco, but, that August, he arranged to go back east. He met Louise in New York where they spent a happy ten days before Wood went up to Boston and then to Washington. He and Louise were married on November 18—the day the battleship *Maine* was launched—in the Field drawing room with the entire Supreme Court as witnesses. The newlyweds spent a few more days in New York and then went to Boston and Cape Cod before taking the train through Cincinnati, New Orleans, San Antonio, Los Angeles, and on to San Francisco.

On October 22, 1892, Leonard Wood Jr., weighing a whopping eleven pounds, was born. That fall, Wood found a new passion to go along with fatherhood. A week after Leonard Jr. was born, the lieutenant played his first competitive football game with the Olympic Club against the University of California.

In August 1893, Wood received the unwelcome news that he was to be transferred to Atlanta. Wood protested to his commanding general who suggested he keep his peace and follow orders.[4] Fort McPherson met his expectations: "Was never more disgusted with a post[5] . . . a dull, stupid post, absolutely without interest."[6] The only saving grace was that there were a few people who might be enticed to play a little football.

In fact, Wood arranged to play on the Georgia Technological School's team. He later claimed to have enrolled in a wood shop course so he could qualify as a student although there is no record of his ever having attended a class.[7] The Tech team had only been organized a year earlier, had a volunteer trainer, and lacked a coach. In 1893, Wood and James Spain became Georgia Tech's first coaches with Wood doubling as left guard, halfback, and kicker. Wood sealed his reputation for toughness when he cut his eye during practice. He bandaged it and kept playing; after practice, the team found the army surgeon in front of a mirror suturing his own laceration.

Their first game was against the University of Georgia, and an entire train was chartered to take the team and its supporters to Athens for the initiation of one of football's great rivalries. Even before the game, rumors had circulated that Tech's team was not entirely legitimate. The *Atlanta Journal* said the team was "a heterogeneous collection of Atlanta residents—a United States Army surgeon, a medical student, a lawyer, and an insurance agent, with here and there a student of Georgia's School of Technology thrown in to give the mixture a technological flavor."[8] Moreover, the umpire was the Tech trainer's brother.

The game was a vicious affair in which one Georgia player drew a knife on a Tech opponent and Wood received a "cruel blow in the head" from a rock thrown by a spectator.[9] Wood was, however, the star of the game. The *Atlanta Constitution* wrote, "Dr. Wood, who is believed by all Athens to be a surgeon of the United States army, stationed at Fort McPherson, and who, it is said, was matriculated in the Technological School for the purpose of playing football, could handle his opponent guard, who was a much lighter man, almost as if he were a child."[10] Wood also played halfback and scored three touchdowns, and Tech won the game 28–6. Even as their fans protested, Georgia was trying to get Wood to play for them against Vanderbilt the following week, an offer the lieutenant declined.[11] Wood's Tech team went on to beat Mercer 10-6, to lose to St. Albans of Radford, Virginia 6-0, and to play Auburn to a scoreless tie.

The next season, Wood organized a Fort McPherson team that beat Tech 34-0. In one play of that game, Wood ran the ball twelve yards with an opponent chewing on his ankle "like a snapping turtle," a foul that earned Tech's respect and a twenty-five-yard penalty.[12] Without Wood, Tech lost all its games in 1894, including a 94-0 rout at the hands of the Auburn team they had tied a year earlier.

The two years in Atlanta passed with Wood playing football, learning to ride a bicycle, and studying French, Spanish, and Latin, but his career was stagnant and he was bored. By 1895, Wood was thirty-five years old and had spent eight years doctoring at sleepy forts on the American periphery. He badgered Miles for transfer to a line command; the medical corps was only nominally part of the army, and doctors lacked the respect afforded to real officers. Nothing came of the requests, so, having completed his tour at Fort McPherson and convinced he was permanently consigned to the medical corps, Wood requested assignment in Washington where a military physician could at least treat government officials instead of malingering privates. In fact, Surgeon General George Sternberg had promised him the Washington post months earlier, but politics were in a fair way to cancel the pledge; Wood had only two high profile supporters in the capital and both were on shaky footing with President Grover Cleveland.[13]

Miles, now the army's commanding general, had been out of favor with the White House since spiriting Geronimo off to Florida, and the president was not inclined to transfer the general's personal doctor to the capital. Justice Stephen Field had even greater liabilities. The judge had publicly opposed several of Cleveland's political appointments and had aggravated the president by refusing to retire. It was generally accepted that Field stayed on the bench solely to deny a Democrat the opportunity to name his successor. Aware that Field desperately wanted his niece with him in his waning years, Cleveland pointedly kept Lou Wood and her husband in the hinterlands.[14]

On June 20, Sternberg wrote that the post of surgeon to West Point was available and perhaps Wood would "prefer this station to Washington." He told Wood that the secretary of war for "reasons of his own, which you understand" preferred that he not come to the capital. Sternberg admitted he had promised Wood the Washington job, but asked that the captain not subject him to the embarrassment of having an appointment reversed by the president. If Wood absolutely insisted, he would honor his promise, but the surgeon general predicted the appointment would result in an "unpleasant complication." If Wood agreed to go to West Point, Sternberg promised a transfer to Washington when the political climate was more favorable. He also reminded the captain that discretion required he hold the communication in strictest confidence.[15]

The warning was a waste of good government ink. Wood went over Sternberg's head and had Field and Miles pull every string still available to them while righteously informing the surgeon general that he expected him to honor his promise. Sternberg tersely responded that he would "bring the matter up again" and find out once and for all whether the secretary of war's problems with Wood were insurmountable. Again, he cautioned Wood to keep the matter "entirely confidential until it is finally settled."[16] Twelve days later the surgeon general wrote Wood that he had spoken with the secretary and the latter agreed to let the captain come to Washington, but that Wood was to understand that "the detail is made upon my recommendation and quite independently of any outside influence." Sternberg, fully cognizant of Wood's machinations, chastised his subordinate: "I regret that you stirred up your friends after receiving my confidential letter of June 20th." Wood got his way by testing the limits of insubordination, learned a perilous lesson in political manipulation, and made a permanent enemy of Sternberg.[17]

Leonard and Louise Wood moved to the capital in September 1895 as the tidal basin Indian summer steamed to an end. Grover Cleveland was finding the season difficult for more than heat and humidity. He had narrowly broken a string of Republican victories in the 1884 election, lost the office to Benjamin Harrison in 1888, and reclaimed it in 1892. His second victory was overshadowed by Wall Street's 1893 collapse, and his Democrats fared poorly in the midterm elections. Reaction to the economic crisis compounded by riots at Andrew Carnegie's steel works, the march of James Coxey's army of Civil War veterans, and the American Federation of Labor strike against the Pullman Company cost Cleveland's party a staggering 113 congressional seats and their majority in both houses. It was hard to tell whether the president was more unpopular with the country at large or his own party.

The first family's health was the responsibility of senior members of the medical department and Wood, a very junior member, spent his days making house calls on army officers scattered around the District of Columbia. Although work was a chore, evenings were considerably livelier than they had been in out-of-the-way military bases. Wood faced both the social demands of an army officer and those of spouse to a Supreme Court justice's favorite ward. Washington in the 1890s was a small town and, sooner or later, even junior officers got to meet just about everybody. Miles and Field made sure the Woods were included on the best social lists, so it was only a matter of time before Wood came to know the president. He and Cleveland got along famously. They fished together, the captain was included in the president's legendary poker games, and, in the bittersweet days after the 1896 election, Wood joined the lame duck president on an extended trip to North Carolina's outer banks.[18] William Jennings Bryan and the Democrats lost the White House to William McKinley, but Cleveland, philosophically closer to the Republicans than to his own party, predicted that McKinley's Washington would not be a bad place for a military surgeon with political connections.

Three people who changed Wood's life came to Washington with the Republicans: Ada McKinley, Mark Hanna, and Theodore Roosevelt. McKinley's wife was an incorrigible hypochondriac who became utterly dependent on Wood who, in consequence, enjoyed unique access to the oval office. Hanna, the power broker behind McKinley's successful political career, became one of Wood's most implacable enemies. Roosevelt became Wood's most enduring friend.

Ada McKinley lost two children early in life and never fully recovered. Her husband spent hours at her bedside hoping for a break in an endless string of ailments. In Leonard Wood, the first lady found another devotee, and she summoned the young physician to the White House almost daily to examine and consult (though rarely to treat, since the complaints almost never had a physical basis). Wood was a confidant and willing ear who accumulated a store of political capital out of all proportion to his rank and station.

Roosevelt, McKinley's assistant secretary of the navy, had a felicitous habit of writing (and saving) mountains of letters, so we know exactly when he and Wood first crossed paths. In the summer of 1897, Roosevelt's wife was at Oyster Bay, leaving the assistant secretary on his own in Washington. On June 18, he wrote his wife, "In the evening,

I dined at the Lowndes', who were just dear. There was a very interesting Dr. Wood of the army there; he had been all through all those last Apache campaigns, which were harassing beyond belief."[19] Roosevelt and Wood walked home that evening trading stories of Arizona Apaches and New York gangs, each finding in the other a kindred soul. Both were ambitious risk takers more secure in their physical than their social skills. In the subsequent months, Wood and Roosevelt hiked in Rock Creek Park, swam in the Potomac, and played football wherever they could find a flat patch of ground. In the winter, they tried Roosevelt's new skis on the hills and paths around Washington. To a city whose males ranged from corpulent to obese and who spent their days protecting the creases in their stove pipe pants and the starch in their collars, thirty-year-olds in knickerbockers, hiking shoes, and slouch hats were absurd. Roosevelt and Wood were inseparable.

Meanwhile, Spain was stuck in a decades-long struggle to retain the last of its New World possessions. Since 1868, a smoldering Cuban rebellion had periodically erupted into outright revolt with each flare-up followed by inconsequential political compromises and waves of repression. The most recent armistice collapsed on February 24, 1895, with a spate of fighting in Santiago Province where the predominantly black and mestizo population was especially volatile. The war started under Bartolomé Masó, a wealthy rancher from Manganuillo; Guillermo Moncada, a black who, like the others, affected the rank of general; and mulatto Antonio Maceo who sported a road map of scars from previous revolts. Ten days into April, a German freighter put two more key revolutionary leaders ashore at the eastern village of Playitas. Dominican General Máximo Gómez was a relic of the last revolt, described by one American correspondent as "a chocolate-covered, withered old man . . . a resurrected Egyptian mummy."[20] Gómez, a prototypical terrorist, was infamous for allowing rural villagers the choice of joining him, taking refuge in the cities, or dying. He had no illusions about his ability to defeat the Spanish in battle, but he knew he could make the island ungovernable. With Gómez came poet-politician José Julián Martí y Pérez, who had spent the previous two decades leading a group of New York–based Cuban exiles and who would become the revolution's soul.[21]

In truth, the conflict was as much about money as nationalism. A large part of the island's upper class, having fled insurrections in South America and Haiti, was viscerally opposed to revolution. Wealthy

Cubans were mostly willing to forego political power (which Spain had reserved to Iberian peninsulars) for personal security. Taxes were another matter altogether. The Cuban government's average annual revenue between 1893 and 1898 was $25 million, $10.5 million of which serviced the island's $400 million debt (a crushing $283.54 for every man, woman, and child on the island), most of which was held by German investors. Another $12 million went to support the occupying Spanish military and naval forces and the island's civil and ecclesiastical establishments, leaving only $2.5 million for all public works, education, and other government services.

Slavery overshadowed economics for the island's predominantly black and mixed-race population. The Spanish agreed to emancipation as part of the armistice ending the Ten Years War, but slavery was not abolished until 1888. As the blacks were freed, they pressed for the economic tools necessary to self-sufficiency. At the same time, the Cuban Creoles, many of whose families had been refugees from Haiti's slave revolt, had a horror of Negro unrest. That paranoia was not lost on the Spaniards, one of whom confided to an American diplomat that fear of the Negro was Spain's single best weapon against insurrection.[22] Finally, in the mid-1890s, the financial burden of economic colonialism outweighed the threat of anarchy and the scales tipped in favor of rebellion. A reciprocal agreement allowing the island to trade directly with the United States rather than through Spanish ports had been reached in 1891, but the United States tariff on Cuban sugar rendered even that belated concession moot.[23] The value of trade between the United States and Cuba fell by one-half in only two years. Cuban sugar production plummeted from 1 million tons in the 1894–95 season to only 25,000 tons in 1898–99, due to a lethal combination of trade barriers, competition from European sugar beets, and physical destruction of plantations by the spreading insurrection.[24] In 1897, the Spanish governor, Captain General Arsenio Martinez de Campos, gave up in frustration and was replaced by the ruthless General Valeriano Weyler y Nicolau. "Bloody Weyler" came with instructions to do whatever was necessary to eliminate "El Chino Viejo" (Gómez) and his rebels.[25]

At the same time, America was drifting away from George Washington's century-old admonition against foreign entanglements. The Atlantic seaboard colonies had unexpectedly acquired trans-Appalachian territory after the Revolutionary War and had, just as unexpectedly, acquired the Louisiana Territory twenty years later. Looking across the continent, Democratic newspaperman John O'Sullivan wrote, "Our manifest destiny is to overspread the continent allotted by Providence for the free development of our yearly multiplying millions." And, within a generation, Texas, Mexico north of the Rio Grande, and the southern part of the Oregon Territory fell to the United States and fulfilled O'Sullivan's prediction. In the greatest human migration in history, those multiplying millions streamed across the Great American Desert, and, in 1883, Frederick Jackson Turner declared the frontier closed. Across the Atlantic, Social Darwinists proclaimed Anglo-Saxon racial superiority and set about carving up Africa and Asia. Chauvinistic Americans, having spanned the continent and having killed or contained the Native Americans, were casting about for their next manifest destiny.

Alfred Thayer Mahan seductively argued that sea power determined a nation's international position and, with specific regard to the United States, he emphasized the importance of an isthmian canal to link the nation's two coasts.[26] Command of the Caribbean's narrow entrances, two of which were adjacent to Cuba, was central to the canal project.[27] Henry Cabot Lodge (who became one of Wood's staunchest allies) saw the importance of Cuba as early as 1895. In the pointedly titled "Our Blundering Foreign Policy," he wrote, "We should have among those islands at least one strong naval station, and when the Nicaragua Canal is built the island of Cuba . . . will become to us a necessity . . . for future expansion and present defense."[28]

The American business community pushed McKinley to intervene in Cuba for economic and geopolitical reasons, but war fever in the general public sprang from rampant nationalism, and Roosevelt and Wood were in the vanguard of the chauvinistic expansionists. One morning, McKinley sardonically asked Wood, "Well have you and Theodore declared war yet?" Wood pulled himself up and responded, "No, Mr. President, we have not, but I think you will, sir." McKinley, a Civil War veteran, shot back, "I shall never get into a war until I am sure that God and man will approve. I have been through one war; I have seen the dead piled up; and I do not want to see another."[29] By January 1898, Roosevelt and Wood were frantically looking for a way into the war they were certain McKinley could not avoid. Wood wanted a line commission and Roosevelt wanted whatever would get him into battle, but their cascade of letters to various National Guard commanders brought no positive responses.

The army was not prepared to operate beyond the nation's immediate borders. The regular forces comprised only a handful of regiments —mostly cavalry and old Indian fighters—scattered over fifty or so minor posts, almost all of which were on the western frontier. Behind the regular forces lay a patchwork of state militias under the general aegis of the National Guard. The Guard was "lamentably weak in artillery, cavalry, or the necessary technical branches; its infantry units were in all stages of inefficiency, and it was endowed in addition with a unique, a truly American, concept of military discipline."[30] Its officers were chosen by popular election and its rifles fired smoky black powder that was worse than useless in modern warfare. These citizen soldiers were expected to mobilize into an army of hundreds of thousands sustained by instinctive American martial ability. The units were untrained, underequipped, and commanded by men whose qualifications were popularity and political connections.

The confusion and ossification of the volunteer system and the tiny regular army led by superannuated Civil War veterans were two reasons Roosevelt chose the navy when the Republicans won the White House. He thought the navy was amenable to constructive change while the army clearly was not. Roosevelt had indeed changed the navy; working with (and around) his superiors he was well along toward modernizing the fleet, even though it was still smaller than those of Venezuela and Chile—and Spain.

But for war with Cuba, the army was where Roosevelt and Wood needed to be; it was Wood's chosen career, and Roosevelt had no hope of naval command. With luck and judicious application of political influence, they might just get regiments in the new volunteer force. They fired off letters to everyone they thought might possibly nominate officers when new units were mobilized.

On February 15, the battleship *Maine,* in Havana on a mission that was somewhere between dubious and intentionally inflammatory, blew up under mysterious circumstances, and Congress, the press, and public opinion united to paint McKinley into a corner. America had contemplated absorbing Cuba for most of the nineteenth century—in 1848, Cubans sequentially approached Jefferson Davis, Robert E. Lee, and the governor of Mississippi, searching for leaders who could help separate the island from Spain and make it part of the United States. Fear of upsetting the balance between slave and free states put back any talk of annexation, but, after the Civil War, the question resurfaced. In the spring of 1898, William Randolph Hearst organized the "Cuban Commission," composed of Senators Jacob H. Gallinger of New Hampshire, Hernando de Soto Money of Mississippi, and John Thurston of Nebraska and Representatives Amos J. Cummings of New York and William A. Smith of Michigan, to "consider" American involvement in the island.[31] The report of their visit to Cuba (predictable since the commission members were chosen specifically for their interventionist views) announced that, since Spain's government was a failure, the island's future was patently American. The report arrogantly concluded that, after twenty years of independence enhanced by American tutelage and money, the island should be ready for annexation.[32]

For a time, McKinley remained unconvinced, but, beset with mounting jingoism from the press and his own party, he finally surrendered to the interventionists. In an April 11 message to Congress, the president justified American involvement in Cuba on four grounds: the need to end misery and death in Cuba, protection of United States lives and property, protection of trade, and the expense of enforcing neutrality laws in the waters around Cuba. His disingenuous solution was to exercise "hostile restraint" on both the Spanish and the Cuban *insurrectos*. In an arrogant extension of Monroe's doctrine, McKinley asserted that the United States had the responsibility to determine the island's future with absolute discretion not "subject to the approval or disapproval" of any other government.[33]

On April 18, he asked Congress to declare war. The House Committee on Foreign Affairs authorized forcible intervention in Cuba to stop the insurrection and to establish "by the free action of the people thereof a stable and independent government of their own in the island." The Republican-dominated House, however, defeated a Democratic resolution calling for recognition of a Cuban republic.[34]

On April 16, the Senate adopted three resolutions, two of which called on Spain to relinquish control of the island and withdraw, adding that the Cuban people "are, and of right ought to be, free and independent" and that the Cuban Republic was the "true and lawful government of that island." The last came as an amendment crafted by Republican Senator Joseph Foraker of Ohio and Democrat David Turpie of Indiana whose name it carried. Foraker was opposed to an involvement he thought was "to be deliberately turned from intervention on the ground of humanity into an aggressive conquest of territory." Orville Platt of Connecticut made the major speech in opposition to Foraker, arguing that intervention was for the highest of moral reasons. Republicans loyal to the administration supported Platt, but there were enough defections to the Democrats that the Turpie Amendment passed 51 to 37.[35]

An amendment written by Senator Henry M. Teller of Colorado and passed without debate on a voice vote added, "The United States hereby disclaims any disposition or intention to exercise sovereignty, jurisdiction, or control over said island except for the pacification thereof, and asserts its determination when that is accomplished to leave the government and control of the island to its people."[36] The debate on the other articles had been intense, but the amendment that determined Cuba's future passed with scarcely a whisper. It may be that it received so little notice because the Senate, having already voted to recognize the Cuban Republic, overlooked the fact that recognition lacked any mechanism of realization whereas the Teller Amendment was operational and rigidly defined the parameters of occupation. Detail triumphed over rhetoric.[37]

Back at the navy department, Roosevelt was frantically angling for a place on General Fitzhugh Lee's staff, but the elderly general, nephew of the Confederate hero and recent consul-general in Havana, had no place for the young New Yorker; nor did General James H. Wilson whom Roosevelt thought the one most likely to see early action in Cuba. For his part, Wood deluged Massachusetts Governor Roger Wolcott with letters of recommendation from Generals Miles, Forsyth, and Graham, from his old commander Colonel Lawton, and even from Secretary of War Russell Alger, but had no more success than Roosevelt. Wood tried New York's governor, but with no luck there either. Undoubtedly, his frenetic quest for command was not helped by the fact that the commander in chief did not want his wife's favorite doctor off fighting in the islands.[38]

Wood's and Roosevelt's solution came from Arizona whose territorial governor Elmer Hawley was an old friend of the president. Hawley had been a Republican congressman and, until he lost his seat in 1890, occupied a desk next to McKinley's in the House chamber. Since February, the Arizonan had bombarded the president with requests to recruit a 1,000-man volunteer cavalry regiment to fight in Cuba, but McKinley, not even having decided to declare war, put him off.[39] In the waning days of the debate over the Volunteer Army Bill, South Dakota Adjutant General Melvin Grigsby, also anxious to raise a regiment of frontiersmen separate from the National Guard, went to Washington to petition his old friend Francis X. Warren, chairman of the Senate Committee on Military Affairs. Grigsby wanted the bill amended to allow an independent frontier regiment.

The amendment, added as Section 6 and drafted exactly as Grigsby dictated it, allowed for the president to "authorize the Secretary of War to organize companies, troops, battalions, or regiments, possessing special qualifications, from the nation at large not to exceed 3,000 men."[40] To satisfy the bill's requirements, Alger authorized three "cowboy regiments." The First United States Volunteer Cavalry was to be raised in the four territories (Arizona, New Mexico, Oklahoma, and the Indian Territory). The Second was to come from Wyoming, commanded by Judge Jay L. Torrey, a Wyoming friend of Senator Warren, and the Third, from the Dakotas, was to be recruited and commanded by Grigsby.

Telegrams went out from Alger's office on April 25 to the governors of Nevada, Arizona, New Mexico, Idaho, the Dakotas, Montana, Wyoming, Utah, Texas, and the Indian Territory, authorizing enlistment of "good shots, good rifles, to form a company in a mounted rifles regiment."[41] In less than a day the responses came back asking only two things: Where should they send their men? and Could they increase their allotment? Theodore Roosevelt was offered command of the First Volunteer Cavalry, but, pleading lack of military experience, took the lieutenant-colonelcy on condition that Wood be named colonel.

Early attempts were made to raise volunteer companies from the ranks of such unlikely groups as Wall Street brokers and bankers, Johns Hopkins students, the Sons of Benjamin social club, "braves" of Tammany Hall, and indicted criminals who offered to serve in return for not being tried. All but the criminals were rejected.[42] The Volunteer Law was amended a few days later to allow one other non–National Guard group besides the cowboys; Secretary Alger, anticipating the invading force's worst problem, was authorized to recruit six regiments from Gulf Coast states where residents were presumed immune to yellow fever.

The public and press were predictably enamored of the First United States Volunteer Cavalry. The *New York Times* heartily approved of Roosevelt's gallantly taking second place to Wood, describing the latter as "a fighting doctor" who "knows the men of the plains and they know him." Wood promised to recruit 1,200 men who "know how to live out of doors . . . understand horses . . . and can take care of their beasts and themselves." Roosevelt extolled the martial virtues of cowboys: "Living as they have and do live in a country where there is heat enough a large part of the year to shrivel up the unacclimated, they would bear the heat of Cuba without much distress, and they would get along with such food as the country would provide and not murmur."[43]

Wood and Roosevelt reckoned that, since the men already had their own horses and guns and were in perfect fighting condition on account of their outdoor life style, they could be recruited, trained, and ready for war in a few weeks, blatantly playing to Americans' self-image as independent frontier warriors with God-given military talent. The public was ecstatic. With officers like Medal of Honor winner Wood and Roosevelt, "a hunter of big game in the West . . . accustomed to hardship and peril and . . . one of the best shots in the country," the regiment's success seemed a foregone conclusion.[44] Wood and Roosevelt received hundreds of telegrams from friends, acquaintances, and people they had never met. In the end, instead of having enough men for a regiment, they had enough for an entire division.

Wood had spent two years in Washington learning the arcane intricacies of the war department and he meant to make the best of what he knew. Roosevelt readily acknowledged that he, innocent of the department's Byzantine complexity, could not match Wood's ability to organize and equip a regiment. The recently converted surgeon's first act was to collect a cadre of veteran sergeants whom he shoehorned into his cramped office and set to scrounging arms and equipment before other new unit commanders could requisition equipment that was certain to be in short supply.

Uniforms were a special problem; blue tunics had been out of production since Miles, having served through Arizona's brutally hot summers, had jettisoned the cumbersome flannels that had been standard since before the Mexican War. In April 1898, he had ordered one hundred "light and serviceable" canvas uniforms colored gray-brown to be "difficult to distinguish from the earth, grass, cornfields, or dead leaves." The pants were to be buckskin-colored leggings and the blouses' collars and cuffs were colored to denote the branch of service: blue for infantry, red for artillery, and yellow for cavalry. The hat was to be canvas as well and turned up on the left side, pinned with a rosette, and decorated with a feather.[45] Unfortunately, there was, in the entire United States, only enough canvas to make a few demonstration uniforms and no supply of rosettes or feathers.

It would be mid-June before the first of Miles's new uniforms actually reached the troops. Wood, looking for an alternative, remembered that army fatigues—work uniforms for manual labor around the bases—were also of canvas, albeit not nearly so dashing and of dark rather than light brown and (fortunately for tropical use) of lighter weight than that selected by Miles. There were plenty of fatigues available, and Wood pronounced them "serviceable and perfectly adapted to the climate of Cuba," producing a "neat, although odd appearance."[46] He augmented the baggy canvas pants and tunics with what blue shirts he could find and issued blue and white polka-dotted neck kerchiefs as a regimental badge. Some of his officers wore regulation blue uniforms cadged from existing supplies or left over from previous service, and those who could afford it (including Wood and Roosevelt) had uniforms privately tailored after Miles's new design.[47]

Arms were a bigger problem. There were no cavalry sabers to be had, so Wood substituted machetes and declared that the Caribbean cutlass was a frightening weapon that could be "used to great advantage by the troops in slashing their way through the dense thickets and underbrush in Cuba."[48] Besides, they were cheap and could be gotten by the case. Rifles were the biggest problem of all. Some of the men would bring their Remingtons, but the government planned to issue only outdated, black powder Springfields to the volunteers. Unless he had modern rifles and smokeless powder Wood was sure he would not be allowed to fight alongside regular units who had no desire to have their location marked by clouds of black Springfield smoke.

The Krag Jorgensen rifle was designed by Norwegian Captain Ole Hermann Johannes Krag, director of the Royal Norwegian Arms Factory. In 1892, the U.S. military chose the Krag to replace its single-shot Springfield in a competition which included the Mauser (the standard Spanish weapon), the Mannlicher, and more than forty other entrants. Because a number of American manufacturers objected to the foreign design, a second competition was held in 1893, and again the Krag was the only weapon to pass the tests. Ultimately, 442,883 Krags were manufactured under license at the Springfield Armory, but only about 53,000 of those were available in 1898. Worse, there were only four factories in the United States capable of producing anything but charcoal-based powder, and one of those had blown up in March.[49] The side-mounted magazine made the Krag slow to load, but the U.S. Army, which emphasized careful aim over high-volume volleys, did not see that as a particular disadvantage. The weapon was considered effective at a range of 600 yards against infantry and 650 yards against cavalry. Rough Riders were issued the 1896 model of the weapon which weighed 8.94 pounds, was 49 inches long, and fired a .30–.40 cartridge. The rifle's chief disadvantage was that the five-shot magazine could only be reloaded by looking down, opening a magazine cover, and fitting in new shells. This forced the rifleman to take his eyes off his enemy and was so cumbersome that an experienced man could fire almost as many rounds using the weapon as a single-shot rifle as he could reloading the cartridge. But, with Krags, Wood's men could fight alongside the regulars.[50]

Wood put his training camp in San Antonio for two reasons. It had easy rail access to the western states from which his volunteers would come, and it had Fort Sam Houston's stockpiles. Wood established temporary recruiting stations in Arizona, New Mexico, and the Indian Territory of Oklahoma and left Washington for San Antonio as soon as he was able. Once he gave Wood and Roosevelt their "Cowboy Regiment," Alger, tired of being badgered for arms and supplies by his would-be warriors, wanted them out of Washington and out of his hair as quickly as possible. Roosevelt stayed behind long enough to finish his personal arrangements and formally submit his resignation before going to Texas. Wood left him with the last few details, and the frenetic assistant secretary found the military bureaucracy almost as frustrating as they found him. He wrote Wood that he had "been rushing about all day making the lives of the Quartermaster General and the Chief of the Bureau of Ordnance a burden to them," but was "nearly crazy" at his inability to energize the bureaucrats. Could Wood even imagine that orders from Washington to the Rock Island Arsenal for Krag rifles had been sent by regular mail rather than telegram? Roosevelt finally coerced the Quartermaster into guaranteeing that the unit's equipment would be in Texas by May 11, although he found the Bureau of Ordnance's foot dragging over rifles and ammunition "entirely unsatisfactory."

One bit of good news was a change in the regiment's authorized strength from 780 to 1,000—an increase Roosevelt exploited to add more of his eastern friends and associates, several of whom were already on their way to Texas when Roosevelt breezily wired Wood, "Please have them enlisted." Finally, Roosevelt entered a personal plea:

I suppose you will be keeping me here for several days longer; but there is one thing, old man, you mustn't do, and that is run any risk of having me left when the regiment starts to Cuba. Of course I know you wouldn't do it intentionally, but remember that at any cost I must have a chance to get with you before you start.[51]

Volunteer training camps named for their commanding officer were being hastily set up across the country. Camp Wood, three miles south of San Antonio on the Edison streetcar line, occupied six hundred acres of the International Fair Association grounds at Riverside Park. The Arizonan contingent, on the wings of Governor Myron McCord's enthusiasm, was the first to arrive. McCord had picked forty-nine-year-old West Point graduate Alexander O. Brodie as his major. Brodie had served as an officer in the First Cavalry in the Indian Wars before resigning in 1877. He tried ranching in Kansas for a few years before reenlisting as a private in 1883 to serve with Crawford's Sixth Cavalry in the Apache Campaign. When Geronimo returned to the reservation, Brodie, relegated to garrison duty, again quit the army. He remained in Arizona and wandered from business to mining to politics. He became close friends with printer, newspaperman, and Prescott Sheriff and Mayor William "Buckey" O'Neill, and the two pestered political authorities for permission to raise a volunteer cavalry regiment as soon as it looked like there might be a war. In March Brodie wrote both McCord and President McKinley offering his services. The following month Mc-Cord wrote McKinley that Brodie's offer should be accepted as part of an overall Arizona contingent. The governor reminded the president that his Arizonans were, of necessity, good riders, well acquainted with firearms, and spoke Spanish. Many of them had fought in the Indian Wars and were used to difficult climate and terrain. The governor promised that "no better material for cavalry purposes can be found anywhere in the world, than among the cowboys of Arizona."[52] Before the Voluntary Army Bill ever came up for debate, O'Neill and Brodie were out recruiting in Arizona's northern counties.

At the same time their friend, James H. McClintock, who covered territorial news for the *Los Angeles Times* and the Associated Press, was recruiting in the southern part of the state.[53] As a result, it only took seven days after Alger authorized the "Cowboy Regiments" for Brodie to assemble his men at Fort Whipple. Brodie divided his unit according to geography, naming O'Neill captain of his northern troop and Mc-

Clintock captain of the southern one, and began scrounging rail transportation to San Antonio. He had a problem when men began arriving before he had either the authority to swear them in or the money to feed them.[54] On May 4, just ahead of a mutiny, the unit finally received orders to leave for Texas and the war.

Fort Sam Houston and the city of San Antonio had only learned they were to receive the new regiment on May 1, and the military purveyors were scrambling to collect supplies.[55] Local newspapers were filled with rumors about the regiment, some of which bordered on truth and nearly all of which violated military secrecy. Roosevelt told one reporter that the Rough Riders would be the first unit deployed and would leave from Galveston in order to save the time and expense of joining the expeditionary force assembling at Tampa.[56] Another reporter claimed the unit would initially be the only force on the island and would join with Gómez's rebels in southeastern Cuba to isolate the southern coastal provinces from Havana, a mission of "immense strategic importance, as it is clearly the intention of the Spanish to use the southern coast as a base of supplies for the beleaguered city."[57] It was rumored that Wood had gone directly to Key West to await transfer of his regiment as soon as it could be assembled, a misconception made evident two days later when the colonel appeared in San Antonio.[58]

Meanwhile, the quartermaster at Fort Sam Houston, charged with mounting and supplying 1,000 men, was frantically trying to find horses for volunteers on their way to Camp Wood. The day he arrived in Texas, Wood was seen in the fort's quadrangle "busily sizing up several dozen cayuses"; the next afternoon he laid out the camp at Riverside Park. The San Antonio Daily Express, politely suppressing its disappointment that Wood and not Roosevelt had come to organize the facility, described the colonel as "just the kind of man one would expect to see at the head of a regiment of Western volunteer cavalry."

Wood had intended to set up a proper military camp under canvas on the fairground's grassy plain, but Fort Sam Houston could only come up with twenty tents, so the colonel compromised by putting the men and their mess kitchens in the barn that had been the fairgrounds exhibition hall. As quickly as that decision was made—in fact, the same day—men and supplies began to arrive. One train brought 189 pack mules from St. Louis as others arrived with troops from Arizona and Oklahoma. Wood summarily rejected two carloads of saddles. The new style was smaller than the friendly old "Arapajo" ones on which he had spent months in Arizona and Mexico, and his cowboys dismissed them as mere postage stamps.[59] The first trainload of Arizonans came on the Southern Pacific Railroad at 8:00 A.M. on May 7 and marched directly to the fairgrounds for breakfast just in time for Brodie to join Wood and Major George Dunn for an initial tour. Dunn, who accompanied Wood from Washington, had been a lawyer in Denver but had most recently worked in Washington where he had "been a leader of outdoor sports among the smart set" and master of the fox and hounds at the Chevy Chase Club.[60]

The Oklahoma troops arrived later in the day. Brodie and Oklahoma Captain R. B. Houston self-consciously assured anyone who asked that their men were carefully selected volunteers and not rowdies, stressing that many had left large ranches or important businesses to join the fight and were "the flower of Western manhood . . . splendid types of American citizens, cultured and educated," and were called Rough Riders in reference to their equestrian abilities and not their behavior.[61] Both the officers and men were quick to differentiate the troops from the usual run of soldiers. One recruit told a reporter, "I would rather march in the ranks among such men as these and under such commanders as Roosevelt, Wood, Dunn and Brodie than to be a captain in any other volunteer regiment in the herd." One lieutenant announced, "I wouldn't swap my commission in this regiment for the adjutant generalship of the militia of any state in the Union."

The men got to Camp Wood before their equipment but not before their name. The papers had tried out Teddy's Terrors, Teddy's Texas Tarantulas, Teddy's Gilded Gang (for the eastern contingent), and Teddy's Riotous Rounders. Mercifully, none stuck. "Rough Riders" had first appeared in the *Arizona Weekly Star* on April 21 in reference to that state's recruits.[62] The press, unable to resist an alliteration, changed it to Roosevelt's Rough Riders. Cowboy Cavalry and Wood's Regiment were proposed, but the name was set. Roosevelt initially objected, worried that "people who read it may get the impression that the regiment is to be a hippodrome affair." He wanted the public to know that his men would be "orderly, obedient, and generally well disciplined a body as any equal number of men in any branch of the service."[63] But the publicity-conscious Roosevelt arranged for several newspapermen, including Stephen Crane, Jacob Riis, and Richard Harding Davis, to accompany the regiment.

Roosevelt slipped in a collection of his eastern friends without Wood's knowledge, although the colonel never objected. The New Yorker mined the ranks of upper class amateur sportsmen, especially those who had been involved in Ivy League athletics. He enlisted Woodbury Kane, William Tiffany, and Craig Wadsworth of the Knicker-bocker Club; August Belmont, Oliver Hazard Perry's great nephew; and Hamilton Fish of the New York political family;[64] and he asked the vice president of the National Fox Hunters' Association to assemble one hundred volunteers from his membership.[65]

The Texas papers, not entirely convinced that their cowboy regiments should be diluted with eastern interlopers, grudgingly allowed that the athletes' "experience on the gridiron, the diamond and in the racing shell has given them just the physical development necessary for the service they are entering upon," and that most of them knew how to ride "Western style" and some had even had ranch experience. The journalists were less sanguine about "society" recruits due to arrive the next day. Advance rumors had the "Fifth Avenue Rough Riders" coming with a trainload of valets, trunks, and golf equipment.[66] The papers heaved a collective sigh of relief the following day when the men arrived without personal attendants, golf sticks, or dress suits and looked as if "they could stand the hardships of campaigning and could also fight."[67] One trooper later described the assembled unit as "Twelve hundred . . . millionaires, paupers, shyster lawyers, cowboys, quack doctors, farmers, college professors, miners, adventurers, preachers, prospectors, socialists, journalists, insurance agents, Jews, politicians, Gentiles, Mexicans, professed Christians, Indians, West Point graduates, Arkansan wild men, baseball players, sheriffs and horse-thieves."[68]

Wood was not actually sworn into the line army until May 9, when Lieutenant Colonel S. H. Whitside of the Fifth Cavalry was ordered to "muster into the service of the United States Capt. Leonard Wood, Assistant Surgeon U. S. A. as Colonel of the First United States Volunteer Cavalry."[69] Although he would not be sure of it for several more years, Wood had permanently abandoned his medical career for that of a combat officer and administrator.

Unsolicited volunteers continued to drift into camp and Wood, with many more men than allotted places, was forced to cull them; the criterion he chose perfectly reflected his prejudices. Wood told his examining surgeon to ignore the usual standards of training and experience and to reject any man whose stomach was bigger than his chest.

The men varied in height from a bandy-legged five-foot two-inch cowboy to the regiment's six-foot six-inch color sergeant, almost none had any military training, and most neither knew nor cared about the protocols of rank and tradition. The colonel picked his officers for leadership rather than social standing. Millionaire New England socialites found themselves washing dishes for Wyoming ranch hands and taking orders from Arizona sheriffs. The men were, however, young, adaptable, and ineffably convinced that they were elite by virtue of being in the Rough Riders with or without the embellishment of rank.

By the middle of May, Wood had a full, albeit marginally trained, complement of men, but they remained sadly underequipped. He had 800 horses more or less broken, but only 150 saddles so Brodie— serendipitously—trained his Arizonans on foot. The men would eventually receive Krag-Jorgensen rifles, but those who had not brought their own guns were unarmed. When the first shipment of Krags arrived, it was preallotted to the First Squadron, and men in the other squadrons were so anxious to have guns that they offered $25 to any man from the First who would transfer and leave his rifle behind.[70] They at least had an ample supply of brown fatigues and machetes, although neither did much to make the unit look like soldiers.

On May 6, Roosevelt had been sworn in as a lieutenant colonel in the United States Volunteers by Army Adjutant General Henry C. Corbin. Roosevelt made sure there were reporters present to appreciate "the plainsmen and rough riders . . . in broad-brimmed sombreros" projecting "an unmistakable evidence of their ability to round up a herd of refractory steers."[71] His staff presented him a silver-mounted cavalry saber (destined for early retirement) which he proudly kept on his desk to impress anyone who happened through before he left for San Antonio.[72]

The lieutenant colonel was greeted with mixed enthusiasm when he got to Texas. The cowboys who knew him only by his reputation as a dandified New York politician were particularly put off by his spectacles, a certain mark of urban softness. In fact, the wearing of glasses had been lumped with rupture, lung disease, flat feet, and heart troubles as mandatory disqualifying physical defects back in Arizona. They were considered a major impediment for an effective fighting man since "aside from the fact that it is difficult to keep glasses clean in the field in battle, the smoke and dust would so cloud them that they would be more of a detriment than a benefit to the wearer."[73] The westerners were also put off by Roosevelt's Harvard accent and a tinny voice that, in moments of excitement, edged past tenor in the general direction of soprano. One trooper commented that he might like the lieutenant colonel better if he would quit skinning back his teeth every time he opened his mouth.

In the few weeks at San Antonio, Wood earned respect for his willingness to stretch protocol, for working long hours, and for sharing the most menial of tasks with his men. He was, however, not outgoing, and the ebullient Roosevelt quickly became a camp favorite. In the end, the men trusted Wood, but they liked Roosevelt. Although they were diametrically different in attitude and approach—Wood icily formal and Roosevelt frenetically enthusiastic—both got on well with the recruits and the affection was mutual.

Still, it only took a few days of camp life for the cowboys to start getting restless. They hated the food, they hated marching and drilling, and they hated the fact that Camp Wood was dusty and bone dry in more ways than one.[74] If they were to fight a war, they wanted to get on with it. In typical Wood fashion, the colonel attacked the problem by ignoring protocol and going directly to the top. On May 22, he wrote McKinley that he had meant to be in touch sooner since the president had "expressed so much interest in this particular regiment." The letter enthusiastically praised his "exceptionally fine body of men . . . all intelligent, honest and full of enthusiasm," and extolled Roosevelt's interest in the regiment and willingness to work "like a beaver from morning to night." Then Wood got to the point: "We are all hoping to get our orders to get off with the first expedition and shall be much disappointed if we do not."[75] Wood was, however, less than reassured by the terse response from the president's secretary, noting that McKinley had "read with a great deal of pleasure your very interesting letter" and assuring the colonel that his commander appreciated so complete a report. There was no mention of deployment.

While the Rough Riders waited, they drilled. Reveille at 5:30 A.M. started a day of riding and marching. The men rode in column three miles down the road to the San Juan mission; they acted out cavalry charges on the small prairie in front of the fairgrounds grandstand; they rode half way up the hill adjoining the camp, dismounted, and acted out a foot charge to the top of the incline in the face of pretended enemy fire. And they kicked up Texas dust, sweated, and waited. Wood tried to put the best face on it. He told reporters:

> We are now ready to move whenever the order comes but, of course, every day that we are allowed to remain in camp is of the utmost value to us. Many of the men and officers being inexperienced in military matters need all the training they can possibly receive before leaving for the front.[76]

Rumor had it that they would go to Cuba as soon as Admiral William Sampson found and destroyed the Spanish Atlantic fleet, but no one knew when that would happen, so Wood made things tougher. A new shipment of tents arrived and the men were moved out of the exposition hall into dog tents and the hall was placed off limits.[77]

On May 23, the adjutant general wired asking when the regiment would be ready to move. Wood fired back that he *was* ready and hopefully requisitioned extra supplies and horseshoes from Fort Sam Houston's long-suffering quartermaster for the anticipated deployment. "Ready" was relative; the previous day's mounted exercises had been marred by "some rather stirring equestrian episodes," including marginally trained mustangs bucking, plunging, charging, and generally refusing to cooperate with army regulations, but Wood and Roosevelt were sure the men could smooth over the rough spots on the way to Cuba.[78]

Finally, on Saturday May 28, Wood received a telegram from Alger ordering him to Tampa. The colonel smiled, handed the telegram to Roosevelt, and quietly shook his hand; the lieutenant colonel tore off his hat, jumped in the air, and whooped. The following morning Wood, Roosevelt, 1,060 men, and 1,280 horses and mules boarded twenty-five day coaches, two Pullman cars, five baggage cars, eight box cars, and sixty stable cars at the Southern Pacific's Union Stock Yards and decamped for Florida.[79]

The amateur regiment had trained just over a month, but both the men and the public had no doubt the Rough Riders would crush the numerically superior professional Spanish army. The prediction, save for the fact that it proved correct, was ludicrous.

As the month in San Antonio passed, the American war plan staggered to life. In the beginning, Miles and Alger were faced with conquering two large islands (Cuba and Luzon) occupied by a potpourri of inhabitants variably loyal to their Spanish governors with the assistance of an unknown number of rebels whose fighting ability was doubtful at best. Cuba was garrisoned by an estimated 80,000 Spanish regulars seasoned to tropical warfare and armed with excellent rifles. The Spanish fleet's ability to resupply and augment their forces and the United States Navy's ability to carry out a two-ocean blockade while protecting the American coasts were equally uncertain.

Best estimates were that the regular army could field about 16,000 men, to which the Cuban insurrection could add perhaps 4,000 more.[80] To augment that anemic force, Miles had to rely on a patchwork of even more poorly equipped and officered National Guard units and his cowboy regiments. The National Guard had an astounding 10,378,118 men liable for duty, but, realistically, fewer than 115,000 were even remotely usable. Of these, since the National Guard by statute could not be required to serve outside the country's borders, only volunteers would be available, and Miles was convinced the volunteers would be "absolutely unsafe in the field against regular troops." One of his officers, although professing respect for the militia, said "it cannot be considered as a regular army, is not seasoned for active campaigning, lacks the solidarity and cohesion of regulars, and cannot be depended on for stubborn fighting, or even for aggressive movements."[81] Wood, tarred with the same brush as the rest of the volunteers, faced a real problem gaining acceptance from the regulars and it was entirely likely that, given a choice, the army would keep all the volunteers out of the fighting.

Although war with Spain had been discussed for half a century, no actual strategy had been formulated; now the press and Congress demanded action within weeks if not days. Alger wanted to send small units to fight with the Cuban rebels whom he proposed to arm and supply. Miles preferred to send supplies only and defer risking American troops until a regular army force large enough to invade and occupy the island could be trained and organized. The strategically sensitive argument was carried out in full view of the press where subtlety and secrecy vanished beneath 48-point headlines.[82]

Just at the moment, high-level arguments were of secondary importance to Wood and Roosevelt, who were occupied with the mundane vicissitudes of forcing 1,200 horses and mules onto rail cars without loading ramps. Officers and men were sick of hundred-degree days and dusty brush country wind. Admiral George Dewey had taken

Manila, and there was more than a little worry that the Spanish would capitulate before the Rough Riders could get into the fight. Admiral Pascual Cervera y Topete's Spanish fleet was said to be sailing the Antilles everywhere from Venezuela to Florida while other reports had it docked in Curaçao, Martinique, Haiti, and Puerto Rico. As Wood's men packed their gear, Admiral Winfield Scott Schley (with the help of a spy in the Havana telegraph office) found the Spanish ships in the protected harbor at Santiago on Cuba's southeast coast. If Schley defeated the Spanish, the war might abruptly end. On the other hand, if he only blockaded them the focus of the land campaign would definitely be Cuba's southern coast, where it had long been rumored the Rough Riders would be sent. They needed to be in Tampa.

The train from San Antonio was unique. It carried nearly 1,000 adventure-seeking cowboys from an outpost on a vanishing frontier across five states that had, only a generation before, suffered through the Civil War. On its way to America's first exercise of international power politics, the train physically traversed the American South and metaphorically passed from one era of American history to another.

Once underway, Wood divided his time between maintaining order among his wayward troops and arguing with railway employees. (At one point he took possession of the train at gunpoint and forced a passenger train off the single track.) Roosevelt spent the days reading Camille Desmoulins' *Supériorité des Anglo-Saxons*.[83] During the day the men mostly slept, so that when the trains stopped at night they could "work like dogs" feeding and watering the stock.[84] The monotony of four days on the train was punctuated by enthusiastic crowds in virtually every town and station. Roosevelt saw that the men had a constant supply of coffee, and townspeople along the rail line brought food, flowers, and adoration. The trains pushed through Texas and the Gulf states —Houston, Lafayette, New Orleans, Biloxi, Mobile, Pensacola, Tallahassee, and south to Tampa. The men gloried in fields of flags, both Stars and Stripes and Stars and Bars, waved by men and women who had not forgotten defeat and reconstruction. Wood wrote, "All the cost of this war is amply repaid by seeing the old flag as one sees it today in the South. We are indeed once more a united country."[85] The Spanish War helped heal states where the memory of the last war remained strong although much of the social and physical devastation would survive another fifty years.

In the last two weeks of May, 13,000 of the regular army had been transferred to Tampa along with about 15,000 of the most serviceable volunteers lucky enough to escape camps awash in hapless, typhoid-ridden National Guard troops, many of whom would die of disease and few of whom would ever leave the United States.[86] The chaos in the camps was matched only by that of headquarters in Washington. Lacking the hierarchy and clarity of a general staff system, McKinley made strategic decisions based on uncoordinated or frankly contradictory input from Commanding General Miles, Secretary of War Alger, General Paul Schofield (his personal military advisor), and Adjutant General Henry Corbin. The plans for the Cuban and Puerto Rican invasions changed daily. It was left to the quartermaster general and the head of the Bureau of Ordnance to supply, arm, and transport the regular army and the flood of new volunteers. The two unfortunates, isolated from the decision-making process, had to guess what resources they would have to supply and scrounge them where they could. There was never any one officer charged with organizing the camp at Tampa or the transport of men from Florida to Cuba. As with Wood, it was each commander's responsibility to see that his men were clothed, armed, trained, and transported to Florida while the bureau chiefs squabbled and vacillated.[87]

By May 26, it looked as if Cervera's fleet was both trapped and unassailable in a harbor accessible only through a narrow, heavily mined channel protected by overhanging cliffs studded with Spanish cannon.[88] The only way to defeat the Spanish admiral would be to land an invasion force east or west of Santiago, take the city from land, and force the fleet to sea. McKinley ordered Major General William Shafter to take his Fifth Corps (including Wood's Rough Riders) to Santiago forthwith.[89]

Shafter had spent forty-seven of his sixty-five years in the army, first as a Medal of Honor winning soldier in the Civil War, and then in an agonizingly measured ascent to brigadier general in a succession of remote western garrisons. In a rare demonstration of consensus, he was the unanimous choice of Alger, Miles, and McKinley for promotion to major general and command of the Fifth Corps, although his physical appearance offered no hint of what his superiors found so impressive. He had a mustachioed, leonine head on top of a squat body one of his commissary officers (in a unique position to know) bluntly called "beastly obese."[90] Shafter could barely carry his own weight and had a reputation as a bad mannered bully. Worst of all, like the rest of the American senior officers, he had not commanded a unit larger than a few hundred men in almost forty years. The presence of tens of thousands of men needing rapid supply and organization bewildered him. Shafter's only salvation came from his surprisingly competent officers and the fact that the Fifth Corps comprised the cream of the American forces.

On May 25, Wood's trains pulled to a stop on a lonely stretch of track miles from Shafter's camp. Between the Rough Riders and Port Tampa's single pier stretched ten miles of sandy pine barren with no road and only a single railroad spur; the hardest part of getting to Cuba would be getting to the ships. Tampa's railhead had only a few warehouses, trains were arriving in the hundreds, a thousand cars jammed the limited facilities, and as many more backed up on sidings all the way to South Carolina. Two different rail companies served Tampa, but Henry Plant operated the single line from the city to the port, and he refused to allow a competitor's cars to use his tracks. The cars were being unloaded at an excruciating two or three a day when frustrated soldiers took things into their own hands, pried open the mountains of unlabeled containers and appropriated whatever seemed useful.

Responsibility for finding ships to ferry the men to Cuba fell to Quartermaster Marshall I. Luddington. He had commissioned a survey of every available merchant ship on the east coast, but was hampered by the fact that federal law only allowed him to charter ships operating under the American flag, and there were pathetically few of those. To compound his difficulties, the waters around Cuba and Puerto Rico were too shallow for the transatlantic vessels that comprised much of the available fleet, and American shipowners, worried about postwar competition, blocked transfer of registry for ships not already under the U.S. flag. What Luddington found were mostly smaller vessels meant for freight rather than men, and the abrupt decision to invade left him only a few days to convert them. Ships sailed from New York with workers still hammering and welding in the holds.[91]

In the end, the quartermaster's department assembled thirty-one shallow draft coastal freighters, one collier, and two water boats along with three small lighters, one tug, and two barges for an epic amphibious landing. Real amphibious craft were still well in the future, and the coast on either side of Santiago, exposed to prevailing southeasterly winds, rendered landing an uncertain proposition at best. Most of the men and equipment would either have to come ashore on one of the few available lifeboats or swim. In the end, Luddington's entire armada could only accommodate 17,000 of Shafter's 25,000 troops. The other 8,000, including a group of bitterly disappointed Rough Riders, stayed in Tampa.[92]

Shafter's Fifth Corps started loading transports on May 26 but did not complete the job for eleven days. Plant had built Port Tampa as a jumping-off point for excursions to Key West or Cuba, and it was served by a single dock that could accommodate only two ships at a time. The army had extended the single track onto the pier but most of the lading had to be done by stevedores who carried their loads on their backs across fifty yards of sand and up steep ramps onto the ships.[93] It was exhausting, insufferably slow work, and every day Shafter was bombarded with telegrams from the president or the secretary of the navy who were worried that Cervera would escape and might even attack the United States east coast.[94]

On May 31, the war department sent the formal, encoded instruction:

> You are directed to take your command on transports, proceed under convoy of the navy to the vicinity of Santiago de Cuba, land your force at such place east or west of that point as your judgment may dictate, under the protection of the navy . . . to capture or destroy the garrison there; and . . . with the aid of the navy capture or destroy the Spanish fleet now reported to be in Santiago harbor. . . . On completion of this enterprise, unless you receive other orders or deem it advisable to remain in the harbor of Santiago de Cuba, re-embark your troops and proceed to the harbor of Port de Banes. . . . When will you sail?[95]

Three nights later Wood and the Rough Riders were still feverishly trying to get to Port Tampa. Roosevelt wrote, "There was no one to meet us or to tell us where we were to camp, and no one to issue us food for the first twenty-four hours; while the railroad people unloaded us wherever they pleased, or rather wherever the jam of all kinds of trains rendered it possible."[96] The trains, provisioned in San Antonio for a three-day trip, ran out of food before they got to Tampa, and Roosevelt and Wood fed the men out of their own funds. The morning after they arrived, they formed the regiment into columns of fours, commandeered what wagons they could find, and walked to Shafter's camp.

When they got there, they were met with a scene "rather curiously combining aspects of a professional men's reunion, a county fair, and . . .

a major disaster."[97] Wood wrote Louise that "we found everything confused and in a most frightful mix. Streets packed with soldiers and a
foot deep in real beach sand. Confusion, confusion, confusion."[98] They
were one of the last units to arrive, and rank after rank of tent rows
stretched from Lakeland thirty miles north of Tampa to the port nine
miles south of the city.

Within a day Wood laid out streets with officers' tents and kitchens
at the ends, cleaned and policed the area, and started drilling the men
—first on foot to let the horses recover from the trip and then in
mounted formations across the pine-covered flats. Their dirty brown
canvas uniforms may not have looked as military as the regulars' blue
blouses, but it was the general opinion of the gaggle of foreign observers that the Rough Riders had the best organized camp in the corps
and were the only unit who looked as if they might possibly function in
the field. Wood, acutely conscious of his standing with the regulars, allowed that the praise "while very flimsy makes the others feel a little
jealous."[99]

Shafter had established his headquarters at the surrealistically or-
nate Tampa Bay Hotel, a five-story Moorish confection built by Plant
with the anachronistic hope of drawing tourists to Florida's west coast
from whence he could whisk them off to Key West on his steamer
Olivette. The hotel's six-acre grounds sported a golf course, a casino,
dining rooms, and elaborate ballrooms, but, for Shafter and his officers,
its main attractions were the broad, comfortable balconies, leading correspondent Richard Harding Davis to term these few days the "rocking
chair period" of the Spanish War. Roosevelt disingenuously dismissed
the hotel as a place where Rough Riders "spent very little time,"[100] conveniently forgetting that he had brought his wife to Tampa and spent
about half of the nights before leaving for Cuba in the hotel with her.
The businesslike Wood tersely wrote his Lou, "Would give anything to
see you but don't come. Am selected for the first expedition with 400
men."[101]

Wood's camp was a source of limitless curiosity. Tampans, already
subjected to several weeks of questionable behavior from underem-
ployed regular soldiers and prewarned about the Rough Riders' Wild
West origin, were not as welcoming as San Antonians. In fact, the citizenry asked that the westerners not be paid until the day they were
to leave in hopes that impecunious soldiers would be forced to stay in
camp. Newsmen and foreign observers were anxious to see if the reg-

iment lived up to its reputation. Roosevelt spent the better part of his time granting interviews, hosting visiting dignitaries, and grinning. Wood, elbowed out of the limelight by his flamboyant subordinate, saw to organization. To the public, it was Roosevelt's regiment, but the work of command had been done and continued to be done by Wood.

Meanwhile, the loading staggered along. Settled in his oversized rocker, Shafter was bombarded by telegrams from Washington asking when he would sail and inundated with complaints from his officers that they had not nearly enough of anything. They lacked arms, food, uniforms, supplies, and what they needed was hopelessly lost in the indecipherable welter of railroad cars stretching back over three states. Alger, out of patience, wired on Monday June 6 that Shafter and 25,000 men ought to be able to unload any number of rail cars and that, if he could not, he might reserve one fast ship to catch up with whatever was lacking and just leave with what he already had on board. The Fifth Corps had loaded the last of their animals and supplies that morning, but the men were still on shore.

Unsurprisingly, the single track to the port was entirely insufficient for moving 25,000 men in a day, especially since Mr. Plant was also using the track for trainloads of paying tourists and dignitaries. Admiral Sampson did not help the situation when he cabled, "If 10,000 men were here, city and fleet would be ours within forty-eight hours. Every consideration demands immediate Army movement."[102] Demands from Washington went from urgent to strident: "You will sail immediately." "Time is the essence of the situation." "Early departure of first importance." And, finally, at 8:50 in the evening, "Since telegraphing you an hour since the President directs you to sail at once with what force you have ready."[103]

Wood had already been told that there was not transport space for all his men or for any but a few of the senior officers' horses; now he was forced to tell four of his twelve troops that they were to be left behind. Brodie and Roosevelt got to go; Hersey and Dunn did not; without horses, Roosevelt's Rough Riders (probably courtesy of a wag from the ill-fated Seventy-First New York Volunteers) temporarily became "Wood's Weary Walkers." In the last minute rush, Wood was informed that only those men who could be on a ship by June 7 would be in the invasion. The whole regiment was at risk, and it was up to their colonel to figure out how to get the men and supplies to Port Tampa's pier and onto a transport before Shafter left for Santiago.

Wood was told to assemble his men at the tracks carrying their bedding, their Krags, 125 rounds of ammunition, and a haversack full of food at midnight. He complied, but no transportation appeared, and the men were left sleeping by the tracks while Roosevelt and Wood badgered every railroad man they could find. Finally, at 6:00 A.M., after a fruitless march to yet another empty siding, a line of coal cars appeared on a return trip from the port. Wood commandeered the cars, loaded his men, and ordered the engineer, who had no place to turn around, to steam in reverse to Port Tampa. The Rough Riders arrived sleepy and sooty, but they were on the dock and the ships were still there.

Unfortunately, there were some 10,000 other men milling around the dock, and no one seemed to have any idea what to do next. The coal train left the Rough Riders at the farthest end of the quay, and the men unloaded while Roosevelt and Wood frantically hunted for someone who could assign them a ship. Finally, a harried dock master told them to talk to the depot quartermaster who was probably asleep on one of the transports, and, after an hour-long search, they rousted the man who distractedly told Wood, "Get any ship you can get which is not already assigned. There's one coming in now. You can go on her if you can get her."[104] Wood confiscated a launch, rowed into the channel, and seized the boat. Roosevelt went back to the regiment which he divided into a guard detail that he left with the equipment and the rest of the troops whom he quick-marched to the pier. Wood had learned that the *Yucatan* (the vessel in question) had also been assigned to the Second Regular Infantry and the sarcastic Seventy-First New York Volunteers, and he correctly assumed that occupation implied ownership.

Wood brought his captive vessel to the pier as Roosevelt marched the men into position. Just as they boarded and sent a detachment back to get their supplies, the other regiments appeared, being, as Roosevelt noted, "a shade less ready than we were in the matter of individual initiative."[105] Wood ultimately made room for four companies of the Second Infantry, but the rest were chased away by a hail of coal retrieved from the ship's hold.[106] Roosevelt did manage to find room for two Vitagraph Company photographers; the lieutenant colonel understood historical significance.[107] A transport designed to carry a maximum of 500 men was packed with 43 officers, 773 enlisted men, and the two movie makers.[108] (In fact, Shafter's army was accompanied by 89 reporters, a number significantly greater than the force's total contingent of surgeons.)[109]

The soot-stained Rough Riders spent the rest of the day at the back-breaking job of carrying their equipment down the long quay and walking it onto the *Yucatan*. By nightfall, thirty-six grueling hours after their first order to depart, the ship pulled out into the bay to await sailing orders. And therein lay a problem. Shafter had loaded as many men as humanly possible and the invasion was almost underway when a telegram from Alger brought the procession to an abrupt halt. "Wait until you get further orders before you sail. Answer quick."[110] A navy scout vessel (the converted yacht *Eagle*) reported sighting a Spanish armored cruiser and a torpedo-boat destroyer in the St. Nicholas channel, and red-faced naval officers belatedly realized they had no idea whether all or only part of Cervera's fleet was in Santiago. The convoy's naval escort was sent out to sweep the channel while Sampson detailed a scouting expedition to look into Santiago harbor and count the ships.

For six sweltering days 16,000 men sweated and cursed in airless holds under steel decks waiting for the navy to declare the seas free of Spanish ships. Tepid drinking water turned green as the algae bloomed and grew. Unwashed, the men stank. Stock died and garbage rotted alongside in the stagnant harbor water. Wood and Roosevelt tried to keep the men occupied by going over the manual of arms and studying whatever books on tactics they could bring to hand. Some men relieved the heat and boredom by diving over the side, but most, either unable to swim or put off by the sharks sniffing through the ships' trash, stayed on board and suffered.[111] Wood's light-weight canvas uniforms were marginally less miserable than the regulars' blue woolens, but it was slight comfort in the lower holds where the temperature hovered around 120 degrees.[112]

Finally, on the evening of June 13, the navy declared the channel safe and Sampson reported all Spanish ships accounted for. The convoy recoaled, rewatered, reprovisioned, and resailed. Roosevelt wrote that the armada "went slowly ahead under half-steam for the distant mouth of the harbor, the bands playing, the flags flying, the rigging black with clustered soldiers, cheering and shouting to those left behind on the quays."[113] As usual, he exaggerated. The "cheering and shouting" throngs comprised three black women, three soldiers, and a few stevedores, but the first American army to attempt an overseas invasion in half a century was underway.[114] In all, the flotilla carried 819 officers,

16,058 enlisted men, 30 clerks, 89 newspaper correspondents (not counting Roosevelt's two photographers), 11 foreign observers, 272 teamsters, 107 stevedores, and 2,295 horses and mules. They also carried 114 six-mule wagons, 81 escort wagons, and a pitifully inadequate seven ambulances along with sixteen light guns, four 7-inch howitzers, four siege guns, one Hotchkiss revolving cannon, eight 3.6-inch mortars, and a dynamite gun that had been donated to the Rough Riders. One of Wood's men hung a sign over the side that announced, "Standing Room Only," to which was wryly appended, "And damn little of that."[115]

The troops were divided into two divisions of infantry (one under Brigadier General J. Ford Kent and the other under Wood's old friend Brigadier General Henry Lawton), one division of dismounted cavalry (there being no room for the horses) under Brigadier General Joseph Wheeler, one independent brigade under Brigadier General John C. Bates, and four batteries of artillery. The Rough Riders were the only volunteer regiment in "Fighting Joe" Wheeler's cavalry division.[116]

As the convoy gathered steam and eased out of Tampa Bay, the thirty-two transports sorted into three long columns, but two transports towing a barge and a schooner filled with water set the flotilla's agonizing pace. Richard Harding Davis wrote, "Sometimes we moved at the rate of four miles an hour, and frequently we did not move at all."[117] The naval escort spent the next six days trying to keep the hapless transports into something resembling a convoy. The navy, unable to convince Shafter to split his slower ships into a separate group, was reduced to shepherding the wandering flock into whatever semblance of order they could manage. Davis said, "We could not keep in line and we lost ourselves and each other, and the gun-boats and torpedo-boats were busy rounding us up, and giving us sharp, precise orders in passing, through a megaphone, to which either nobody on board made any reply, or everyone did. The gun-boats were like swift, keen-eyed, intelligent collies rounding up a herd of bungling sheep."[118] The convoy, lights carelessly blazing, passed along Cuba's north coast close enough to see Spanish soldiers outside their barracks.

The men remained surprisingly healthy, the weather remained good, and the Spanish remained ashore. The flotilla enjoyed the luck of the innocent and the Americans were convinced that heaven intended it that way. One general said, "This is God Almighty's war, and we are only His agents."[119] Less sanguine, Wood noted, "A good dashing Spanish commander could get into this fleet and put out a good portion of it before he could be located."[120] The European observers were simply appalled.

The men suffered in hastily constructed three-tiered wooden bunks growing lice and subsisting on hardtack, coffee, and gray beef canned half a decade earlier for the Sino-Japanese War. Heat, close quarters, inedible food, and the rocking summer sea gave many of the cowboys their first taste of motion sickness and left their officers worried that they might not recover in time to fight. Wood had the bunks torn out and made into gratings to span open spaces so the men could sleep on deck. The makeshift bunks were taken up during the day so there would be space for drilling and exercise.[121]

Only a handful of senior officers knew whether they were bound for Havana, Puerto Rico, or Santiago until the day the ships turned southwest and the easterly trades which had been in their faces were off the port quarter. Wood wrote:

> Painted ships on a painted ocean. Imagine three great lines of transports with a warship at the head of each line, steaming in long lines, 800 yards from each other over a sea of indigo blue, real deep blue, such as I have never seen before. Air warm and balmy, with a gentle breeze stirring up the water. No swell or disturbance. Simply a great peaceful marine picture. Hard it is to realize that this is the commencement of a new policy and that this is the first great expedition our country has ever sent overseas and marks the commencement of a new era in our relations with the world. . . . North of us about ten miles away is the Cuban coast with high beautiful mountains rising about six thousand feet directly up from the water's edge. The sea is as smooth as a mill pond.[122]

He reassured his mother, "We hardly know what is in store for us at Santiago but I do not think we are going to have a very hard time. The general impression is that after this we will be sent by ship to Puerto Rico, to take that island."[123] He was wrong on both counts.

On Monday June 20, they could see the Sierra Maestre with Santiago nestled between the blue mountain haze and Sampson's fleet. Shafter spent the next two days coordinating his invasion with the navy and García's insurgents. Shafter and Sampson, accompanied by their staffs, the British and German military attachés, and several reporters (including Frederic Remington and the ever-present Davis), came ashore twenty miles west of Santiago at Aserraderos to meet with the patrician, white-linened general whose silver-haired good looks were marred by a weeping bone-deep furrow plowed exactly between his eyes by a self-inflicted gunshot wound from his days as a Spanish prisoner. Sampson's gig was met by a squad of half-naked Cuban soldiers who, anxious to preserve the Americans' boots and uniforms, waded out into the surf and carried them ashore on their shoulders.[124] Shafter's one-sixth-ton bulk was hauled to General Calixto García's camp on an unlucky but "stout-hearted" mule.

García and Shafter decided to land at Daiquirí, a small village seventeen miles west of Santiago, and attack the city from behind. Sampson, having planned for the army to capture Morro Castle at the mouth of Santiago's harbor and disable the mines at the harbor entrance so his ships could attack the Spanish fleet while it lay at anchor, was furious.[125] An assault from behind might very well cause the Spanish admiral to surrender before the navy could get into the action. Shafter dismissed the admiral's objections and pressed on.

There was little to recommend Daiquirí except that everywhere else was worse. Guantánamo had an excellent harbor but was forty miles from Santiago.[126] All the other potential landing sites were open to the ocean and had rudimentary docks. Daiquirí's only landing facility was a tall pier used to load ore from the Juragua Iron Company's disused facility, so the men, the animals, and the bulk of the equipment would have to come ashore on a beach open to the prevailing winds and pounding surf. The final plan called for Sampson to divert the Spanish by shelling Santiago while García's troops isolated Daiquirí from inland. Once ashore, Shafter's men were to march west along a narrow coast road that the Americans expected to be defended by Spanish regulars. It was García's job first to see that the Spanish did not amass a force from Santiago to oppose the landing and then to prevent reinforcements coming overland from Havana to attack Shafter from behind. The expedition was under some time pressure since the rainy season, yellow fever, and malaria were only a week away.

Fortunately for Shafter, Lieutenant General Arsenio Linares Pombo, Spanish commander of the Department of Santiago, had no idea where the landing was to take place; one unprotected, unimproved harbor seemed to him as likely as another. He had spread his 36,582 troops (about 12,000 of whom were in the immediate vicinity of Santiago) throughout the eastern part of the province, leaving no potential site unguarded, but none guarded adequately. On June 22, before the three hundred troops at Daiquirí could endure even a single shot from the naval bombardment, they simply withdrew and let Shafter's men land unopposed.

Using steam launches, lifeboats, and whatever light craft the navy could muster, Shafter got 6,000 men and a fair number of his horses and mules ashore. The first animals were simply pushed overboard, and a number of the disoriented beasts headed out to sea before an enterprising trooper began blowing "Charge." The horses turned to the call, and all but thirty (including Roosevelt's Rain-in-the-Face) managed to get to land. Later, the animals were strung together and led by boats to the breakers where they were cut loose to be pulled ashore by soldiers who had waded out after them. All of the men except two, who were dragged to the bottom by their heavy packs (in spite of Captain "Buckey" O'Neill's diving in and trying to pull them back to the surface), came safely ashore.

Shafter had planned for Lawton's Second Infantry Division and four Gatling guns to be the first on the beach, followed by Bates's brigade with Wheeler's dismounted cavalry (including Wood's troops) last ashore. The landing started at 9:40 in the morning and, to the delight and surprise of the troops watching from ships, was entirely unopposed. Wood decided not to wait for his regiment to land. He stole a boat and sent Albert Wright, the oversized sergeant; Henry La Motte, the regimental surgeon; and Clay Platt, the unit's trumpeter ashore with the Arizona squadron's flag.[127] They climbed to a blockhouse on Mount Losiltires which overlooked the harbor from the east where they encountered reporter Edward Marshall who intended to raise "a small flag belonging to the *New York Journal*" in the same place. Marshall bowed to military precedence and, after several failed attempts at climbing the roof, the Rough Riders' flag went up.[128] There followed, "A quarter of an hour of whistle shrieks, cheers, yells, drum flares, bugle calls and patriotic songs."[129]

Meanwhile, Wood and Roosevelt were frantically trying to get their men ashore. They realized that the general confusion of the landing would force them—assuming they kept their assigned order of debarkation—to spend the night on board the *Yucatan* while the infantry was preparing to march toward Santiago and the enemy, but Roosevelt saved the day. He found a lieutenant who had once been his aide commanding the converted yacht *Vixen*. The young officer had a Cuban pilot who was able to maneuver the *Yucatan* within a few hundred yards of shore (and directly in the path of the launches ferrying the infantry to the beach) while the rest of the transports cautiously hovered a mile and a half from the beach.[130] Wood, anxious to be on land before dark, took his men ashore with the *Yucatan*'s lifeboats. By dark, Lawton's division, Bates's brigade, and the entire Second Cavalry Brigade (6,000 men in all) were on the beach. Linares had pulled his men back from Daiquirí and Siboney a few miles to the west and taken up a defensive position three miles down the road to Santiago.[131]

When they got ashore, the Rough Riders made camp next to the Negro Tenth Cavalry in a field east of Daiquirí where they were immediately besieged by a horde of Cuban civilians and shabby *insurrectos*. The Cuban irregulars were armed with a hodgepodge of weapons, mostly stolen from the Spanish; some wore rags, and many were naked except for torn shirts. One sergeant, comparing the Cubans to Indians he had fought in the Southwest, wrote:

> ... in all my travels I never saw such a dilapidated, hungry, undressed group of men in my life as these Cuban soldiers were. The only thing they wore was a cartridge belt, mostly empty, to this some of them would arrange a "G" string. Some of the more energetic would fabricate sandals out of the fiber of the Maguay, Spanish dagger, or coca leaves, fastening them to their feet with thin grass cords.[132]

It was evident to Wood and the rest that the Cubans would be of little use in the fighting to come. When one foreign correspondent (who had been a major in his country's army) was asked whether he thought the Cubans could fight, he sardonically replied, "I guess they'll fight. I don't quite see how such ragged fellows can, with modesty, turn their backs upon the enemy."[133]

The afternoon of June 22, Shafter ordered Lawton to move several miles west along the road to Santiago and take Siboney. When he arrived in the town the following morning, the American general found himself in uncontested possession of the harbor, a locomotive, and thirty barrels of whiskey and wine which he judiciously placed under armed guard.[134] Shafter began landing troops and supplies at Siboney the following morning.

A narrow path led northwest over the cliffs behind the town and then over jungle-draped hills and across a series of ravines cut by streams running out of the mountains to the sea. The "Camino Real," little more than a track worn over the centuries by farmers and their mules, was the only approach to Santiago's inland side.

Wood and his men spent a nervous night plagued by mosquitoes and land crabs, and, unable to believe they had been allowed to land unopposed, waiting for a counterattack. Wood, sympathizing with the tired cowboys, did not insist on his usual orderly camp, and the night was punctuated by gunshots as jumpy sentries mistook jungle crustaceans for Spanish soldiers. To make things worse, it stormed all night, and the few men who managed to sleep through the thunder and random rifle fire were tormented by voracious land crabs trying to make a meal of toes, fingers, and ears.[135] The more resourceful troops alleviated their misery with captured stores of Jamaican rum and Spanish wine, and the sun rose on tired soldiers with cotton mouths and swollen heads.

Shafter had planned for Lawton's infantry to lead the way to Santiago with the dismounted cavalry in reserve, but Wheeler conveniently misinterpreted his orders. Shafter assumed that the cavalry would, like Lawton, take a leisurely two days to come to Siboney from Daiquirí, an assumption that underestimated both Wheeler and Wood. In his official report, Wheeler blithely stated that "in obedience to instructions given to me in person on June 23rd, I proceeded to Siboney." Riding alone, the old cavalryman was able to get well ahead of Wood's men and the rest of Young's dismounted cavalry. As soon as he got to the village and found that the Spanish had decamped, he tracked them up the Santiago road and found the main body dug in about three miles away. He sent word for Wood to come with all available speed.[136]

The Rough Riders, baking in the airless afternoon heat, grumbled, loaded their equipment, and, joined by General Samuel B. M. Young and two squadrons of regular cavalry, marched eight and a half miles to Siboney. Roosevelt later wrote, "It was a hard march, the hilly jungle trail being so narrow that often we had to go in single file. We marched fast, for Wood was bound to get us ahead of the other regiments."[137] Reporter Edward Marshall added, "I shall never forget the terrible march to Siboney. . . . The heat was absolutely terrific, and before we had marched two miles every uniform was so soaked with perspiration that the men looked as if they had been ducked."[138] The men set out carrying ammunition, clothing, blanket rolls, shelter tents, and various supplies that weighed about sixty pounds in all. As they marched along the jungle trail, they discarded one item after another to be scavenged by trailing Cubans. Wood, veteran of hotter, longer, and more difficult marches, dismissed the day as "a hot one and a very hard one, as the men had become rather soft during their two weeks on ship and consequent lack of exercise."[139]

It was well past dark when the Rough Riders made camp next to the old commandant's residence where Wheeler had established his headquarters in Siboney. Throughout the night, under searchlights from the ships and firelight from the shore, Shafter landed men and equipment while Wood and Young slipped their troops past Lawton's infantry to camp a precious few yards closer to Santiago. The men had long since emptied their canteens, and the Spanish had cut the pipes that brought clean mountain water into Siboney. Wood, reverting to his role as physician, refused to let his men fill their canteens or cooking pots with the fetid water collected in pools around the village. Grumbling troopers remained thirsty until clean water was carried from the surrounding hills, but, unlike Young's men who drank from the ponds, none of the Rough Riders were sick the following day. The noise from the beach, a drenching two-hour thunderstorm, and anticipation made sleep impossible. Three miles west, the Spanish were preparing to defend the Santiago road at a nondescript wide spot in the trail called Las Guásimas.

That night Wheeler gave Young and Wood the next day's plan. Shafter had ordered the old Confederate to assume a defensive position until all the men and supplies were landed, but the commanding general was still on board his yacht and Wheeler, being the senior officer on shore, saw an opening. As soon as his men arrived, he exercised his dubious authority as "senior officer ashore" and changed Shafter's plan. Rebel General Demetrio Castillo reported having attacked an enemy force of some 1,500 men during the day and said he had left the Spanish dug in at Las Guásimas. The dubiously accurate Cuban general also reported that the Spanish position was "extremely strong," and that Linares himself was bringing an additional 1,500 Spanish regulars to defend it.[140] Roosevelt said Wheeler was "anxious . . . to get first blood, and he was bent upon putting the cavalry division to the front as quickly as possible."[141] Nothing could have pleased Wood and his lieutenant colonel more.

"Fighting Joe" Wheeler's career stretched back to the Civil War in which he had commanded the Army of Mississippi's cavalry, finishing the war at Appomattox as a lieutenant general before being imprisoned with Jefferson Davis in the custody of Wood's mentor, General Nelson Miles. He had, with two short breaks, served in the United States House of Representatives since 1881, where he earned a reputation for promoting southern business and fostering reconciliation between the north and south. His appointment as general in the Cuban expedition recognized both his military and political skills. McKinley reckoned that having a southern hero in command of the cavalry would help generate support for the war in the old Confederacy. Although sixty-two years old, Wheeler's five-foot two-inch frame remained trim, ramrod straight, and decidedly more military than that of his corpulent commander or the ursine Lawton.

The "Camino Real" from Siboney led up from the beach into the jungle and over the surrounding line of hills, but was only a muddy path in a valley between the mountains paralleling the coast. Left of the main road to Santiago and three hundred feet up the valley wall ran an even more difficult path that wound through the jungle to rejoin the main road three miles inland at a junction named for the surrounding guácima (hog-nut) trees. The Spanish were dug in on a ridge to the right and just north of where the two tracks joined. The plan was for Young's two squadrons (362 men) along with Castillo and 800 Cubans to take the main road. They would also take the two Hotchkiss revolving cannons and Wood's dynamite gun. Wood was to take his 574 Rough Riders up the jungle track and rejoin the regulars at Las Guásimas, where the volunteers would attack the Spanish right flank while Young's men engaged their left.

Linares had missed an opportunity to stop the invasion when he allowed Shafter to land his men at Daiquirí and Siboney; Las Guásimas was his second chance. If he could successfully hold the road he would not only prevent the Americans from attacking Santiago, but also trap them on a narrow, malarial strip of coastal land to be decimated in the rapidly approaching fever season. Wheeler—even though his motives were tainted by ambition—was undoubtedly correct in pushing the attack before the Spanish could strengthen their defenses. He managed to sneak 1,000 men (the Rough Riders and one squadron each from the First and Tenth Cavalry) past Lawton to a camp where they could slip out in the predawn darkness before Lawton's officers knew they were gone.[142]

Wood, having the more difficult terrain, started first on the morning of June 24. He woke his men at 3:15 A.M.; neither he nor Roosevelt had slept at all. Edward Marshall wrote that Wood was drawn and haggard with a voice cracked with fatigue. The usually punctilious colonel was uncharacteristically short with his soldiers and packers. Finally, as Robert Harris of the *Chicago Record* wrote, "Col. Wood jumped up and snapped his watch shut. 'We start in five minutes. Any one who isn't ready will be left behind.'"[143] At 5:40 they were marching.

The first part of the track was a seven-hundred-foot climb so steep that the men had to crawl and pull themselves up the rocks clinging to vines and undergrowth. The Rough Riders, loaded down with blanket rolls and ammunition and still tired from a long march and a short night, repeatedly dropped to their knees to rest. The climb left exhausted men supine and panting on the hill top while transports swung peacefully at anchor in the picturesque harbor below. Between the summit and the bay, there rose the first soft sounds of distant trumpets waking Lawton's sleeping infantry.

From the hilltop the trail went into a thick growth of trees festooned with luxuriant broad-leafed vines. The trail was so narrow that, for the most part, the men were forced to march single file and crawl over one fallen tree after another. New Yorker Hamilton Fish and Oklahoman Allyn Capron (whom Roosevelt called the best soldier in the regiment) led the way. Fish, whose grandfather had been Grant's secretary of state, had four Rough Riders and two Cuban scouts, and Capron came next with his sixty-man troop of Oklahomans. Capron had requested the lead and Wood, having known him since the Geronimo Campaign, "knew that in his hands the advance was as safe as in the hands of any man living."[144] The trail was too narrow to allow flanking scouts, but, after the first hard climb, it was fairly level and progress was reasonably quick. Wood, Roosevelt, the lieutenant colonel's ubiquitous reporters, and the main force of Rough Riders followed. All except Wood, Roosevelt, two observers from Wheeler's staff, and Davis (suffering from a bout of sciatica) walked. The men on horseback held back out of consideration for the dismounted cowboys obviously struggling in the oppressive jungle heat.

The Cubans, assuming that the Americans would be unable to recognize a guácima tree, had told Wheeler that he would know he was getting close to the Spanish position when he came across the body of a guerilla killed just short of the intersecting trails the day before. Capron and Woodbury Kane found the body and sent word back to Wood who ordered a halt in a grassy opening. The men, still doubting that they would encounter actual Spanish troops, casually unrolled their blankets and stretched out to rest.

Wood's main body was some two hundred yards behind Capron and the scouts, and what happened next remained a source of dispute for years. One Arizona trooper later wrote that Capron's men were fighting the Spanish before Wood ever spread his men out.[145] This version was repeated by disgruntled reporters who, lacking a favored relationship with the two colonels, had been left in Siboney from whence they sent dispatches accusing the neophyte commanders of leading their men into an ambush. Burr McIntosh, the photographer-reporter for *Leslie's Weekly,* was particularly critical: "Those men on that hill tonight are lying there, sacrificed on the altar of a showman's greed."[146] Stephen Crane wrote, "The men marched noisily through the narrow road in the woods, talking volubly, when suddenly they struck the Spanish lines. . . . It was simply a gallant blunder."[147] Even Davis, who was most often the Rough Riders' semiofficial cheerleader, initially described the encounter as an ambush, though in later versions he called it a planned action. In his official report, Wood claimed that he had arranged his men in a skirmish line on both sides of the road before the firing started, suggesting that he had communicated with Capron, realized they were close to the Spanish, and deployed his men. At any rate, the Rough Riders were at war.

The skirmish line ran from the Camino Real across the jungle track and into the plain on Wood's left. That first Spanish volley killed Hamilton Fish and was followed by shots that took the lives of Allyn Capron and six more Rough Riders. Wood went forward, investigated, and returned ordering his men to be silent and to "load chamber and magazine."[148] He later reported that he had heard about the dead guerilla from Capron and had been expecting to encounter the Spanish for some time. Regardless of which version is true, no one questioned Wood's courage once the battle started. Marshall wrote, "Colonel Wood was as cool a man as I ever saw. He gave his orders with the utmost calmness and showed then (indeed, it was true of him throughout the battle) not one sign of excitement."[149] His men called him "Old Icebox."[150] In his official report, Wheeler said, "the magnificent and brave work done by the regiment, under the lead of Colonel Wood, testifies to his courage and skill."[151] Roosevelt, on the other hand, was anything but cool. Mar-

shall said he, "jumped up and down, literally, I mean, with emotions evidently divided between joy and a tendency to run."[152]

Wood ordered half of his men to cross the barbed wire fence and deploy into the open field on his left, and he told Roosevelt to take three
troops into the trees on the right of the path. When Roosevelt crossed
the barbed wire fence into the trees, he became a different man. Marshall wrote:

> It was as if that barbed-wire strand had formed a dividing line in his
> life, and that when he stepped across it he left behind him in the bridle
> path all those unadmirable and conspicuous traits which have so often
> caused him to be justly criticised [sic] in civic life, and found on the
> other side of it, in that Cuban thicket, the coolness, the calm judgment,
> the towering heroism, which made him, perhaps, the most admired
> and best beloved of all Americans in Cuba.[153]

At Las Guásimas, Roosevelt found the steel Wood had found in the
Mexican Sierra Madres twelve years earlier. They were soldiers.

Just before Capron and Fish encountered the Spanish snipers,
Young, marching with his column of regulars several hundred yards to
the right, came upon the main force occupying the ridge overlooking
the Camino Real. Now both columns were actively engaged, Wood's
men firing their Krags and Young's men firing both rifles and artillery.

As Roosevelt's men deployed through the dense underbrush, a hail
of Spanish fire came from his right. The high-velocity Mauser bullets
whistled through the trees clipping off leaves and branches which fell
on troops struggling to push through jungle so thick they could barely
see the men on either side. Smokeless Spanish powder and dense undergrowth made it impossible to tell where the shots came from, and
death rained in an anonymous torrent of lead from a blank green cloud
two hundred yards ahead. The Mauser bullets were unsettlingly different from the Minnié balls that warbled from Civil War Springfields or
even from the hum of a Remington shot. They came with an insectlike
zing which, like a passing train, approached with a steadily increasing
pitch that abruptly dropped as the bullet passed. Sometimes the whine
was punctuated with the click of breaking branches and sometimes
with the sharp clap of a bullet stopped by a tree trunk. Other bullets
were never heard. If the supersonic Mausers struck before their sound
arrived, they simply made a sickening chug as bone and soft tissue

slowed the projectile. Marshall marveled at the fact that these bullets, so much more powerful than those of previous wars, caused whomever they hit to freeze and drop where they stood. Men—even those only hit in an arm or a leg—did not pause to look up, did not spin around, did not drop on a knee, and did not stagger backward. They simply collapsed in a heap as if muscle and bone had suddenly gone soft. Veterans vividly recalled the muffled impact that could be heard two hundred feet away.[154] Mercifully, the Mausers often passed through and through leaving relatively clean wounds, and the survival rate compared to earlier wars was high.

As Wood's men came into a small opening, they guessed the Spanish troops were only fifty to eighty yards away but still could not see them, so the Rough Riders were forced to lay flat in the grass and fire randomly at the green wall in front of them. For a time, still confused by the invisible smokeless powder, they even thought the firing might be coming by accident from Capron's men. They yelled at Capron to stop shooting and gave rise to the inaccurate but persistent story that the Rough Riders had fired on their own troops. At the time, the shouting only made it easier for the Spanish soldiers to find targets. Davis wrote, "It was an exceedingly hot corner. The whole troop was gathered in the little open place blocked by the network of grape-vines and tangled bushes before it. They could not see twenty feet on three sides of them, but on the right hand lay the valley, and across it came the sound of Young's brigade, which was apparently heavily engaged."[155] Unable to advance, Roosevelt took his men and a growing number of wounded back across the road to the left while Buckey O'Neill and two troops of Arizonans pushed right into the valley to join up with Young's troops.

In the field on the left of the path, Wood began a sweeping motion intended to circle the right side of the Spanish skirmish line and force it back toward the main road and Young's brigade. Roosevelt came back from the woods and across the fence to take command of the left end while Wood ranged up and down the line. He stood upright but could only see his men as indentations where they lay in the waist-high grass. Wood had dismounted and walked in front of his men leading his horse, Charles Augustus. Marshall noted that Wood could easily have placed the horse between himself and the Spanish line but opted for the more exposed position. Marshall (who was, himself, brought down by a gunshot wound to the spine) wrote:

I shall never forget how he looked as he stood there with his face burned to a brown, which was almost like that of the Khaki uniform he wore. His sandy mustache, too, had been grizzled by the sun until it fitted into the general harmony of tone, and he stood there brave and strong, like a statue in light bronze. The Cuban grass reached almost to his waist. There was not a breath of air, and yet the grass about him moved, once, slowly, as if a breeze were blowing it. At first I had no right idea of what had caused this, but presently the thought came to my mind that it might be bullets. And then I realized that Colonel Wood, forming, with his horse, the most conspicuous item in the view before the Spaniards, was naturally the target for all the bullets they could shoot. It was the effect of volleys fired from Spanish trenches and from the bush across the valley that made the grass wave about his feet.[156]

Through it all Wood looked vaguely distracted. When Marshall later asked him what had been going through his mind, the colonel admitted he had left managing the battle to his officers whom he trusted to carry out his orders and, having nothing specific to do, had let his mind wander to the unfortunate fact that he had neglected to take advantage of a $100,000 life insurance policy offered him before leaving for Cuba.[157]

All the while the men crept forward toward the unseen Spanish. The easterners crawled or walked forward bent over until they figured out that, partially visible above the grass tops, they were better targets than westerners who had fought Indians on the Great Plains and knew about staying down in the weeds. Soon they all inched ahead on their stomachs, intermittently getting up to run a few yards before falling back into the protecting grass. The invisible Spanish continued to fire low into the grass from the green wall ahead. The men, suffering in the heat and humidity, shed clothing and equipment until they were stripped to the waist and carried only weapons and cartridge belts.

For much of the time, only three figures were consistently visible, erect, and out of the grass's protecting cover: Wood, Roosevelt, and Dr. Robert Church. As wounded men fell, "Bob" Church (former Princeton football star and one of the eastern "swells") went into the grass, and kneeled over the wounded to stop bleeding and dress wounds. If the men could not crawl back to his "field hospital" under the trees, he picked them up and carried them to the rear on his shoulders.[158] Wood and Roosevelt stood so they could follow the action, give orders, and remain visible to their men who stayed amazingly well organized, advanced on command, fired when told, and did that most difficult thing —held fire when instructed to do so. In describing his two colonels' leadership, Young wrote in his official report, "Both . . . disdained to take advantage of shelter or cover from the enemy's fire while any of their men remained exposed to it, an error of judgment, but happily on the heroic side."[159]

The men pushed forward—one, two, three hundred yards through the high grass. The grass gave way to scattered trees and low brush, and, after an hour of bitter fighting and painstaking advance, the Americans came to abandoned Spanish positions littered with spent cartridges. Unbelievably, the line stayed together as it wheeled in on an old distillery where the Spanish made a last ditch stand. Young later commented that, during the whole advance, the troops had fired only an average of ten rounds a man. Young called the discipline with which Wood's men fought "remarkable, and I believe unprecedented, in volunteer troops so quickly raised, armed, and equipped."[160]

As they approached the old distillery, Wood decided to take a chance. He spread his entire force into a thin line and brought them slowly forward *without firing a shot* to within 300 yards of the Spanish who continued shooting into the grass. When Wood's troops got close, he ordered them to open fire and, in what came to be called "Wood's Bluff," he got the men on their feet and charged.[161] The Spanish, certain this was the vanguard of a much larger force, broke and ran. When Roosevelt and Wood got to the buildings, all they found were two dead Spaniards and a pile of spent casings. One of the Spanish soldiers later said, "When we fired a volley instead of falling back they came forward. That is not the way to fight, to come closer at every volley." Another complained, "The Americans were beaten but persisted in fighting, and we were obliged to fall back; the Americans tried to catch us with their bare hands."[162] Wood wanted to pursue the retreating soldiers, but Young ordered him to stop, consolidate his position, and wait for the rest of the army. Wheeler later wrote that the men were too exhausted to pursue the fleeing Spaniards, but, in fact, Wood and the Rough Riders stopped only because they were not allowed to advance.

In the midst of the battle, regimental adjutant Lieutenant Tom Hall had fled to the rear announcing that the regiment had been cut to pieces, that Wood was dead, and that Roosevelt was wounded, telling everyone he passed that he was on the way for reinforcements. When one of

Wood's officers later suggested charging the man with cowardice, the colonel, intent on preserving the regiment's reputation, demurred. The offending officer was reinstated and fought at San Juan where he again ran and was finally cashiered, and became a primary source of the rumor that the Rough Riders had been led into an ambush, an accusation that haunted Wood for years to come.[163]

Meanwhile, Young and Wheeler attacked the main Spanish position to the right of the Camino Real. Wheeler, afraid they were losing, reluctantly sent word to Lawton to bring reinforcements. Just as Lawton's Seventy-First Infantry arrived, however, the Spanish broke and the battle was over. The enemy raced toward Santiago and Wheeler gave the war one of its great anecdotes when he jumped to his feet, slipped into some earlier conflict, and triumphantly yelled, "We've got the damn Yankees on the run!"[164]

It is worth pausing to consider the fervor the officers and men (both regular and volunteer) brought to the Cuban Campaign. The regular officers had—with the exception of the few of senior rank who had served in the Civil War—seen combat only in the dispiriting Indian wars where they struggled against a guerilla opponent who almost never fought face to face. Winning more often than not involved returning their adversaries to a reservation from which, within a few months, they escaped and had to be chased again. They fought not only Indian men but also their wives and children, and their careers had been long on sacrifice and short on honor. The chance to prove themselves against a seasoned European army, even a second rank one, was a splendid opportunity.

For both the regulars and the volunteers, officers and enlisted men alike, there was another reason to be eager for Cuban action. Few of them had been off the North American continent, and many had never seen a body of water larger than a lake. The Cuban expedition was not just a chance to broaden their personal horizons, it was a chance to show the world that the fractured American nation was ready to unite and export its particular and particularly successful brand of popular democracy to the rest of the world. They were taking themselves and their nation onto the world stage and, with the encouragement of publicists like Hearst and Pulitzer, even the least sophisticated understood precisely what they were about.

At Las Guásimas, the Americans sent just under one thousand men against fortified positions and lost sixteen killed and fifty-two wounded; of approximately fifteen hundred defenders, the Spanish lost ten killed and twenty-five wounded.[165] Las Guásimas was, to be fair, only a skirmish, but the Americans, especially the inexperienced Rough Riders and their novice officers, performed well. Inexperienced, under-trained volunteers commanded by a former medical officer whose entire combat résumé was a few months fighting Indians and a professional politician whose dubious military credential was a stint as sheriff in the Dakota Territory won a heated battle against an entrenched force of well-armed, battle-seasoned regular troops. They advanced across difficult terrain and maintained fire discipline throughout the engagement. Of the nearly five hundred Rough Riders, only one was a coward. The regiment of cowboys and eastern athletes had done exactly what their prewar publicity said they would, and nothing stood between Shafter's invading force and Santiago's perimeter defenses.

In a letter to his wife, Wood described the battle:

> I don't want to boast, but we really had a most brilliant fight. . . . It was exciting when the entire Spanish line would come up on the knee and pour in a volley at short range and if they would have shot as our people did we would have been wiped out, but one and all of our fellows went on obeying every command, ceasing firing and advancing in good order and pouring in a splendid fire when they were ordered. After over two hours' hard fighting and slowly beating them back from rock fort to rock fort, the whole force broke and ran like sheep. . . . Praise God I am all right and we won our first big fight.[166]

Lawton promised Wood a regular army brigade and Young recommended him for a star. Lawton was not as happy with Wheeler whom he informed that he would never again tolerate part of the army sneaking out of camp to be the first in battle. He advised the older general that Shafter had given him command of the advance and he proposed to keep it, even if it meant posting guards to keep reserve troops in the rear.[167] Lawton was too late. The press had already made heroes of Wood and Roosevelt, and the politically savvy McKinley had forwarded his congratulations for their "gallant action." Since it was clear that Roosevelt was due for promotion and command of the Rough Riders, Wood's promotion to general was inevitable, but the speed with which it came was a surprise.[168] The day after Las Guásimas Young was stricken with fever, Wood replaced him in command of the dismounted cavalry, and Roosevelt got the Rough Riders.[169]

The Santiago road from Las Guásimas ran west in a valley flanked by the coastal hills on the left and the Sierra Maestre eight miles to the north. Three miles west of Las Guásimas, the road was crossed by a series of ridges, the tallest of which was San Juan Hill. The path was paralleled by the Aguadores River which, as the rains came, overflowed its banks and turned the road into a quagmire. The track was sunk two or three feet below the jungle floor and the bush around Las Guásimas was so dense that Wheeler had to bivouac his men in whatever small openings he could find in the tropical underbrush.

Wood and the Rough Riders settled in two miles west within sight of the Spanish fortifications and waited for the rest of the troops and supplies to come up from Daiquirí and Siboney. The wet season had started and they were drenched with two to three inches of rain a day. The rain meant mosquitoes, and, although Wood knew that yellow fever came with the rain, he did not yet know the insidious relation between the deadly disease and the annoying insects. The nights were cold and the men longed for the blankets dropped on the march up from Siboney and long since vanished into Cuban huts whose occupants blandly claimed them as family heirlooms. The blankets were not all that was missing. The men had dropped their packs on the trail before the battle started and, by the time the fighting was over, the voracious Cubans had stolen virtually all the food and most of the equipment.[170] Cuban plundering was so common that the Americans came to regard their quondam allies "with that same delicate consideration and pleasure with which they looked on land crabs."[171]

The muddy, single-track road made it nearly impossible to move supplies over the mountain ridge to their camp, so Roosevelt took forty of his Rough Riders on an impromptu commissary raid and requisitioned enough beans and bacon for a regimental feast. Wood also took a detachment and raided the docks at Siboney where he had part of his men form a double line armed with picks and shovels while the rest pilfered crates and boxes for goods to take back to camp.

On June 29, Shafter lumbered up from the coast and set up his advance headquarters to prepare for the final attack on Santiago. The cumbersome commander had significant logistical problems. It was hurricane season and there was the constant threat that his transports would be driven to sea before their supplies could be off loaded, guaranteeing that his army would be trapped to die of disease or starvation. Even if all the supplies could be gotten ashore at Siboney, there was the nearly insurmountable problem of transporting them up a muddy path that crossed one unbridged stream after another to his line outside Santiago. Much of the trail was too narrow for both a wagon and a man on foot to pass abreast, and almost none of it would allow two wagons to pass in opposite directions, so the comings and goings had to be meticulously timed. Wagon wheels churned the path into a foot-deep quagmire of gelatinous muck that made it nearly impossible to even get food to the front, much less stockpile supplies for future operations. Food took priority, but what distressed the men most was lack of tobacco. They tried to talk Cubans into sharing their cheroots, and when that failed, they took to smoking grass, roots, and dried manure. On the other hand, there was no shortage of Cuban rum. A plug of black market tobacco cost nearly as much as a private earned in a week, but a can of government-issue beef could be traded for enough rum to get a man joyously drunk.[172]

Shafter's troops could not stay in the trenches for long. First there came a distressing report that 8,000 Spanish regulars had left Manzanillo with cattle and supplies, broken through the insurgent lines, and were expected in Santiago within two or three days.[173] At least as worrisome was the looming threat of disease. Shafter had studied the repeated failures of previous Cuban invasions and knew it was a matter of time before malaria and yellow fever would defeat him as well, but the commanding general had no idea how extensive the Spanish fortifications around Santiago had become. Linares had been digging trenches in the hills surrounding the city for two months. As his men dug, they removed the dirt instead of piling it in front of the trenches so that, when Wheeler turned his binoculars on the heights he mistakenly judged them unoccupied and undefended. In fact, the city's perimeter was protected by four thousand yards of trenches, almost all in two or three echelons. Behind earthen breastworks lay rows of barbed wire interrupted by stone block houses anchored on the northern end by the fort at the village of El Caney. Kettle Hill, on the north end of the San Juan Ridge, overlooked the spot where two tracks of the Camino Real emerged from the jungle, and Linares had guns and rifles on the hill's crest trained exactly where he knew the Americans would appear.

Shafter's troops were scattered in campsites along the ridge ranging north to south from Las Guásimas toward Santiago and the sea. El

Pozo Hill rose above the road a mile or so from the campsites next to where the Aguadores River turned and crossed the path. Standing on El Pozo, Shafter looked across a jungle basin toward El Caney in the foothills of the Sierra Maestre on his right. Four miles to the south he could just make out the hills in front of Santiago. With field glasses he could even see the Santiago army barracks and the red crosses on the roof of the city hospital through a gap in the San Juan Heights. The heights ran north to south from El Caney to the village of Aguadores, five miles east of El Morro Castle on the coast. San Juan, the highest hill in the group, had a vertical blockhouse on its crest and the Camino Real at its base. Taking the road and gaining access to the city meant taking the hill and the block house. Of his 12,000 troops, the Spanish commander had about 500 at El Caney and, inexplicably, only 1,700 more to protect the San Juan Heights.[174] On June 30, Shafter at last decided it was time to move.

The commanding general felt he had to take El Caney for three reasons. First, the village prevented an American flanking attack on the northern and western perimeters of Santiago. It also stopped the Americans from interrupting Santiago's water supply which was piped in from the west. Finally, it prevented Shafter from intercepting the reinforcements on the way from Manzanillo. On the other hand, it was only an outpost and in no way threatened the Santiago road, but, on balance, Shafter decided El Caney justified dividing his forces. One group would mount a frontal assault on the heights, but only after the Second Infantry under Lawton (along with one battery of field guns) had taken El Caney. Almost half of Shafter's force was assigned to take the village in hopes that it would fall quickly. As soon as El Caney had fallen—a project expected to take only a couple of hours—Lawton would turn and march south to join the main assault on San Juan Heights.

The road from El Pozo to Santiago ran almost straight west through a patch of jungle paralleling the Aguadores River. After about 1,000 yards, the Aguadores joins the southward flowing Guamas Creek and then the San Juan River. After a few hundred more yards, the road crosses the San Juan River and emerges from the jungle at the foot of the heights. As the jungle opened up, one could see Kettle Hill (named for a large iron pot left over from an old sugar refinery) on the right. On the left of the road rose San Juan Hill and the blockhouse.

Shafter mounted his remaining battery atop El Pozo to provide artillery support. He sent the First Infantry Division and the Cavalry Division (under Brigadier General Samuel Sumner who had temporarily replaced malaria-stricken General Wheeler) west down the road to San Juan Heights with Wood in command of Young's brigade. Just at the jungle's edge they were to divide with Brigadier General Jacob F. Kent's three infantry brigades to form a skirmish line on the left of the road and Sumner's cavalry to do the same on the right. As soon as they received word that Lawton had secured El Caney, Kent and Sumner were to attack. Wood was supposed to remain in reserve.

The main group was to have started at daybreak, but it was 4:00 in the sweltering tropical afternoon of June 30 before they finally assembled themselves, their regimental band, their Gatling and dynamite guns, their ambulance and supply wagons, and the Vitagraph Motion Picture Company camera and set out.[175] The Rough Riders marched all day in the crowded lines of advancing infantry and 100 degree heat until, shortly after dark, they finally reached the top of El Pozo Hill, only a little more than a mile from the San Juan Heights. They settled in around Captain Allyn Capron's (father of the Rough Rider killed at Las Guásimas) artillery battery which had been posted on the hilltop to provide covering fire for the assault. The campsite was a disastrous choice. Capron's guns lacked smokeless powder so that a gray cloud hovered for one or two long minutes after each round. Not only did the smoke make it impossible to reaim the gun, but it also gave the Spanish a perfect target. After the first few American rounds, the Spanish artillery was sighted in and shrapnel rained down on Capron's guns and Wood's soldiers.

Roosevelt admitted that he temporarily lost control of his men as they fled into the trees to escape the Spanish shrapnel, but, to their credit, they ran toward rather than away from the Spanish lines.[176] Wood barely had time to remark to Roosevelt that he wished they had found someplace else to camp when the latter's horse was killed by flying metal.[177] This is the only recorded instance in which the Rough Riders lost their discipline under fire. Roosevelt initially reported that the men had scattered without orders, but, in a later, redacted description, he said he "hustled my regiment over the crest of the hill, into the thick underbrush, where I had no difficulty in getting them together again into column." This was the new colonel's first experience with independent command and, although he was an astoundingly quick learner, he was still less of a commander than Wood.[178] The press criticized Wood for camping his men so close to artillery, although he apparently did so under direct orders. In any event, it was an inauspicious start to the Rough Riders great battle and Roosevelt's "crowded hour."

Lawton, who had already moved his 5,000 men part way to El Caney, attacked at 6:15 A.M. on July 1, expecting to reduce the village and be on the road to San Juan by midmorning. After four hours of bitter fighting, he was still not in control of the village, and Shafter was convinced that the remaining half of his forces would not be able to take the well-defended heights. Wood had been ordered to follow the First Cavalry Brigade down the road and to deploy to the right at the edge of the jungle until he could join Lawton's troops when they marched south from El Caney.

The day was cloudless and the high blue sky threw the tall palms and the distant mountains into sharp relief against the dark green of the jungle basin in front of El Pozo. Wood's men left camp with five days of food and two hundred rounds of ammunition each, but the day was hot and the march through the airless jungle exhausting. The men discarded first the food and then their blanket rolls before inverting their cartridge belts so the Spanish could not aim at a gleaming buckle.[179] As usual, the supplies were picked over and stolen by Cuban hangers on as quickly as the soldiers were out of sight.

The road through the jungle was narrow, concentrating the men and leaving them vulnerable to Spanish artillerymen who knew quite well where the track ran. As if that were not enough, a misguided army engineer launched an observation balloon that followed the column down the road and furnished a perfect target. Wood bitterly called it "one of the most ill-judged and idiotic acts I ever witnessed."[180] The balloon and its six support wagons had gotten to Cuba and then to El Pozo with great difficulty. It was the only balloon the army possessed and was, by consequence, the entire United States military air force. The troops were not impressed, and men on both sides cheered when over two hundred punctures from Spanish shrapnel finally brought the balloon to earth.

The worst of the fire came where the road crossed the San Juan River. The entire force of 16,000 men was expected to exit the forest at a single point, where the ten-foot-wide road crossed the shoulder-deep river and emerged into the open field in front of the heights. The men and wagons bogged down in the muddy river bottom and the line backed up behind, making a perfect target at what came to be called "Bloody Ford."

When they finally got the men across the river and spread in a north-south line at the jungle's edge it became brutally clear that the operation was in serious trouble. Wood was ordered to stay where he was until word came that Lawton was on the way from El Caney, but his men were in direct line of Spanish fire and were protected only by the underbrush and an occasional palm tree, the soft trunks of which would barely slow a Mauser bullet. There was no word from Lawton as the Spanish poured deadly fire into the trees. The road back toward El Pozo was vulnerable to Spanish fire as well, and there were camouflaged snipers (reputedly recruited from Spanish prisons with promises of clemency for any survivors) hiding in the tops of palm trees behind American lines. The snipers were shooting men as they forded the San Juan River and killing the wounded as they lay beside the muddy trail. Retreat was not an option.[181]

The only choice was to rush the Spanish positions. Shafter was confined to his headquarters a mile and a half behind El Pozo by the combined vicissitudes of heat prostration and gout and had effectively ceded control of the battle to two of his staff officers, Lieutenant Colonel E. J. McClernand and Lieutenant J. D. Miles. In a triumph of ambiguity, he had his adjutant send word from El Pozo that "The Commanding General would deplore any loss of life, but he does expect general officers to use all their men to best advantage."[182] Finally, conferring with Kent and Hawkins, Lieutenant Miles made the command decision. He told the two major generals, "I am entirely of General Hawkins's opinion and I will, if you have no objections, in the name of General Shafter and with his authority, direct General Hawkins to advance with his brigade and capture the hill."[183]

For Wood, whose men were being pounded from the top of Kettle Hill, the decision could not have come soon enough. He had been begging for permission to take the hill, and later suggested that he had made the decision independently writing, "We lay under heavy fire, losing men constantly, until finally, weary of the inaction and constant loss, I ordered my brigade to advance."[184] Wood sent word to Roosevelt, who was on the far right of the line trying to make contact with Lawton, that they were ready to attack. He collected the First and Tenth Cavalry Regiments and members of the 1st Brigade scattered in the grass awaiting orders and set out across the millet field at the base of Kettle Hill. Fortunately, Lieutenant John Parker had hauled his Gatling guns up the muddy road from Siboney and positioned them at the river edge where they provided covering fire. Wood came out of the trees on Charles Augustus and rode him right to the base of the hill where he was stopped by a barbed wire fence. He calmly dismounted, tied his horse to a fence post, and resumed the climb on foot.

Remington's famous painting notwithstanding, the "charge" up San Juan Hill was anything but a mad rush at the Spanish defenses. Richard Harding Davis described the action:

> I have seen many illustrations and pictures of this charge on the San Juan hills, but none of them seem to show it just as I remember it. In the picture-papers the men are running up hill swiftly and gallantly, in regular formation, rank after rank, with flags flying, their eyes aflame, and their hair streaming, their bayonets fixed, in long, brilliant lines, an invincible, overpowering weight of numbers. Instead of which I think the thing which impressed one the most, when our men started from cover, was that they were so few. It seemed as if someone had made an awful and terrible mistake. One's instinct was to call to them to come back. You felt that someone had blundered and that these few men were blindly following out some madman's mad order. It was not heroic then, it seemed merely terribly pathetic. The pity of it, the folly of such a sacrifice was what held you.
>
> They had no glittering bayonets, they were not massed in regular array. There were a few men in advance, bunched together, and creeping up a steep, sunny hill, the top of which roared and flashed with flame. The men held their guns pressed across their breasts and stepped heavily as they climbed. Behind these first few, spreading out like a fan, were single lines of men, slipping and scrambling in the smooth grass, moving forward with difficulty, as though they were wading waist high through water, moving slowly, carefully, with strenuous effort. It was much more wonderful than any swinging charge could have been. They walked to greet death at every step, many of them, as they advanced, sinking suddenly or pitching forward and disappearing in the high grass, but others waded on, stubbornly, forming a thin blue line that kept creeping higher and higher up the hill. It was as inevitable as the rising tide. It was a miracle of self-sacrifice, a triumph of bull-dog courage, which one watched breathless with wonder.[185]

It was also carried in large part by volunteers who had been soldiers for less than two months and most of whom had seen their first battle only a few days before.

By now the Third, Sixth, and Ninth Cavalries and the Rough Riders had joined Wood and the First and Tenth on the hill and swept the Spanish from the summit, but they were far from secure. Lawton, after eight hours fighting, was still at El Caney. Kettle Hill was exposed to Spanish fire from the west and to counterattack from three sides. To make things worse, Kent's attack on San Juan Hill from the left side of the road had bogged down. The volunteer Seventy-First New York Infantry (a National Guard unit armed with black powder Springfields which fully one-third of the men had never fired) had broken and had to be herded off the road into the jungle to make way for the advancing regulars. The Sixth and Sixteenth Infantry, under withering Mauser fire from the hilltops, decided at almost precisely the same time as the charge on Kettle Hill that the only answer was to advance.

Wood urgently sent for reinforcements, but Lt. John J. Pershing returned with word that there were none. Bates's independent brigade— Shafter's only reserves—had gone to El Caney to help Lawton. There was no artillery west of El Pozo, so Wood moved Parker and his Gatling guns to the hilltop and told his men to dig in. By 1:30 in the afternoon, Sumner's cavalry division was, at least temporarily, in control of Kettle Hill and Kent's infantry was closing in on the apex of San Juan Hill. The Spanish, still in control of the higher elevations to the left of Kettle Hill, were pouring murderous small arms and shrapnel fire on Wood's men. Clearly, they needed to mount a second charge on the right end of the San Juan ridge and help Kent's men take the heights.

Roosevelt, determined not to miss a moment of the action, ran over the top of Kettle Hill and on toward San Juan to his left before he realized he had outstripped his regiment and was charging almost alone. He went back to get his men who apologized for having lost him and proceeded to take the north end of the ridge just as Kent took the main hill. When they reached the first line of trenches, the Rough Riders found them filled with Spanish bodies. The vast majority were dead rather than wounded, having been brought down for the most part by bullet wounds to the head and neck most of which (in ominous presage of the world war to come) were inflicted by Parker's 900-round-per-minute Gatling guns.

Wheeler left his sickbed just in time to see the end of the action.[186] An infantry captain, asked whether he had any trouble getting his men to charge the hills, laconically answered, "No, sir, but I had considerable trouble keeping up with them."[187] As Pershing noted in disbelief, a mixture of northerners and southerners, blacks and whites, volunteers and regulars had charged an entrenched professional army and routed them. The American army had come of age. Wood wrote with justifiable pride, "That dismounted Cav. Should have been able to charge regular infantry in strong position supported by artillery and the general lay of the land, seems almost incredible yet this is exactly what the Cav. Div. of the 5th Army Corps did in this fight, passing over a long zone of fire and charging steep hills topped with works and block houses."[188]

Kent held San Juan Hill, Wood had Kettle Hill, but Lawton was still in a desperate fight at El Caney. Lawton had started the morning intending to take the three objectives and march straight through to Santiago. Now, at about 2:30 in the afternoon, the Americans wondered if they would even be able to hold the high ground they had won with such difficulty. Through the afternoon, the retreating Spanish kept up a raking artillery and small arms fire, making it all but impossible for the Americans to come out of the trenches. Lawton did not take El Caney until after 4:30, and there were no reserves to repulse a Spanish counterattack. Although there had been only 1,700 defenders on the heights, there were still nearly 6,000 Spanish regulars, volunteers, sailors, and marines in Santiago, and the Americans were tired, had no food or water, and were short of ammunition.

In the midst of the hot, nervous afternoon, Wood temporarily reverted to a former role and made a lifelong friend. Early in the charge, he had dispatched Lieutenant Frank McCoy to Shafter with a message. McCoy barely started before being hit in the leg, his wound later inexpertly dressed by a trooper from the Tenth Cavalry. Wood found the lieutenant lying next to an artillery limber and told him, "I am a doctor and I think I can do better with those bandages than your trooper." He took down the old dressing and, using his own first aid kit, rebandaged the wound. McCoy later said the general had "braced me up with his sympathy and interest so that I was a devoted admirer from that moment." McCoy, who eventually became a general and aide to President Woodrow Wilson, remained Wood's loyal supporter through the rest of their careers.[189]

Wood's and Kent's men occupied the Spanish trenches and settled in to hold the hills. Parker's Gatling guns were brought to the top of the ridge and, on the one occasion the Spanish looked as if they might leave their second line of trenches and try to retake the heights, the rapid fire automatic weapons drove them back. Artillery was initially brought up with vague instructions to shell the Spanish but with no suggestion as to which targets the guns might address. Their first ineffective salvos left a cloud of smoke that, just as at El Pozo, prevented further aiming but furnished a perfect target for return fire. The guns were withdrawn forthwith.

Darkness came quietly, but there was no rest for troops who had slept only three or four hours the night before and fought all day. The Spanish trenches on San Juan Heights were on the wrong side of the hill and defensive trenches had to be dug on the south side. The ground was rocky and, by morning, most of the American ditches were, in spite of the men working all night under sporadic Spanish fire, only a foot or so deep and less than four feet wide. The men spent the next day baking in their shallow dugouts while Spanish riflemen harassed anyone who dared raise his head. Water and food could not be delivered and relief only came from men who crawled to the north side of the trenches and lay in the grass until the trench's occupant could crawl out and let the new man roll in. There were almost no trenches large enough to accommodate two soldiers at once.

Most of Linares's troops had survived to retreat into the city, and the Americans were not at all sure they could hold their precarious position if faced with a counterattack. In fact, Wood later wrote that "throughout the afternoon and night the enemy attempted to regain his lost position without success."[190] The diary entry reflected worry more than reality since the Spanish never mounted a concerted attempt to retake the heights. The Americans were three-quarters of a mile from Santiago, but a worried Wheeler told Shafter, "The lines are now very thin as so many men have gone to the rear with the wounded, and so many are exhausted. . . . We ought to hold tomorrow, but I fear it will be a severe day."[191] A tenth of the American troops were either dead or wounded (a quarter of the Rough Riders were casualties), and there was still the threat of Spanish troops coming from Manzanillo to attack his men from behind. What Shafter did not know was that Linares was wounded, the city was critically short of food and water (Lawton had captured and interrupted Santiago's fresh water source), and disease was rampant. The Spanish had lost a bit over 500 men at El Caney and about 400 more in the unsuccessful defense of the San Juan Heights, and the fleet was bottled up by a vastly superior American force. The Spanish spent that night under the pall of certain defeat. The Americans, having advanced without blankets or food, spent the night sleeping on the ground after eating scraps of bread, salted fish, rice, and beans the Spanish had left behind.[192]

Back at El Pozo, Shafter nearly made a catastrophic error. Describing headquarters on July 2, Davis wrote, "One smelt disaster in the air. The alarmists were out in strong force and were in the majority."[193] Shafter polled his generals on the advisability of abandoning the heights and retreating toward Siboney. In fairness to the commanding general, he believed that a relief column was on the way, and he knew there was a large Spanish force about twenty-five miles away at San Luis, 7,000 troops around Guantánamo, and 10,000 more at Holguín. He thought he was surrounded. Fortunately, only Kent was in favor of withdrawal; the others were adamantly opposed to giving up what they had won. Shafter wired Alger, "I am seriously considering withdrawing about five miles and taking up a new position on the high ground between the San Juan River and Siboney." He went on to complain that he had "been unable to be out during the heat of the day for four days" although he was still in command.[194] Even the redoubtable Roosevelt was worried. He wrote Cabot Lodge, "We are within measurable distance of a terrible military disaster; we *must* have help—thousands of men, batteries, and food and ammunition."[195]

Hoping for help from the navy, Shafter sent a message to Sampson: "I urge that you make effort immediately to force the entrance to avoid future losses among my men, which are already very heavy. You can now operate with less loss of life than I can."[196] Sampson refused to move until the harbor defenses were taken and the mines were disabled. Through the day, the Spanish kept up constant fire on the American trenches, making it nearly impossible to deliver even hardtack and coffee to the weary defenders although Wood did send some of his sharpshooters back into the trees to hunt down and kill the Spanish snipers harassing men on the road to the coast.

On the morning of July 3, hoping his commander would be in better spirits, McClernand woke Shafter with the novel suggestion that they request a Spanish surrender. There was nothing to lose and Shafter, perhaps more rested or perhaps not fully awake, tersely said, "Well, try it." At 8:30 McClernand sent a message to General José Toral, in command of the Spanish forces following the injury to Linares, informing him that, unless he surrendered, the Americans would shell the city. All foreigners, women, and children should leave immediately. What he planned to shell with is not exactly clear since his dynamite gun was inoperative and he had only sixteen 3-inch field guns and eight light mortars, the siege guns having been left either in Siboney or Tampa.[197]

The demand was rendered moot when the men heard the deep-throated rumble of naval cannon from over the horizon; at 9:30 that morning Cervera had brought the Spanish fleet out. The narrow harbor entrance forced the Spanish ships to emerge one at a time to be systematically destroyed over the next four hours. Spain lost six ships and 474 men killed and wounded while the Americans suffered almost no damage to their ships and lost only one man killed and two wounded. The last vestige of Spanish power in the Western Hemisphere was gone. Toral still refused to surrender, but every soldier in the trenches and the city knew the battle was over.

Toral did request a truce to allow noncombatants to leave the city, and over the next two days, 20,000 civilians fled Santiago while 3,600 (not the rumored 8,000) Spanish troops from Manzanillo slipped past the Cuban insurgents who were supposed to stop them. Unfortunately for the Spanish, there were not enough men in the relief column to allow Toral to fight Shafter or to break out of the city; they merely added to the drain on his dwindling supplies. Shafter continued to move supplies to his front lines and settled in to starve the defenders. With the Spanish navy gone, the American troops knew victory was certain and their morale, like that of their commander, surged back. On July 10, Sampson began shelling the city from the sea. Reinforcements (and General Miles) arrived from the United States, and discussions with Toral dragged on for two more days. Shafter offered to accept an "honorable" surrender and to arrange for the Spanish soldiers to be returned to their homeland at American expense, while the general informed his superiors in Madrid that surrender was inevitable and that he was only prolonging the agony by holding out.

Shafter had problems of his own. Fever sporadically appeared among his troops and fear of yellow fever outbreak was a lowering dark cloud over the camp. The rainy season arrived in force and the roads were, as Wood wrote, "absolute canals of mud such as you never saw or imagined."[198] Back in Siboney, conditions were also deteriorating.

Cuban refugees spent their days on the beach, defecated in the bushes, and left half-eaten food rotting in the streets. At night they retreated to the bush seeking shelter from the cold rain. Dead mules rotted in standing pools at the town's edge and, by July 10, there were thirty confirmed cases of yellow fever. At El Caney, Shafter had to feed both his soldiers and the army of Santiago refugees. There were only 300 houses in the whole village and people crowded fifty to a room. Clara Barton's Red Cross labored valiantly but fruitlessly to get food up from Siboney to relieve impending starvation while the total lack of sanitation guaranteed an epidemic that would inevitably spread to the American soldiers.[199] In the trenches, the men were tormented by flies and mosquitoes. Many had not changed clothes in weeks and the only place they could bathe was a small pond between Kettle and San Juan Hills that had the misfortune of being the lowest point around and a natural sink for filth from latrines on higher elevations.

Besides fever, the rainy season promised hurricanes; even a brief storm could stop the flow of supplies and threaten the entire army with starvation. Even without storms, the army (20,000 and growing) had trouble supplying food to its soldiers and was now also responsible for feeding 4,000 Cuban insurgents and the refugees.[200] The men were getting frustrated. In his diary, a disgusted Wood wrote, "No effort being made to get up artillery or to do anything which seems to me ought to be done. A most awful state of affairs." He called the dearth of food and ammunition "simply criminally negligent."[201] One bright spot came on July 8, when Wood received formal notification of his promotion to brigadier general, following which he proudly wrote his wife requesting a new khaki shirt, riding trousers, four pairs of socks, and four single stars.[202]

Also on July 8, Davis toured the rifle pits and wrote a long dispatch to the *New York Herald* describing the "serious nature" of Shafter's situation. The dispatch brought the reporter a firestorm of criticism and even accusations of treason when it was reprinted the following day in the Paris *Herald* from which it was forwarded to Madrid and probably telegraphed on to Toral. In fairness to Davis, if Toral did receive the information he must have paid it little attention; by that time he only wanted an honorable way to abandon the city.[203]

July 11 was stormy; tents blew over, trenches ran with water, and the roads turned into a sticky, smelly, foot-deep slurry. Living became a misery and moving provisions from the beach a near impossibility. Privately, Wood had nothing good to say of his superiors. He complained to his wife of "the awful mismanagement of this campaign" in which every single department had failed. He was sure that, with adequate leadership and a little artillery, they would have been in Santiago a week earlier rather than trapped in muddy trenches awaiting the inevitable arrival of yellow fever.

> Shafter was not *out of* his ship until *3 days* after my first fight and did not see the battlefield of Santiago until four days after the fight. . . . Wheeler runs a news correspondence stand and while a dear old man is of no more use here than a child. . . . The medical department is a failure.[204]

Clearly, something had to be done. Miles and Shafter decided to land a contingent of reinforcements west of Santiago's harbor entrance, have Sampson enter the harbor with his ships, and simultaneously attack from the San Juan Heights, but the attack, scheduled for July 14, never occurred. Miles, Shafter, and Toral met that day; Toral had finally gotten permission from Captain General Rámon Blanco to surrender, although in an attempt to salvage some honor, he insisted that he be euphemistically allowed to "capitulate" and his men be allowed to keep their small arms. In fact, Spanish law forbade a commander in the field to surrender while he still had ammunition and food, and Toral was well aware that he would eventually have to defend himself in a Spanish court.

On July 12, Miles had written the secretary of war that Toral's terms, although more lenient than he would ordinarily have accepted, should be considered since there were now one hundred yellow fever cases in his camps and the number was sure to increase.[205] Indeed, one day later the estimated number of cases had risen to 150 and Shafter was very nervous.[206] To Miles's surprise and gratification, Toral turned over not only the 16,500 men in Santiago City but also 12,000 more scattered about the province and completely beyond the American army's reach. The papers were signed on July 16, and, on Sunday July 17, Toral and one hundred of his officers formally "capitulated" in a field outside Santiago after which his men turned their rifles over to American guards at the city armory. The Americans, led by Shafter and Wheeler, then Lawton and Kent followed by the rest of the generals, their staffs, an honor guard, and the ever-present reporters rode in column of twos to meet the Spanish party. The Americans congratulated Toral on his men's bravery and honored him with the sword taken from General Joaquín Vara del Rey who had fallen at El Caney. Shafter accepted the surrender of the single remaining Spanish gunboat. At exactly noon, the Stars and Stripes replaced the red and gold Spanish flag that had flown over Cuba for four centuries. Two parties were conspicuously absent from the ceremony—the Cuban insurgents and the United States Navy. Shafter had deliberately excluded the former and neglected to invite the latter until it was too late for a representative to arrive.

Wood, in spite of the hardships, was fast acquiring a real affection for Cuba. Cubans, accustomed to foreigners being captivated by their island's beauty since the first European came there, refer to the "Sindrome de Colon," and Wood was a victim. He wrote his wife:

> This is God's own country in many ways. As beautiful as a dream— great mountains green to their tops, valleys filled with cocoanut and great royal palms and all kinds of superb trees. Water is fine and at night you want two blankets over you. Dear quaint little towns, hundreds of years old but so dirty. . . . No roads, but now and then a relic of an old bridge, arched and well built. . . . A country full of ruins, all buried in the great mass of semi-tropical vegetation.[207]

Reality was less idyllic, and Wood must have seen what lay ahead on that first day in Santiago. Dead Spanish soldiers had been hastily tucked into shallow graves, and the ubiquitous vultures had already scratched many of the bodies to the surface and were openly feeding on the human carrion. Dead animals, many still saddled, littered the streets. The stench was overwhelming.

When the Americans took possession of the city, Shafter appointed Lawton military commander of Santiago province and named Chambers McKibben military governor of the city. McKibben began his military career as a private in the Union army but received a field commission soon after enlisting. He was promoted first lieutenant in June 1864 and captain two months later. He stayed in the army after the war and spent the next twenty-five years without a promotion before finally being named major in 1892 and lieutenant colonel four years later. He went to Cuba with the Twenty-Fifth Infantry and was promoted brigadier general of volunteers after the surrender of Santiago, a jump in rank one grade greater than Wood's but without the attendant controversy.[208] The promotion made McKibben eligible to be military governor of Santiago City, leaving Wood to command a garrison force of black "immunes." The promotion was an honor for which the ailing old soldier had no stomach. After only two days facing the Augean task of sanitizing and civilizing the city, he stepped down. On July 20, Wood received a handwritten note from McClernand:

> The Commanding General directs you take charge of the City of Santiago, and see that order and quiet are observed—arrest all disturbers of the peace, and permit no armed men to enter the city except such of our own men as come on duty.

6

Santiago, 1898–1899

IN MAY OF 1494, Columbus jibed west out of Guantanamo Bay along Cuba's southeastern coast sailing almost exactly on the twentieth parallel of north latitude. Forty miles along the ironbound coast, a 180-yard gap in the rocks opened into a magnificent bay two miles wide, seven miles deep, and fifteen miles around. It was far and away the best harbor Columbus had seen in the New World and, when Diego Velazquez circumnavigated the island seventeen years later, he made it the site of Cuba's second city and moved the island's capital from Baracoa.[1] Santiago, with its perfect harbor and easy access to Santo Domingo, remained Cuba's most important city for almost eight decades. Even when the capital was moved to Havana in 1589, Santiago remained the heart of the island's eastern provinces.

By 1898, Santiago de Cuba was a thriving mining and agricultural city of 40,000—over half of whom were former slaves and their descendants—occupying 6,000 pastel, tile-roofed houses on winding, climbing cobblestone streets. Three quarters of a mile farther east and 150 feet higher lay San Juan Hill and the Spanish trenches occupied by Wood and his men. In the tropical August heat the blue harbor, the variegated green hills splashed with red flowers, and the tidy azure, yellow, and red colonial city seemed exotic and seductive.[2]

But looks were deceptive. Santiago's underlying problems had been centuries in the making, but the insurrection and the American blockade had left the city starving, disease-ridden, and near collapse.[3] Houses, mottled with black mildew, were built around garden courtyards long since converted to stables, privies, and cesspits. On the odd occasions when sewage was removed, it was heaped in the streets to stink and evaporate. There were no covered drains, little paving, and few sidewalks; only the bravest or poorest traveled on foot. Filth accumulated in the streets until rain and gravity carried the sludge to the harbor's edge to give low tide a pungency that could be appreciated ten miles out to sea. The entire city reeked of garbage, feces, and the sick-sweet smell of decomposing flesh. One American reporter reckoned that Santiago was the dirtiest city in the world.[4] Over one hundred people died every day that August.

The *reconcentrados* camps on Santiago's outskirts were even worse than the city. The only shelters were bark strips and palm leaves tacked over tumbledown frames. They lacked floors and windows, and smoke from the cooking fires was left to find its way out through the innumerable holes in the walls or ceilings. Fifteen-by-twenty-foot hovels housed a dozen people on dirt floors eating with their hands from open kettles.[5]

Then there was yellow fever. Doctors had helplessly watched the fever kill for centuries and knew quite well how it behaved, but none knew where the disease came from or how it was transmitted. Both yellow fever and the *Aedes aegyptii* mosquito that carried it came with West African slave ships. The first Spanish and Portuguese explorers, accustomed to the African Fever Coast and equating tropical climate with tropical disease, were amazed at the healthfulness of the American tropics, but that was temporary. The first recorded cases of Western Hemisphere yellow fever occurred almost simultaneously in Havana and the Yucatan in 1648, and, for the next 250 years, epidemics were a regular event in coastal cities as far north as Philadelphia and Boston.[6] When Napoleon sent 25,000 troops to put down the 1802 slave revolt in Saint Domingue, all but 3,000 died of yellow fever. The emperor ordered the survivors home and, disgusted with the New World and its pestilence, sold his remaining continental possessions to the United States. Haiti's blacks declared independence, drove out the whites they did not kill, and left a fear of slave revolt that colored Caribbean (and American) politics for the next century.[7]

The fever, with its yellow skin and black vomit, was horrifying. The initial chills and headache often brought a sense of impending doom. Then the temperature rose, muscles ached, and vomiting became uncontrollable. When the liver failed, bile pigments accumulated in the skin and the victim took on the color from which the disease got its name. Clotting factors normally produced in the liver disappeared, and the skin, the lungs, and the mouth, stomach, and intestines bled. The unfortunate victim hemorrhaged from every external and internal body surface and orifice. In a population without immunity, about half died. There was—and is—no treatment.

Discoveries by Louis Pasteur and Robert Koch convinced scientists that yellow fever was infectious, but the origin, method of spread, and responsible agent were an enigma in 1898. Giuseppe Sanarelli of the University of Bologna had received worldwide acclaim for discovering *Bacillus icteroides* that he claimed to be the cause of yellow fever. The announcement was taken badly by Sternberg, who had claimed his own *Bacillus x* as the etiologic agent. Walter Reed and the Yellow Fever Commission, organized three years later under Wood's authority, would prove that a filterable virus caused and a mosquito transmitted the illness, but, in 1898, Wood faced an epidemic armed with incomplete, incorrect, and largely unhelpful information.

One reason the war department had pressed Shafter to move from Tampa as quickly as possible was to get the troops back in the United States before fever season. In fact, fear of yellow fever had been more important than Admiral Sampson's badgering in the expedition's timing. Fever would come with the summer rains. The only question was how severe the epidemic would be, and native Cubans predicted a bad season.

By July 13, yellow fever had already broken out among Shafter's troops.[8] On July 14, Corbin's doctors, who knew that low lying marshes fostered fever, ordered Shafter to withdraw his army to the hills.[9] A day later Shafter informed Washington that he had 150 yellow fever cases and was adding new ones at a rate of thirty a day. Resigned to the inevitable, Alger ordered Miles to stop all troop movements to Cuba until the fever had "had its run,"[10] and the secretary, afraid Shafter would lose his entire force, proposed replacing the white soldiers with two regiments of "colored immunes."

There were only two ways to combat the fever—sanitation and isolation—and the army vigorously employed both. When soldiers fell ill, their entire units were moved to separate camps. When possible, the ill were removed to quarantine hospitals in the United States, mostly on poorly provisioned transports that were pathetically short of doctors and nurses. The Florida quarantine camps were on bare, sandy coastline surrounded by barbed wire fences to protect locals from soldiers. The troops were consigned to these bug-ridden prisons until they had been fever-free for at least ten days. Transports that had brought the sick to Florida returned loaded with alcohol, bicarbonate of soda, cathartics, strychnine, carbolic acid, bismuth, iron sulphate, brandy, beef extract, and condensed milk, none of which were of any use whatever against yellow fever.[11]

As bad as conditions were on the ships and in the camps, in Santiago they were immeasurably worse. Averting a major epidemic was Wood's first order of business. Lawton could remove most of his soldiers to the hills and allow only the absolutely essential or presumptively immune into the pestilent city. Ironically, it was at just this time the army discovered the "immune regiments" were not immune at all when fever broke out in the Fifth Immune Regiment, forcing the whole unit into quarantine.[12]

Wood did not have the luxury of moving sick and exposed civilians out of the city. His only recourse was to sanitize the city, and he did that with a vengeance. Even before the Americans had taken Santiago, Wood had recommended that the entire city of Daiquirí be burned on the grounds that its filth might breed fever, and Santiago was every bit as bad.[13]

By mid-August, half of Shafter's men were too ill to report for duty —one troop of Rough Riders could only muster eight men. Most had malaria or dysentery and would likely recover, but the lethal specter of yellow fever was on every mind.[14] Death rates from disease, although not made public until months later, were rising exponentially and every soldier had only to look at the empty bunks around him to know he was at risk. In May the army, still in camp in the United States, had a modest 0.46/1,000 death rate from disease. By June, the number rose to 8.4, then 25.8 in July, when the bulk of the forces were in Cuba, and a daunting 48.6 as the fever season struck in August.[15] For every man who died, there were ten or twenty who were unfit for duty. Shafter's army teetered on the edge of disaster.

The ever-vocal Roosevelt was worried about his Rough Riders and had no hesitance about using his considerable political influence to protect them. On July 23, he wrote Alger (in what he intended to be a private letter) that he wanted his men removed to Puerto Rico as soon as possible. Roosevelt reasoned that the move would protect their health, and, in a bit of tactless braggadocio, added that his volunteers were three times as good as any other state troops and deserved special consideration.[16] Alger curtly replied that the Rough Riders were "no better than other volunteers," and had succeeded only because of "an advantage in their arms, for which they should be grateful."[17] They would stay right where they were.

Alger had legitimate reasons for keeping the Fifth Corps in Cuba. Negotiations for Spain's surrender of the island and its other colonial possessions were near completion, and McKinley did not want it widely publicized that his army—still sharing Cuba with a potentially formidable contingent of Spanish regulars—was essentially nonfunctional. The volunteers who were to replace Shafter's army were untrained and unreliable. Finally, the war department was afraid that returning soldiers carrying yellow fever would trigger a domestic epidemic. In fact, Alger had been visited by a parade of New England senators protesting relocation of the troops to a camp being built on eastern Long Island, a site chosen with the thought that the men would be far from any city and their contagion would be blown out to sea.[18] It was no secret to Shafter's Fifth Corps that they frightened American civilians, and rumors circulated that they might just be left in Cuba to die.

Alger opened Camp Wikoff on Montauk Point on August 1 to healthy troops so they could be reunited with their horses in preparation for an invasion of Havana.[19] The troops were furious when they learned that anyone not certified fever-free was to stay in Cuba.[20] Shafter wired Alger that an epidemic was imminent and he wanted his men home immediately, but the war department and Sternberg decided it was best to keep the men in Cuba and move them farther into the mountains. Even had he believed that higher elevations were safe (which he did not), Shafter knew most of his men were too sick to march. He thought the order was ridiculous.[21]

Fearing the loss of his whole army, Shafter summoned his division commanders and medical officers to Santiago on August 3.[22] Shafter and Wood occupied adjoining offices that opened on a common anteroom where the generals and the doctors congregated to consider Alger's order. Roosevelt, although only a colonel, was invited for several reasons. First, he commanded the semiautonomous Rough Riders. More to the point, he was outspoken and impulsive, he had political influence, and he had no army career to ruin. It is likely he was included expressly to author a protest. Roosevelt suggested a press conference to denounce the secretary and the Washington bureaucrats, and an Associated Press reporter, in a bit of suspicious serendipity, just happened to be in the room taking notes. Wood and the other generals convinced their impetuous comrade that a letter to Alger would be more effective and less inflammatory than a press release.[23]

Roosevelt was more than happy to write the letter and later excused his insubordination, claiming that Shafter called the meeting specifically to generate a "united action of more or less public character."[24] He minimized his own role, saying "I wrote a letter to General Shafter, reading over the rough draft to the various Generals and adopting their corrections."[25] Nonetheless, Roosevelt minced no words. He said fever had rendered the command "so weakened and shattered as to be ripe for dying like rotten sheep." He dismissed plans for isolation in the mountains as "quarantining against the toothache" and predicted disaster if the men were not immediately removed from Cuba.[26] The colonel and the newspaperman took the letter into Shafter's office and Roosevelt claimed that, when he attempted to hand the letter to his commander, the general shoved his hand toward the reporter without reading it.

What happened in the anteroom while Roosevelt and the reporter were with Shafter is unclear. Herman Hagedorn said the newly appointed governor only joined the meeting because he overheard the generals' voices from his own office.[27] Regardless of when or under what circumstances Wood joined the group, the decision was made to draft a second letter demanding the evacuation for all the generals to sign. Wood said he only took what other officers told him to write and dictated it to his secretary; both Shafter and Roosevelt claimed Wood actually composed the "Round Robin" letter. A third letter, similar to that from the generals, was drafted by the medical officers.

The generals' letter was marginally more temperate than Roosevelt's. It claimed there was no yellow fever to threaten American civilians, but that the army was afflicted by "malarial fever to the extent that its efficiency is destroyed," and was physically incapable of moving to the interior. The Round Robin letter, signed by Wheeler, Kent, Bates, Chaffee, Sumner, Ludlow, Ames, Wood, and Roosevelt, demanded immediate evacuation from the island and charged that "persons responsible for preventing such a move will be responsible for the unnecessary loss of thousands of lives."[28]

Wood was delegated to deliver the letter to Shafter, and, accompanied by the ubiquitous correspondent, he laid the note on the senior general's desk. Wood said he tried to get Shafter to pick up the letter rather than allow the reporter to copy it, but the general refused: "I don't care whether this gentleman has it or not."[29] Shafter later claimed that the Associated Press had all three letters before he ever saw them.[30]

Ensuing events say more than the bowdlerized recollections of the participants. Shafter wired Alger that he was about to receive a telegram containing the views of his senior officers and doctors concerning the "health situation," but neglected to inform the secretary that the press already had the telegram. Roosevelt had convinced the Associated Press to pay the astronomical $1700 cost of privately cabling the three documents to the United States in return for the right to publish the letters. The Round Robin and Roosevelt's "cover letter" appeared on front pages across the country on August 4.

Alger and McKinley were furious, but the secretary had the troops on ships for Long Island within three days. McKinley, acutely aware of the potential effect of the letters on peace negotiations, called an emergency meeting with Alger and Secretary of the Navy John D. Long looking for ways to ameliorate the "grave impression abroad" that United States forces were sick and ineffective.[31] McKinley caustically cabled Shafter that the Round Robin had been "unfortunate from every point of view."[32]

As rumors circulated that Roosevelt was demanding that those who had kept his men in Cuba be brought to trial, Alger counterattacked.[33] He released Roosevelt's "private" letter denigrating the volunteer regiments. Roosevelt's charge that state troops were only one-third as good as the Rough Riders was especially inopportune since he planned to run for governor of New York and the poor performance of that state's Seventy-First Volunteer Infantry was a sore point. Alger, who later wrote that "It would be impossible to exaggerate the mischievous and wicked effects of the Round Robin," felt entirely justified in causing Roosevelt whatever embarrassment he could.[34]

Shafter and Wood took cover. On August 4, Shafter wrote Alger that "It was not until some time after that I learned their letter had been given to the press. It was a foolish, improper thing to do, and I regret very much that it occurred."[35] Shafter wrote McKinley that he could "readily see what intense excitement the publication must have occasioned; a great deal more than the situation warranted." He went on to say that Wheeler, Lawton, Kent, and Bates agreed, but Wood and Roosevelt were conspicuously absent from the exculpatory list. He wired Adjutant General Corbin that the letter had been so strong only because 75 percent of his men were ill while assuring Corbin that "The joy of this Army at receiving orders to return is intense."[36] The press winked at the Round Robin as "a commendable indiscretion."[37] Sternberg launched a press campaign assuring the country that there was no yellow fever, only sickness "of a malarial type," in the army and that returning soldiers posed no threat.[38]

When Shafter had summoned Wood to the governor's palace on July 20 and told him he was in charge of Santiago, he ordered the young general to "maintain order, feed the poor, and do everything possible to facilitate the prompt re-establishment of business."[39] He made Wood absolute ruler of a city of 40,000, virtually all of whom were hungry and one-third of whom suffered from typhoid, malaria, or yellow fever. Nearly 18,000 refugees had straggled back from El Caney, leaving a trail of emaciated bodies—mostly the very old and the very young—dead and dying along the roadside. Wood also had 4,000 Spanish prisoners, many of whom had malaria or other fevers.[40]

People with jaundiced skin draped over wasted muscles shuffled along streets ankle-deep in garbage and excrement, their slow progress occasionally redirected around the swollen, fly-blown corpse of a horse or mule.[41] When Wood took command of Santiago, the city's sanitary needs were in the hands of twenty hopelessly overburdened men and a legion of vultures and stray dogs. The general had been ordered to restore Santiago's business as soon as possible, but he knew that if he did not sanitize the city there would be no one left to do business. Most of the American soldiers were allowed into Santiago only on unavoidable official errands, so Wood drew his workforce from the city itself.

The new governor was not optimistic: "The people are almost impossible and simply will not work under any condition if they can help it and one simply has to drive them to keep them at work."[42] He added that "Such stupid and downtrodden people you never saw and our patience is sorely tried at times."[43] But he had power and he meant to use it. He wrote his wife, "My authority is absolute, even to life and death if I choose to use it. I have not shot any one but have pardoned a great many of the poor devils of Spaniards who were in jail."[44] He held audience for a steady stream of obsequious city leaders and put Cubans and Spaniards who misbehaved in irons and fed them bread and water.[45]

Wood retrieved shovels from the Spanish trenches and had prisoners make twig brooms.[46] He divided the city into five districts, each with its own medical and sanitation officer and drafted 100-man work crews (with absolute disregard for social status) from the citizenry. The poor were induced to work by trading food for labor, and the wealthy were conscripted. Those who resisted were taken into the streets and horse whipped. Wood requisitioned every wheeled vehicle and every surviving draught animal to haul garbage.

Wood's chief sanitary officer was Major George Barbour, an independently wealthy volunteer who had made a public service of cleaning Chicago's streets. A man of "somewhat peppery and irascible temperament," the major was deaf to claims of social privilege or the sanctity of private property, and he convinced the city he was serious when he publicly whipped a man for refusing to dig a new privy.[47] He put a military physician in each of Santiago's districts with directions to prioritize the clean up so the worst threats to health could be attacked first.

Before anything else could be done, the streets had to be cleared, but there were more bodies—human and animal—than could be conveniently buried. Cemeteries were traditionally the province of the Catholic Church for whom death was a singularly lucrative franchise. Since a basic funeral cost the equivalent of $4.50, a sum well beyond the means of most Cubans, families left corpses in their shacks to rot, closed the doors, and moved on. Cemeteries were owned by the church and grave sites were rented. If the rent was not paid, the corpse was exhumed and the bones, stripped clean by quicklime, were thrown in a communal pit. Wood ordered the priests to perform services regardless of pay and to leave the bodies buried.[48] When they objected, the governor threatened to put them on street cleaning brigades.[49] Funerals resumed and exhumations stopped, but even with its best efforts, the church could not cope with the mountains of bodies so Wood and Barbour established crematories on the city's outskirts where eighty to ninety corpses at a time were burned on pyres of grass, sticks, and kerosene.[50] When kerosene ran short, local merchants raised the price to $1.00 a gallon. Wood brought the shopkeepers into his office, accused them of being no better than murderers, and put the price back where it had started.[51]

Barbour's "whitewings" went house to house, inspected every courtyard, and ordered owners to transfer all the manure and garbage to the street where it could be collected. Of the city's 7,413 privies, 1,160 deemed beyond repair were destroyed and the rest were scrupulously cleaned. The city water system, built in the 1830s and riddled with leaks, was hopelessly inadequate. Without water, washing was not an option, so contaminated surfaces were scraped clean with hoop iron and dry scrubbed with either iron sulfate or lime. Cesspools were emptied bucket by bucket. The crews worked twelve to sixteen hours a day and, one month after Wood took command, every house in Santiago was sanitized.[52]

Wood then ordered the streets, formerly dirt tracks with drainage washes down the middle, paved and "macadamized" with a center crest and proper gutters. The edge of the harbor, with its 360 years of accumulated filth, seemed to him particularly unhealthful and he made plans to have it dredged. Believing that the yellow fever germ resided in filth, Wood was afraid that stirring up the "great mass of corruption" exposed at low tide would be "unhealthy and dangerous" during the summer fever season, so he reluctantly waited for fall.[53] Four thousand of the city's dogs—no longer needed as scavengers—were poisoned and burned.[54]

Wood personally inspected the city's bakeries and found only two he deemed clean enough to leave open. Most were unceremoniously shuttered and locked, and the most egregious owners were jailed. Groceries, markets, and slaughter houses were either cleaned or closed.

Santiago had once been surrounded by fertile fields, but, during the insurrection, the rebels and the Spanish took turns burning the houses and barns. Weyler transported the women and children to concentration camps while the men escaped to join the *insurrecto* armies.[55] In the extended tropical growing season, it took only weeks for neglected fields to revert to jungle. An American reporter wrote, "There was hardly an eatable thing growing within ten miles of Santiago in any direction."[56] Crisis had become catastrophe when the American blockade prevented importing food from other parts of the island.

There was almost no water since most of the city's supply came from the neighboring mountains in pipes that had been laid in 1839 and never repaired. It needed weeks of tedious, back-breaking labor to dig up the pipes and repair the thousands of leaks. Fortunately, there were still a number of ancient cisterns to supplement the supply. Wood divided the city into sections and turned on what water he could get one area at a time in volumes small but sufficient for survival.

The Spanish had stockpiled considerable amounts of bacon, sugar, hardtack, and rice that Wood commandeered for distribution to hospitals, religious institutions, prisons, and the public. He wrote, "When we first opened the ration stations for the distribution of food, the sights were indeed pathetic. Long struggling lines of human beings, tattered and starving, some barely able to stand, others still strong, but all fierce with hunger, swayed and pushed and fought fiercely for their places in line."[57] Cuban civilians besieged the army camps for American left-overs. One soldier complained, "Our camp is always crowed with hungry, starving Cuban men, women, and children, some of them naked and the rest only partially clothed. They will do almost anything for our hardtack."[58] Famished children scoured the piers for stray grains of rice spilled from military shipments.

Within four weeks Wood was distributing 935,000 meals a month (as many as 50,000 in a day) from the captured Spanish supplies augmented by private sources.[59] Clara Barton's Red Cross sent the steamship *Texas* filled with food, and the German vice-consul fed 5,000 people a day from his own funds.[60] From the looming catastrophe, Wood created policy; food was desperately needed and he had food, so he used it to control the city. Only those who worked ate. Citizens of every class and background were drafted to help clean Santiago and were paid either $.75 a day, $.50 and enough food for one person for a day, or three to four rations and no money for ten hours work.[61]

Starvation might have led to civil disruption, but Wood did not allow that to happen. He fixed bread prices and, when the bakers tried to decrease the size of the loaves, he threatened to jail them. Merchants caught using fraudulent scales were imprisoned,[62] and thieves and looters were shot on sight.[63] Within two weeks the city was under control. By August 15, Charles Cottrell of the Red Cross reported that "The work of distribution has gone on beautifully at this point and we have heard no complaint, and believe that every hungry mouth is filled."[64] Three weeks after she brought the *Texas* to Santiago, Clara Barton announced that "Little Santiago is served and overstocked" and redirected her efforts to other parts of the island.[65] Cottrell worried that, if the Red Cross continued to give away food, it would find itself competing with the local merchants.

Having weathered the immediate crisis, Wood started on Santiago's rehabilitation. For the city to be self-sufficient, the surrounding farms had to be returned to productivity. The land and the climate afforded three or four harvests a year, but the men had to be retrieved from the insurgent armies, returned with their families to the countryside, resupplied, and fed until the first crop came in. To do that, Wood used a two-part strategy. First he paid the men to help clean Santiago, anticipating they would use the money to reestablish their farms. Second, emulating Crook's Apache policy, he relocated food stores to rural depots so the men would stay on their farms rather than coming to the city for supplies.[66] By January 1899, the farms were sending sweet potatoes, beans, and the occasional chicken or pig to Santiago's markets, and the number of distributed rations had fallen to 261,000 a month.[67] By rotating men through 2,000 paid jobs, Wood was able to get 6,000 families a year financially stable and working to feed the city.

Even better, he paid for the project with captured stores, tariffs, and license fees and required virtually no money from Washington.[68] Tariffs had been the traditional support of Spain's colonial administration and a major irritant to the Cubans. Rates were high, corruption was pervasive, and most revenues that escaped the local administrators' pockets went to Spain. Wood insisted that tariffs be collected and, for the most part, refused to lower rates. He did, however, eliminate bribery and smuggling and kept the receipts for local projects. He augmented the tariffs with graduated license fees based on a business's estimated profit as determined by a four-man commission, half of whom were American and half Cuban.[69] Typical annual fees were: for a bank, $1,000; for an electric light company, $800; for a telephone and telegraph company, $300; for a bread, fruit, or candy stand, $6.[70]

Wood felt strongly that Cubans were too poor to pay direct taxes, which he dismissed as blood money and extortion.[71] Short on revenue, he slashed government salaries and, whenever possible, coerced office holders into donating their services. He wanted to spend as much as possible on public works that would both improve the city and provide income for its residents. It was the antithesis of Victorian colonialism and quite similar to the modified socialism Theodore Roosevelt's cousin would champion three decades later.[72]

Wood was relieved of a considerable burden on August 25 when the last of the Spanish soldiers left for home. With almost all their food diverted to civilians, the prisoners of war had been at real risk of starvation. As the Spaniards finally staggered down the docks to be taken home, they had "faces that looked like death's heads, every line of the skull marked on the yellow skin, protruding teeth over which lips would not close." And those were the healthier men who carried the litters with their sicker companions.[73]

The governor had been obliged to keep American soldiers in Santiago to protect the sick and starving Spaniards from the Cuban revolutionaries and the general populace. Most of the regular army and better volunteer troops had gone home, replaced by an influx of "immune" regiments, largely southern blacks. The United States' experience with volunteer black troops in Cuba was a stormy medical and social experiment. Alger felt blacks should be integrated into the army on as equal a basis as possible, but that was not a popular position. When Major Jesse Lee resigned command of the Tenth Volunteer Infantry because he was expected to dine with his black troops, the *New York Times* leapt to his defense, calling Alger "a politician of the old scheming kind, who no doubt still cherishes the belief which all sensible men dismissed many years ago that social equality between the races can be established only by forcing them to associate."[74]

It was also assumed—though, as far as one can tell, with no supporting evidence—that most blacks would not get yellow fever; having grown up in the South where the disease was prevalent, they must have been exposed and acquired immunity. One early plan for the Cuban invasion even proposed sending a small force of "colored immunes" to join García's forces in Santiago province from whence they could gradually push the Spanish north and west to be trapped by a larger white American contingent that would land near Havana after the yellow fever season ended.[75]

The regular army had only a small black cavalry, and, if Alger was to exercise his "colored immune" plan, he had to recruit, train, and arm a large group of new volunteers. The National Guard units were overwhelmingly white, so the secretary created several de novo regiments manned by southern blacks intended to be officered by northern West Point graduates. The plan was later tempered with the commissioning of nonprofessional whites and a number of black officers, although the latter appointments outraged the press both on account of race and because the commissions were mostly awarded for political connection rather than talent or experience.[76]

Shafter intended to garrison Santiago with as many blacks and as few whites as possible. When Wood assumed command of the city and later the province, he concurred with removing the regulars as quickly as feasible, but he preferred that Cubans do the actual police work, reserving American troops as mostly passive symbols of support. As it turned out, Wood's decision to rely on the Cubans was fortuitous since the immune regiments proved both difficult to control and virtually impossible for the Cubans—especially those of the middle and upper classes—to accept.

The black volunteers had even less military training than the hapless National Guard units, and most of their officers had little ability and less experience.[77] Discipline was a recurring problem both in training and after deployment, and relations with Cubans were a constant problem. The Second Volunteer Immune Regiment was one of the first American units in Santiago and was the first removed from the city. In less than two weeks the troops had been accused of public drunkenness, disorderly conduct, and stealing from and physically abusing the city's inhabitants. On August 16, Shafter removed the regiment to a camp in the hills and replaced them with another "colored regiment" from Illinois. He had more confidence in the "sobriety and discipline" of the northerners than he did in the raucous southern immunes.[78] Unfortunately, even getting the immunes out of the city did not entirely solve the problem. Within two months of Santiago's surrender, Shafter had been forced to segregate all the immune regiments in camps around San Luis, twenty-five miles north of Santiago. The units remained poorly disciplined with frequent reports of the officers and men drinking and carousing together at the expense of the village inhabitants.

Cubans feared and mistrusted the American blacks. Slavery had only been abolished in Cuba for a decade, and racial divisions played a major role in the nineteenth-century Cuban wars for independence, especially the most recent one. The majority of the *insurrectos* were black while virtually all of those who remained loyal to the Spanish crown were white. The vast majority of blacks were illiterate and landless and, conversely, almost all the educated and propertied were white.

One early rumor had it that the United States planned to colonize Cuba with southern blacks. The Santiago paper *El Porvenir* wrote, "On account of the terrible crimes of the negroes, there exists at the bottom of the Yankee mind a wish to evict the negroes from the country. American intervention in Cuba favors the sinister design . . . (but) Cubans must not consent to a single negro landing on our shores."[79] Upper class Cubans feared a repeat of the Liberian experiment or a new Haiti.

At first, Wood, who sympathized with Alger's feelings about integrating the blacks into American society, tried to isolate his black troops from the Cuban populace long enough to turn them into usable soldiers.[80] He thought that, if he could train his troops while using native Cubans for most police work, the system might succeed. After three months of constant trouble from the immunes, he gave up.[81] In a personal letter to McKinley, Wood noted that the population of Santiago, although itself largely black, had a "cordial and almost deadly hatred" for the American Negroes. The white citizens liked them even less, and Wood requested that his immunes be distributed among the other Cuban provinces and replaced by a single regiment (or even half a regiment) of white cavalry.[82]

Wood decided from the outset to rely on the "better class" of Cubans to build his government and to push the *insurrectos* and the *reconcentrados* back to farms in the countryside. He did not, however, completely exclude Cuban blacks from local government. He included former rebel troops in administrative positions and made a point of publicly showing equal respect to members of every social stratum.[83] The insurgents, however, had expected to assume positions of authority abandoned by the Spanish and were bitterly disappointed when García was barred from the city.[84] To make things worse, McKinley had ordered that existing civil officials should be left in place except in cases of egregious misconduct. Shafter had promised García control of the province's civil government, and the latter had named General Demetrio Castillo governor. Then Shafter, in response to McKinley's order, named Leonardo Ros, who had been mayor of Santiago under the Spanish, provincial governor. Of course, Shafter commanded all American military in Santiago, Lawton was military governor of the province, and Wood was military governor of the city. All five were headquartered in Santiago, and each assumed he was in charge.[85]

It was Wood who grabbed the reins of power. Castillo was never permitted to take office, and on August 14, Wood offhandedly commented, "Ros is no longer Civil Governor and I am now in charge."[86] Shafter had his eye on Havana and command of the entire island, and Lawton was careening toward a personal breakdown. The methodical, indefatigable Wood was right; he really was in charge.

The only credible threat to Wood's authority was García and his 23,000 armed, unemployed *insurrectos* in the countryside around Santiago.[87] Again, Wood got his solution by emulating Crook. Whenever possible, he made the soldiers trade their arms for food and sent them back to the farms. He proposed giving every veteran one *caballeria* (33 1/3 acres) of public land to farm, although that proposal was never adopted.[88] He turned those he could not convince to become farmers into policemen in a newly constituted Rural Guard. Those who refused to do either he declared bandits and had hunted down and shot.

By the beginning of October, Santiago city was self-supporting. The people, although still poor, were no longer starving or dying from uncontrolled epidemics. Unruly American soldiers were almost the sole source of civil unrest. Wood had spent a quarter of a million dollars of the city's tax revenues on sanitation, and Santiago had gone from being one of the world's dirtiest cities to one of its cleanest.[89] In August a public market that had been a "foul stinking pest hole" was clean enough to satisfy a New England housewife, and bakeries, butchers, and groceries were either cleaned or closed.

Santiago also had an American bank, a weather station (essential in the hurricane-prone Caribbean), and post boxes on every street with service two or three times a week to other cities in the province.[90] The streets were being paved (a contract for $30,000 a month had gone to an American road builder) and $1,000 a week went to keep them clean. The death rate had declined from 100 a day to thirty or forty a week.[91] In spite of those expenses and a municipal payroll in the thousands, Wood had amassed $250,000 in the city treasury, mostly as a result of his government's efficiency and scrupulous honesty.[92] The volume of imports to Santiago's harbor had actually decreased somewhat from their Spanish colonial peak while tariff rates had remained the same, but revenues had increased from $30,000 a month to over $70,000 and, at least for the moment, all the money stayed in the local treasury to which Wood added $500,000 a year from municipal taxes and his license fees.[93]

How did a young man with no experience so quickly become one of the most successful colonial administrators in history? Lord Cromer, the archetypal "pro-consul" and administrator of Egypt, told the British Foreign Office that there was only one man in the world capable of taking his place but, unfortunately, Wood was an American. Charisma certainly played a role. Wood was an acceptably handsome, erect, muscular man who stood out in a crowd. He had cultivated an athletic, military bearing that demanded respect. His Calvinist morality and rigid commitment to honesty and obedience (to him if not from him) stood in sharp contrast to the venality of the colonial government he replaced. If he sought personal gain it was in reputation rather than money. But merely having the bearing and character appropriate to a benevolent dictator would not have been enough. Had he not been in a position of extraordinary autonomy he could never have fully exercised his unexpectedly effective leadership skills.

Through a series of governmental accidents and generally poor planning, Wood found himself an essentially independent agent. Lawton had no interest in governing Santiago and was seldom sober; besides, his nominal control over the province terminated in an early departure. Shafter had no real interest in Santiago; he spent all his energies angling for command of the whole island and in getting his troops home before they were caught in a yellow fever epidemic guaranteed to generate a career-ending political firestorm. Miles was diverted first by the Puerto Rican invasion and then by his political battle with Alger. Alger was fully occupied with preserving his job in the face of rising public anger over his conduct of the war. McKinley had his hands full with the growing Philippine insurrection and had yet to give much thought to the mechanics of administering the new American possessions. Wood was left with unlimited power locally and with no oversight from the chain of command above. For the time being he was (at least until General Douglas MacArthur got to Tokyo half a century later) as near to a dictator as any American could be.

When Lawton precipitously departed after a barroom altercation, Wood's fiefdom expanded to the whole of Santiago province. Conditions in the rest of eastern Cuba were, in many ways, worse than in Santiago. Guantánamo had suffered even more than the capital from the war. A fourth of the city's 15,000 inhabitants had starved during Sampson's blockade, and the children who were still alive staggered through the streets with "five-year-old bodies and fifty-year-old faces."[94] Holguín had 3,000 active cases of smallpox.[95]

Wood divided the province into four sectors and set out to reproduce his Santiago City success. He sent twenty-five-year-old Colonel Duncan Hood and a regiment of immunes to Holguín. Hood brought food from Wood's coastal stockpiles to feed the starving, quarantined the smallpox victims in hastily improvised hospitals, and sent a group of American and Cuban doctors to vaccinate the entire population.[96] In a month the number of new cases of smallpox leveled off and the disease was fully controlled four weeks after that. As in Santiago City, the healthy citizens were put to work cleaning and scraping the city and burning garbage that had been accumulating for decades. Hood enlisted the Rural Guard to restore order, a job they took with such diligence that a later investigator was forced to excuse their enthusiastic elimination of criminals or just "people who led bad lives."[97]

By spring people were back in their houses and businesses were reopened. Colonels Ray at Guantánamo and Wylly at Baracoa undertook similar (though slightly less drastic) efforts while Brigadier General Ewers assumed Wood's place as governor of Santiago City. Wood's two assistants, Lieutenant E. C. Brooks and Second Lieutenant Matthew Elting Hanna, and Cuban Captains Mestre and Mendoza rounded out Wood's administrative team.[98] Although he was later accused of taking credit for his subordinates' accomplishments, Wood was, in fact, a model leader. He remained personally involved in the affairs of all his provincial sectors, making frequent visits to remote parts of eastern Cuba while lavishly praising the men under him both in public and in private.

Once the immediate sanitary and public health emergencies came under control, Wood turned his attention to organizing a civil government. The Spanish had divided Cuba's provinces into "municipalities," each of which was responsible for both a population center (town or city) and the surrounding countryside and each of which had a mayor and an administrative council. Wood opted to retain the system but, to avoid "factional quarrels and disorder," either he or one of his colonels appointed all office holders from a list submitted by locals of the "better class."[99]

Wood was much more comfortable with the Spanish and Cuban upper classes than with the insurgents, who had putatively won their revolution, and who were furious when he weighted his appointments toward Spaniards who chose to remain on the island. The New York–based leaders of the self-styled Cuban provisional government were an annoyance to the governor. Although Wood had disposed of García, his army, and his governmental "appointments," the New Yorkers persisted in efforts to participate in Santiago's government. Wood complained that "The people who will cause the most trouble are the political Cubans in N.Y. who, too cowardly to fight, are now keen to publish their inflammatory articles and keep everything in a ferment."[100] McKinley complicated the situation by maintaining contact with Tomás Estrada Palma and his "provisional government" in New York, although he never officially recognized them.[101]

Wood, however, left no question as to who was really in charge in Santiago. Referring to his Cuban appointees, he said "The only condition attached to the exercise of their authority was the stipulation that every resolution adopted or appointment made by them should be subject to the approval of the American district commander, or, upon appeal, to that of the Commanding General of the province."[102]

In sharp contrast to his complete control of the administrative hierarchy, Wood granted the Cuban people a degree of personal freedom they had never known. He published a list of universal rights modeled (with a few signal exceptions) on the United States Constitution's Bill of Rights. All Cubans citizens were to have:

The right of assembly
Freedom of religious choice
Universal access to the courts
Freedom from seizure of property
Protection from self-incrimination
Protection from double jeopardy
The right to bail, habeas corpus, and a speedy trial
Protection from excessive fines and cruel and unusual punishment
Protection from unreasonable search and seizure, and
Freedom of speech and the press.[103]

Wood was certain his government could not succeed unless the Cuban people agreed to respect civil authority without being subject to military force.[104] He feared that, if control relied on the army rather than consent of the governed (not to be confused with their participation), Cubans would drift back to a corrupt bureaucracy. Wood, benefiting from a lack of the career soldier's military prejudices and the professional politician's ideological ones, combined despotism and personal freedoms in a way more typical of pre-Enlightenment Europe than of American democracy.[105] He was convinced that, in order to win Cuban trust, transparent honesty was more important than universal participation. Like Cromer, he understood that free expression of dissent (as long as it was verbal and not physical) was a stabilizing rather than an unsettling influence. Wood told the New York Union Club, "I have allowed (Cubans) to hold public meetings without limit, and the result is that there are no more public meetings and everything is as quiet as a New England village."[106] If the people were fed, busy, and allowed to speak, they would cooperate even though suffrage was conspicuously absent from the "Santiago Constitution." Wood, in an incongruous mixture of Polonius and Abraham Lincoln, wrote:

What is needed in Cuba at present is a firm but liberal and just government of the people, for the people and by the people, under American military supervision, for the time being; this supervision to extend only to such time as the civil government shall have become fully established and running smoothly.[107]

Wood fought another battle key to establishing authority and trust. Almost as soon as Santiago came under United States control, American businessmen flocked to Cuba looking to make money. One reporter on the way to Santiago late in the summer of 1898 found as shipmates Americans who had "lived and worked in Alaska, Siberia, India, China, Japan, Siam, Africa, Turkey, Armenia, Mongolia, Manchuria, Mexico, Honduras, South America, the Caucasus, Mexico, and the Malay Archipelago."[108] Wood made the "absolute necessity of keeping Americans and all others than the inhabitants of the island of Cuba out of office in Cuba" one of his most immutable policies.[109] For some jobs for which there were no local sources like road building and dredging, he allowed Americans to provide the services on an open bid basis with the condition that they not establish a permanent presence on the island. He was determined that Santiago province not become a windfall for a new generation of carpetbaggers. He proudly told a New York audience that "All public places were filled by representative Cubans, without exception. There has not been a single American appointed to office in my department of Santiago" (save for those who had come with the original expeditionary force).[110]

Besides absolute authority, scrupulous honesty, and civil liberty, Wood relied heavily on his direct, personal presence. He tirelessly visited jails, schools, courts, hospitals, and seats of government throughout eastern Cuba. He wrote, "I am strongly of the opinion, that, if we are to have a successful civil government, each Department Commander has got to be physically able to make extensive tours of inspection, to be a great deal among the people, and to give the greatest amount of personal attention to all the details of the civil work in his Department."[111] What he demanded of his department commanders, he demanded of himself many times over. Theodore Roosevelt, explaining his friend's surprising success in Santiago, credited Wood's honesty but, even more, his unlimited capacity for hard work.[112]

Eastern Cuba, especially in the late nineteenth century when there were few roads and almost no railroads, was geographically difficult. The coast west of Guantánamo ascends abruptly into the Sierra Maestre that parallel the coast and effectively isolate the coastal cities from the interior. North of the coastal range are discontinuous ridges of jungle-covered mountains, rising as much as 8,000 feet and extending all the way to the north coast. In 1899, much of Santiago's interior had not been mapped, and parts had not even been explored. Besides the dense jungle, the area was cut with canyons and ravines that were dry in the winter but became thundering, impassable rivers when the rains came. The only railroads were short spurs, connecting the port cities to mines or plantations, and even the roads no longer connected the eastern provinces to Havana which was, in consequence, five days away by ocean steamer. Communication between Santiago and the interior city of Holguín was by mountainous mule track. The other major cities (Manzanillo, Baracoa, and Guantánamo) were best reached by water. The province was, for all practical purposes, an island of its own, and Wood had to bring this wild country under a central control. He needed roads and telegraph lines to communicate with his district commanders and municipal governors. He needed a civil government with laws, courts, and prisons. He had to establish relations with the Catholic Church, and the island's children had to be educated.

Wood's "military supervision" ranged at times from petty to tyrannical. Bullfighting, a traditional favorite of Cubans of every social stripe, offended his New England sensibilities and he banned it outright along with cockfighting and the lottery. To stop cattle theft he ordered that all livestock be branded and registered with the military government. He ordered his Cuban police to shoot on sight anyone who was caught stealing or had the temerity to resist arrest.[113] Wood fervently believed that citizens had to anticipate equal treatment under the law, but the existing Spanish institutions were hopelessly corrupt and inefficient. Wood maintained the Spanish three-tiered judicial system but replaced all the judges with his own appointees.[114] Wood found the courts "swimming with untried cases" with the accused, most of whom were too poor to post bail, languishing in filthy jails for months.[115] In one of his daily forays into Santiago's slums, Wood came upon a pile of scrap paper about to be sold for fuel. The pile proved to contain nearly all the province's mine and land records and a significant portion of the district's court records. Wood bought the lot for $2 and restored the records to the courthouse.[116] By December 1898, all three judicial levels were fully functional and were operating at half the cost of Spanish colonial courts.[117]

The jails were places of "intolerable cruelty and injustice" which constituted for the island's new rulers "a national disgrace," where "assassins, brigands, sodomites, pickpockets, and young men charged with disorderly conduct" were thrown together in crowded cells.[118] The prisoners slept on bare stone floors carpeted with vermin and their own feces. In one jail only 2 of 151 inmates had actually been convicted; the rest were awaiting trials which occurred at a frequency of about two a day, a fraction of the rate at which new prisoners were arriving.

One Santiago town had three mayors, each of whom claimed an annual budget of $10,000 out of total municipal revenue of $4,000, so Wood fired all three and found a man willing to take the job without pay.[119] In general, Wood paid as few municipal administrators as possible and paid the few he hired as little as he could. His tendency to enlist members of the upper class continued to distress the *insurrectos*, who were almost without exception from outside that social stratum. In November, he appointed Emiliano Bacardi mayor of Santiago, although he told an aide he was not so sure how news of his naming the scion of the great rum-producing family would sit with his mother's Puritan neighbors.[120]

Personal involvement was the hallmark of Wood's administrative style. He visited churches and hospitals, schools and orphanages, construction sites and city dumps. He wrote McKinley that "The civil government of this Province, for a time at least, has got to be one almost of paternalism. . . . one has got to go among the people, advise them, help them, and in fact give one's personal attention to the greatest extent possible, considering no detail too small to be worthy of careful investigation."[121]

Reasonably sure that he would be in Cuba for the foreseeable future, Wood began plans to move his wife and two sons to the island.[122] He had already rented *Guao,* a grand house that had formerly housed the British consul and occupied a hill a mile east of the city with a stunning view of the harbor. Wood missed his family and virtually every letter home complained of a lack of communication, packages, or other evidence of appropriate concern from his wife and children. On August 21 he wrote his wife, "Your last letter was written July 29, 1898 and you don't know how delighted I was to hear from you dearest. I am simply wild to see you and hope . . . that you will soon come down here or I go up there."[123]

A month later the yellow fever season was waning, and he told Louise that the time was right to give up the Washington house, pack and store the furniture, and come to *Guao.*[124] In November, Lou, Len, and Osborne Wood arrived with an assortment of chickens, a cow, a horse, a buckboard, and a cook. Mrs. Wood brought the social skills of a Washington political family and, within days, she was entertaining the local dignitaries and their wives in a series of afternoon "levies" at the residence.

Although a remarkably energetic and fit man, even Wood could not escape Cuba's debilitating illnesses. In August, he had written his wife that he had "had a bad dose of some sort of fever" and had been "pretty well knocked out."[125] He was careful not to name the disease; euphemisms such as malaria, malignant fever, and "some sort of fever" carried much less emotional baggage than yellow fever. A week later he assured his mother that, though he had had a "rather nasty turn of fever," he was confident that he had "stamped out" the dreaded yellow fever in the city.[126] He was wrong, probably on both counts. Two weeks later, he assured his wife that he was entirely over his bout of "malarial fever," although the episode had given him "quite a shake."[127] Wood's "malarial fever" caused his skin to discolor and his temperature to rise over 105 degrees and his weight to go down more than twenty pounds. Although he continued to work, one reporter saw him stagger against his office wall and nearly lose consciousness on standing. Wood never caught yellow fever thereafter, in spite of spending most of his life in the tropics, and, in all likelihood, he was one of the disease's lucky survivors.

For five months, Leonard Wood was the United States' sole proconsul, and he governed virtually without supervision. By November 1898, there were only 8,000 American troops in the province, 6,000 of whom he wanted to send home.[128] García's insurgent army was either disarmed and returned to farming or incorporated into the Rural Guard. The *reconcentrado* families were back on their farms. Death rates from disease were the lowest that had ever been recorded. City streets had been cleaned, macadamized, and were being paved. Dumps and septic tanks were sanitized and running water had been restored to the cities. Cuban civil officials had been appointed and the courts were functioning. The province was in the black by October 1, 1898, and had $250,000 in the treasury by the beginning of the New Year.[129]

Henry Cabot Lodge wrote, "You are advised that the work accomplished by you in the rehabilitation of the city of Santiago is worthy of the highest commendation."[130] Roosevelt published articles praising Wood and wrote letters extolling his performance to Secretary of State

John Hay[131] and Attorney General John Griggs.[132] The citizens of Santiago named a street for him.[133] Working without direct supervision and allowed to bring every aspect of his energy, intuition, and intellect to bear, Wood was triumphant, but, while his reputation soared, trouble loomed in the form of General James Brooke.

Brooke was a mesomorphic, rigid sixty-year-old Pennsylvanian whose regular army career stretched back to 1861. Like most Civil War veterans who had lingered in the military, he had spent three decades languishing in a variety of frontier outposts and glacially ascending the promotion ladder. After a brief, scandal-plagued stint in command of the training camp at Chickamauga, he joined Miles's invasion in Puerto Rico, fought a few minor skirmishes, and emerged by dint of seniority as military governor of that island. Shafter, Wilson, and Lee had all wanted to be Cuba's military governor, but stolid, conservative Brooke got the job.

On December 22, 1898, McKinley sent Brooke "a few unofficial suggestions" that, although intentionally vague, formed the basis of the latter's authority. The president asserted that American authority over Cuba derived directly from "the law of belligerent right over conquered territory."[134] Neither the United States Constitution nor its laws had provisions for governing colonies. The Paris Peace Treaty, signed twelve days earlier, provided that Spain was to relinquish sovereignty over the island and that the United States was to occupy Cuba thereafter. The treaty was silent on the transfer of sovereignty.[135]

The Military Department, established by the war department as part of the Division of Customs and Insular Affairs on December 13, 1898, was to administer Cuba, Puerto Rico, and the Philippines.[136] As department commander and military governor, Brooke was given sole authority in Cuba, answering only to McKinley until Congress saw fit to legislate otherwise. Realizing that his autonomy would vanish when the rest of the island passed to United States control, Wood spent the fall of 1898 staking out his position. He argued in speeches, in print, and in private communication with government officials all the way to McKinley that the provinces required hands-on administration and should be allowed to function in a semiautonomous federal system. He lost the argument, and Brooke came to command with virtually unfettered control over Cuba's government and finances. McKinley obliquely offered Wood a second star as a consolation prize.

When he arrived in Havana, Brooke lived up to Wood's worst fears. The new governor general abrogated the "Santiago Constitution" and restored Spanish laws. Worse, Brooke decreed that all tariff revenues from the port of Santiago would henceforth flow directly to Colonel Tasker Bliss's customs office in Havana for redistribution to the various provinces. Only $10,000 a month was allocated to Santiago City and only $30,000 to the entire province. Wood had been spending $4,000 a month on street cleaning alone, and the new budget promised to immediately put up to three thousand Cubans out of work.[137]

All local taxation was to stop pending development of an island-wide system of revenue generation. All expenditures except those for emergency sanitary projects were to be approved in Havana and all civil appointments had to go through Brooke. All administrative salaries were to be cut by 20 to 30 percent—a uniquely bitter pill in Santiago where Wood had already cut them in half.[138] The new postmaster A. Estes Rathbone (who reported not to Brooke but directly to the postmaster general in Washington) initiated what became a vicious, protracted war with Wood when he closed all the governor's popular interior post offices, a move he justified as fiscally necessary since only those postal facilities in port cities had immediate access to the outside world.[139]

Brooke added salt to Wood's wounds by spreading the power between his office and an appointed Cuban government. He divided the Military Department of Cuba into six subdepartments and the city of Havana. Each department and the city was under an American general, who had charge of the civil government and command of the American troops in his area.[140] Unlike Wood, Brooke preferred to keep a certain distance from the gritty details of daily government, and he meant to use Cubans as the buffer. He divided the civil government into four departments, each with a Cuban secretary: Justice and Public Instruction under José Antonio Gonzales-Lanuza; Agriculture, Commerce, Industry, and Public Works under Adolfo Saénz-Yanes; Finance (although Bliss and the North American Trust Company controlled tariff revenues and the island's treasurer was an American army officer) under Pablo Desverine; and the powerful State and Government Department under Domingo Méndez Capote. The six provincial civil governors and the mayors of the municipalities reported to Capote. It was general knowledge that, under Brooke's laissez-faire administration, "The American governor reigns but the Cuban secretaries govern."[141] The Cuban cabinet was the island's new power broker.

Furious, Wood reacted on three fronts; he by-passed Brooke and complained directly to the war department, he enlisted his powerful Washington friends, and he went to the public. The public campaign began in Santiago. The city's merchants liked Wood's tax policies. Graft had stopped, rates were predictable, and the money was spent on visible, necessary public projects. Sending tax receipts to an American official in Havana smacked of colonial exploitation, and Santiago's papers published irate editorials encouraging businessmen to take to the streets in protest. Regardless of whether (as one author suggested) Wood organized the strikes and mass meetings or merely allowed them to take place, the reaction from Havana was swift and angry.[142]

Brooke's chief of staff, Major General Adna Chaffee, fired an icy letter to Wood, whom he addressed not by name but only as "Commanding General, Department of Santiago," instructing him that it was the will of the president "to disburse customs duties for the benefit of the Cuban people." Brooke interpreted that to mean the Cuban people as a whole, and it was not the prerogative of the citizens of Santiago to dictate to the president how these revenues were to be allocated. Wood was to instruct the local editors that any further criticism or calls for mass meetings would lead to suspension of publication. As for Wood, he was to exercise "tact and discretion" and to conduct the department's affairs "along lines *prescribed for guidance,* repressing with your influence, power if necessary, all acts that may tend toward interference with an orderly execution of, and adherence to, every regulation prescribed by the President for the government and business affairs of the island." There was no "Yours truly" or "sincerely," merely "By command of Major General Brooke." Chaffee meant to leave no doubt as to who was in charge.[143]

Back in Washington, Wood's friends rallied to his support. Roosevelt wrote a paean to his abilities in an article unambiguously titled "General Leonard Wood: A Model American Military Administrator."[144] The new governor of New York claimed the article was not so much personal praise as a description of how an island colony ought to be run—Wood's way and not Brooke's. "First class men" (like Wood) should be given "the widest possible latitude" (and not be subject to interference from meddlesome superiors like Brooke) to solve the problems they encountered. The United States could not "afford to let doctrinaires or honest, ignorant people decide the difficult and delicate questions bound to arise in administering the new provinces."[145] Without actually naming Brooke, Roosevelt was brutally clear.

Wood also cabled Secretary of War Alger for permission to come to Washington and personally plead his case. When Brooke found out about the request he furiously protested, but Wood was already on his way home. Leonard Wood had only been away from Washington for eight months, but in that time had risen from army physician to national hero, and his return was a triumphal event. Wood started his grand tour at the White House, where his standing ovation stopped a reception in progress and virtually forced the president to invite him into the receiving line. He spoke at the Union League Club in New York, where he advised that all Cuba's provinces be allowed to follow the model he had established in Santiago.[146]

Wood spent two days testifying before the Senate Committee on Military Affairs, mostly about what he had done in Santiago and what he planned to do if given the freedom and resources. He also testified before General Grenville Dodge's Commission to Investigate the Conduct of the War Department in the War with Spain. Wood had previously sided with Roosevelt in criticizing Alger's management of the war, but now considered it impolitic to publicly chastise his superior. Accordingly, he changed his stance, proclaiming that he had been feeding his own family on army issue canned beef—the same "embalmed beef" that had been the center piece of the public attack on the secretary. Wood's volte-face annoyed Roosevelt who had made Alger's removal a crusade, but the rift proved temporary.

Wood was honored by the Metropolitan Club in Washington before returning to Cuba in early February, where Brooke and his staff waited, determined to bring him to heel. Wood kept after his Washington friends. Lodge reassured him: "I think the Cuban matter will work out all right, though there will be annoyances and many drawbacks. Your success in Santiago shows how very possible it is, and I also think that events in other parts of the island are all tending in the same direction."[147]

The "events in other parts of the island" to which Lodge alluded were anything but smooth. In fairness to Brooke, Wood had a five-month head start and a relatively prosperous province. He also had a much smaller area and less populous cities to clean and govern. Havana was nearly as dirty as Santiago had been and was four times as large.

Some of the poorer provinces, especially Matanzas, could not generate the revenue to clean the streets and pay teachers and municipal workers. Most municipal treasuries had no money. Less than one school-age Cuban child in ten was enrolled in classes and only half of those enrolled actually attended. In some areas 90 percent of the population was illiterate. The rest of the island had precisely the same problems as Santiago half a year earlier.

Unlike Santiago, the Havana government was a hodgepodge. Brooke had overall command of both the civil administration and about 24,000 American troops. Colonel Tasker Bliss ran a customs service staffed partially by American officers and civilians and partially by Cuban civilians. The island's treasurer was an American army officer, but the North American Trust Company of New York was a virtually independent fiscal agent. Senator Mark Hanna's crony Estes Rathbone ran the postal service as a personal bank account. The Quarantine Service was run by the United States Marine Hospital Service and telephones and telegraph were the purview of the Army Signal Corps. Behind all this were the Cuban secretaries and their network of provincial and municipal officials. Wood had been in direct charge of all those areas in Santiago prior to January 1, 1899.

From Santiago, Wood was relentless. In high dudgeon, he requested an official court of inquiry into Brooke's criticism of his administration. He complained that Brooke "tried in every way to hamper, hinder and discredit" his work and that "every statement he made was a lie" and that when one contemplated "the character of the work done here and the present situation" it seemed "rather low down to run an obstruction policy."[148]

Mired in growing animosity with his commanding officer and the regular army power structure and with no certainty that he would not be unceremoniously returned to the rank of captain, Wood was tempted by an offer of lucrative civilian employment. On May 24, New York financier F. L. Pearson cabled that the Washington Traction and Electric Company would like the general as president with a $20,000 salary that dwarfed the $5,500 he got from the army.[149] Roosevelt, aware of Wood's tenuous position and lack of outside resources, urged his friend to take the job for his family's sake. Wood toyed with the idea but abandoned it when he received confidential assurance of his imminent transfer to the regular army.

Once Wood made his decision, Roosevelt swung into action. He wrote Attorney General John Griggs that, in his humble opinion, Wood should be "put in absolute control of all Cuba, with no one to divide authority with him in any way." He asked to present his argument to McKinley directly, confessing that he did not know whether the president would care to hear it or not, but provocatively suggesting that the appointment would be in the best interests of the Republican Party and McKinley's reelection.[150] He wrote Secretary of State John Hay that Wood should be put "in immediate command of all Cuba, with complete liberty to do what he deems wisest in shaping our policy for the island." Roosevelt, anticipating regular army resistance to Wood's appointment, went on, "The objection will at once be raised that Wood is a young man who has already had a very rapid promotion and that he should not be put over the heads of his seniors. Undoubtedly to take such action would invite a great deal of criticism of the wooden-headed sort. To this criticism absolutely not one particle of heed should be paid, and the objection counts for literally nothing." He concluded that, if the United States intended to administer Cuba "on the seniority plan," it might just as well give up the job at once.[151]

In June, Wood and his family returned home so he could receive an honorary doctorate of laws from Harvard, and, on the way to Boston, he detoured to visit McKinley who was vacationing in Massachusetts. Wood hinted just enough at the Washington Traction and Electric offer to elicit a promise of a regular army appointment "at the first opportunity," although he had already decided to stay in Cuba regardless. He went on to Boston where, his less than respectable departure from Boston City having been forgotten, he was honored at his medical school's commencement. He took the opportunity to assure reporters that "The Cuban problem can be easily solved. With the right sort of administration everything could be straightened out in six months. Just now there is too much 'tommyrot.'"[152] *Colliers* magazine and the *New York Times* surmised that Wood might be named secretary of a new Department of the Colonies.[153]

Just as Wood began to settle in for a summer vacation in New England, word came from Santiago that yellow fever had again broken out. The news came as a bitter disappointment for Wood, who had assumed that his rigorous sanitary measures had stopped the disease. Worse, it had broken out not in the city at large but in a barracks housing American troops. On June 22, Wood ordered the garrison restationed in the hills behind El Morro after four soldiers died of the disease.[154] The general, who had placed so much faith in the efficacy of sanitation, told reporters that the cases must have originated in the seedy Army and Navy Bar, "a liquor place of bad repute" frequented by soldiers, sailors, and Caribbean transients. He was confident that closing such establishments and returning to rigorous sanitary measures would stop the outbreak.[155] He was wrong.

New cases were reported every day and, after a brief July 4 holiday, Wood returned to Santiago. The *Times* wrote, "It would be expressing it very mildly to say that Gen. Wood was surprised and shocked at the situation which confronted him when he arrived Monday morning."[156] There were 150 active cases of yellow fever, thirty of whom had already died, almost all Americans. Two of Wood's clerks and one of his household staff were hospitalized. He laconically wrote his wife, "I must say all hands were a trifle blue as every officer who had the fever had died and it looked deucedly bad."[157]

Here was an emergency Wood could manage without interference from Havana. He placed the entire city under quarantine. His whole headquarters save for a handful of "immune" clerks were moved with all the office records and supplies to Cristo in the hills. Santiago was placed off limits to all government officers and employees. Those infected with yellow fever were placed under military guard. All hotels and bars were closed and liquor sales were banned. Railroads and steamship lines were forbidden to bring Americans into the city. No ship could touch a wharf. No traveler could leave the city until he spent five days in quarantine.[158] American and Caribbean vagrants were rounded up and confined in camps.[159] An American physician caught hiding an English yellow fever victim who was a private patient had his house fumigated and was jailed.[160]

By mid-August, the outbreak had receded (although probably not as a result of any of the draconian quarantine measures) and Wood was free to resume his attempt to supplant Brooke. He complained to Roosevelt, "I have had a great deal of trouble with General Brooke. Whether he is guilty of the policy of obstruction, derogatory criticism, or all round hostility, I do not know and do not care. The only thing is that it is discouraging and disgusting under the circumstances."[161] Brooke's accusation that Wood was foolishly spending money on roads and submitting reports that were "a disgrace to the army" brought back the old demand for an official inquiry. Wood was particularly irate about Brooke's having ceded power to his Cuban secretaries ("these little rascals") and raised the possibility that, if the Cubans were not rooted out soon, the Americans would lose control. Roosevelt replied that the letter made him "worried and indignant" and that he would, in confidence, place it before Elihu Root, who had just replaced Alger as secretary of war. Roosevelt thought Root was "a thoroughly good fellow" who could be counted on to do the right thing.[162]

Brooke was having problems with the Cubans as well. General García had been bitterly disappointed when he was banned from the Spanish surrender of Santiago, but the insurgents naively continued to assume that the United States would only occupy urban enclaves on the island and that the overall government would pass to them. The Cubans had even formed a revolutionary assembly under General Máximo Gómez to assume power. Initially, the United States did establish control in the port cities with their revenue-producing customs houses, and, for the most part, left the interior to the rebel armies. (Santiago, where Wood had control of the entire province, was the obvious exception.) When Wilson took "control" of Matanzas, he estimated that 350 towns in his province were occupied by Cuban troops.[163] Even though García's army in Santiago had disbanded and surrendered its arms, Brooke still faced 40,000 men under Gómez scattered through the western provinces.[164] Like García before him, Gómez did not participate in the Havana surrender ceremonies on January 1, 1899. The old Dominican said he did not wish to come unless he could bring his army. Brooke said he was afraid he could not prevent violence between the Cubans and Spanish citizens and soldiers still in the city; a five-day celebration planned by the *Habañeros* was cancelled and the Cubans were left to seethe in silence.[165]

When Brooke took control, Cuba (with the exception of Santiago) was in pitiable shape. The protracted war and Weyler's reconcentration policy had killed a fifth of the population and the American naval blockade had left many of the survivors near starvation. As in Santiago, the roads and railroads were a shambles and the burned out farms and plantations were well on their way back to jungle. One-third of the island's agricultural land was no longer in production and over 80 percent of the cattle were gone. In 1899, the island produced only one-sixth of the tobacco and one-third of the sugar that it had in 1894. The coffee industry was destroyed and never recovered.[166]

Brooke organized emergency food distribution but, lacking the warehouses full of abandoned Spanish supplies from which Wood had benefited, had to rely solely on Bliss's customs revenues. Ludlow, following Wood's model, divided Havana into sanitary districts and began house to house decontamination, but he lacked Wood's paid local workforce so the project dragged. The battle against malaria and yellow fever raged furiously and remained a political open sore both because of the risk to Americans serving in Cuba and the worry that diseases would spread from Cuba to the United States. In August, a special commission of the Marine Hospital Service confidently announced that Professor Giuseppe Sanarelli's *Bacillus icteroides* was the true and only cause of yellow fever (wrong), that yellow fever was transmitted through the air (wrong), that Sternberg's *Bacillus x* was not the cause of yellow fever (boldly correct since Sternberg was still surgeon general), and that yellow fever could surely be controlled by vigorous sanitary measures (profoundly wrong).[167]

Except in Matanzas, where Wilson insisted on forming his own police force, part of the insurrection army was recruited into a Rural Guard after Wood's model. In Havana, Ludlow imported an ex–New York police superintendent and an ex–New York detective sergeant to organize an urban police force whose marginal efficiency was mercifully masked by a generally law-abiding and tractable population. Root sent Charlton Lewis (president of the Prison Association of New York) to examine Cuban courts and prisons in the latter half of 1899 and got back a scathing report of a "frightful situation." Abuses in the prisons for which the United States was now responsible were "a national disgrace." Most prisoners had never been tried and were being held only because they lacked the money to bribe a corrupt judge or his staff. At Cienfuegos Lewis found 157 prisoners only two of whom had been tried and convicted. He concluded that "to be accused in Cuba is practically to be confined under torture during the arbitrary pleasure of an irresponsible judge." And the judges, besides being lazy, were "habitually and systematically corrupt." Nonetheless, Brooke refused to investigate any court officer without irrefutable proof that a bribe had been accepted. A prisoner who actually had been tried might serve twelve years for murder or life for speaking insolently to an officer. Lewis's complaints to Brooke brought only referral back to an unresponsive Cuban civil government.[168] In Santiago, Wood had already emptied the jails, fired the judges, and directly supervised appointment of new court officers.

Brooke was saved from an influx of American opportunists by the Foraker Amendment to the February 1899 Military Appropriations Bill, which banned granting of Cuban concessions and franchises to American companies.[169] Before the law, scores of potential street builders, railway operators, and telegraph entrepreneurs had begun circling Havana as replacements for the buzzards newly chased from the streets. A law establishing Cuban schools was not issued until November 2, and new boards of education under American educator Alexis Frye were not appointed until December. The first of the schools were finally opened on December 11.

In contrast to the chaos on the western end of the island, the situation in Wood's eastern provinces steadily got better. Wood sent his chief surgeon, Major Valery Havard, on a tour of the province in early September where he found "a decided general improvement" in conditions. Fields were cleared and back in production, the people were fed, small children traveled the road unmolested, and stock grazed safe and unguarded. The Rural Guard had reestablished peace and had the confidence of the populace.[170] Albert Robinson, one of Wood's most vociferous critics, grudgingly assessed the difference between the younger general's government in Santiago and Brooke's in Havana: "General Brooke's Cuban appointees made a tool of their chief. General Wood made tools of his Cuban appointees. General Brooke's cabinet established an elaborate bureaucracy. General Wood established autocracy and met with notable success in his effort."[171]

Behind the details of Brooke's difficulty lurked the fundamental question of America's actual intentions toward Cuba. Was the United States merely a beneficent neighbor trying to allow Cuba to create a government of its own or was the larger country involved in its own version of the Scramble for Africa?

At first, McKinley had obdurately opposed any Cuban intervention. When circumstances and pressure from the press and a thoroughly propagandized public forced him to action, he did so under the restrictive Teller Amendment which specifically forsook any territorial ambitions in Cuba. In his 1899 report to Congress Root said, "Our temporary occupation of the island of Cuba involves a very simple plan of operation. . . . The control which we are exercising in trust for the people of

Cuba should not be, and of course will not be, continued any longer than is necessary to enable the people to maintain order and discharge their international obligations."[172] Wood's view, that of the public, and even that within the White House were not nearly so straightforward.

Wood began his job in Santiago saying (and to every appearance believing) that it was his job to reestablish civil order and economic stability so the Cubans could create their own government. His success with an autocratic regime blended with the failures of Brooke's more participatory policies and leavened by a considerable dose of personal ambition changed that attitude. The United States could not rely on people with no experience of self-government to immediately possess the skills necessary for that enterprise. Wood still thought establishment of a Cuban civil government would be "easy of accomplishment" and should be "effected as quickly as possible," but easy and quick looked harder and longer than they had a few months earlier.[173]

Some domestic opinion was even less generous. General H. O. Ernst, recently of Brooke's staff, told the *Times* that, although annexation to the United States was not generally discussed, there was "a decided sentiment tending that way," particularly among the ubiquitous "better class of Cubans."[174] Bellicose Captain Robley Evans who had fought with Schley proclaimed that, in his estimation, the Cubans could never govern themselves and that "when the time comes that the Government of the United States can guarantee a stable Government in Cuba, you will find it inhabited by Yankees."[175]

Even the president's own personal commissioner to Cuba, Robert Porter, was not aligned with the official renunciation of territorial acquisition. He wrote, "If, at the conclusion of military occupation, Cuba is made an independent republic, it will be because the people of Cuba and the people of the United States, acting jointly, so decide. If, on the contrary, the future of Cuba shall lie in the still greater independence of American Statehood, it will be by the mutual consent of the people of the two countries."[176]

International politics in the closing years of the nineteenth century was a maelstrom of colonial acquisition and Americans were not immune to the frenzy. Mahan had made a compelling case for a strong navy and overseas projection of power. McKinley, clearly influenced by Republican American businessmen, decided that American interests in China and East Asia mandated outright possession of Guam and the Philippines, even though it meant being dragged into a profoundly unpleasant local insurrection. Mahan argued forcefully and convincingly for a Central American canal so the United States Navy could be a two-ocean force, and Cuba was key to any canal project.

Wood was proud of his accomplishments and enjoyed his power and, as 1899 progressed, he drifted farther from the Teller Amendment and closer to Mahan, Porter, and the acquisitionists. In June, he told a reporter that, although independence would come in time, it could not be "rushed upon a people thoroughly unaccustomed to handling themselves and controlling their own affairs." If the Cubans were hurried to self-government, "the most disastrous results" were sure to follow. He added that "a military supervision must necessarily exist for some time."[177] On the other side, Brooke, who knew his tenure was limited, and Lee, who knew he would not get Brooke's job, agitated for American withdrawal but in vain since public opinion had swung sharply in favor of staying.[178]

Through the late summer and fall Wood continued his indirect campaign for the governorship, an effort in which his wife proved one of his most formidable allies. When Wood went back to Santiago to deal with the yellow fever epidemic, she stayed in Washington. Mrs. Wood belonged to the capital's inner social circle and sought every opportunity to corner the president and his advisors. She arranged a private meeting with Senator Platt's wife during which she managed to buttonhole the powerful legislator who obligingly said, "Your husband is just what we are looking for . . . he is the man of the future." Mrs. Wood acerbically told her husband, "There was no necessity of this diced-up little old codger giving me such taffy about you if he didn't mean what he said."[179] The "diced-up little old codger" went on to write an amendment that, besides being enacted into United States law, was included verbatim in the Cuban constitution and defined Cuban-American relations until 1934. Mrs. Wood dined with General Miles and the Roosevelts and kept in constant touch with Root. All those contacts were important since Wood, now sure that Brooke was on the way out, was worried that Wilson or Lee might grab the governorship.[180]

Mrs. Wood also called directly on McKinley and his wife. Turning up uninvited at a White House reception, she got next to the president, who solicitously inquired after "Leonard" and once again assured her that the transfer to brigadier general of the line was in the offing. McKinley did caution against Wood's annoying tendency to pull strings, warning that such practice would do "more harm than good" since Wood had all he needed in "the political influence of the President of the United States."[181]

Wood dropped a personal letter to McKinley suggestively pointing out that things in Santiago were orderly and quiet, yellow fever was under control, the people were fed, and prospectors were discovering new sources of valuable minerals every day.[182] Western Cuba might be a mess, but Wood's provinces were doing just fine.

Roosevelt was not idle either. Although he badgered Root until the secretary told him he had heard all he wanted of Cuba, Roosevelt could not resist one more barb, saying he was sure Root must realize "Brooke's unfitness" and was also sure Root "could not but see Wood would have to have the island." Just in case Cuba did not work out, Roosevelt had approached Admiral Dewey (also a victim of Mrs. Wood's attentions), who allowed that the military government would love to have Wood in the Philippines where they were sure he "could settle matters in short order."[183]

On October 31, Mrs. Wood wrote that she had had another private conversation with McKinley in which he told her he had a secret she must keep—Wood was finally to get his second star. She also heard that Wood's old friend and commander Lawton was to go to the Philippines.[184]

By November, the papers were openly discussing Brooke's imminent departure and speculating on his replacement. The *Times* noted that, although Ludlow, Lee, and Wilson had admirable records, Wood's was the best and Cubans, even of the "agitator class," could find little ill to say of him.[185] On November 23, Wood was summoned to Washington. Root would only say the trip was for "business," but it was obvious to everyone familiar with the situation that Wood was about to replace Brooke. His new title, in keeping with the fact that he was still not a member of the regular military establishment, was to be civil governor of Cuba. Rumors had briefly circulated that he was to return to the medical corps and replace Sternberg as surgeon general, but Wood scotched them: "My relation with the medical department of the army, so far as any further duty in the medical corps is concerned, is at an end, and whatever duty I may perform in the army in the future will be in the line."[186] Of course, he was not yet a member of the line, but he was never one to miss the chance to influence events in his own favor. On December 13, 1899, Root appointed Wood Cuba's 168th governor general.

7

Havana, 1900–1902

DAWN BROKE over Cuba clear and cool on December 20, 1899, as the steamer *Mexico* finished a "pleasant and uneventful" four-day voyage from New York and entered Havana harbor.[1] A launch brought the pilot and an assortment of dignitaries to the ship before it slipped past the imposing Castillo de Los Tres Reyes del Morro (El Moro), the ancient symbol of Cuban nationalism guarding the harbor's eastern entrance. Like Santiago, Havana was attractive from a distance, but, like Santiago, it was scarred by four centuries of administrative neglect and indifferent sanitation.

The gaily colored flags in the *Mexico*'s rigging were just visible from the shore as the sun broke over El Moro. Wood's appointment had been announced only five days earlier leaving scant time to organize a proper welcome, but the city put its heart into the reception. As the steamer slowed and entered the 1,400-yard neck of the bay, Wood was greeted with a major general's thirteen-gun salute from the Americans at Cabanas Fortress followed by a twenty-one-gun governor general's salute from the Cubans at La Punta. The pilot gingerly steered the ship past the *Maine*'s ghostly superstructure, still breaking the surface in midchannel, and turned to drop anchor. As the chain clanked from the hawse hole and the anchor bit, the *Mexico* swung into the wind to be surrounded by a swarm of ferries, barges, launches, and rowboats hung with brightly colored bunting. In spite of the short notice and the early hour, virtually every craft in Havana harbor turned out. Three bands played for over an hour as Wood impatiently paced the deck.[2] Finally, twenty-one rockets bearing Cuban and American flags were fired and the newly minted major general went ashore in a line of boats led by Colonel Estes Rathbone. The young general was about to become absolute ruler of 1.5 million Cubans.

Although Wood's party was met at Machina wharf by a large enthusiastic crowd of Cubans, only a few Americans came and Brooke was conspicuously absent. The outgoing general had held a farewell ball the night before and the reception committee, concerned that a quayside ceremony "might show a want of proper respect for Brooke," left the official welcome to the natives.[3] Brooke had no inclination to greet the man who had engineered his removal, and his staff was in full agreement.

In many ways Wood had rather an easy time of it in Santiago. He had minimal supervision and his subordinates, mostly from the volunteer army, harbored little professional jealousy. His main tasks—restoring order, relieving starvation, and controlling infectious diseases—had been difficult but straightforward, and Wood had had the resources necessary to do the job. The Cubans of Oriente were mostly rural, had little taste for political intrigue, and were too exhausted by five years of fighting to cause much trouble. Wood brought peace and food, and the natives had responded with gratitude and obedience.

Havana was a venerable, densely populated urban capital whose upper class considered itself culturally and intellectually superior to the Yankee interlopers. The Americans in Havana, unlike Wood's Santiago volunteers, were career officers and civil servants, many of whom had decades more experience than the parvenu physician who had vaulted over them on the promotion list. Murmurs of discontent had circulated since word first leaked of Wood's appointment. Early rumors had it that, since the new governor was not a member of the regular army, McKinley planned to change his title from military governor to civil governor, a modification with ominous implications of permanency. Worse, a change from military to civil authority might open Cuba to plunder by a flood of commercial concessions.[4] In the end the president pleased both Wood and the Cubans by retaining the military title.

To give Wood the best chance of a propitious start, Root sent Horatio Rubens, the New York Junta's long-time legal advisor, to Havana to smooth the way. Rubens, who had known the revolutionary leaders for years, was charged with convincing the rebels to cooperate with the new governor. After ten days of hard negotiation, Rubens convinced the Cuban generals to be at least cordial, but their soldiers, not always willing followers, remained a potential problem.[5] In 1899, the Cuban power structure, such as it was, was divided into three parts: the émigrés of the New York Junta, despised by the Cubans who had stayed and fought the Spanish but with the closest relations to Washington's politicians; the insurgent generals who had a questionably loyal standing army and were destitute; and an ad hoc Assembly principally composed of the island's businessmen and professionals. The Assembly had convened at Santa Cruz del Sur on the Camagüey Province's Caribbean coast in October 1898, elected Bartolomé Masó president of a provisional government with Domingo Mendez-Capote as vice president, and promptly fired Calixto García for trying to establish a military dictatorship in the interior of Santiago province.

The middle-class Assembly was leery of the largely black, illiterate army and sharply critical of its generals, especially Gómez and García. In November 1898, they voted to dissolve the army with a commitment to borrow enough money to pay the soldiers back wages promised since the beginning of the insurrection. The proposed loan was clearly meant to forestall a mutiny and to convince the insurgents to disband and leave the Assembly to assume power when the Americans left.[6] García and Gómez ignored the Assembly and held much of their army together in the smaller towns and cities of Cuba's interior. Instead, the generals approached the Junta which, in late 1898, was essentially the only line of communication between Washington and the Cuban nationals.

In November, the Assembly sent its own commission to Washington putatively to clarify the terms and duration of the American occupation, but really to be recognized as Cuba's legitimate government. García, his personal resources exhausted, abandoned Gómez, accepted a minor administrative position in the military government, and joined the Assembly delegation to Washington. The Assembly planned to get administration approval of their loan to pay off the soldiers, but McKinley's staff understood that granting the right to borrow money was tantamount to official recognition. In a White House meeting, McKinley cagily asked how much money would be needed to satisfy (and demobilize) the army to which García quickly responded $3 million. It is likely the old general was preprogrammed with the answer because, although $3 million was a fraction of the amount promised the soldiers, it was precisely what was left over from the original congressional allowance for the Cuban invasion and would have gone back to the treasury if not spent. The president, not allowing even a moment for discussion, announced to the stunned Cubans that they had reached a deal. McKinley's "gift," all the soldiers would get until the American intervention ended, sent the Assembly home with no official standing. García, unable to tolerate the cold northern climate, caught pneumonia and died before he could return to Cuba to be pilloried by public opinion.[7]

Gómez still had about 40,000 armed insurgents, mostly scattered through small towns in the western interior, and, in January 1900, McKinley sent Robert Porter to negotiate directly with the old Dominican, who agreed to accept the $3 million and disband the army in return for assurance that the American occupation would be temporary. Porter neither consulted nor contacted the Assembly. The men of Santa Cruz still had one last gasp. They privately negotiated a loan with the New York firm of C. M. Cohen for $20 million which, after interest and fees, would have netted $12.4 million to pay the army. They also charged Gómez with insubordination for accepting Porter's offer and, unable to take the risk of firing him outright, simply abolished his rank of general-in-chief and left him unemployed. They also censored the New York Junta and Tomás Estrada Palma for their role in getting Porter and Gómez together.[8]

Brooke wanted to dissolve the Assembly outright, but McKinley was more subtle. First he announced that any debt incurred by the Cubans would not be recognized by the United States, effectively canceling the Cohen deal. Then he announced that the American government did not recognize the Assembly, and he arranged for Gómez to be officially invited to Havana. The old general's progress from his headquarters at Remedios to the capital was a triumph capped by a boisterous welcome from thousands of cheering Habañeros. In March, the Assembly, recognizing that it had no support either at home or in Washington, quietly dissolved itself and left Wood the only power in Cuba.[9]

The day after Wood's arrival, La Lucha said, "Gen. Wood, although promising nothing, speaks volumes by his quiet democratic manner of taking charge of affairs. He has captivated everyone."[10] The paper added, "No other American would be received with such heart felt rejoicing."[11] Gómez was convinced as well. In a note with elegant penmanship but tortured English, the general assured Wood his revolutionary mission had ended "when the last shot was discharged," adding that he had no personal political aspirations except "helping with neither interest, for the liberty of this Country." He promised to cooperate with Wood to that end.[12] Wood offered the general $5,000 a year to chair a veteran's committee, but the proud old man, as good as his word, declined. Wood assured the rest of the generals that it was the American government's and therefore his policy to work for Cuban independence. They took him at his word and the army ceased to be a problem.

Wood still had to deal with the Americans held over from Brooke's administration. Under Alger and Brooke, the military government, if not entirely rudderless, had shown little indication of knowing its course. Alger was a successful businessman and a force in Republican politics, but his widely criticized failure to manage a wartime military bureaucracy left him bitter, ineffective, and mired in a losing fight to keep his job. Brooke had all the administrative creativity one would expect from a man whose career had been spent on small frontier outposts commanding handfuls of troops and chasing bands of Indians. Alger never gave Brooke clear marching orders, a fact the general later stressed in his own defense. Brooke, for his part, kept the Cubans and their problems at arm's length.

Wood and Root brought an entirely different style. Elihu Root was one of the remarkable characters in a period of American history replete with gifted public servants. Root was born in upstate New York to a demanding mother and a scholarly father who taught mathematics in a local college. The personable younger Root did well at Hamilton College and New York University Law School and acquired a coterie of influential friends. He was a tall, strikingly handsome man with high cheekbones and a strong jaw who used his good looks and good connections to build a stellar career in law and politics.

Where Alger and Brooke had waffled, Root and Wood went at Cuba head on. Wood walked into the Hotel Inglaterra, dropped his bags, and proceeded directly to a meeting with Gonzalo de Quesada, the unofficial Cuban "chargé d'affaires" who had arrived from New York the same morning. By nine that morning, Wood was closeted with Brooke's Cuban cabinet. The appointed administrators were intensely unpopular among both Cubans and the American district commanders, and it was widely assumed that they would be sacked. Wood had actually intended to keep them for a time, and he was somewhat taken aback when they announced their unanimous intention to resign immediately. He asked them to take a night to think it over and to meet with him the next day.

When the secretaries came back the next day, Wood accepted their resignation, wiring Root that "Public opinion is such that they could not continue, and they realize that it would be fatal to their future prospects to remain longer."[13] As the disaffected cabinet walked out of Wood's make-shift office, Brooke's disgruntled department heads, none of whom had come to Machina wharf to meet their new commander, walked in. Wood saw Havana City's Ludlow and his staff followed immediately by Wilson and his staff. (Lee, out of the city, met later.) Again there is no record of the meetings, but, since Wood got a job both Ludlow and Wilson wanted, since both were senior to Wood in age and tenure, and since the three quarreled almost constantly thereafter, it is safe to assume the sessions were not entirely congenial.

Wood had an astonishing capacity for work, characteristically being up by 5:00 A.M. and often working until midnight. Within a week of arriving in Havana, the governor was seeing over two hundred people a day in his office. One of his first jobs was to reorganize and repopulate the advisory cabinet. He named Diego Tamayo, a justice of the Cuban Supreme Court, secretary of state and government; Enrique Varona, recent editor of La Patria and "the most conspicuous figure intellectually in the Island,"[14] secretary of finance; José Villalon, an American-educated engineer and chief of public works in Santa Clara, secretary of public works; Luis Estevez, another justice of the Cuban Supreme Court, president of the National Party, and a major financial supporter of the revolution, secretary of justice; Juan Ruis Rivera, "a man of excellent character and reputation"[15] and in Wood's opinion the cabinet's most radical member,[16] secretary of agriculture, industry, and commerce; and Juan Bautista Hernandez, dean of the legal faculty at the University of Havana and a long-time supporter of the revolution, as secretary of public education.[17] Wood's choices, while certainly not the most radical Cubans, had good enough credentials and enough revolutionary background to win the almost universal approval of the Cuban press. Rubens, Root, and McKinley had taken care of the army, the Assembly, and the Junta, and Wood had won over the public and the press.[18]

Wood still needed a working agreement with his American subordinates. Cuba was under direct war department control, and Wood's military command was split into four districts. Oriente, comprising the eastern provinces of Santiago and Puerto Principe, was now under a colonel who reported directly to the governor. Wood planned to run the eastern end of the island with a large degree of civil autonomy but under his personal supervision. Fitzhugh Lee had the provinces of Havana and Pinar del Rio, James Wilson the provinces of Santa Clara and Matanzas, and William Ludlow the city of Havana. Wood also inherited Brooke's talented chief of staff, General Adna Chaffee.

The portly, silver-haired Lee had a distinguished record as general of cavalry in his uncle's Army of Northern Virginia. He had served as governor of Virginia and American consul to Havana before being named major general of volunteers when the Spanish War broke out. Lee was sixty-five years old and had, at least on the basis of longevity and experience, a legitimate claim to the job Wood occupied.

Wilson was only two years Lee's junior and had been a Union brigadier general when Wood was three years old. After the war he became wealthy building railroads and was active in Republican Party politics. In 1898, he, like Lee, was named major general of volunteers and participated in the Puerto Rican invasion before being named military governor of Matanzas. Wilson had close ties to a number of powerful Republicans and had campaigned hard for Brooke's job before settling for Matanzas and promptly initiating a campaign to replace him. It is likely that Wilson rather than Wood would have succeeded Brooke had his aggressive pursuit of the position not offended McKinley, and he remained bitter and disaffected at having been passed over by a forty-year-old, whose experience as a line officer could be measured in days.

Ludlow and Chaffee had both served under Lawton as brigadier generals in the assault on El Caney.[19] Adna Romanza Chaffee (whose son would become the first great American tank commander) was eighteen years Wood's senior and had been a regular army officer since the Civil War. Ludlow, a civil engineer by trade, had made an impressive start in cleaning up Havana although, because of the greater magnitude of the job and Wood's six-month head start, the capital remained considerably filthier than Santiago.

In all, Wood faced a group of men older and more experienced than he; some, like Chaffee, resented his having displaced Brooke and some, like Wilson, Ludlow, and Lee, had wanted the job themselves.[20] Prior to December 1899, they had all outranked him. On the face of it Wilson was the worst problem, and before Wood left Washington, he and Root settled on a code name ("Wheeling") so they could, in official correspondence, secretly criticize the general. Wilson was committed to two paradoxical policies that were anathema to Root. He wanted to loan as much money as possible to Cuban farmers with the expectation that they would default, allowing consolidation of their property in American hands. He also wanted early Cuban independence, believing that a failed government would force abrogation of the Teller Amendment and precipitate the island's outright annexation. Wood and Root considered both ideas impractical and morally objectionable. Root knew Wilson would try to make Wood's life a misery so he brought the older man to Washington for "consultations" early in 1900. Also knowing that Senator Joseph Foraker was one of Wilson's closest political allies, Root blocked Foraker's appointment to the Committee on Relations with Cuba so the two could not conspire to undermine Wood.[21]

Root and Wood wanted a gradual progression toward Cuban independence, starting with municipal elections to be held as soon as a census could be completed. The elections had to wait at least until April, the date set by the Treaty of Paris for Spanish residents of Cuba to decide whether to be citizens of the island or the peninsula. As soon as he had details of the island's population, Wood meant to adjust suffrage so the "right sort of Cubans" would be elected. Wilson, hoping for a failed government, wanted immediate elections and universal suffrage, expecting a radical, incompetent set of office holders. He refused to support Wood's plan, and the governor told Root he needed him "moved from the island as soon as possible."[22] Chaffee, on the other hand, took Wood's accession with unexpected grace and grew into an invaluable resource.

Although Havana's 250,000 inhabitants were jammed into only 20,000 houses, the city was blessed with an abundant supply of clean water and, if the trash could be removed and the streets paved and sewered, it could be washed. The need to sanitize the capital had not escaped the Spanish who had commissioned plans for paving and draining the city before their forced departure. Unfortunately, along with rudimentary drawings, the Spanish left a horde of bond holders and builders with conflicting financial claims on the projects. Ludlow, confident of his own engineering credentials, had little interest in the existing plans and none at all in the investors. By late 1899, Ludlow was in open conflict with Havana's citizens and newspapers. The press was bitterly critical, and the general responded by fining the papers for every article he deemed "scandalous." The editors happily paid the fines and went on berating him.[23] Wood advised Ludlow to settle his problems in court rather than by military fiat, but the general missed the point and demanded the papers be closed altogether.

Wood looked to other administrators to solve the problem, especially Lee, who proved unexpectedly helpful. He privately suspected that Lee's tractability was more from indolence than benevolence, but he told Root the old Virginian was "cooperating loyally" and was, for the most part, getting along with the Cubans. Wood suggested that the department of the city of Havana be merged with Lee's provinces of Havana and Pinar del Rio under Ludlow's adjutant Hugh Scott.[24] The plan had three advantages: Ludlow would be out of a job; Wood could keep Scott whom he liked and trusted; and Cuba's government would be one step nearer consolidation. Ludlow recognized he was fighting a losing battle and requested a leave. On February 13, Root told Wood that he had "seen for some time that Ludlow was getting into an awkward situation" and had offered him a job organizing the new War College.[25] Wood was rid of the first of Brooke's leftover generals.

Meanwhile, Wilson returned to Havana. Root told Wood that when he first got to Washington the general had been "wholly irreconcilable," but, after a few days, "seemed to feel much better" and had given "the most absolute and unconditional promise to do everything in his power towards carrying out the policy of the Administration in Cuba."[26] Although Wood worried that Wilson was still working behind the scenes to undermine him in Congress, the recalcitrant general (at least in public) stayed quiet.[27] In two months, Root had protected Wood from an assortment of potentially powerful enemies while teaching him fundamental lessons in administration. For his part, Wood had made more progress toward centralizing the Cuban government in eight weeks than Brooke had in a year.

Root put legal and penal reform squarely at the top of Wood's list of priorities. General Order Number 184 of December 28, 1898, placed all Cuban prisons under the war department's direct control. An army of unwashed, unclothed, unconvicted Cuban women and boys sharing bare stone cells with hardened criminals had all the earmarks of disaster.[28] On his first day in office, Wood personally toured Havana's prison and penitentiary. Privately, Wood confessed: "The condition of the prisons here in Havana was found to be very bad and unless you had seen the records you could hardly credit the abuse of authority and the absolute disregard of the rights of those held." He found cells full of women who could only be interviewed one at a time because the whole cell shared a single dress. Their attendants were often male, and women who had been in jail seven or eight years were nursing newborn infants.[29]

Although ultimate responsibility for the prisons lay with the war department, the day-to-day operations were under Cuban civil administration headed by the *fiscal,* an officer roughly equivalent to an attorney general in the United States. Wood found the sitting *fiscal,* socially prominent Federico Mora, "an insincere humbug, conceited, shallow and an enemy to public order and public peace," and summarily fired him. Wood then directed that untried prisoners either be brought to court immediately or freed and ordered that remaining sentences be publicly posted so prisoners would know exactly when they were to be released. He also segregated the women and children from the general prison population and mandated minimum standards of sanitation.[30]

The courts were another point of signal vulnerability for Wood's government. Cubans had, with ample justification, never trusted the Spanish judicial system, and things had seemed no better under Brooke. The judicial system as a whole bore only the vaguest resemblance to Anglo-Saxon jurisprudence. An accused citizen was held incommunicado, was not necessarily informed of the charges against him, and had no inherent right to legal representation. Trials were before a panel of judges rather than lay juries. Wood instituted police courts to deal summarily with offenses involving sentences of less than six months or fines less than $30. He experimented with five-person juries but found Cubans almost universally unwilling to convict their fellow citizens, so he reverted to trial by judge, but provided lawyers for the poor in hopes of gaining the trust of Cuba's lower classes.[31] Wood demanded adequate records and established schools of typewriting and stenography to train court reporters. Then he funded new and renovated buildings to house the records and the proceedings. Judges and clerks had traditionally been supported by a floating scale of fees paid by the litigants, and, in a move designed to "teach the Courts and people that they have but two things to consider and those are the law and the evidence in the case," Wood put all officers of the court on salary. Hereditary notary and clerk positions were abolished, and the right of habeas corpus was enforced.[32] When Wood came to power there was no penalty for (and not even a legal definition of) perjury, a deficit the governor remedied by fiat.

Besides the courts and prisons, Wood found himself in charge of tens of thousands of Cubans too young, too old, too ill, or too disturbed to care for themselves. For reasons unclear, but having nothing to do with either training or experience, it fell to Major Edwin St. John Greble to create a law and a bureaucracy for the island's hospitals and charities. The Spanish government and the Church had created a reasonable charitable endowment, but what had not been squandered on bloated administrations and poor management had been overwhelmed by the prolonged insurrection. Charitable facilities across the island were in hopeless disrepair and were disastrously overcrowded. When Wood ordered Greble to clean up a particularly offensive insane asylum at Mazona outside Havana, the major said, "General I'm afraid I don't know much about insane asylums." Wood shot back, "I don't know much about being a military governor. Find out how much it will cost, how long it will take, what machinery you will need, what you will have to do for discipline, and report."[33] Before leaving Cuba, Greble spent $400,000 on the Mazona asylum and left it as good as the best in the United States.

The insurgency left Cuba overrun with sick and undernourished children and a critical shortage of both hospitals and trained medical personnel. Wood constructed large temporary hospitals around the island, supplemented Cuban physicians with American military surgeons, and built nursing schools modeled after those in the United States to generate new personnel. By 1902, Greble's department was running 5,500 hospital and asylum beds on the island.[34]

One additional bit of administrative housekeeping was necessary early in Wood's term. Root had dismembered the Assembly, the army, and the Junta, but the general still had to establish some relationship with Cuba's politically inclined citizens, especially those living outside Havana. With that in mind, he invited the island's civil governors and an assortment of prominent civilians and former revolutionary officers to Havana on January 1, 1900, having, as he told Root, "simply a desire to explain to them our policy." Wood told the gathering what was going to happen and advised that all Cubans "of the right kind" were expected to help him.

Wood and Root were convinced that any long-term relationship between Cuba and the United States had to be based on the willing cooperation of the Cuban people. Both men believed in democracy, but the general and the secretary were also firmly convinced that universal suffrage was a recipe for disaster. As Root put it, there was no way "any people three quarters of whom are contented to remain unable to read and write, can for any very long period maintain a free government."[35] The secretary thought it obvious that literacy was the only way to avoid "the perpetual revolutions of Central America and the other West India Islands."[36]

When the Americans came to Cuba there was not a single building on the island devoted solely to primary education. What public instruction there was took place in the teachers' homes and, in December 1899, on an island where 66 percent of adults were illiterate, only 21,000 students were enrolled in schools, and few of those attended class regularly.[37] Wood spent money on schools at a staggering rate. Under Spain, Cuba's annual education budget had totaled $400,000, a figure Brooke increased to $750,000 in 1899. In 1900, Wood spent $4,009,460.31 out of a total government budget of slightly over $17 million.[38] Average school enrollment in 1899 had been 21,435. During the American intervention, it peaked at over 256,000.[39]

Teachers were a serious problem. There was no indigenous pool, and Wood was strictly opposed to recruiting from the United States. The administration made a contrary choice in the Philippines, where the government actively recruited American women to teach Filipino children in English, intending to use schools to bind the new colony to the United States. Six hundred of these enthusiastic ladies came to Manila on the steamer *Thomas* to foster Americanism in the archipelago's young people, and bitter memories of the uninvited "Thomasites" adversely effected Philippine-American relations for an entire generation.[40]

Wood was convinced that Cuban children should be taught in Spanish by people raised in their own traditions. That meant he had to recruit from among literate Cuban women, essentially all of whom were from the upper classes and expected generous salaries. Only three districts in the entire United States paid their teachers more than Wood's Cubans, making schools on the island an extraordinarily expensive proposition.[41] The average cost of educating a Cuban child was $25.50 a year compared to $22.50 in the United States as a whole and a mere $8.00 in some southern districts.[42]

Once hired, these ladies, none of whom had teaching experience, had to be trained. Although he was opposed to colonies, Harvard President Charles Eliot was an educational zealot and training teachers was his forte. He and a group of his Boston and New York friends, including financiers Henry Higginson and W. Cameron Forbes (both friends of Wood as well), set out to raise enough money to bring the teachers to Harvard for the summer. After three months of badgering their friends and business associates, Higginson, Forbes, and Eliot scraped together $70,000. Wood talked the military into transporting the teachers for free and sent 1,450 women to Cambridge.

Wood's education department was also responsible for the University of Havana, a venerable institution founded by the Dominicans in 1734 that had degenerated into a sinecure for 107 faculty members shepherding a handful of students toward poorly regarded diplomas. (The faculty of letters had fifteen professors and only seven students and the faculty of science, twenty-five professors and eleven students.) Some professors lived in Spain and paid surrogates to perform their duties in Havana.[43] On June 30, Wood had his Secretary of Public Instruction fire the entire faculty. Twenty-five professors were rehired, departments were consolidated, a new curriculum was developed, and competitive examinations were announced for the remaining forty-five teaching positions.[44] There was surprisingly little upset, and 479 applicants sat for the examination. Wood boasted to Root that there were not half a dozen men outside the fired professors who did not approve of what he had done. The governor used money saved from faculty salaries to lower tuition to $60, which resulted in an increase of enrollment to 632 for the 1900–1901 academic year. He shopped Europe for microscopes and equipment to build proper chemistry and histology laboratories and opened a medical school in the old Spanish barracks.[45]

Even as things were coming together, Estes Rathbone nearly wrecked the government. The first whiff of corruption drifted out of the Cuban postal department less than a month after Wood came to Havana when the war department wired the governor that postal audits for 1899 were suspiciously deficient.[46] About the same time a clerk, whom Wood had known as one of Gómez's staff officers, claimed that postal officials were paying personal bills out of government funds.[47] Fully aware that their "democratic friends in Congress" would like nothing better than to uncover fraud in Cuba in the middle of the presidential campaign, Wood ordered all departments to prepare an extensive audit. Ominously, he warned Root that the postal auditor had furnished no expense vouchers but reassured the secretary that he could count on "everything being kept quiet and such irregularities as are discovered, if any are, will not become matters of public information."[48] The postal situation was anomalous in that the department was under the American postmaster general and outside Wood's direct authority. Rathbone got his job as a result of his political association with Marcus Alonzo Hanna, a turn-of-the-century Republican political icon. Round-faced, round-bodied, pink-skinned, Hanna had appropriately made his fortune in pig iron. Roosevelt, who actually liked him, described Hanna as a "Good natured, well meaning, coarse man, shrewd and hard headed."[49] Wood found him an implacable enemy.

Hanna took on McKinley as a personal project, managing his 1896 presidential campaign and funding it with $100,000 of his own money. When McKinley won, Hanna was Republican Party Chairman and the second most powerful man in America, a status that was only enhanced in 1897 when he became a United States Senator. An inexperienced young governor in Havana could attack one of Hanna's protégés only at considerable peril. Responding to Wood's first suggestion of trouble, Root cautioned that Rathbone was under the authority of the postmaster general in Washington, and the latter had been at pains to remind the secretary that Wood's investigation was "an infringement upon his authority." Root advised Wood to "run matters along quietly, avoiding any possible clash."[50] At first Wood tried to pursue the investigation behind the scenes, but it proved impossible to keep it secret. Havana postal auditor C. F. W. Neely's accounts were short at least $100,000, and fully 10 percent of the Havana post office's $13,000 monthly budget was being spent on Rathbone's salary and personal expenses.[51] The war department had been correct; the postal department never submitted a financial accounting, and now Neely and the records had gone missing.

Neely had been moving up to $500 a week to a personal account in Baracoa, and he and Rathbone had even bought a brick factory outside Havana. When Neely disappeared, he left behind a bond for $30,000. Wood collected the evidence and had his auditor, Colonel C. H. Burton, hand carry the packet to Root. He thought it important enough to have Burton sail directly to Fortress Monroe in Virginia so he could circumvent Florida's quarantine delays.[52] By now Root had changed political strategy and decided to pursue the whole affair in full public view, taking the righteous stance that Wood and his government would never tolerate corruption in Cuba. The open pursuit of fraud suited Root's moral sense better anyway, and he told Wood, "I want you to scrape to the bone, no matter whose nerves are hurt by it. The first essential of administration in this island is that we shall be perfectly honest with ourselves."[53] Of course, the first nerves to be hurt would very likely be Wood's.

Neely had escaped to New York but, on May 5, he had been apprehended in Rochester and was doggedly resisting extradition. Roosevelt, who was no stranger to prosecuting postal fraud, was pulled into the fracas. As civil service commissioner under Benjamin Harrison, Roosevelt had battled with Postmaster General John Wanamaker over firing twenty-five Baltimore officials involved in election fraud, and it was widely believed that public airing of Republican dirty linen had contributed to the 1892 presidential defeat. Nonetheless, Roosevelt was determined to help Wood. He wrote, "My legal advisors here did not want me to surrender to you that criminal, stating that there was no constitutional warrant for it and that I would render myself liable to an action for false imprisonment. However, I am a broad constructionist in constitutional matters and I told them I would risk the false imprisonment business. I am no believer in technicalities in a business such as this."[54] Neely fought on as damning evidence accumulated. He had been selling stamps marked as burned and had imported large quantities of stationery for "postal use" (avoiding costly tariffs) before selling the supplies to Havana merchants. Meanwhile Wood, having heard that Rathbone was about to flee the island as well, arrested him. In a brief visit to Washington, Wood encountered Hanna in a capitol anteroom where the senator asked if he planned to try Rathbone and threatened that "If you bring my friend to trial you will never get to be more than a captain doctor in the army."[55]

Domestic newspapers were more supportive. The *Washington Post* praised Wood's "candor and enthusiasm" and opined "That Genl. Wood may be trusted to antagonize the whole vile conspiracy which evidently exists, no honest man will doubt. That, if left to his own devices, he will ventilate the scandal, detect and punish the criminals, and in every other way illustrate the fidelity and the righteousness of the American people in their dealings with these new possessions, is as certain as that the sun shines above us."[56] The Republican convention was only six weeks away and Wood was in the eye of a political and public relations hurricane.

Meanwhile, Wood arrested one of Neely's assistant auditors, James H. Reeves, and held him under house arrest until he agreed to testify against Rathbone.[57] The governor was having difficulty getting specific evidence that the postal director was a thief, although he was convinced of the impossibility of Rathbone's being unaware of Neely's "defalcations."[58] In Washington the political situation was tense. Senator Orville Platt wrote Wood that the Democrats were "seeking every opportunity to charge, and where they cannot charge, to insinuate that everything is wrong in Cuba." They were determined to tar the whole military government with the postal scandal's dirty brush. Platt warned Wood that Congress was "nervous, liable to take the bit in its teeth and say we ought to get out of Cuba."[59] Root cautioned that the war department was "flooded with resolutions of inquiry from both houses of Congress, relating to pretty nearly everything the army has done for the past two years."[60] Somehow, Wood had to keep matters in hand until Congress adjourned on June 6.

With Rathbone under arrest and the case against him building, Wood reassured Root that the whole matter was, for the moment, under control.[61] As the trial approached, efforts to incriminate Rathbone to a degree that would satisfy Hanna and his Washington cronies reached fever pitch. The postal cases finally came to trial in February 1902, and Neely, Reeves, and Rathbone were convicted in March. Neely was sentenced to ten years in prison and fined $56,000. Rathbone was also sentenced to ten years in prison and was fined $35,000; Reeves received the same sentence as Rathbone but was pardoned by Wood. Roosevelt, now president, directed Wood to have the case reviewed by the Cuban Supreme Court which upheld the convictions, but the new Cuban national government freed the two as part of a general independence amnesty.[62]

Wood also had to make a going financial concern of the economic shambles he had inherited from Brooke and the Spanish. Prior to 1898, Spain had mercilessly milked the island. Cubans had been presented bills for the cost of suppressing their Ten Year War for independence, for the cost of the 1895 revolution, for Spain's costs in the 1863–65 Santo Domingo revolution, for the 1866 expedition against Peru, for the cost of maintaining Fernando Po military prison, for the costs of all Spain's embassies and consulates in the Americas, and for Christopher Columbus's pension in perpetuity. As if that were not enough, the Cubans also had to pay for the Spanish army of occupation. Unable to generate taxes sufficient to pay all those bills, Spain had floated $500 million in loans guaranteed by the island's revenues, $171 million of which was privately held by Europeans and Cuban residents. Notes held by the Bank of Spain were guaranteed by import duties, the island's only reliable source of revenue. When the United States took control, McKinley expressly declined sovereignty so the debt did not transfer. The notes were simply allowed to lapse and were presumed uncollectible so Wood started with a clean slate.[63]

The private sector was not so fortunate. For export purposes, Cuba was a two-crop agricultural economy, although there were still a few coffee farms, small truck farms, and some mines, mostly in the eastern provinces and mostly American-owned. Export earnings, however, came from sugar and tobacco. The sugar industry had suffered from the emergence of tariff-protected beet sugar in Europe and the American west over the previous decade. To compound the problem of competition, both the Spanish and the insurrectionist armies had targeted cane fields and sugar refineries in the economic terrorism that accompanied the wars of independence. Plantation owners emerged from 1898 with debts that often exceeded the value of their land and were paying interest rates as high as 40 percent. Between 1898 and 1900, 3,700 farms a year were sold or foreclosed.[64] The situation would have been even worse had it not been for the "stay laws" which provided a partial moratorium on debt collection and bankruptcy. Of 1,100 sugar mills operating in 1894, only 297 survived the war, and many of those remained out of operation as late as the 1900–1901 crop year.[65] Wood wanted to restore Cuban agriculture by providing public service jobs so individual farmers could earn enough to bring their land back into production without borrowing money. For the sugar industry, he eliminated excise and export taxes on cane and its transport, he cut the import duty on farm equipment to 5 percent, and he assigned Rural Guards to protect the cane fields from extortion by arsonists. Wood also initiated a frustrating battle with protectionist Republicans to lower the United States tariffs on Cuban sugar and tobacco.[66]

Wood spent $100,000 to import oxen from Mexico that he sold to the Cubans at cost[67] while lobbying Root and McKinley to abrogate the stay laws and force the farmers to either pay their debts or fail.[68] Fiscally,

Wood was Calvinist to the core. When asked his criteria for Cuban self-government, he answered, "when money can be borrowed at a reasonable rate of interest (6 percent in his opinion) and when capital is willing to invest in the island, a condition of stability will have been reached."[69] If a few farmers failed along the way, so be it.

There were actually few ways Wood could materially help the Cuban economy. He sent geologists into the hinterlands looking for exploitable resources but found only marble, asphalt, and a bit of iron ore. His ability to develop Cuba's infrastructure was hamstrung by the Foraker Amendment which was meant to prevent American entrepreneurs plundering Cuba but virtually eliminated American investment in anything but bankrupt farms. From his first weeks as governor, Wood lobbied to have the amendment repealed or modified so he could attract American money, but the anti-imperialists allied with western-state farmers worried about potential competition and united against him. With one exception the amendment stood.[70]

Although Root and Wood were convinced an educated populace was prerequisite to full democracy, they felt obligated to take a few steps toward limited self-government. Root had ordered a Cuban census in the summer of 1899, and Wood came to Havana with instructions to arrange municipal elections as soon as the census results were available. The task was a daunting one; he had to arrange the first political campaign in four centuries for 500,000 literate and 1,000,000 illiterate Cubans. The potential electorate comprised former slaves, insurrectionists, refugees who had been in the United States for decades, and peninsular Spaniards who had opted to stay in Cuba. The island had no election machinery and no election laws.

The first decision was who should be allowed to vote. Masó and the insurrectionist leaders favored universal (male) suffrage, a prospect that terrified the Cuban upper classes. On the one side, the former insurgents were overwhelmingly poor, illiterate, and black. On the other, the upper classes were educated and mostly of either European descent or first-generation descendants of French refugees from Toussaint l'Ouverture's slave revolt in Haiti.

The Americans found the upper classes, especially the Iberians, easier to relate to than native Cubans. The municipal election's outcome would most certainly be determined by who voted, and Wood and Root did not want the poor and illiterate at the polls. On February 16, 1900, the governor appointed a thirteen-member election commission most of which was Cuban, but two of whom were Wood's men, to consider the question. The committee submitted two reports: the majority recommended universal suffrage. Wood's representatives favored sharp restrictions, and the governor accepted the latter.[71] Any twenty-one-year-old male who was either a native of the island or a Spaniard who had surrendered his Spanish citizenship, who had no felony convictions, and who had lived at least thirty days in his municipality, could vote provided he met one of three additional qualifications: he must be able to read and write, or he must own real or personal property worth $250, or he must have served in the Cuban army prior to July 18, 1898. The last pacified the insurgent generals by giving their soldiers the vote, but had limited effect because only a small minority of Cubans had actually fought in the revolution.[72] The one other group Wood wanted enfranchised were Cuban exiles who had taken American citizenship. These men were educated, politically active, and mostly favored American annexation.

Wood pressed for adoption of the qualifications and immediate elections, but Root insisted they wait for the results of the census. Publicly Root claimed that, since they had justified the census as the data on which to base suffrage, they were obligated to wait for the numbers. More likely, the secretary wanted to avoid demographic surprises that would force him to change the rules after they were published. Wood fretted that he was running out of time to register voters, nominate candidates, and print and distribute ballots before the election which had already been announced for May. He was also running short of time to personally campaign for candidates he wanted elected.

The census came available in early spring. Of 1,572,845 Cubans, 365,000 were males over twenty-one. Of these, 188,000 were white, 127,000 were black, and 50,000 were Spanish entitled to Cuban citizenship. Of the million and a half residents of the island, 105,000 met the suffrage requirements and could vote.[73] When the numbers became public, there was an uproar, but Wood assured Root that the reaction was "only a few agitators" howling and that any change in suffrage would be a sign of weakness.

After seven months in Cuba, Wood was an unabashed Anglo-Saxon Social Darwinist convinced that broadly based democracy was dangerous. He told his boss, "In dealing with Latin races it is not advisable to yield under pressure, unless one is prepared to give up everything and submit to be ruled. Moreover, I believe that universal suffrage would destroy the standing and influence of our government among all thinking and intelligent people in the Island." He added, "There is a feeling of genuine alarm among the educated classes, lest the absolutely illiterate element be allowed to dominate the political situation. Giving the ballot to this element means a second edition of Haiti and Santo Domingo in the near future."[74]

Root held firm on suffrage and the elections for mayors, municipal judges, police court judges, and city councils were pushed back to June. Although Wood exerted as much influence as he could in favor of the more conservative candidates, the radical part of the restricted electorate took a lead so great that the conservative Union Democratic Party and its candidates withdrew to avoid embarrassment. Scrambling to maintain control, Wood insisted that minority parties be guaranteed representation regardless of the vote and that "for such a time as will be deemed proper" any action of the elected Cubans be subject to veto by the governor.[75]

The results were not what Wood wanted or expected, but elections had "passed off without disturbance of any kind," and the Cubans had voted for the first time in their history.[76] Root wrote, "I congratulate you on the successful accomplishment of the Cuban elections. It was a great thing to secure the peaceful adoption of the basis of the suffrage upon which we had agreed and to carry Cubans through their first real election so quietly and satisfactorily." Considering the course of imperialism in the rest of the world at the turn of the century and the fact that the United States had only been in Cuba two years, the election was surprisingly successful.

Before Wood had time to enjoy his success, Cuba's lethal yellow genie escaped yet again from its bottle. There were a handful of cases among the soldiers and the Habañeros, but, all in all, 1899 had been a remarkably good year. Officials in Washington began congratulating themselves; sanitation and good Yankee engineering had rendered one of the world's most dangerous cities in the world safe. American officers even began keeping their families in Cuba rather than sending them home for the fever season.[77] Cubans who had seen the fever wax and wane over the decades were unconvinced.

The skeptical Cubans were right—1900 was a yellow fever year. In May, the disease surfaced in Quemados, a village next to Columbia Barracks where several American soldiers kept offbase homes. Between May 16 and June 30, there were thirty-two cases in the village and eight deaths. Three American soldiers got the disease, but all survived.[78] Wood minimized the problem, telling Root, "Everything is going well at Columbia Barracks: no fever there excepting one or two cases picked up at Quemados. Quemados cases are more or less among those living in houses formerly occupied by natives."[79]

Nevertheless, the winter cases were ominous, and one more thing worried Wood. There had been, during 1899, a huge influx of Spanish immigrants, all of whom were nonimmunes and few of whom paid even cursory attention to personal hygiene.[80] Although Wood moved his men into isolated camps in the hills when fever season approached, eighteen of his Havana troops got yellow fever by the end of July, and four had died. His chief surgeon, Jefferson R. Kean, barely survived. All the "infected" bedding at Quemados was burned, and every "fever house" and its contents were thoroughly disinfected. All "salons and resorts" in the village were closed, but the cases kept coming.[81] As more soldiers died, the quartermaster, who refused to use flags that had adorned fever coffins for any other purpose, assigned one "yellow fever flag" that was cleaned and reused until it faded into an unrecognizable rag.[82] By late July, five of Wood's staff and forty-eight of his civilian employees had the fever and seven had died—and all lived in areas sanitized under Ludlow's and Wood's supervision. Wood moved all but a skeleton administrative staff out of the city, and those who remained hopefully burned sulfur candles on their desks to ward off germs.[83]

The papers pointed out that yellow fever had not been a problem when Ludlow was in Havana and wondered where Wood had failed. The governor, unable to come up with any other explanation, blamed the data. When the *New York Evening Post* pointed out that 1900 was a worse fever year than 1899 or even 1898, Wood replied that the higher reported incidence was merely a reflection of the fact that he, unlike Brooke and Ludlow, issued regular disease reports, a claim the reporters reworded into an accusation that the previous military governors had hidden the disease.[84] Ludlow was furious. He wrote Wood demanding a retraction "as direct and public as is the charge itself."[85] Wood replied that he had merely said sanitary conditions in Havana were "better than ever," and that he was furnishing disease information that had never before been made public. Besides, as he had informed the press, the death rate the month before he took office had been the worst in years.[86] That was hardly the apology Ludlow was looking for, and he initiated a formal complaint with the war department.[87] Wood decided a strategic retreat was in order, and wrote Oswald Villard of the *Evening Post* that he had never meant to imply that Ludlow was hiding yellow fever and he wished the editor would "correct the impression produced by the articles" and the injustice done to Brooke and Ludlow.[88] He wrote similar letters to the editors of *Outlook* and the *New York Sun* who had also carried the story.[89] He wrote Ludlow that he was sure the senior general could "appreciate fully the impossibility of guarding against deductions and conclusions being made which are entirely contrary to the spirit and intention of the interview."[90] Wood wrote the adjutant general that the whole episode, though unfortunate, had "a good deal of unnecessary importance" attached to it and that he had "said very little and that the newspaper reporter inferred a great deal."[91] In fact, Wood had tried to avoid responsibility for the epidemic, had indicted his predecessor by implication, and had gotten caught.

That summer and fall, Cuba and its governor were in trouble, but what might have been a disaster metamorphosed into one of Wood's greatest triumphs. Sternberg was a medical microbiologist by vocation, and Cuba was a hotbed of yellow fever, malaria, hookworm, tuberculosis, leprosy, smallpox, and glanders, so the surgeon general formed a commission under Major Walter Reed to investigate infectious disease on the island.[92] The commission (Reed, James Carroll, Aristides Agramonte, and Jesse W. Lazear) was not originally charged with investigating any one disease, although Sternberg hoped they would disprove his rival Giuseppe Sanarelli's claims for *Bacillus icteroides* as a cause of yellow fever. Carroll and Reed had both trained at Johns Hopkins and worked in William Welch's famous pathology laboratory. Both had also worked with Sternberg, and Reed had recently been professor of bacteriology at the Army Medical School. Lazear was from a well-to-do family and, like Reed, held a degree from Bellevue Medical College in New York, and, like Reed and Carroll, had worked with Welch. Agramonte was born in Cuba but raised and educated in the United States and worked as a bacteriologist for the New York City Health Department before applying for a post as an army contract surgeon.

Lazear and Agramonte were assigned to Havana as contract surgeons six months before they were picked to join Reed and Carroll on the commission. The team came together for the first time on June 25,

1900, at the Columbia Barracks officers club. They started work at the height of the Quemados outbreak and almost immediately proved that Sanarelli's bacillus did not cause yellow fever. They also inferred from the widely known but little publicized fact that nonimmune nurses seldom got yellow fever that the disease was not transmitted by airborne infectious droplets. Two long-held theories of yellow fever causation and transmission were put to rest in a matter of days.

Carlos Finlay, an avuncular, white-goateed Havana physician, had argued for years that yellow fever was transmitted by the *Stegomyia fasciatus* (later *Aedes aegyptii*) mosquito. His theory had brought him little but ridicule and, since there were no animals known to suffer from the disease, the idea had never been tested in a laboratory.[93] Most of Reed's team had little interest in Finlay's theory, but Lazear was intrigued, and, since they had nothing better to investigate, he persuaded the team to explore the Cuban physician's idea. Testing the theory meant experimenting on humans, not a plan for which Sternberg harbored any enthusiasm. Sanarelli had injected his bacillus into humans and three of his subjects died during the experiment. Sternberg had a very good idea how the public would react if human experiments authorized by the surgeon general resulted in more deaths, and he ordered Agramonte to undertake no trials without the "full knowledge and consent" of the subjects. Frankly, it would be best if no such trials took place at all.[94]

Forewarned, Reed's team decided to blunt the objections by experimenting on themselves first. The decision to proceed with Finlay's mosquitoes was made August 3, 1900. Finlay had tried feeding the *Stegomyia* on yellow fever patients and having them bite volunteers, but had failed to realize that the mosquitoes must harbor the disease for nearly two weeks before they could transmit it, so the Cuban never passed the disease from mosquito to man. Reed arranged to be in Washington when the experiments started, and Agramonte was excused because he had been born in Cuba and was presumed to be immune. That left Lazear and Carroll. Lazear was bitten first but did not become ill. Then Carroll tried using a mosquito that had fed on a yellow fever patient twelve days earlier. On August 29, Carroll's temperature rose to 104 degrees and, over the next few days, he shook, became confused, turned yellow, and nearly died. On September 7, he began a long, slow recovery.

Lazear had Carroll's same mosquito bite another volunteer (Private William Dean) who developed a mild but definite case of yellow fever. He then had himself rebitten on September 13 and, twelve days later, died in a pool of black vomit. His wife, who had delivered a baby the previous month and who did not even know her husband had been ill, received a simple telegram: "Doctor Lazear died at eight P.M. this evening."[95] Reed, although professing some guilt for his absence, never personally participated in the experiments, arguing that risking yellow fever would be "foolhardy in the extreme" since being "an old man" of forty-nine, he risked being "quickly carried off."[96]

The remaining experimenters and Chief Surgeon Kean were convinced they had found the cause of yellow fever. Reed, worried that someone would publish the mosquito hypothesis first, rushed back to the United States where he presented his preliminary findings to the American Public Health Association meeting in Indianapolis. Jaded by previous claims that the fever's riddle had been solved, professors and editors scoffed, pointing out that Dean, Lazear, and Carroll had all been around a number of yellow fever patients and had no doubt been infected by simple exposure. Nonetheless, Reed had protected his claim to priority and could return to proving the theory beyond doubt.

Knowing that Sternberg was unlikely to support the necessary human experiments, Reed went to Kean for help. The chief surgeon took him to Wood on October 12 to ask for money and permission to experiment on Cuban civilians.[97] At his fortieth birthday party on October 9, Wood had already announced that his army physicians had found the cause of yellow fever and that the disease would be eradicated worldwide within five years.[98] When Reed asked the governor for $10,000 to conduct his experiments, Wood said, "I have this morning signed a warrant for that amount to aid the police in the capture of criminals. This work is of more importance to Cuba than the capture of a few thieves. I will give you ten thousand dollars, and if that proves insufficient, I will give you ten thousand more."[99] Wood was taking a risk; he knew Sternberg had misgivings and he knew all the subjects would be either Cuban civilians or American soldiers. Lazear had already proven that deaths were likely, and a public uproar was not long in coming. On November 21, *La Discusion's* front page trumpeted:

HORRIFIC . . . IF IT'S TRUE!
Yellow fever transmitted to Spanish immigrants by mosquitos!

ALERT THE AUTHORITIES!

A rumor of an act so horrific, repugnant and monstrous has come to us, that hesitating to believe in its existence, almost daring to deny it, we do not hesitate to record it—only by way of rumor—in our columns, because in that way the popular version will arrive directly and quickly to the authorities, and they; if as we hope the deed turns out false, will dispel alarm and if—what we do not believe—it were true, will impose upon its authors an exemplary punishment, whose importance is at the height of the monstrous magnitude of the crime.[100]

Trained in scientific medicine, Wood not only understood the magnitude of the problem, but also the rationale and the necessity for well-designed experiments to prove the mosquito hypothesis, and, as military governor, he had the power to make the experiments happen. Wood had good reason to take the risk; eradication of yellow fever had been one of his primary charges, sanitation had failed, and the governor was under withering attack from the American press.

Reed decided to experiment on recently arrived Spanish immigrants, reasoning that they were unlikely to be immune, that they would need the money, and that the reaction if they died would be less than if an American soldier or a Cuban citizen succumbed. Knowing that he might get a reaction from Madrid, Wood approached the consul, Spain's senior representative in Havana, who agreed to let his country's citizens participate provided they were at least twenty-four years old, were volunteers, and were paid.[101] The Spanish "volunteers" were offered $100 in gold and immunity certificates that entitled them to wages twice those of a nonimmune. If they got the disease, they were promised $250 and the "best treatment" by American doctors and nurses, although no treatment had any effect on the disease and Reed knew it.[102] The pay was generous enough to attract the attention of American soldiers who campaigned for the right to participate. They even scattered bones on the path the Spanish volunteers had to walk to reach Reed's office and spread the rumor that they were remains of previous experimental subjects.[103]

On November 20, Reed's team pitched seven tents a mile from the nearest town, quarantined the area, christened it Camp Lazear, and inoculated their first five volunteers, four of whom got yellow fever.[104] Reed then started controlled experiments designed to prove the mosquito hypothesis beyond question. He built two 14 x 20 foot frame houses, each with two tiny, well-screened windows and two similarly screened doors. The buildings were specifically designed to limit sunlight and ventilation which might lessen the risk of infection. Each had a coal stove to keep the temperature over 90 degrees and basins of water to make the rooms drip with humidity. In Building #1, the "Infected Clothing and Bedding Building," volunteers were locked up for twenty days with clothes, sheets, blankets, and pillows soaked with blood, vomit, and feces ripened for two weeks after having been used by yellow fever patients. The first volunteers retched and staggered out but were eventually able to tolerate the steamy, fetid room, and none got the fever.

Building #2, the "Infected Mosquito Building," was identical in construction to the other except it was divided in half by a screen. All contents of both sides were decontaminated, and fifteen infected mosquitoes were put in one side along with a volunteer who had spent a month in quarantine so there would be no question of prior infection. Two other volunteers were placed in the nonmosquito side. Only the "mosquito side" volunteer got the disease.[105]

Carroll went on to prove he could transmit the disease by injecting infected blood that had been passed through an earthenware filter fine enough to trap any known bacteria. Yellow fever was, without question, caused by a "filterable virus" transmitted by the *Stegomyia* mosquito. As expected, papers in Havana and the United States excoriated Reed and Wood for the experiments' design, but none questioned the results.[106]

As military governor, Wood was in a unique position to apply Reed's results. Through Kean, he ordered that all barracks be covered with "mosquito bars" and that all standing water around barracks and hospitals be drained. Water barrels were layered with kerosene and had taps put in their bottoms.[107] Wood extended the order to all Cuba on December 31, 1900. Wood's chief medical officer, William Gorgas, was initially skeptical of mosquito control and tried vaccinating volunteers with serum taken from patients with a "light case" of yellow fever. When the vaccinations resulted in several deaths including the highly publicized demise of an American nurse, he joined the mosquito control campaign that brought him worldwide acclaim.[108] Gorgas redefined disinfection from sanitation to removal of insects and recommended fumigation of infected houses with sulphur, formaldehyde, or insect powder. Since the *Stegomyia* was known not to fly far, any occurrence of yellow fever in an army facility was taken as prima facie evidence of negligence by the camp commander.[109]

Next, the measures were extended to civilians. Wood ordered district commanders to report all fever cases and to "investigate the prevalence of mosquitoes, their species, the extent to which they produce malaria and yellow fever infections, the measures adopted to prevent their propagation, and the success thereof."[110] Mayors were notified that the nearest United States Army post surgeon would henceforth be the local medical inspector and would be responsible for mosquito control. It was made a misdemeanor to have mosquito larvae on any premises. Cisterns and water buckets had to be screened or kerosened and army carpenters were supplied to drill taps at the bottom of storage barrels. Gorgas's sanitary officers divided Havana into twenty districts and inspected every house monthly. Homeowners in violation of mosquito regulations were fined $5, although the fines were returned when the violations were corrected (2450 of 2500 fines were eventually remitted).[111]

By September 1901, yellow fever in Havana had essentially ceased to exist, and mosquito control had almost eradicated malaria as well. From 1898 to 1900, malaria killed 1,047 people in the city each year. In 1901, 151 died; in 1902, there were 77 malaria fatalities; from 1902 to 1912, an average of 44 died each year; and, in 1912, only a single malaria death was recorded in all Havana.[112] There had been 103 yellow fever deaths in Havana in 1899, 310 in the grim 1900 yellow fever year, only eighteen in the first nine months of 1901, and none in the next nine months.[113] In 1902, the death rate among American soldiers stationed in Cuba was the lowest of any billet in the world and one-third that of men stationed in the United States.[114] By the end of 1900, Havana, which had been one of the world's most dangerous cities, had an infectious disease death rate lower than Dublin, Munich, or Le Havre.[115] Wood called the conquest of yellow fever "worth the cost of the war, and probably the most important (advance) in the field of medicine since the discovery of vaccination."[116]

Besides keeping the island healthy, Washington wanted Wood to minimize American costs in Cuba. Under Spanish rule tariffs had been essentially the only source of revenue. Colonel Tasker Bliss, appointed director of customs by Brooke, cut many rates nearly in half, but, because he collected the duty efficiently and honestly and because the revenues all stayed in Cuba, there was actually more money available for public improvements than there had been prior to 1898. It was a good thing. Shortly after coming to Cuba Wood wrote the secretary, "We want this coming year all the revenues we can get. This will be apparent when you consider that we have barely commenced the real establishment of civil government, that there are light houses to be built, nearly all the principal harbors to be buoyed, beacons to be constructed, school houses to be built, bridges to be reconstructed, in fact our revenue is only a drop in the bucket compared to what we really need."[117]

Food was one place Wood felt he had to sacrifice tariff income. A good part of Cuba's basic food supply had to be imported and prices had to be lowered if the people were to avoid starvation. Since most of the imported goods came from American farms, the reduction was popular in Washington.

Wood recognized that tariffs would not be a sufficient tax base in the long run, and, considering the fact that Cuba's was an agricultural economy, he opted to support the island's municipalities with tax revenues based on property value rather than income. The drawback to valuation tax was the complete lack of assessment rolls, a situation Wood remedied in his first two months in office.[118]

Wood's tax reforms were thwarted in one key area. He looked to American corporations doing business in Cuba as a potentially fruitful source of revenue, but they were also a source of political mayhem. When he proposed taxing two American banks, the institutions appealed straight to Root. Wood defended his idea: "The talk about taxation is all nonsense. . . . The only two corporations who have protested are two who have their entire revenues from the government of the island." The North American Trust Company was paid $60,000 a year to act as Cuba's depository and paid "not one penny of taxes." The Maryland Fidelity Company held virtual monopoly on the sale of Cuban bonds and had paid a mere $250 in taxes. Nonetheless, both had powerful senatorial allies and Wood was forced to back down.[119] It was one of the rare times during Wood's tenure that American companies were allowed to siphon money out of Cuba.

Brooke left a balance in the treasury of just over $2 million with outstanding bills of over $1.5 million. With revenue limitations and a seemingly endless list of demands on that income and with no possibility of help from Washington, Wood was forced to be both frugal and creative. He went to great lengths to run the island as efficiently as possible, and he insisted that all finances flow through Havana. He told Root, "I want to see how every dollar is spent in Cuba and have the opportunity to examine and approve the outlay and, when in this position, I am more than willing to be held directly accountable for all expenditures here."[120] The irony of that demand in view of his battle with Brooke over centralization was evidently lost on the governor.

By mid-1900, Wood had paid all municipal debts back to June 1899, put judges and court employees on salary, funded hospitals and charities, spent $600,000 on school buildings and supplies, was spending $350,000 a month on education, and still accumulated $2.5 million in the treasury.[121] Wood saw to it that, with very few exceptions, no American civilian working for the Cuban government was paid more than $250 a month (although he received a relatively handsome $15,000 a year, half of which was his major general's salary paid by the army and half his salary as governor general paid by the Cuban government).[122]

A large part of Wood's success came from his ability to centralize power. By July 1900, he had consolidated the whole island into two military departments and, shortly thereafter, he got Root to abolish those departments (and the other generals' jobs) in the interest of "efficiency."[123] Having consolidated his island, Wood set out to take control of the chain of command between Havana and Washington. Technically, he reported to the adjutant general in his military capacity and to Root's assistant secretary, G. E. Meiklejohn, in his role as governor general, and Wood wanted to be rid of both. He wrote the secretary, "Would it not be possible for me to receive orders only through the Adjutant General? I get a good many orders, telegraphic etc. from Mr. Meiklejohn signed by Edwards which are not always in accord with our policy here. It is confusing." Just to be sure there was no mistaking his intent, Wood added, "Speaking candidly, Mr. Meiklejohn knows almost nothing of affairs in Cuba nor of the necessities of the situation here and I should feel a much greater sense of security and satisfaction if orders received emanated from you directly through the Adjutant General."[124] The young general and recent captain surgeon was calmly telling the secretary of war how he would receive his orders. A few days later the brazenness of the request must have occurred to him. Wood retreated:

"What I wrote you the other day about orders from Mr. Meiklejohn is not a matter of tremendous importance, but it is a trifle nagging, and I am very anxious to avoid any disagreeable issue with him as I believe that he generally means well."[125] Wood, however, got his way and, after June 1900, his orders all came, not from the adjutant general, but directly from Root.

Finally, Wood had to solidify his relationship with the nascent Cuban government. McKinley and Root had made it clear that they wanted Cuba prepared for self-government, but Wood wanted to remain in charge while the process played out. As he put it, autonomy should be established "under our control and supervision for such time as will be deemed proper; but the government should be completely organized as a Cuban government with the exception of the Governor of the Island, who should remain for the present an American commanding the Military Forces of occupation and holding an absolute power of veto."[126] Wood ordered that all legal disputes go through the Cuban courts but that the governor have the final right of appeal. He insisted that no Cuban appeal go around him directly to Washington: "if they get the idea that they can call the Military Governor to account and keep up an extensive correspondence through the War Department, it is bad for us here, and I'm sure only gives an unnecessary burden to the War Department."[127] He disingenuously assured Root that "I am not hunting after petty authority or absolutism or anything of the sort." Whether Wood wanted petty authority might be arguable, but his desire for absolute authority was unquestionable. Under Brooke civil orders were prefaced: "The military Governor directs the publication of the following order: . . ." Wood changed the formula to: "I, Leonard Wood, Military Governor, by virtue of the authority vested in me, direct the publication of the following order: . . ."[128]

By 1901, Wood had gone even farther; he forbade appeal to either Cuban courts or the secretary of war of any of his decrees. As he euphemistically put it, "Administrative action here has a very large scope and is sometimes almost legislative in character." He added that "it would be a very dangerous expedient to place in the hands of any Court the power to reverse the administrative action of the Military Governor."[129] Wood appointed a domestic Administrative Council with the putative though entirely conditional right to review his decisions, while stating, "Appeals against executive action . . . cannot be tolerated under this form of government without jeopardizing its existence."[130] In six-teen months the administrative tyro created an autocracy in which he could not be challenged from below, in which he had no peers, and in which his only superiors were the secretary of war and the president of the United States.

In spite of his successful accretion of power in Cuba, Wood's mili-tary future still hung from the slender thread of a commission in the volunteer army. When that army was dissolved, as was rumored might happen any day, the major general would automatically revert to cap-tain in the medical corps. McKinley had repeatedly promised Wood a regular army commission as brigadier general, but the young firebrand had accumulated enough political enemies—notably Senator Mark Hanna—to make the necessary congressional approval anything but certain. Regular army promotions were glacial, usually coming only as the result of advancement, retirement, or death of someone higher on the list. When Wood heard that Miles had been promoted lieutenant general and Merritt had retired, he approached Lodge, reminding him that he had been "definitely assured on various occasions" of a brigadier general's appointment. He reminded the senator that his "tremendous responsibility" in Cuba had necessitated his making pow-erful enemies and left him in no position to look after his own inter-ests.[131]

Wood complained to Roosevelt that men who had not fought in the Spanish War were being promoted ahead of him, that it was unfair after all he had done for the United States government in Cuba "to remain without substantial recognition in the Regular Service." Worst of all, the Democrats might win in the fall and send him back to the medical corps "about ten thousand dollars poorer in property and with the unavoid-able effect of three years of hard work in the tropics."[132] He asked Lodge "both as a friend and as my official representative" to help get past his congressional enemies.

In the end, even though Wood had to sweat out the 1900 election, McKinley came through; in February, Wood's appointment went to Congress. The press was hardly unanimous in its support; Wood's old nemesis the *Evening Post* complained, "We do not believe that any other service in the world would reward an army doctor with the rank of brigadier general because of military duties comprising, in all, eight weeks in the command of a volunteer regiment."[133] But Wood had his line commission and, based on his tender years, was virtually certain to one day be the army's senior general.

Wood's problems with the press were not confined to editors in the United States; he had difficulties with the fourth estate in Cuba as well. When the press had attacked Ludlow, the new governor loftily opined that "Nothing can be more fatal in Cuba than interference with its gossipy and at times provoking press; silence is more annoying to them than anything else."[134] He assured the president that "the only justification for interference with the press must be the preaching of dangerous doctrines tending to jeopardize public order and the printing of immoral and obscene matter."[135] Personal attacks on Wood himself evidently fell in one of those categories. When, on Good Friday, one of Havana's papers caricatured Wood and McKinley as two thieves crucified beside the Cuban people, Root had to directly intervene to keep the governor from closing the paper.

Wood had better luck dealing with the first estate than the fourth. Although Cuba was nominally Catholic, the Church neither commanded a great deal of loyalty nor exerted much influence among the majority of Cubans. In 1880, the bishop of Havana complained that only 3,000 of the city's 200,000 residents regularly attended mass although they supported fifty Masonic lodges. When the Church sided with Spain in the insurrection, its credibility reached a nadir. The islanders were annoyed when the Vatican sent an Italian bishop rather than naming a native Cuban after the Spanish left, and they were disappointed when Wood said he could not reverse the appointment.[136]

Wood had to solve two Church-related problems—marriage laws and property rights. The Church's high fees for marriage ceremonies had resulted in a majority of Cubans simply forgoing the formality, and, in an effort to regularize the situation, the Spanish administration decided to recognize only civil marriages. The Church wanted a return to religious monopoly, a change the Cubans "from the President of the Supreme Court down to the working man" adamantly opposed.[137] Wood compromised, recognizing both civil and religious marriage and leaving the choice to the participants. The people were happy and the bishop of Havana fatuously praised Wood as "a wise leader and an able statesman" with "elevated ideals of justice, fairness and true liberty" that were a credit to the United States.[138]

Wood's other Church problem, although more contentious, was easier to deal with as a result of his having successfully navigated the marriage dispute. Some years previously the Spanish had commandeered most of the Church's extensive Cuban real estate holdings but had paid rent for their use. When the Americans came, they continued to use facilities and land that nominally belonged to the Church but stopped paying rent. The bishop demanded that Wood either pay back rent, purchase the property outright, or return it. The cash demands were exorbitant, with the amount due on one building alone being $2 million and the total demand in excess of $5 million. Wood delegated Frank Steinhart to negotiate with the prelate, and the stolid German convinced the bishop to cut his demand in half, with the stipulation that the state could later buy the land outright and deduct part of the rent from the purchase price, a much better deal than the quagmire the United States fell into in the Philippines over the same issue.[139]

Cuba's railroads proved a more complex problem. In 1900, there were 124 different railroads on the island, seventeen public roads with 1,226 miles of track and 107 private lines with 871 miles of track. The private lines mostly served one company's mines or plantations and brought goods to the nearest dock. The public roads were almost all owned by British investors and 90 percent were in the western end of the island. There was no connection between Havana and any city east of Santa Clara (roughly half way along the island's axis). Not only were the public railroads inadequate, but also any failure to protect property or any attempt to regulate them risked British intervention.[140] About the time Wood became governor, Sir William Van Horne, an American-born entrepreneur who had recently built the transcontinental Canadian Pacific line, assembled a group of investors including General Grenville Dodge, political power broker Thomas Fortune Ryan, James J. Hill, and Levi Morton into the New Jersey–based Cuba Company.[141] Van Horne and his partners were "looking into the feasibility and desirability of building a line from Santa Clara to Santiago with off shoots to open up Cuba's eastern half."[142]

The investors' main stumbling block was the Foraker Amendment which specifically banned granting Cuban governmental concessions to foreign (including American) investors. The amendment was intended to prevent American capitalists from plundering the island, but it also prevented Wood's granting Van Horne the right to cross public roads and waterways. Wood wanted the amendment repealed, but the Senate, still in a froth over the postal scandals, was in no mood to comply. Root, the clever lawyer, devised a solution; he saw no reason why allowing Wood to exercise eminent domain in Van Horne's behalf violated the amendment. Root solved the rivers and roads problem by issuing "revocable permits" to cross government property which since they were not permanent, presumably fell outside the constraints of the Foraker Amendment. The railroad opened for business in December 1902 and, for the first time, there was a reliable overland connection between Cuba's capital and its second oldest city. Wood correctly predicted that the railroad would be "one of the great features in the reclamation of the island."[143]

Besides having a dearth of track, Cuba's railroads were plagued with an exorbitant, arbitrary, and constantly changing rate schedule. It cost four times as much to move sugar sixty miles from a plantation to a dock as it did to carry it from Cuba to New York. Wood estimated that rail profits were at least 40 to 50 percent higher than they should be. The lines were owned by British (and a few French) who, in the governor's opinion, had "absolutely no interest in the Island except what they can get out of it" but whose governments, accustomed to exploiting colonies, would make an international incident if the investors were disturbed.[144]

Once again, Root's legal expertise furnished a solution. In October 1901, Wood asked McKinley for permission to establish a "Commission somewhat similar to the Interstate Commerce Commission" that could regulate rates and modify charges "prejudicial to the public interest."[145] The idea was really Root's who saw a parallel to regulation of public utilities as was done in America and "practically every civilized country," and, wondering why they had not done it in Cuba sooner, authorized the regulatory body with the sole caveat that the investors should still be allowed a "reasonable return" on their investment. However, he left the definition of reasonable to the governor. Cuba's Commission to Standardize Freight Rates was not actually formed until shortly before the Americans left the island, but, under the terms of the Platt Amendment, the incoming government was not allowed to change its rate schedule.[146] That schedule was drafted with the assistance of two members of the Interstate Commerce Commission as well as less neutral input from Van Horne and Dodge, and, although it clearly worked to the benefit of the Cuba Company and its American investors, it furnished much needed relief to Cuban farmers.[147]

By mid-1901, it was time to make good on the Teller Amendment's promise; Wood and Root agreed that, if the municipal elections came off without major problems, a constitutional convention would be held. In fact, Wood had been thinking about a constitution for Cuba since June 1900, and he meant for the elected convention to discuss and presumably approve a document he would submit. He told Root, "I am going to work on a Constitution for the Island similar to our own and embody in the organic act certain definite relations and agreements between the United States and Cuba."[148] He told Senator Nelson Aldrich that the constitution should embody a legislative assembly and such laws as were necessary to regulate marriage, divorce, and property, but that the governor should retain an absolute power of veto.[149]

On July 25, 1900, Wood announced elections for the coming September, and, as the summer progressed, his ideas for the convention crystallized. Wood remained convinced that the Americans had to stay in Cuba, a conviction reinforced by the rise of the proindependence Nationalist Party. The governor decided the convention would have thirty-one delegates divided among the six provinces and that slates would be apportioned to guarantee representation to "the conservative and intelligent classes" since it was obvious those classes would be in a minority.[150] Wood initially thought the municipal elections were an aberration that would be corrected when the wealthier, conservative Cubans realized they would have to be politically involved, but, as the summer progressed, the radicals developed a substantial lead. Wood decided to tour the island to personally convince the Cubans that "they must not trifle with this Constitutional Convention and that if they send a lot of political jumping jacks as delegates they must not expect that their work will be received very seriously."[151]

His discussions with the Cubans did convince him of one thing; any attempt to embody the subject of United States–Cuban relations in the constitution would lead to trouble. He warned Root that the Cubans wanted "entirely separate documents" and advised that the separation was "worthy of consideration." The next hundred years might well have been different had Root listened.

Wood's tour of the island was not reassuring. He found some proposed delegates acceptable, but most were "rather bad." He also found a "certain feeling of alarm and apprehension concerning the coming Constitutional Convention" and worried that radicals would make "extreme declarations" in favor of early and complete separation from the United States.[152] Although he thought four of the secretaries from his advisory cabinet and three or four of his Supreme Court justices might be nominated, there were also "a good many undesirable individuals" who looked sure to be elected.[153] Looking at the convention's likely makeup, he again warned Root that the question of Cuban-American relations was too delicate to be included in the constitution.

Wood opened the constitutional convention at the Teatro Marti on November 5, 1900. Root overruled Wood's suggestions regarding intergovernmental relations and the governor, in his opening speech, charged the delegates with two jobs: adopt a constitution and formulate "what, in your opinion, ought to be the relation between Cuba and the United States."[154] He also pointedly reminded them that their duties had only to do with future events and would have no influence on the existing military government. Since the most pro-American Cubans were not in the room, there were only two ways the United States could maintain an influence on the island: prolong the occupation (the alternative Wood favored) or restrict the new nation's sovereignty. Root opted for the latter, advising Wood that creating a Cuban legislature subject to a military governor's veto power was not safe and that there needed to be a "clean cut" between the intervention and the new Cuban government. He went on to say that the convention had to deal with the issue of relations and they needed to "disabuse their minds of the idea that they are certain of being protected by the United States" if they did not "accord to this government the authority and facilities for her protection."[155] Root painted United States supervision "not as a favor to us but a favor to them," and he warned against letting "the Americans get the impression that Cuba is ungrateful and unreasonable."[156] The secretary added that the Treaty of Paris left America with an obligation to protect Cuba and the Monroe Doctrine made it a right. The argument was tenuous and Root knew it, but he also knew Britain and Germany were anxious to prevent any special relationship between the United States and Cuba.[157]

The Cubans offered a compromise: in the "spirit of the Monroe Doctrine" the island would "proceed in all cases, in peace as well as in war, in common accord with the United States." They also offered the United States one port of its choosing on Cuba's north coast or two in the south and an agreement to go to war with the United States whenever the latter thought war necessary "to defend or protect the independence of the States which constitute the entire American continent." They did not, however, want the agreement to be integral to their new constitution.[158] The delegates, realizing after the fact that the offer was too generous, tried to scale it back to a lease of coaling stations, United States supervision of Cuban foreign policy for two years, and shared occupation of Cuban forts for the same period.[159] Other suggestions included United States control of ports and customs, control of Cuban foreign policy for ten years, an offensive-defensive military alliance, and a monetary union.[160] Root turned to Congress to solve the impasse, later claiming to have been influenced by Cuban conservatives who, fearing a radical government, asked that Cuba be annexed. Root said the Platt Amendment was his attempt at a compromise to protect the Cubans. It was, in fact, a transparent attempt to hold Cuba as close as possible to the United States.[161]

Wood cautioned Root about the constitutional delegates and the convention's possible outcome: "I think Congress should be told very plainly that the men who have been elected to position of authority in Cuba are in no way competent to protect the present interests or develop the future prosperity of the Island." He added that Congress should under no circumstances let Cuba be self-governing until "competent men come to the front." Bowing to the Teller Amendment, he said, "I believe in establishing a government of and by the people of Cuba and a free government, because we have promised it, but I do not believe in surrendering the present Government to adventurers who are now in the Convention."[162] Wood was still convinced that the property owners and Cubans outside the radical cities wanted the United States to be in (or possibly of) Cuba.

For Wood, the situation seemed clear: "It is an extremely delicate situation, both from the sentiment at home which is that we have got to give these people their independence—a thing which all of us want to do—and the question whether we are keeping faith with them or with ourselves if we push them into a condition which we know means their failure and the ruin of their aspirations."[163] The Cubans should be allowed a trial of independence, but not yet.

For his part, Root had come to a decision. After discussions with McKinley and Wood, he drafted an eight-point resolution to be adopted as an amendment to the 1901 Army Appropriations Bill. It is ironic that the three laws that defined (and perverted) Cuban-American relations for at least the first half of the twentieth century, were all amendments to military appropriations bills. The Teller Amendment of 1898 barred colonization of Cuba, the Foraker Amendment of 1899 prevented economic exploitation, and the Platt Amendment of 1901 constrained Cuban independence for the next three decades. Together, they reflected turn-of-the-century American ambiguity toward imperialism and predicted, in microcosm, twentieth-century American foreign policy. All three were a radical departure from sixteenth- and seventeenth-century Spanish, Dutch, and Portuguese imperialism and the eighteenth- and nineteenth-century British, French, and Russian empires.

The Platt Amendment stipulated that American troops and the military government could be withdrawn from Cuba only if the new constitution expressly provided that (1) Cuba make no foreign agreements that would "impair or tend to impair" its independence, (2) the government of Cuba contract no debts it could not pay back out of "ordinary revenue of the island," (3) the United States would have "the right to intervene for the protection of Cuban independence, (4) all acts of the military government be validated and maintained, (5) current sanitary plans and measures be maintained,[164] (6) the status of the Isle of Pines be a subject for future negotiation,[165] (7) Cuba would sell or lease naval and coaling stations to the United States at "specified points to be agreed upon," and (8) all seven stipulations would be made part of a permanent treaty with the United States.[166]

On February 27, 1901, the Senate passed the amendment 43 to 20, and the House of Representatives passed a similar version 161–137 two days later. On February 12, the Cuban convention had belatedly appointed a committee to consider Cuban-American relations, but Root had already forwarded a final draft of the Platt Amendment to Wood with instructions that the convention was to accept the stipulations without alteration.

Wood then made the whole discussion immeasurably more difficult. The governor had planned a crocodile hunting trip to the village of Batabanó south of Havana, and, rather than cancel the excursion, he summoned representatives of the convention to join him on the train ride, during which he presented Root's ultimatum. Although Wood later claimed the delegates thoroughly enjoyed the jaunt, word filtered back that they were deeply offended at being forced away from deliberations they took very seriously.[167] Root, in an unusual handwritten note, told Wood he had heard from a "private source" that the insulted delegates were "less inclined to be reasonable" because of the incident.[168] Wood countered that "relations between the Committee and myself are of the most friendly character imaginable and any statement to the contrary is without foundation in fact."[169] Given the governor's low opinion of the convention, one doubts the accuracy of his estimate. In fact, the same letter goes on to assure Root that he could make the Committee "accept pretty much whatever we propose," and if the "ungrateful lot" had the temerity to make trouble, they would certainly appreciate a show of authority and, he went on, "if necessary *we must show it.*"[170] The Teller Amendment was forcing him out of Cuba, but Wood was not giving up power gracefully.

While he browbeat the convention, Wood was also manipulating congressional debate on the Platt Amendment. On February 26, the governor summoned Gómez to the palace, after which he quoted the Cuban general as saying that, if the Americans left, "Within sixty days the Cubans would be fighting among themselves." Gómez later denied saying any such thing, but the quote had appeared in American papers and Platt's amendment passed. After the fact, Wood told the Havana papers he had, unfortunately, been "misquoted."[171]

The convention, meanwhile, was adamantly opposed to the amendment. After two weeks of heated debate, they approved a report from the Committee on Relations that found the demands "not acceptable inasmuch as they modify the independence and sovereignty of Cuba."[172] Wood, still assuring Root the delegates would come around, suggested that the Key West naval squadron "visit" Cuba.[173] On March 2, a torchlight parade brought a letter of protest to the governor's palace. There were additional demonstrations on March 3 and 4 and, on March 5, a few papers even suggested that Cuba go to war with the United States. Wood still reassured Root: "The people of Cuba lend themselves readily to all sorts of demonstrations and parades, and little significance should be attached to them."[174] Nonetheless, the governor considered disbanding the convention and giving emotions time to quiet.

Root was unyielding; there would be no Cuban government unless the Platt Amendment was incorporated into the constitution. Moreover, the Cubans could expect no tariff reductions or other United States assistance as long as they showed "ingratitude and entire lack of appreciation of the expenditure of blood and treasure of the United States to secure their freedom from Spain."[175] The convention threatened to adjourn itself to avoid bringing the Platt Amendment to a vote, an idea Wood thought had some merit since it would temporarily disperse radicals who were encouraging one another, but Root impatiently wrote that, if the current convention would not act, the United States would get one elected that would.[176]

Wood still hoped the convention might accept the amendment. It had occurred to him that restricted independence might just be the transitional step that would lead to a Cuban request for annexation.[177] Root would not budge. He wrote, "No constitution can be put into effect in Cuba and no government can be elected under it, no electoral law by the Convention can be put into effect, and no election under it can be held until they have acted upon this question of relations in conformity with this act of Congress."[178] He did offer one bit of mitigation, authorizing Wood to tell the convention that the intervention clause should not be taken as "synonymous with intermeddling or interference" but was only a restatement of rights the United States already possessed under the Monroe Doctrine and the Treaty of Paris.[179] Root had blithely anticipated Roosevelt's corollary to the doctrine. Wood carried the olive branch to the convention leadership who suggested that a small group go to Washington for direct discussions with Root and McKinley. Wood promised Root that the convention had already accepted the Platt Amendment and wanted to make the trip only to save face, and the secretary wired back that the president would be "pleased" to receive a committee representing the convention.[180]

The committee went to Washington and, contrary to Wood's expectations, drafted a counter to the amendment as soon as they got back to Havana. Root, out of patience, brought out a new argument for the recalcitrant Cubans. He abandoned the international law justification and pointed out that only the president could withdraw the military government, and he was under specific instructions from Congress (in the form of the Platt Amendment) as to when he might do that. Until the congressional terms, including verbatim incorporation of the amendment into the Cuban constitution, were met, there would be—could be —no independence.[181] The convention made one last try to ameliorate

Root's terms on May 28 when they passed a modified version of the Platt Amendment by a vote of 15–14. Root, noting that the altered version did not answer "the requirement of the act of Congress," refused to accept it. By June, Wood was frustrated and beginning to doubt the convention's outcome. He wrote a long summary of the deliberations designed to demonstrate to Root and the rest of official Washington that they had "done everything possible to enable (the convention) to accept the Platt Amendment with as little humiliation to themselves as possible." He went on, "The time has come to state clearly the position of the Government, and to state it as an ultimatum, of which will be no further reconsideration or discussion."[182] Of course, that was precisely what Root had already done. On June 12, the convention, realizing they were out of options, accepted Root's ultimatum and incorporated the amendment into their constitution by a vote of sixteen to eleven with four abstentions. After the vote, Wood laconically commented, "There is, of course, little or no independence left Cuba under the Platt Amendment."[183]

Now Wood urged Root and McKinley not to turn the island over to the Cubans until it was beyond question that they could form a stable government that would protect the lives and property of upper class Cubans and Spaniards who had opposed the revolution.[184]

In a last grasp at autonomy, the convention tried to pass an electoral law under which they rather than Wood's military government would supervise Cuba's first elections, but Wood rejected the plan.[185] Elections for the new government were held in December 1901 and went off quietly with, "No disturbance, no coercion, no interference by the military government and no intervention directly or indirectly, by any officer or soldier of the United States Army."[186] At least by no officer other than Wood.

On February 21, the newly elected Cuban Assembly formally signed their constitution to the tepid accompaniment of less than half a minute of subdued applause. Wood's military government sent no representatives, and the event passed without public demonstration or notice. A band had been hired and played an abbreviated version of the new national anthem as delegates filed somberly up to sign the document. One man's shout of "Viva la Republica Cuba" drew scattered applause. Washington's response was equally unenthusiastic. Root said, "I do not fully agree with the wisdom of some of the provisions of this Constitution, but it provides for a republican form of government; it was adopted after long and patient consideration and discussion; it represents the views of the delegates elected by the people of Cuba, and it contains no features which would justify the assertion that a government organized under it would not be one to which the United States may properly transfer the obligations for the protection of life and property under international law assumed in the Treaty of Paris."[187] Cuba had qualified independence under a government neither Wood nor Root wanted, but the mechanism was in place to turn an island that had spent four centuries as a colony into a nation state.

It is instructive to look at Wood's version of imperialism alongside other contemporary models. Nineteenth-century imperialism was of two general types—cultural and economic—and varied from country to country, based on whether the imperial power thought the colony capable of or worthy of being brought to the level of the metropolis.

Great Britain occupied a spot near the middle of the spectrum. In both of their empires (North America/Oceania and Africa/Asia), they imposed their language and laws, often to the benefit of the colony, but structured trade and government to the economic benefit of the metropolis and held fast to the conviction that residents of the colony, either native or immigrant, were incapable of cultural, economic, or political equality with citizens of the home country. The colonies often started as trading bases meant to unload Britain's excess manufactures in return for underpriced local sugar, spices, timber, metals, or minerals. The trading bases grew to include the local area necessary to their protection, then to the surrounding countryside, and finally to territorial hegemony.

The French were economic imperialists similar to the British but differed in the cultural aspect. The underlying assumption of the *"mission civilizatrice"* was that the colonials could, with proper education and encouragement, be made French and could (as in Martinique, Guadeloupe, and—for a time—Algeria) become integral to the metropolis. The Mongols who colonized China occupy an odd extreme. They did not just believe the colony could be brought to the level of the colonizer; they thought it culturally superior and integrated themselves into the conquered culture. At the far opposite extreme lay the colonizers who assumed the indigenous population impossible to civilize. In this case, the native population was either removed or destroyed. The only other nineteenth-century American experience (and Wood's only experience) with imperialism was with the Indians and was of precisely that type.

In spite of his western experience, Wood came to Cuba as a cultural imperialist. He thought the Cubans capable of one day being part of the United States, and he was adamantly opposed to economically exploiting the island in the process. He had a Social Darwinist's low opinion of the island's illiterate former slaves, but he liked and respected the educated Cubans and especially the Cuban Spaniards who he thought might bring the island to American statehood. In retrospect, he fatally underestimated the island's lower class and overestimated the upper.

There was sharp disagreement in the United States as to whether absorption of Cuba was a good idea. Anti-imperialist arguments generally fell into two categories, constitutional and racial. One set of arguments revolved around what the Constitution said, or did not say, about owning colonies. Ewing Wilson epitomized that argument in the *North American Review*, pointing out that in neither document did the founding fathers make any reference to the acquisition or governing of colonies, so the United States was, by implication, constitutionally barred from that activity.[188] The positive side of the constitutional argument was that the Declaration of Independence pronounced all men to have been created equal, a stance expressly incompatible with colonizing other peoples.

The only way an overseas colony could be constitutional was if it was afforded statehood, and that introduced the more emotionally charged racial argument. Senator Benjamin Tilman of South Carolina delineated the position held by most of the southern anti-imperialists. First, an empire required a large standing army, anathema to a region barely out of the shadow of its own occupation and reconstruction. Second, the assimilation of Latin and Oriental populations was abhorrent. Tilman argued that "The Anglo-Saxon is pretty much the same wherever you find him, and he walks on the necks of every colored race he comes in contact with."[189] There was no logic in adding nine million "Malays, Creoles, and black Spanish ex-slaves" to the six million American Negroes, themselves "not fitted for or entitled to participate in government."[190] Representative Champ Clark of Missouri shuddered, "How can we endure our shame when a Chinese Senator from Hawaii with his pigtail hanging down his back, with his pagan joss in his hand, shall rise from his curicle chair and in pigeon English proceed to chop logic with George Frisbie Hoar or Henry Cabot Lodge?"[191]

The eastern intellectual anti-imperialists—Carl Schurz, Andrew Carnegie, Charles Eliot, Charles Eliot Norton, Mark Twain, and E. L. Godkin—came to terms with the Cuban intervention on humanitarian grounds but opposed permanent acquisition of either Cuba or the Philippines lest their inferior racial makeup dilute the American blood-line. Schurz found, "the prospect of the consequences which follow the admission of the Spanish creoles and negroes of the West Indian islands and of the Malays and Tagals of the Philippines to participate in the conduct of our government" too alarming to contemplate seriously.[192] Yale economics professor William Graham Sumner agreed: "The prospect of adding to the present Senate a number of Cuban senators, either native or carpet bag, is one whose terrors it is not necessary to un-fold."[193]

The imperialists countered that there was nothing in either the Con-stitution or the Declaration of Independence guaranteeing the right of self-government. Indeed, the slavery provisions of the Constitution specifically denied that right to inferior races. We had always governed slaves, Indians, and free men of color, and their consent or dissent were irrelevant. In fact, "It made no difference what their wishes were, or to what they opposed."[194] The editors of *Outlook* agreed that asserting the right of every race to govern itself was foolish. They wrote, "We might as well say that it is an inalienable right of every man to read or every animal to fly as to say that it is an inalienable right of every community to govern itself . . . self government is not a right at all—it is a capac-ity."[195] The editorial went on to say that America had betrayed the Indi-ans by not trying to prepare them for self-government and the Negroes by giving them self-government before they were ready for it. As jarring as this argument sounds today, it was precisely Wood's conception of the Cuban situation.

Throughout 1901, Wood still hoped for a transitional independence leading to annexation. He told Root that a government under the Platt restrictions would be "of short duration and will be followed by an-nexation in some form or another."[196] On another occasion, he told the secretary, "My belief is that if encouragement were given, the people of Cuba would with almost one voice ask to become a state in the Union."[197] In the fall he said, "The sentiment looking towards annexation to the United States is strong and growing everywhere."[198] Perhaps Wood was hearing only what he wanted to hear, perhaps he was trying to convince Root of something he knew to be unlikely, or perhaps it was a bit of both.

Wood's orders from Washington were, however, clear; Cuba was to be independent. That being settled, Wood assured Roosevelt (now president after McKinley's assassination) he was still confident the Cubans would eventually ask for annexation since, with "little or no real independence left Cuba under the Platt Amendment" the more sensible Cubans realized their only course was to join the United States. Still, the "sensible" Cubans to whom Wood was speaking were neither the majority nor the elected. Wood had given the Cubans an efficient government, but the majority of the islanders, after four centuries as colonials, wanted independence.

Although he favored limitations on Cuban independence, Wood wanted the island to be as financially autonomous as possible. The revolution had devastated Cuba's two cash crops—sugar and tobacco— but two years of peace had begun to restore output by the summer of 1900. Unfortunately, the market for Cuban sugar collapsed just as production increased. There were two reasons for the collapse. Europe and the United States had, over the previous four years, developed large, heavily subsidized beet sugar industries, and the new supply profoundly depressed the price of raw sugar. Besides a depressed market, the United States also had tariff barriers restricting entry of Cuban sugar, and producers had to pay a Cuban excise tax to export sugar. At one point, the duty alone equaled the wholesale price of raw sugar on the New York market, and every pound of Cuban sugar sold cost the growers money.[199]

Wood lobbied hard for a tariff reduction beginning in early 1900, and his requests became more urgent as the summer and fall progressed and the magnitude of the planters' financial disaster became evident.[200] By December 1900, Wood was convinced a 50 percent reduction in duties on sugar and tobacco were necessary to save "the class to whom we must look for good government and building up of the Island."[201] A few day's reflection convinced the governor that 50 percent was unrealistic and he apologized to Root, saying he supposed the secretary must have been "astounded" at the request and that 25 or even 20 percent would be enough to "win the greatest amount of affection and good will" from the Cubans.[202]

McKinley was shot on September 7, 1901, and died seven days later bringing Wood's old friend and supporter Theodore Roosevelt to the White House. Roosevelt was, by conviction, a protectionist, but he, like Root, was susceptible to the moral argument that, having intervened in Cuba, the United States was responsible for the island's well-being. Wood polled his Cuban mayors and judges for comments on the sugar crisis and forwarded the resulting pleas for aid to Washington in October. The governor wrote the new president that a tariff reduction was "of vital importance" since the warehouses were still full of unsold sugar and tobacco from the previous year's crop. The planters were near bankruptcy, and, without the income from sugar and tobacco, there would be no way to maintain the schools, courts, hospitals, communication systems, or any of the other necessities of good government. He went on, "We have had the Island of Cuba absolutely under our control for three years. We have announced to all the world its ruined condition and our charitable organizations of all classes have contributed largely to alleviate conditions of distress etc., but our government has not taken any action tending to stimulate the two great industries whose increase will speedily put Cuba back on her feet."[203]

Convinced, Roosevelt sent the issue to Congress on January 15, 1902. Root had been warning Wood for a year that the political climate was against him and that any attempt to decrease the tariff would create "a great outcry and a strong pressure on the part of the cane sugar, beet sugar, and tobacco people."[204] The senators, tired of Wood's badgering, complained to Root. Platt informed the secretary that, in his opinion, no tariff discussions could be even started until Cuba had achieved sovereignty and could be treated like any other trading partner.[205] When Cuba was a real nation, tariff reductions could be undertaken on a reciprocal basis. Reciprocity became the centerpiece of a two-week congressional debate, and the reduction foundered on the specious argument that reciprocal reductions would primarily benefit the sugar trust who could get cheaper raw product instead of the Cuban growers. The reductions did not pass.

Meanwhile, Tasker Bliss was trying to develop a tariff schedule Congress would accept. This was a difficult problem since import duties were Cuba's primary source of revenue and any reduction in duty on American goods inevitably diminished the funds available for public works. American control of Cuban tariffs led to a few odd situations. Some imports, such as trained animals, portable theaters, wax figures, wallpaper less than forty centimeters long, and gold bars were duty free. Some things—firearms, ammunition, explosives, paintings offensive to morality, and (in a bow to Wisconsin dairy farmers) oleo margarine—could not be imported at all.[206]

In an attempt to satisfy Congress, Wood's fiscal needs, and the Cuban planters, Bliss proposed a reciprocal reduction with the lost island revenues to be made up by increasing the duty on goods imported from Europe. When Congress refused to report out a Cuban tariff reduction, Roosevelt sent a special message in which he painted the reduction as the cost of American influence in the Caribbean and a foreign policy imperative. The president suggested a modest 20 percent reduction in American tariffs on Cuban agricultural products. In return Cuba would decrease tariffs 20 percent on items customarily bought from the United States, but up to 40 percent on items they had traditionally bought from Europe such as cheese, perfume, and luxury goods.[207] Wood was convinced that some relief was necessary to keep Cuban farmers solvent, but his incessant lobbying finally exhausted even Roosevelt and Root.

In February 1902, there was still no agreement and the Americans were two months from leaving Cuba. Republican Senators, most of whom were protectionists, were tired of Wood's flood of letters and published articles criticizing their inaction. Root ordered Wood to desist. The contrite governor responded, "I regret exceedingly if my correspondence on the question of duties has given you any trouble or annoyance."[208] Wood never got his bill, tested friendships, risked his reputation, and added to his burgeoning list of enemies. He paid this price for two reasons: He felt that a trade agreement would bind Cuba to the United States and might lead to annexation and also that lack of an agreement would drive Cuba back toward Europe. When Congress finally agreed to a modest reduction in 1903, it was because the Cuban government had begun forming ties with European governments.[209] In less than a year Cuba moved out of the near-exclusive financial dependence on the United States that Wood had crafted and annexation was a faint memory.

On another level, Wood genuinely felt a moral responsibility for Cuban welfare. He was criticized for spending all Cuba's resources on public works and education and for failing to improve the island's economy and productive capacity, but that criticism is unfair. Cuba's was a two-crop agricultural economy and, with no immediate possibility of diversification, the only way to increase revenue was to increase output of one of those crops. In 1902, only 3 percent of Cuba's arable land was in cultivation, and two-thirds of that was in production for export. Half the island was covered with unproductive pine forest, even though Cuban sugar cane could grow fifteen feet in a year and the land would produce up to three tobacco crops a year. If markets could be found, an acre of Cuban farm land could earn $1,000 every twelve months.[210] Wood reestablished ruined farms and built railroads with predictable, fair rates to get the crops to harbors buoyed and lighted and safe for ocean transport. The result was warehouses packed with product without a market. Wood then risked his reputation and influence to expand those markets until he was directly ordered to stop. Wood crafted a series of successful programs for Cuba and, at the last step, could not overcome a wall of American self-interest.

But in the spring of 1902, a new Cuban government was being formed and plans for transfer of power progressed. Two men ran for president, the elderly Creole general Bernardo Masó whom Wood dismissed as being in his second childhood and expatriate Tomás Estrada Palma. There had been an early push to make Gómez president, but the old Dominican declined and, fearful of a radical government under Masó, Wood threw his support behind Estrada Palma. In spite of the fact that he never left New York to campaign, Palma benefited from fear of Masó and Wood's help. The governor, in spite of repeated claims that the electoral process was free of interference, fired mayors who supported Masó and appointed the five-man election supervisory board entirely from Palma's campaign executive committee. Masó decided he had no chance and withdrew, advising his supporters to boycott the election.

On February 24, Cuba held its first national elections, and the new congress convened in Havana on May 5, where they ratified their own elections and that of Estrada Palma. The new president had come back to Cuba two weeks earlier and made a triumphal passage from the port city of Gibara to Havana. Formal ceremonies transferring the government to Palma and the new legislature were held on May 20—"a fine

Cuban May day"—in the marble hall of the government palace packed with representatives of the United States government and army, the Church, foreign governments, and the Cubans. Reading the documents of transfer took only ten minutes, after which Wood and Gómez, by prior agreement, adjourned to the palace roof where they were to raise the new Cuban flag. To their surprise, someone had already run the banner up, and McCoy was frantically trying to get it down before the old general noticed (although the flag had been seen by ships in the harbor and ceremoniously saluted). When Gómez got to the roof and raised the flag for the second time, the halyard broke so the flag had to be lowered and raised a third time; Wood called it "a rather inauspicious sign."[211]

The banner finally having been successfully raised, Wood returned to the great hall for a final round of farewells. Wood left Frank Steinhart to manage the last American business and to be custodian of some thirty tons of military government records.[212] He left the island in reasonable financial shape; the government had no long-term debt and $689,191.02 in the treasury, not counting $100,000 reserved to complete "winding up the affairs of the military government" with the provision that any funds left over would go back to the Cuban government.[213] At the time of transfer, almost half of all government revenues went to education, sanitation, and public works. Only $482,000 a year was spent on administration. Ironically, Cuba imported $11.2 million from the United States and exported $16.6 million. America as colonial custodian spent essentially all the island's revenues in the island to the direct benefit of its citizens and actually had a negative balance of trade with the "colony."

Two virtually insurmountable problems became evident almost before Wood's ship cleared Havana Bay. First was Cuba's obligate two-crop agricultural economy. If sugar and tobacco failed, the Cuban economy was bound to fail, and the inability to get meaningful tariff relief for the Cuban farmers guaranteed that the island would remain impoverished. The second failure was more directly attributed to Wood's administration. In retrospect, his and Root's decision to limit the vote to the Spanish and Creole upper classes and to effectively disenfranchise the majority of Cubans had its first repercussions only four years after the military government retired and resulted in the second United States intervention. Ultimately, the narrow upper class base on which the island's government was supported rotted and the whole structure was toppled by another populist revolt from Oriente. The result was (as Wood predicted) a militarist despot, but from the left rather than the right. Much of the good that Wood had accomplished was either lost or reversed by the economic problem he could not control and the governmental one he might have.

8

Zamboanga, 1902–1908

WOOD, EXHAUSTED from slogging through paperwork until midnight every day of his last week in Havana, came aboard the USS *Brooklyn* ready to rest:

> Once in my stateroom with the doors closed I felt for the first time a feeling of complete relief and satisfaction that the work was done and the transfer over, although I felt and feel it would have been much better for the Cuban people if we had remained several years longer in Cuba and give [*sic*] them a chance to settle down on a much more sound basis, and the relations between Spaniards and Cubans to become more firmly established, and, above all things, to have accustomed the people to the ideal of restricted suffrage, restricted within such reasonable limits as would exclude the ignorant and the criminal from the polls.[1]

From May to July, Wood finished the last details of his Cuban administration, having sent his wife and children to spend the summer in Europe. In July, Root sent three generals—Wood, Corbin, and Young—to observe French and German military maneuvers. During the passage, Wood was accorded the deference ordinarily reserved to a head of state, and his suite boasted its own bath, a four poster bed, an electric fireplace, and "everything to make travel pleasant."[2]

The French military attaché and the district commanding general met Wood at Le Havre and saw him safely onto the train for Paris. The following morning, the general left for Spain, arriving at Valdecilla the next evening, where Wood joined his family and spent the next few days driving and picnicking in the vineyards and olive groves of the southern Pyrenees. The general saw his first (and last) bull fight: "While there are some pretty features it is on the whole a disgusting sight. . . .

Wished throughout the performance that the bulls would be successful in disposing of some of their tormentors."[3]

On August 17, Wood and Lou left the children and their nurse in a rented villa at St. Jean de Luz and, with McCoy, left for Paris. From the French capital they embarked on an American tourist's transit through France and Germany; a day in Bordeaux, a week in Paris (Luxembourg Palace, the Louvre, the Pantheon, Les Invalides, Notre Dame—all "very interesting and instructive"), a day in Cologne, a day in Heidelberg, a day in Nuremberg, a day in Dresden, and on to Berlin to rejoin Corbin and Young.

On September 6, the Americans were escorted onto a manicured green plain outside Berlin where 40,000 of Germany's most elite regiments passed before 50,000 cheering spectators and the Kaiser and Kaiserin. The emperor, whom Wood noted spoke better English than King George, impressed the general with his knowledge of Cuba. Wood was captivated by the empress and entirely taken with Berlin's order and cleanliness. From the capital, the Americans traveled to Frankfurt for field maneuvers. Wood was impressed with the German troops and suspected they must be secretly developing a better artillery piece than the one they presented in public which was no match for the French seventy-five.

The Kaiser sought Wood out and spent the better part of an hour inquiring about Roosevelt's Cuban experience, the president's personality, and his attitude toward Germany. He stressed that Germany intended to concentrate on economic development and naval and colonial expansion rather than risk a war with France or Russia. He pointedly suggested that it would be "a very great misfortune" for the three greatest Christian powers (England, Germany, and America) to have a falling out.[4] The Kaiser finished with an invitation for Roosevelt to visit Germany. Wood was entirely won over: "The impression the Emperor made upon me was an extremely favorable one. He spoke with an air of sincerity of his desire for peace and certainly his arguments were logical and conclusive as to the desirability of it from the German standpoint."[5]

Maneuvers resumed the following morning, and Wood had the exhilarating opportunity to ride in the midst of a full tilt charge by sixty squadrons of cavalry, the largest collection of men and horses he had ever seen in a single body. He wrote Root, "We have many things to learn from these people and can probably give them a good deal in

Boston City Hospital House Officers, 1884. Leonard Wood is seated at far right. Library of Congress.

Wood at Fort Huachuca, 1885. Library of Congress.

The Olympic Athletic Club football team, 1891. Wood is seated fourth from the left. Library of Congress.

Wood as a medical officer, 1891. Library of Congress.

Louise Condit-Smith, 1891.
Library of Congress.

Ada McKinley from Murat
Halsted, *Life and Distinguished
Services of William McKinley,
Our Martyred President.* N.s.
Memorial Association, 1901.

The USS *Maine* sunk in Havana harbor, 1898. Courtesy of the Philip S. Hench Walter Reed Yellow Fever Collection, Historical Collections & Services, Claude Moore Health Sciences Library, University of Virginia.

Wood (at right) and Theodore Roosevelt in Rough Riders Uniforms. Reprinted with permission, City of Las Vegas Museum and Rough Riders Collection.

Confusion on Port Tampa dock en route to Cuba, 1898. Library of Congress.

Rough Riders on the SS *Yucatan*, 1898. Reprinted with permission, Theodore Roosevelt Collection, Harvard College Library.

From left to right, Major-General Joseph Wheeler, Wood, and Roosevelt, 1898. Library of Congress.

Landing at Daiquirí. Reprinted with permission, *Harper's Weekly*, July 16, 1898.

Marching to Las Guásimas, 1898. Reprinted with permission, National Archives.

Wood. Reprinted with permission,
Harper's Weekly, December 5, 1903.

Moro warrior from Hugh Lenox Scott, *Some Memories of a Soldier* (New York: The Century Co., 1928).

Front row, left to right, Luisita Wood, Osborne Wood, General Wood, Mrs. Wood, and Leonard Wood Jr. in 1914. Back row, Orderly Henzuan, Captain Matthew Hanna, Captain Edward Carpenter, Captain Frank McCoy. Library of Congress.

Cavalry training at Camp Funston, 1917. Library of Congress.

Wood and aides at Camp Funston, 1917. Wood is in the foreground.
Library of Congress.

Wood, at Theodore Roosevelt's funeral, Oyster Bay, New York on January 8, 1919. Wood is in the foreground, in uniform. Library of Congress.

Wood and Louise campaigning, 1920. Library of Congress.

Wood and presidential candidate Senator Warren G. Harding at Republican Headquarters, Marion, Ohio, July 10, 1920. Library of Congress.

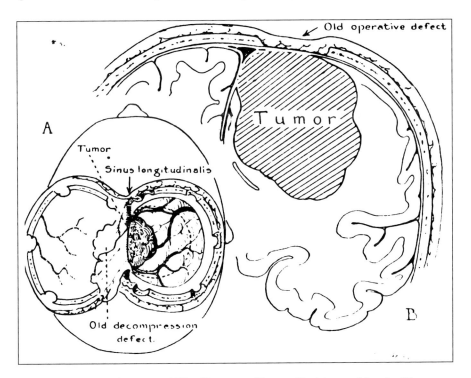

Harvey Cushing's drawing of Wood's tumor. Harvey Cushing and Louise Eisenhardt, *Meningiomas: Their Classification, Regional Behaviour, Life History, and Surgical End Results* (Springfield, Ill., Charles C. Thomas, 1938).

Wood. *Literary Digest*, cover, March 6, 1920.

return."[6] Wood thought the Americans inferior in artillery and in physical conditioning, and was amazed that cavalry could ride twenty-eight miles before an all out dash over ploughed fields and still be fresh, although he doubted that mounted charges would be of any use in the next war.[7]

From Germany, Wood collected his family and went to London where he pursued a friendship with Field Marshal Lord Roberts ("Bobs," commander-in-chief of the British Army, and vociferous advocate of preparing for war with Germany) whom he had met in Berlin. Lord Roberts, who had seen combat from Bloemfontein to Kandahar, suited Wood's taste for men of action and reinforced Wood's conviction that great nations needed great armies. He arranged for the Woods to lunch with King Edward VII and to meet Prime Minister Arthur Balfour, Joseph Chamberlain, Lord Lansdowne, the Duke of Devonshire, Henry Campbell-Bannerman, and the bishop of London. Balfour told Wood he thought the Cuban work, had it been done in the Empire, would have been worth a peerage and several thousand pounds to which the general wistfully replied that it promised to bring him "nothing but a row" and that he expected a fight just to keep his commission.[8]

Arthur Lee, Lord of the Admiralty and former military attaché in Havana, invited Wood to a House of Commons debate. When the question of how the general would enter the chamber arose, it was suggested that he be introduced as an "absolute ruler of a foreign country" and be seated next to the Prince of Wales. Wood enjoyed the stir and consternation as members and gallery tried to figure out just who he was, but he knew he had to return to Washington where the pomp and prestige would end.

With Cuban affairs winding down, Major General Wood needed a job. Managing the Panama Canal, which had been suggested to him by New York attorney Nelson Cromwell on the passage to Europe, came up again, and Wood had serious discussions with Roosevelt about taking charge of the project. The general, however, wanted exclusive authority and the president was committed to spreading the power through a commission. Wood, more interested in a military than an administrative career, declined the opportunity with no real regret.[9] The International Banking Corporation offered him $25,000 a year and a block of stock to become president, but, ignoring his chronically fragile financial position, the general declined that as well.

Almost a year earlier, Wood had written Roosevelt that "If there should ever be a change in the Philippines, I should like to have a go at the situation," provided it came with the same authority he enjoyed in Cuba.[10] Roosevelt, who had wanted the Philippines job himself before being forced into the vice presidency, understood the archipelago's appeal. However, William Howard Taft had been named governor general and the Philippines slipped from Wood's mind until he chanced to meet the incoming bishop of Manila, who suggested there might still be an opportunity in the Pacific possession.

While Wood was governing Cuba, Root and the army had struggled with the Philippines, which were proving measurably less tractable than the Caribbean protectorate. Rear Admiral George Dewey opened fire on the Spanish fleet in Manila Bay in the predawn hours of May 1, 1898, and the last Spanish shot came just after noon. The navy had, however, only occupied the shipyards, leaving Spanish troops in control of the city and the rest of the Philippines. Actually, the Spanish had been fighting a sputtering insurrection since 1840, most recently led by General Emilio Aguinaldo, the educated young son of a part Chinese lawyer. Aguinaldo had been named president of the provisional Philippine government and commander-in-chief of the rebel army in March 1897. In December, he succumbed to Spanish pressure (or Spanish bribes) and agreed to amnesty and exile. However, the rebel armies stayed more or less intact when he and a number of his closest supporters decamped for Hong Kong. Aguinaldo wandered on to Singapore where United States Consul E. Spencer Pratt convinced him to cooperate in the event of American involvement in the Philippines—an involvement that Pratt strongly suspected was imminent. The consul very likely guaranteed independence in return for rebel assistance, but Dewey, who dismissed Aguinaldo as a "soft-spoken, unimpressive little man,"[11] had no intention of honoring such a promise. Nonetheless, the United States revenue cutter *McCulloch* brought Aguinaldo home to reassume his role as president of an unrecognized government and commander-in-chief of a fragmented, ill-equipped army.

On August 12, 1898, American Secretary of State William R. Day and French Ambassador to the United States Jules Cambon (acting for Spain) signed the armistice that ended fighting in the Spanish War and left McKinley with a dilemma. He knew next to nothing about the Philippines and had no idea what to do with them. Options ranged from leaving the islands to Spain to leaving them on their own and everything in between. Dewey, whose only army was 5,000 newly arrived soldiers under General Wesley Merritt, favored keeping part of Luzon and giving the rest back. Reinforcements were still somewhere in the Pacific, and the Americans were outnumbered not only by the Spanish behind Manila's walls but also by Aguinaldo's ragged rebels surrounding the city.

Neither the Americans nor the Spaniards wanted Manila in rebel hands so, after a sham battle designed to avert an otherwise obligatory court martial, the city's commander surrendered to Merritt who promptly barred Aguinaldo and his men from the capital. The city changed hands the same day the armistice was signed, but America still controlled only Manila and the bay. Legally, Spain still ruled the rest of the islands, although a request to allow more troops into the archipelago to put down the revolution was summarily rejected. With the fighting stopped and Manila occupied, McKinley was finally in a position to end the war and decide what to do with the spoils. As Dewey set about collecting information on the islands at the other side of the world, America chose sides in a political battle that formed the basis of its twentieth-century foreign policy.

On one side, the navy was systematically exploring harbors and looking for coal with a view toward Mahanian maritime expansion. Lodge and American businessmen touted the islands as a gateway to China's supposedly limitless markets. Indiana Senator and arch imperialist Albert J. Beveridge called the Philippines a "self-supporting, dividend paying fleet, permanently anchored" where they could command the Pacific and make it an American lake.[12] American Protestants were intrigued with the possibility of Christianizing the Filipinos, casually overlooking the fact that 90 percent of the islanders were already Roman Catholic.

On the other side, an odd coalition of anti-imperialists lined up behind Democrats William Jennings Bryan and Grover Cleveland, Republicans George Frisbie Hoar and Thomas Barton Reed, labor leader Samuel Gompers, business magnate Andrew Carnegie, and a bevy of eastern academics who compiled a litany of arguments against Philippine involvement as disparate and unlikely as themselves.

McKinley dithered while Merritt nervously looked over the walls at Aguinaldo's army. Finally, a confluence of special influences impelled the president to a decision. Pressure from businesses wanting access to China; public infatuation with international power; a nagging suspicion that Germany, Russia, France, Great Britain, or Japan might step in if the United States left; and Dewey's reports of spreading anarchy led the president to decide to keep Luzon. And if Luzon, why not the rest of the archipelago? McKinley told the General Missionary Committee of the Methodist Episcopal Church that he had gone down on his knees and "prayed Almighty God for light and guidance."[13] The revelation, five months coming, had arrived. The peace commission arranged to buy the entire Philippines for $20 million, and the treaty ending the war was signed December 10, 1898. After more than the usual amount of senatorial barter (including promises of one federal judgeship, nine postmasterships, and resolution of a prickly legal problem), the treaty was ratified by a single vote on February 6, 1899.

But, as the treaty was being signed, the war between the United States and Aguinaldo's rebels was already two days old. In January, Aguinaldo had issued a statement flatly rejecting United States sovereignty. The Filipinos, looking to the Teller Amendment as a model of American anti-colonialism, were shocked to learn that they were about to be bought outright. With the army in Manila and Aguinaldo's men surrounding the city, it was only a matter of time before hostilities broke out. On February 4, a Filipino, possibly as a result of a language problem, failed to respond to an American sentry, was shot dead, and the war was on. Dewey, understanding that the rebellion would spread sooner rather than later, urgently suggested that McKinley dispatch a civilian commission to formulate some sort of coherent Philippine policy. Root and the president assigned Joseph Schurman, president of Cornell University and anti-expansionist; Dean Worcester, a University of Michigan zoologist who had gone bird collecting in the Philippines and was the only civilian member to have actually visited the islands; Charles Denby, former minister to China; Dewey; and Merritt's replacement, Major General Elwell Otis, to draft a program to ensure peace and order in the Philippines. The commission arrived one month after the fighting started and almost had its report done by fall, but Otis had already been ordered to take military control of the islands in a process McKinley euphemistically christened "benign assimilation." The only experience the United States Army had in assimilating people who did not share their language, religion, or culture (and who had no desire to be assimilated) was the Indian wars. The soldiers had no experience whatever in administering countries 8,000 miles from home, and it showed.

The Philippines War divided into two phases: organized warfare from February to November of 1899, and a guerilla war that dragged on to July 1902—or perhaps to the present day. When Aguinaldo declined an order to unconditionally surrender in May 1899, Otis sent Brigadier General Arthur MacArthur into northern Luzon to root him out. As the summer progressed, it was evident that the Filipinos could not defeat MacArthur in set-piece battles, so Aguinaldo divided his men into small bands and started a war of terror that, in the end, cost the United States eight times as many dollars and many more lives than had the entire war with Spain.[14] The guerilla war was spectacularly brutal on both sides. For the first time, American soldiers fought an Asian opponent whose combatants and civilians were indistinguishable and where the enemy attacked, killed, and melted imperceptibly into the general populace. Fear, leavened with racial bias, swelled into hatred and atrocity.

Filipinos disemboweled captive Americans or buried them to their necks in ant hills after propping their mouths open and painting their tongues with honey. Soldiers were strangled with their own amputated genitalia. Americans, for their part, resorted to the "water cure" in which they crammed open hoses down Filipino throats, filled the captives' stomachs just short of bursting, jumped on them until the water was expelled, and repeated the whole process of "drowning without dying." In an uncharacteristic ethical lapse, even Root excused the torture saying, "Soldiers fighting against such an enemy, and with their own eyes witnessing such deeds, should occasionally be regardless of their orders and retaliate."[15]

The slaughter reached a zenith on Samar, the last great campaign of the war. On September 28, Company C of the Ninth United States Infantry, stationed at the seaside village of Betangigi, were seated around long tables in mess tents just starting their midday Sunday meal. A mob of rebels and local civilians wielding razor sharp bolos broke in and commenced slashing every soldier they could reach. Severed heads fell onto tables and into plates as a handful of survivors, using kitchen knives and throwing anything that came to hand (including canned food), fought their way to the beach and escaped by boat to the neighboring camp at Basey.

Brigadier General Jacob Smith ordered every male over the age of ten killed and the interior of the island turned into a "howling wilderness." There were different views of the resulting carnage. For years, a veteran of the campaign entering a Marine mess was greeted with

"Stand Gentlemen, he served on Samar." The anti-imperialists took a less favorable view, and they had access to the press. The resulting outcry led to a spate of courts martial (including Smith's) and a temporary national self-examination.

Meanwhile, the Schurman Commission had been laboring away, although without Dewey and Otis who refused to participate. The violence convinced Schurman and his remaining colleagues that Filipinos were not ready for self-government, but they still believed that, with an appropriate period of peace and prosperity, they could be taught to be "more American than the Americans themselves."[16] Significantly, and typical of their country's altruistic version of imperialism, the commission recommended that Philippine finances be kept separate from those of the United States and that island taxes and duties be reserved to the exclusive benefit of Filipinos. They understood that tropical countries were exporters rather than importers and, although the Philippines might be an entrepôt for China, they never would be a moneymaker.

The Schurman Commission was succeeded by the Taft Commission, comprising the rotund Ohio judge, every bit as much a reluctant imperialist as Schurman; patrician Judge Luke Wright of Tennessee; Henry Ide, a Vermont lawyer and former judge in the United States court in Samoa; Bernard Moses, a Latin American history professor from the University of California; and Worcester, the only holdover from the previous group. Schurman's commission was sent to study; Taft's was sent to act. They were to replace the military government and were charged with creating an administration for "the happiness, peace, and prosperity of the people of the Philippine Islands," and to involve Filipinos in that administration wherever possible. When the commission arrived in June, MacArthur (now commander of the Philippine division) refused to meet them and saw that they were officed in a miserably cramped single room. He informed Taft that he was interfering in a "settled situation" and that all the Philippines needed was another decade or so of "bayonet treatment." The deceptively jovial Taft, however, held the purse strings and was fully aware of their power.

The guerilla war effectively ended when Aguinaldo was captured in March 1901 by Brigadier General Frederick Funston in an episode of trickery almost as daring as Funston claimed it was. Taft became civil governor on July 4 and ended military rule except in a few areas, especially the Moro province. The resistance outside Mindanao district crumbled as the rebel leaders followed Aguinaldo in taking oaths of allegiance to the United States, and, on July 4, 1902, Taft unilaterally declared the Philippines War over. Despite Taft's declaration the Moros remained fragmented, obstreperous, and altogether ungovernable. "Moroland" needed a military presence that understood tribal guerilla warfare and an administrator who could bring centralized civil government to an area that had, for nearly four centuries, refused to accept it. Roosevelt decided that Indian fighter and ex-pro-consul, Gen. Leonard Wood, was the ideal candidate.

The Moros originally came from Borneo and Malacca, after the breakup of the Islamic Madjapahit Empire in the early fifteenth century, and were still trickling into the southern islands when Ferdinand Magellan arrived in 1521. In the ensuing century, the Spanish took over the northern and central part of the Philippines, but the Mohammedan Malays retained control of Mindanao, Palawan, and the Sulu Islands that stretched south almost to Borneo. The Spanish, having only just driven out their own Mohammedans, named the island Moslems Moros. By 1903, there were about 100,000 Moros, mostly along the coasts of the various islands, leaving the interior to the handful of Negritos whom they chased into the forests. When America took the Philippines, Moros only accounted for 5 percent of the archipelago's population, but they controlled 40 percent of its land area.

The Moslems divided into five general groups: the Maguindanaos of Mindanao's Cotabato Valley; the Yakans of Basilan Island; the Maranaos around Lake Lanao; the Samals of Zamboanga Peninsula; and the Sulus or Joloanos of the Sulu Archipelago and Palawan.[17] Most were sorted into communities of a few hundred to a couple thousand living in fortified villages—cottas—ruled by a chief or dato. (Sulu was a partial exception in that a number of datos pledged at least nominal fealty to a sultan who was also the region's religious leader.)

Orders to American commanders were clear; Washington wanted the province controlled. Roosevelt, in his letter accepting the vice presidential nomination was characteristically to the point. Not controlling the Moros would be equivalent to "granting self-government to an Apache reservation under some local chief."[18] In an effort to comply, General John C. Bates entered into an agreement with the sultan on August 20, 1899, in which he promised the Moros religious freedom and gave the sultan and his datos protection, a limited right to buy guns, and a government salary in return for help with the two problems that most vexed the government in Washington—piracy and slavery.

The Moros were a sea-going people and had made a living for generations by taking what they could from under and on the sea around them. Their predilection for preying on other Filipinos challenged American control, and their stealing from British subjects in Borneo threatened to precipitate an international incident. Moros, morally free to capture and own non-Moslem slaves, preyed on Filipino Christians. Although technically barred from owning other Moslems, they also had a lively market in Moros who, along with their families and descendants, were chattel to unrepaid loans. For an army and nation, many of whose senior officers had fought their own war over slavery, the situation was anathema, but the sultan and the datos, while perfectly willing to take money under the Bates Agreement, had no intention of either stopping their raids or freeing their slaves.

The Moros opposed Aguinaldo and a Christian Filipino government but had no desire to be under American control either. When Taft announced a general amnesty and formation of a civil government, he pointedly excluded the Moro province.[19] Root said, "The establishment of civil government in the Philippines still left a function for the army to perform in the control of the Moros . . . very similar to that which it has long performed in relation to the Indian tribes in the Western part of the United States."[20] The secretary added that, as wards of the state, the Moros would be supervised and controlled just like "denominated domestic dependent Indians."[21] They were not like Spaniards or *insurrectos* or even Aguinaldo's rebels; they were Apaches, and the army and its officers saw them that way. The Philippines were not Cuba and the Moros were not Cubans. By September 1902, Captain John J. Pershing was in the Lake Lanao district inflicting the "severe punishment" demanded by this new "Indian war."

General Adna Chaffee, Wood's former chief of staff and commander of the Philippine division, had concluded that the Moro problem could not be solved by military force alone. Some accommodation would have to be made with local customs and religion, and he thought that could best be done by combining the civil and military governments. Wood was to be the first American to wear both hats in the Moro province.

Governing a recalcitrant Philippine province was a large step down from being pro-consul of Cuba, but Roosevelt promised to make Wood head of the Philippine division if he would take the lesser job on a temporary basis—say six months.[22] Reporters, not believing the general would settle for Mindanao, openly guessed that he was being sent to replace Taft, who was finally to get his cherished Supreme Court seat, a rumor Wood had to deny all the way to the Pacific.

Roosevelt had good reason to get Wood out of Washington; when Nelson Miles retired, Wood became the next brigadier up for promotion, and that required Senate approval which meant public hearings. The president knew Hanna and the Democrats would use the hearings to blast administration performance in Cuba and that his arrogant, short-tempered former governor general would not be the best witness. Wood had jumped past 530 more senior officers when McKinley appointed him brigadier general, but the appointment to major general was in strict order of seniority.[23] To not appoint Wood, Roosevelt would have had to slight his old friend and would have effectively ended any possibility of his commanding the Philippine division. The appointment had to go to Congress, but there was going to be a fight.

Wood arrived in Manila on July 19 and was met by the cutter *Bucky O'Neill* and a contingent of old Rough Riders including Albert Wright, his towering color bearer, and Captain George Curry who was now Manila's chief of police. The day after arriving, Wood called on Taft to assure the governor he was not there to replace him, no matter what the papers said. Wood spent two weeks in Manila visiting with Taft, being briefed on conditions in Mindanao, and catching up on the mail that had preceded him. The last was undoubtedly the least pleasant task— while Wood had been traveling, the storm over his promotion had built and was now blowing a full gale.

In Washington, Estes Rathbone, determined to revenge his Cuban conviction, had formally complained to Platt's Insular Affairs Committee that he had been victimized by false and illegally obtained evidence. When Wood came up for promotion Roosevelt's and Wood's enemies saw their chance. The attacks came in waves from people with whom Wood had crossed swords in Cuba, from political enemies (both his and the president's), and from a military establishment anxious to avenge the insult implicit in the medical officer's meteoric rise. The press—Republican and Democratic—jumped in for both personal and political reasons, and the battle that consumed the next four months was on. To defend himself, the general needed his entire list of friends and political allies as well as all of his wife's diplomacy.

Wood's appointment put Roosevelt in an awkward position. Senator Hanna, chairman of the Republican National Committee, had made no secret of his intention to get revenge for the Rathbone episode. Besides, the erstwhile senator was not at all sure he wanted Roosevelt reelected and was still considering opposing the New York maverick himself. Senator Teller of Colorado, the main beet sugar state, was angry over the Cuban tariff fight and stood staunchly at Hanna's side. On the other hand, Wood had seniority in his favor, had assumed unprecedented responsibility and performed admirably in Cuba, and was popular among the progressives and imperialists who were the heart of Roosevelt's Republican support. Besides, Wood was the president's good friend and would be hurt, angry, and vocal if passed over. The president seldom met a fight he did not like, and he was not going to avoid this one. The politician in Roosevelt, however, knew the battle would be best waged with the mercurial general safely on the other side of the world. When Wood suggested delaying his departure until after the hearings, Roosevelt did everything but help him pack, assuring his friend that the situation would be handled.

General James Wilson, still bitter at having lost the Cuban governorship, joined the fight and brought along the strident, influential *New York Sun*. Wilson convinced the Grand Army of the Republic's civil war veterans that Wood had stepped over a host of their more deserving comrades on his way to promotion. The *Sun* ran a full-page summary of the careers Wood had passed by. The mayor of Boston got into the act, retrieving Wood's records from Boston City Hospital, although the general's opponents ultimately let those indiscretions lie.

Senator Alger told Lou Wood, "I believe, in my soul, the President would rather lose his nomination for the Presidency than fail in the Wood confirmation."[24] Speaking of the general's record in Cuba, Roosevelt told a San Francisco audience:

> He did the kind of government work which should be the undying honor of our people forever. And he came back to what? He came home to be thanked by a few, to be attacked by others—not to their credit—and to have as his real reward the sense that though his work had been done at pecuniary sacrifice to him, that, though the demands upon him had been such as to eat into his private means, yet he has willingly and well done his duty as an American citizen, and reflected honor, fresh honor, upon the uniform of the United States Army.[25]

To Wood, he wrote:

I shall treat what you have done as establishing a claim for which we have not given and cannot give you a sufficient reward and shall hit out as savagely as I know how at those who try to balk your advancement.[26]

Passing through Egypt on the way to Manila, he received a handwritten note from Roosevelt: "The mugwump *Boston Herald* under the lead of Henry Loomis Nelson—a liar—is attacking you more bitterly than ever. The *New York Sun* continues its attack with malignity under the inspiration of General James H. Wilson, whose conduct in this matter has been infamous."[27] The president went on that the *New York Herald* and the *Journal* had spies in Havana looking for anything else they might use against the confirmation. Roosevelt was worried: "If you can by racking your brains think of anything in which they can hang a false accusation send me the answer at once."

Both the president and Wood worried about Brooke and his friends. Wood admitted disagreeing with some of his predecessor's policies, but he assured the president he had always "believed he was an upright and honest man in every way" and that he personally "never had the slightest feeling against him or desire to do other than serve him."[28] No doubt Brooke would have been delighted to have heard that four years earlier. Wood also reminded Roosevelt that had he "not enjoyed the confidence of the administration," he would never have been governor of Cuba.[29] He volunteered to return to Washington for hearings or even a court martial and told Roosevelt he could withdraw the nomination if necessary, but he also reminded him that, if he was not promoted now, it would delay his ascension to commanding general of the army by a decade.

Wood's opponents toyed with creating an in-law scandal. Some of Louise Wood's relatives had come to Havana in search of business opportunities, but nepotism was anathema to Wood, and he pointed his defenders directly to a former Havana engineering officer, who confirmed that he had been specifically instructed to never give the general's relatives any contract if an equivalent service could be obtained elsewhere. Hanna and his allies looked for irregularities in Cuba's finances, but the island's books were scrupulously kept and immaculately clean. Commander Lucien Young, former captain of the port of

Havana, came forward with accusations that Wood had hired detectives to follow him and had hounded him out of his job. Young had come to grief when, after rather too much wine, he had given an after dinner speech critical of Cuba and the Cubans. Wood had, in fact, defended him to Root and Roosevelt so vigorously that the secretary was forced to tell the general he had talked quite enough and that they would let him know their decision in due time. When Young showed up to testify before the Senate, he was so well fortified with "Dutch courage" that his accusations were dismissed out of hand. Young left having secured only one vote against Wood, and that by a senator from his home state.[30]

There was one last weapon in the opposition arsenal, and it was potentially the most damaging. The army establishment resented Wood's Medal of Honor almost as much as his promotions. Wilson testified that he had it on good authority that Wood, far from being a hero of the war in Cuba, had barely gotten through Las Guásimas and then only because Pershing's black troops had kept him from being "badly handled." Moreover, Wilson claimed that Wood had never participated in the Battle of San Juan Hill, having spent the afternoon at the rear "looking for ammunition." Wilson said he had confronted Roosevelt with the accusations, and the former colonel admitted their truth but told the general to keep the conversation secret.[31] Roosevelt told Root the meeting never took place and that Wilson's claims were "a ridiculous untruth," but he wrote Lou Wood that protocol prevented a president becoming involved "in an open question of veracity" with a major general.[32] He did, however, file a confidential denial of the allegation with the war department.[33] The committee sought testimony from three officers known to have been at San Juan with ambiguous results. All agreed Wood had been at Bloody Ford just before noon, but none had seen him again until after the battle. Pershing's support was especially tepid.[34] Finally Roosevelt, though admitting he did not actually see Wood during the charge, said he was quite sure he had been there and the question was effectively settled by J. H. Dorst, who swore to Wood's participation, and Lieutenant Peter Traub, who produced a personal diary verifying Wood's own description of the charge up the south side of Kettle Hill.

By the time formal hearings opened in November, Wood and his wife were tiring. Lou Wood had spent the winter quietly building support for her husband and earning the admiration of much of official

Washington. Chauncey Baker wrote that Mrs. Wood's "close personal relations with the Secretary and with the President, have enabled her to throw certain side lights on this case that would otherwise, perhaps, not have reached their proper parties."[35] James R. Garfield said, "It has indeed been a hard winter for Mrs. Wood, but she has borne herself splendidly, making no mistakes."[36] Wood told Roosevelt, "I have been a good deal worried lest Mrs. Wood would break down under this constant annoyance."[37] The president replied that he had been "very, very sorry for her all this winter,"[38] but that Mrs. Wood was, in fact, doing quite well. The scrutiny was so intense that Wood felt he had to reassure his wife that his record was "absolutely clean."[39] She was smart, strong, politically adept, and managed Washington better than her husband ever could have. The general, on the other hand, spent the winter growing progressively more depressed. He complained to the president, "Unless a man were of a rather philosophical turn of mind, the American Press would make him feel that disinterested public service was to be avoided."[40] In a letter written shortly thereafter, he added, "I am so heartily heartily tired of the systematic campaign of lying and misrepresentation that I feel I made a mistake in coming to the Philippines."[41]

Hearings dragged on through December and, when Congress adjourned for Christmas, Roosevelt took the opportunity to give Wood a recess appointment. The general put on his second star, but the president warned him the fight was "inconceivably bitter" and not yet over.[42] But it was. When they reconvened, the committee voted for Wood's confirmation eight to two. Just as he was warming up for a Senate floor fight, Hanna died unexpectedly, his heart a victim to an excess of passion and good food, and the opposition to both Wood's promotion and Roosevelt's renomination collapsed. By a vote of forty-five to fifteen, Wood got to keep his second star. With an audible sigh of relief Roosevelt wrote, "I have not written you during the four month's conflict, because it really did not seem as if I had the heart to. I could not tell when it would end, and there were months when it appeared as if the result would be very close."[43]

Wood emerged from the confirmation hearings a different man. In Cuba he had been a model administrator, but a year of vicious attacks on his record and his character left him cynical and bitter. If vilification was the reward for his Cuban performance, there was no reason to reproduce that performance in the Philippines. Leonard Wood, the most adroit colonial administrator America had ever had, went to Zamboanga in the Moro province as governor, major general, policeman, and enforcer, but not as nation builder. Hints of Wood's new attitude were evident even before he left Manila. He wrote Roosevelt:

> The Moros at Sulu (especially about the island of Jolo) will, in the opinion of Governor Taft and General Davis, require one severe lesson. I am going to exercise the greatest forbearance and if they do force a fight on us we will attempt to make it such a one as not to require repetition.[44]

The general underestimated the Moros' persistence and overestimated his own forbearance; there would be many lessons and they would be terribly severe.

Wood sent the indefatigable Hugh Scott off to be his governor in Jolo and, on August 6, 1903, came to Zamboanga. The delightful small city sits at the southernmost tip of a peninsula jutting into the Sulu Sea like an outsized right claw of crab-shaped Mindanao. Backed up against steep mountains and washed with a constant sea breeze, it has the finest coastal climate in the Philippines. Wood was assigned the same house in which Spanish Generals Blanco and Weyler had lived during their own futile attempts to civilize the Moros. The house sat between the wharf on one end of the base and an early seventeenth-century fort on the other.

Zamboanga peninsula is a tongue of land several hundred yards wide and just under three miles long with the commandant's house at its tip. From the front of the house, Wood looked up the flat peninsula to rice paddies and foot hills that rose into 4,000-foot mountains. From the back garden wall, he could see Greater and Lesser Santa Cruz Islands and, ten miles off on the southern horizon, Basilan beyond which Jolo, the rest of the Sulus, and British Borneo stretched in a southwestern arc. The grounds were landscaped in tropical flowers, palms, and almond trees that pleasantly contrasted with the Woods' cramped Washington house.

Wood, however, took no time to enjoy his new quarters. On August 8, after tersely writing in his diary, "Major general today," he set sail on his first official inspection of Moroland. Circumnavigation of the province was a 3,000 mile trek, and Wood sighed, "to get around and see things in an eight knot boat, requires time."[45] He started with Lake Lanao in Mindanao's mountainous southern interior, a hotbed of Moro disorder that has persisted to the present. The lake was a volcanic crater in a narrow part of the island near the base of the crab's claw, equidistant from the Mindanao Sea in the north and the Moro Gulf in the south. American soldiers had hacked twenty-mile roads through the forest in each direction and built more or less permanent camps on both sides of the lake. The Spanish had used four gunboats on Lanao to control the obstreperous Moros but had sunk the vessels when they abandoned the island. The lake itself was sixteen miles long, varied from one to twelve miles in width, and was drained by the Agus River cascading through jungle gorges in rainbow-draped waterfalls Wood pragmatically saw as a potential source of electricity.

The land was fertile and supported a population variously estimated between 75,000 and 250,000 in cottas housing from a few hundred to as many as 2,000 souls surrounded by fields of coconuts, hemp, coffee, and betel nuts. Moros in the interior lived by farming and raiding neighboring cottas, had no loyalty to anyone outside their cotta, and fiercely resented outsiders. Wood found the short, wiry, dark-skinned Moros "typical Malay types . . . very hostile and warlike" with "something about them like our Apaches." And that is how he treated them.

Spain had kept 8,000 troops around the lake but, in almost four hundred years, had never controlled the Moros or prevented their pillaging each other and killing any Spaniard foolish enough to be caught alone. The cottas were surrounded by earthworks, moats, and parapets bristling with sharpened bamboo. Most had a single bridge over the moat that opened to a passage just wide enough to admit one man who, if he was unwise enough to force an entry, could be hacked to pieces by kris-wielding defenders. The general spent a week touring the cottas and evaluating their defenses before going back to Zamboanga to catch a boat south to Borneo to call on the British governor.

Wood found the governor's hospitality "as broad as the British Empire and as wet and boundless as the sea."[46] A proper New Englander, he thought warm champagne at 9:00 in the morning a bit much. Wood admitted the British colony was, on the whole, prosperous and efficiently run, but he was put off by the "rather vicious" fact that it was supported by gambling and opium.

On August 19, twelve days after arriving in the Moro province, Wood got down to business; he took fifteen men, a Gatling gun, and a Colt's rapid fire gun and went down into the Sulus after a group of Moros who had the temerity to chase off a customs inspector. Wood found the natives "bitterly hostile . . . rather ugly and suspicious," but appropriately respectful of the Gatling and not anxious to fight. Unable to generate an excuse to discipline the Sulu Moros, he returned to Zamboanga and put together a larger expedition to educate their cousins on Jolo. When Wood got to that island, he summoned a collection of prominent datos and informed them that a "new and very strong country" now owned the islands, would insist on tranquility, and would institute new laws (including a ban on slavery) that the Moros might find disagreeable but would have to obey; any resistance would be "simply suicide."[47] Wood in the Moro provinces was not the same man who had governed Cuba.

There were two more things: the Moros would have to quit raiding Borneo, and attacks by *juramentados* had to stop. *Juramentados* were suicidal Islamic radicals who took their name from their vow (*juramentar* —sp. for to swear an oath) before a Moslem priest to kill a Christian and were promised direct access to paradise if they were killed. The *juramentados* much preferred death to capture considering the dearth of otherworldly rewards in American jails. The preferred weapon was a razor sharp barong capable of bisecting a man with a single swing. One *juramentado* was shot seven times before he cut the leg off a soldier "more smoothly than it could be taken off by a surgeon."[48] The barong could filet pieces off a soldier's chest large enough to expose his beating heart. The *juramentado* dressed in white, put tourniquets on his arms and legs so he would not bleed to death if wounded, and hid in doorways or behind corners waiting for a random victim. At night they would cut tent ropes so, when the canvas collapsed around a sleeping soldier, his outline was visible and he could be sliced up in his cot.[49] Defense was near impossible and fear of the *juramentados* poisoned the American attitude toward Filipinos, in general. Wood decided to go directly after the imams who administered the oaths. He told the datos that they and their priests would be held responsible for the *juramentados'* actions and would be punished as if they had committed those acts themselves.

After the meeting in Jolo, Wood took three companies—two guns, sixty men, forty mules, and eight horses—into the interior to "visit" the Maharajah Indinan, whom the general (without having met him) called "a shifty, slippery fellow . . . insubordinate and treacherous." He surrounded the maharajah's palace just in case his "attitude looked as though he would have to be arrested," but was disappointed again; the Moros still showed no inclination to fight, so Wood pushed on to confront the sultan. That worthy was absent and his brother Raja Muda, acting in place of the leader, claimed illness made it impossible for him to meet the general. Wood sent Scott, a doctor, and 100 men to retrieve the reluctant regent. Scott, informed the leader could not walk because of a boil on the ankle, ordered the Moro's pants leg raised to the ankle, "whereupon the boil jumped to the knee and finally to the crotch."[50] The story changed when the old Moro's entire nether half had been bared and proven free of blemish. He had smallpox and cholera. Scott told him that, if that was the worst he had, he was well enough to meet with General Wood. The Raja loaded himself on the back of a slave and was hauled to meet the American commander.

A week into his Jolo tour, Wood thought he had finally found his battle, but the hostiles, after a brief feint, disappeared into the forest. After marching his men around the beaches and through much of the island's interior without so much as a skirmish, Wood gave up and returned to Zamboanga. He had met virtually every important dato on the island, and none had seen fit to challenge the troops and their Gatling guns. Although he had not actually met the sultan, Wood assured Taft that he was "degenerate, dishonest, tricky, dissipated, and absolutely devoid of principle."[51] He told Roosevelt the sultan was "a rundown, tricky little Oriental degenerate, with half a dozen wives and no children; a state of affairs of which I am sure you thoroughly disapprove."[52] Wood wanted the sultan's and datos' salaries terminated forthwith and a "simple, rather patriarchal government" imposed. He assured Roosevelt that, although slavery would have to be gradually eliminated, the Moro problem was not nearly as serious as they had been led to believe. They certainly had shown no tendency to fight and had deprived Wood of his chance to prove he was a combat commander.

Wood, not having completely forgotten his experience in Cuba, did recommend establishing schools, allowing a degree of local government under the existing chiefs, and creating a constabulary manned by Moros and officered by Americans. But he still wanted to be a fighter and not an administrator. Regarding local government, Wood wrote Senator Francis Cockrell, "as soon as it is in running order, I want to drop it and devote myself to my military work. . . . I had all the administrative work I wanted in Cuba, and I do not know but what it is a misfortune for any officer to take it up. You have the abuse of every shyster in the country whose toes have been trodden on."[53]

After a few days rest, Wood went to Cotabato on Mindanao's east coast, across the Moro Gulf from Zamboanga peninsula. He had been in Zamboanga six weeks and had been in every main district (Lanao, Sulu, and Cotabato) and had found the inhabitants "offish and ugly" but universally unwilling to come out of their cottas and fight. In light of this unexpected tractability, he recommended putting the Moros under general Philippine law since "a Moro has no more right, in his semisavage state, to an independent system of laws than any other of the half civilized tribes, of which Mindanao has a score or more." He also recommended bringing American soldiers to the southern Philippines for mandatory five year rotations, where they could benefit from regular field maneuvers and would be available to "thump a few towns" should the occasion arise.[54]

Early in October, reports of episodic kidnapping and slave raids in the lake district suggested to Wood that there might finally be a chance to "take hold" of the Lanao cottas.[55] He wrote Taft:

> The Moros especially have been maintaining a state of affairs marked by licentiousness, murder, robbery, slavery, piracy, and kidnapping, a condition far exceeding in its crime any which has before come under American control. . . . What is needed, and all that is needed to bring the Moro into line, and to start him ahead is a strong policy and enforcement of the law.

By that he meant American law since the Moro's own laws and customs were "for the greater part rubbish."[56] He told the president, "These Moros will have to be eventually soundly thrashed, especially around Jolo and in the Lanao country. . . . I am prepared to do it whenever it becomes absolutely necessary to do it."[57] Wood, embittered by his congressional ordeal and determined to prove he was a soldier, wanted to prove he was every bit as much Miles the Indian fighter as he had been Cromer the pro-consul.

Dato Priang was the most powerful leader in the Lanao country and had, during the gap between Spanish withdrawal and the American arrival, raided abandoned military blockhouses and armed his followers uncommonly well. He looked like a worthwhile adversary so, late in October, Wood put together yet another expedition. It was the rainy season, and his men slogged twenty miles a day through central Mindanao's swamps contending with vines, snakes, mosquitoes, and five-foot bats. Wood carefully charted each day's march while his men cursed and grumbled. Curious Moros, who had no idea what the blond American was doing, watched from the forest with no intention of confronting him.

Scott rescued the expedition with an urgent message from Jolo. Panglima Hassan, a dato from central Jolo's Crater Lake region, had collected 700 armed followers whom the major suspected were about to attack Jolo Town. Wood marched his men thirty-seven miles in two days ("One of the hardest and roughest marches I have made for a long time") to the coast, commandeered six boats, and took his men to Jolo, stopping at Zamboanga long enough to collect seven companies of infantry, 150 pack animals, three Gatling guns, and 40,000 rounds of ammunition. Although the stop took less than five hours, a number of Wood's weary marchers got roaring drunk and had to be "rather roughly handled."[58] That morning Wood and his tired, hung over expeditionary force sailed for Jolo.

Shortly after landing in Jolo, the American camp was infiltrated by a handful of *juramentados* who were "promptly killed or disabled." They also met their first organized opposition and killed some thirty Moros and wounded a number of others with no American casualties. Scott joined the force later that night with three more companies bringing the total strength to 1,250 men. The next morning Wood set out for Hassan's palace, killing "a very considerable" number of Moros along the way, again without American casualties. Hassan, choosing not to fight, surrendered, escaped, and, in the process, shot Scott's pistol from his hands and cost the American major several fingers. Wood's men swept the area around the palace killing another 150 Moros, but Hassan was gone. Wood wrote, "It has been a very busy day's work and I think has given the Moros a very wholesome lesson."[59] Scott, the only American injured, had two mangled hands.

The next day they killed twenty-seven more Moros and pushed into the jungle after Hassan. Whenever Wood's men came across cottas that "seemed to have hostiles in them," they shelled them. Wood did not differentiate the bodies of men from women and children when he counted them for his official reports, and he never mentioned survivors except to say that he assumed some Moros must have escaped into the jungle. Wood's men had a "pleasant march into Jolo," burning cottas and collecting spears, knives, and copies of the Koran for souvenirs.[60] The official report cited 1,500 Moros killed although Wood reckoned

1,200 or so more likely.[61] Wood lost seventeen men killed and a handful of wounded and was back in Zamboanga by the end of November.[62]

Wood told Roosevelt the Jolo outbreak started with an attack on an American mapping expedition, that he was out numbered two to one, and that he lost only two Americans while killing 400 Moros.[63] In fact, the general did not know about the mapping expedition until after he got to Jolo and the casualty figures are wildly at variance with both the official reports and his own private estimates. As time went on, the numbers continued to drift about and the story changed with the audience. He wrote General Grenville Dodge that the Moros "had to be straightened out" and that "something over 500" were killed at a cost of one American killed and eight wounded.[64]

Wood spent December shooting ducks instead of Moros and doing paperwork. He showed little interest in civil government and no faith in the Moros' capacity to participate in it. He wrote a friend, "The situation here is different from the situation in Cuba. There are whole districts containing many people in which it is impossible to find enough intelligent men to form a civil government. . . . The interior of the island is filled with savage tribes; many live in the trees and others practice human sacrifice and cannibalism. The Moros are treacherous and unreliable, but have one redeeming quality, a certain amount of courage and manliness, out of which we may be able to make something."[65] He thought little of the commission's work, writing Steinhart that "We have a Legislative Council, and are rolling out a municipal code, school laws, anti-slavery laws, etc. etc., in fact a good deal of the old tread mill."[66] Occasionally, a positive thought would surface as in a letter to his English friend J. St. Loe Strachey:

> It is a difficult proposition to establish the kind of government among these Moros which we Americans want, which is, in a way, a government altogether different from the form of government which perhaps suggests itself to Englishmen under similar circumstances. You are quite content to maintain rajahs and sultans and other species of royalty, but we, with our plain ideas of doing things, find these gentlemen outside of our scheme of government, and so have to start at this kind of proposition a little differently. Our policy is to develop individualism among these people and, little by little, teach them to stand upon their own feet independent of petty chieftains. In order to do this, the

chief or headman has to be given some position of more or less authority under the government, but he ceases to have any divine rights.

Root agreed that protection of personal freedom and property rights were natural rights, but, like Wood, he saw no reason to extend Anglo-Saxon imperatives to illiterate island Moslems.[67] He agreed with Wood that the Bates Agreement should be terminated and the Moros brought under general Philippine law.

Late in February reports drifted into Zamboanga that Dato Ali, Priang's son-in-law, was trying to cement a coalition between the Cotabato Moros and those of the lake region. On March 4, 1904, Wood collected five companies of infantry and dismounted cavalry and an artillery battery and started up the Rio Grande River from Cotabato looking for Ali. The Rio Grande estuary was a morass of standing water covered with a mat of floating vegetation thick enough to support small trees but porous enough to drop men, guns, and animals into the twenty-foot-deep liquid muck below. Mosquitoes were so thick the men slept with their faces covered in blankets and smoke, and Wood was afraid the insects would drive them mad. After a brutal two day trek, the troops reached Seranaya cotta, a "well-constructed fort" rumored to hold several thousand Moros. Wood had a 3.2-inch gun dragged up river in a split canoe and spent March 9 "firing into the cotta in a leisurely way."[68] Ali fired back with ancient cannon, but their range, 500 yards less than Wood's artillery was hopelessly inadequate. After two days of shelling, just as Wood was preparing to attack, a white flag appeared on the parapet. When the Americans entered the cotta they found, "many dead and evidences of heavy losses. Many graves, good deal of blood . . . deserted except one wounded man."[69] They captured twenty-one century-old Spanish naval guns mounted on homemade wooden trucks, seventy-two brass lantacas and seven tons of powder, but not Ali.

Wood moved farther up river and took Ali's obese brother Djimbangan, whom the Americans humiliated and nearly killed by bringing him into camp strapped over the back of a carabao that panicked and ran wild when it approached the troops. Ali and his followers escaped, and Wood went back to Zamboanga. He optimistically wrote, "This whole trip will, I believe, have a very good effect on the Moros as Seranaya was supposed to be inaccessible and Ali unbeatable."[70] When he got back, Wood found a cable officially informing him that Congress had finally confirmed his appointment as major general in the regular army. He was to keep his second star.

Within days, word of Wood's shelling at Seranaya cotta reached Manila. Taft sent a sharply critical telegram ordering that Wood refrain from such brutality in the future. Wood wrote the adjutant general in Manila that "recent operations in the Cottabato [sic] Valley were rendered absolutely necessary by repeated hostile acts of Datto Ali." He stretched the truth, adding, "Hostilities were opened by the Moros, who in considerable force attacked the command on the march." Wood promised to "bring about a settlement of this difficulty if possible by peaceful means," and Taft let the matter drop.[71]

Having administered a "thrashing" in Jolo and Cotabato, Wood was left with only the Lake District in need of a lesson. The most disorderly Lanao Moros were in the Taraca district where Pershing had earned first criticism and then promotion for his own brutal attacks. Wood put together sixteen companies of infantry, two troops of dismounted cavalry, and a field artillery battery and embarked on yet another expedition on April 1, 1904. The road was considerably improved since Wood's first trip, and the party was at the lake shore in two days. When they encountered a small group of Moros, they opened fire with shrapnel from 1,800 yards. When the Moros tried to escape in canoes, the Americans opened fire with rifles and left no survivors. After the slaughter, the chaplain addressed the troops, and Wood noted that "He seemed to be filled with the crusading spirit and spoke of the troops being in service in a land of infidels where it had been impossible for the Word of God to be preached in times past. His words seemed to convey the idea that a wholesome disciplining of these people would be approved by him."[72]

Again, as in Jolo and Cotabato, Wood's men went from cotta to cotta, firing from the parapets until there was no sign of life then destroying the structures and everything in them. Wood said, "The people of the valley have been so hostile and intractable for generations that I have decided to go thoroughly over the whole valley, destroying all warlike supplies, and dispersing and destroying every hostile force, and also destroy every cota [sic] where there is the slightest resistance."[73] Only three weeks before, he had promised Taft he would settle the Moro difficulty "by peaceful means."

After three weeks of vengeance, the general returned briefly to Zamboanga before going to Manila to meet his wife. Wood's pleasure at seeing Lou was dampened when he learned that Corbin was to succeed General James Wade as commander of the Philippine division. Roosevelt had promised Wood the job but, after the promotion fight, he was in no mood for another congressional confrontation. The general reacted poorly: "Wrote Mr. Roosevelt a rather long, and, I am afraid, a rather hot letter about it."[74] Roosevelt impatiently reminded his friend that he had just put his reputation and renomination at risk and he should take his second star and go back to Zamboanga. On reflection, Wood admitted that some time with his family in their seaside house might be a good thing.

And the Wood family loved Zamboanga. The boys hunted every day and went on long rides with their father. Luisita (who had been born in Havana four years earlier) learned to swim, and Lou fell in love with the house and grounds. Even the general paused to appreciate Mindanao:

> Great bodies of lotus plants with their enormous pink flowers and floating pads. The whole air is filled with the delicate fragrance, and the sea of pink blossoms, mixed with the green of the rushes and the bronze colored mass of lily pads produces a singularly beautiful effect.[75]

But Dato Ali was still loose and F Company of the 17th Infantry had the misfortune of stumbling upon him in the forest at a cost of two officers and eleven enlisted men. Wood wrote, "I shall go at once to the Cotabato Valley and look into this."[76] Initial attempts to get Ali to surrender were fruitless so Wood led his men and one field gun up the river to Simpetan cotta where Ali was rumored to be hiding. The fugitive was not at Simpetan, but F Company's dead were, hacked up and partially eaten by wild hogs. Wood also found one crazed sergeant and a corporal with a head wound that the Moros had released. They gathered up the remains, burned the enlisted men's corpses (but not the officers') for easier transport, incinerated the cotta, and went back to Zamboanga without having found Ali. Wood agreed with his friend Admiral Folger that "extermination is the only sure method of pacifying the Moro."[77]

A month later, Wood was back in Cotabato where he killed twenty-six Moros but again failed to find Ali. In Jolo, a group of Moros threatened a customs agent, causing the infantry to open fire with a 1-pound gun and a Colt automatic which dispatched twenty-one hostiles. Wood said, "These things are sad, but until the people learn the result of use-less resistance there seems to be no way to handle them but by a deter-mined and prompt use of force."[78] Ali's repeated escapes notwith-standing, Wood's reputation, especially among the American military, was growing. One sailor wrote his father:

> There is only one officer in the Philippines who is feared by the bad Moros, and that is General Leonard Wood, who is run down by a lot of the lazy older officers and people in the Senate who would not know him if they saw him, but who is dearly loved and respected by officers, soldiers and others who come in contact with him personally. He goes out after them himself, takes command himself, and is often to be seen leading an advance column through a swamp or other dan-gerous place. He had subdued lately two of the worst tribes in the Philippines—those of the island of Jolo and the Lake Lanao region of Mindanao. At the first place his report shows, I think, 1500 killed—5000 would be nearer the mark. At Lanao he reports 1000 killed, but I have friends who were with him, and counted that number after two days fighting, which was only one-fourth of the time actually fought.[79]

Scorched earth, destruction, and indiscriminate slaughter of women and children brought undeniable if temporary results. By the summer of 1904, the soldiers of the Moro department settled into gen-eral supervision of the native population by small patrols able to move about the interior unmolested. Piracy and slave raiding nearly stopped, and Moroland was quieter than it had been in half a millennium. Wood and his sons spent the summer reducing the islands' population of wa-terfowl and improving their tennis games. Luke Wright replaced Taft who went to Washington as secretary of state, and the district was so safe that Wood took the new governor on a jaunt up the Cotabato to meet Priang and down to Jolo to visit the sultan. He even took Lou boating on Lake Lanao. Although he occasionally would "have to qui-etly pull some refractory Datto out of his hole," the province was at peace leaving Wood time to dabble in administration. He visited Bilibid prison in Manila and made suggestions for controlling the tuberculosis epidemic among the inmates, and he joined Commissioners Cameron Forbes and Henry Ide in visiting schools and asylums around the cap-ital.

In late fall, Wood had the first indication that his tranquility would not last. On October 26 he wrote in his diary, "Had a nasty turn last night, quite sick for a few hours."[80] The next day he saw the post dentist thinking his teeth might have caused the problem. What he had were seizures caused by the brain tumor that plagued the rest of his life. The episode passed and Wood went back to work, but he suffered increasing weakness in his left side which he tried to exercise out of existence. He spent hours on the rifle range shooting with his uncoordinated left hand and even attempted to prove his fitness by trying out— unsuccessfully—for the division rifle team.

The odd dato, especially on Jolo, still insisted on raiding his neighbors, although most of the problems were handled by intimidation rather than force. Wood cautioned Scott that he had assured Washington Jolo was pacified and they would be harshly criticized if any new unrest surfaced. The general advised his aide to use artillery from a distance to clean up any recalcitrant cotta so as not to risk American casualties. In spite of Wood's warnings, the situation in Jolo deteriorated and, early in May, he took several hundred men and mounted his first large expedition in almost a year. Their first day on the island, Wood's men killed fifty Moros and lost one of their own. The next day, he heard that rebellious dato Perika Utig had attacked Scott and killed three of his men before taking refuge in his cotta. The village was in a valley and Scott had taken a position on a mesa overlooking it. Wood joined him, surrounded the cotta, and reduced it to rubble with a field gun. At 7:30 A.M. the soldiers closed from all sides and overran the village. Seven soldiers were killed, but Wood surmised that most died from friendly fire since virtually all the Moros, along with their women and children, were already dead. Wood excused the deaths by pointing out that the noncombatants refused to surrender, the women were armed, and there were, after all, "very few children."[81] The next day Wood's troops marched to a nearby cotta and again killed "a good many of the defenders."[82] A seaside cotta, threatened by searchlights from two U.S. Navy destroyers, wisely surrendered before Wood quit and went back to Zamboanga.

The Jolo expedition was Wood's last for a long while. In spite of his exercises, the weakness was worse and increasingly frequent seizures rendered his left side limp for hours at a time.[83] A new post surgeon, Dr. William Thornwall Davis, came to Zamboanga late in 1904 and, convinced the symptoms were related to the growing lump on Wood's skull, recommended surgery. The divisional surgeon in Manila agreed with Davis that "there is a bony tumor upon the vault of the cranium, due to an old injury received seven years ago in the line of duty." The surgeons added that Wood required the expertise of a specialist in the United States; they left Manila on May 26.

The Woods stopped briefly in San Francisco to revisit the Presidio and listen to Shafter grouse about Sampson's behavior in Santiago before going on to Chicago and then to Boston where he consulted Drs. Arthur Tracy Cabot and James Jackson Putnam. Putnam had founded the neurology clinic at Massachusetts General Hospital and was Harvard's first professor of neurology. Arthur Cabot was Boston's premier surgeon, had done Massachusetts General's first successful abdominal operation, had built the surgical pathology laboratory with his own funds, and was president of the Massachusetts Medical Society. Unfortunately for Wood, his specialty was urology, not neurosurgery, and he opted to use the private Episcopal hospital at #2 Louisburg Square rather than the better equipped Mass General. There are no notes from the procedure that started at 8:30 on July 7, 1905, but Cabot, not recognizing the nature of the tumor, merely cut out a disc of bone, scraped it, and replaced it. He did not understand that the bone was infiltrated with tumor, and he never saw the tumor lurking beneath the fibrous meningeal membrane over Wood's brain. Cabot removed just enough of the mass to palliate Wood's symptoms, but he left the bulk of the tumor which continued to grow.

Wood spent the day of surgery "thoroughly out from ether," but had no complications. He spent nine days in the hospital before moving to Cabot's country house to continue his convalescence. He had to have a fluid collection in the wound drained ("a rather mean evening") but had an otherwise smooth recovery. In early August, he moved to Cameron Forbes's farm and continued to improve, walking up to seven miles a day, trying a bit of tennis, and taking the time to personally lobby Roosevelt and Senators Aldrich and Kane for Scott's promotion.

Cabot must have known his procedure was incomplete because Roosevelt ordered Wood back to the Philippines by way of London "on business of a confidential nature."[84] The business was a consultation with Sir Victor Horsley, father of British neurosurgery, to determine whether a second operation was necessary. Horsley spent a very long time pushing and probing Wood's head before deciding that, although recovery would likely take three to five years, another operation was unnecessary. Horsley was wrong, but Wood and his wife were delighted and immediately left for Calais.

They spent a month exploring Switzerland and Italy (where they saw Vesuvius erupting from Pompeii) before going east through Suez. On October 9, between the Red Sea and Columbo, Wood noted with satisfaction, "Birthday at sea. Fine weather. 45 years old today."[85] They went through Singapore and Hong Kong and were back in Manila on October 24, where Wood took temporary charge of the Philippine division in lieu of Corbin who was in poor health after a tour of Australia and New Zealand.

The Woods finally got back to Zamboanga and the children on October 27; three days later Wood was off up the Cotabato where, a month earlier, McCoy had run down and killed Ali and three of his sons. Wood could not have been more pleased: "General opinion now of all Moros familiar with the situation is that trouble in the Cotabato Valley is over."[86]

Corbin, sapped by the tropics, wanted Wood transferred to Luzon, but the general, never very good at performing within ear shot of a superior, declined, arguing that he had too much work left with the Moros and wanted to stay in Zamboanga until he actually took charge of the division. Wood's future was a matter of some speculation. He wanted to spend four years in command of the Philippine division and then take the Atlantic division where he could study coastal defense, a plan which he thought would "round out my tour of service so that it will cover pretty much the whole of the United States and its possessions."[87] That rounding out was, of course, in preparation for being general-in-chief. Only Arthur MacArthur still stood in front of Wood on the promotion list, and he had even more political enemies than Wood and would never be the army's commanding general.[88] Wood could afford to be patient.[89]

Wood had been inexcusably brutal in the Moro province, but he had been effective. Slaving and piracy were at an all-time low and coastal commerce was thriving as it never had before. Henry Ide, who replaced Wright as governor general, pronounced Wood's province the most prosperous in the Philippines. Revenues for the third quarter of 1905 were twice what they had been the previous year in spite of abandoning the two main sources of government income—opium and the lottery. The Sulu Moros were paying taxes for the first time in their history. There was more fertile land than people to farm it, and Wood suggested to Roosevelt that he could send any spare southern European immigrants to Mindanao.[90] When William Jennings Bryan and his wife visited the Philippines, Wood showed off the lake region and the Sulu Islands. Bryan was particularly anxious to meet the sultan, although Wood warned him the "palace" would be a disappointment. The general and the sultan later shared a laugh at the politician's expense when a bevy of mischievous boys tipped a wardrobe over on Bryan who thought he had survived a *juramentado* attack.[91]

Corbin never recovered after his Australia trip, and Wood formally assumed command of the division of the Philippines on February 1, 1905. Tasker Bliss succeeded him as military commander in Mindanao although Wood temporarily kept the title of civil governor. The day he took the division, Wood prophetically wrote of the Moro province, "The only serious situation remaining there is the presence of a considerable number of discontented people in the crater and on the slopes of Bud Dajo. These people represent the remnants of all the hostile bands which have been broken up."[92] "These people" came perilously close to ending Wood's career.

But before dealing with the Jolo Moros, Wood's attention was temporarily drawn to a grander issue. Chinese American relations had been tenuous for decades, and the early months of 1906 brought them to crisis level. Railroad construction had slowed and Americans were losing jobs to cheap Chinese labor. Immigration laws were changed to regulate the influx of laborers but, on paper, all other Chinese were still free to enter. In 1882, all immigration of Chinese laborers was suspended for ten years, a ban that was extended in 1894 and made permanent ten years later. Immigration officials used the amended treaty as an excuse to effectively ban all Chinese immigration, and the Chinese responded late in 1905 with a boycott of American imports and revocation of the American concession to build a Canton railroad. Since opening the China market was the putative reason for the Philippine purchase, Roosevelt felt obliged to respond. In the post–Boxer Rebellion climate, response meant armed incursion, and Wood's Philippine division was geographically poised to do the job.

Wood had a long-standing interest in China. He had tried to get Chaffee's job commanding the American contingent in 1902 and, two years later, had told Roosevelt that, if he ever had occasion to send troops to China again, he hoped the president would "give the Army a chance to do the work, which really is its proper work, and if anything is to be increased, let it be the Army and not the Marine Corps."[93] China might yet offer Wood the chance at a career-defining military adventure.

The general was not fond of the Chinese and certainly did not think reinstituting immigration was any sort of answer. He wrote:

> I sincerely hope that no legislation admitting any of Chinese labor into the United States will ever become law. Anyone who has seen the Chinese in the coast cities of China would, rather than see the Pacific coast, or any other portion of the United States, sink into the ocean than covered with these people.[94]

Wood did not want Chinese in the Philippines either. He argued that British colonies that relied on coolie labor were stable only so long as there was a large, well-armed military present. The immigrant laborers had "neither patriotism nor morals" and what revenue they produced came from women, opium, and gambling.[95] As he denigrated the Chinese, Wood pushed for military action, assuring Roosevelt that the boycott and loss of the rail concession had left American businessmen in the Orient feeling hopeless and abandoned, a situation that could only be alleviated by putting all Philippine troops "on a war footing."

Wood proposed to ready 5,000 of his own troops, perhaps augmented with 3,000 of the Philippine Constabulary, to take the forts at the mouth of the Pearl River preparatory to moving upriver to Canton.[96] He went so far as to equip a force of infantry, dismounted cavalry, and engineers with two weeks of rations and 400 rounds of ammunition a man along with a field hospital, 100 bamboo ladders, eight siege guns, twelve howitzers, and six million rounds of ammunition for his Gatling guns and Colt automatics.[97] But, to Wood's disappointment, the beginning of March saw cooler heads prevail; Roosevelt's advisors convinced him to manage the problem diplomatically, and the general's attention turned back to the Philippines.

Bud Dajo is a 2,100-foot extinct volcano rising out of the jungle six miles southeast of Jolo Town. At its lower reaches it is a gentle rise, but, five hundred feet from the summit, it takes on a sixty-degree slope and the last fifty feet to the crater rim are practically vertical. If one does not use one of three trails cut up the sides, the only way to the top is by climbing vines, roots, and tree trunks that hang from the cliff. The crater itself is 100 feet below the rim and about 500 feet in diameter. Bud Dajo's lower slopes and the crater floor are fertile and have an ample supply of water, so anyone taking refuge there could be indefinitely self-sustaining. Wood's last sweep through Jolo had left scores of homeless survivors. Some chose to return to their villages and rebuild, but a few gathered their families, moved into the crater, and replanted their rice, hemp, mangoes, and sweet potatoes on the mountainside. Word of the settlement spread and attracted several hundred more of the island's disaffected Moros.

The Mount Dajo Moros enlarged their farms, sold draft animals to buy rifles, and dug trenches and fortified the crater rim. Their confidence grew with their numbers, and they took to swaggering into neighboring cottas armed and talking about independence. Scott sent Captain James Reeve to investigate in December 1905. Reeve spoke with the datos around the mountain who told him there were about 250 men and 375 women on the mountain who "had gone up there to die, and that they would fight, and further that they would force our hand by committing depredations."[98] The only documented destruction was a raid in which the Dajo tribesmen burned a few huts on Scott's rifle range, and, except for occasional posturing, the Moros posed no real threat to their neighbors or the military. Even Reeve reported that "the greatest danger . . . was not so much from the depredations or raids that the people on Dajo would make, but from the attitude of the entire Moro people."[99]

Wood, however, took the challenge personally: "This is a ridiculous little affair from every standpoint, and should be brought to an end." If Reeve was satisfied that the Moros could not be gotten off then "a couple of columns should take the place some night and clean it up." Wood was quite specific. Something like 100 men with good stamina should sneak up the mountain during the night. When dawn broke, they could open fire from the crater rim and "clean the place out," and Wood wanted to know when the attack was to take place so he could witness it in person.[100]

At first the Dajo Moros said they would leave the mountain as soon as their crops were in, but the harvest came and went and the Moros stayed.[101] Scott still thought he could talk them into leaving the mountain, but Wood had already decided that "affairs in Jolo are in such shape as to require action immediately."[102] On March 3, Wood sent 120 men from Zamboanga to bolster Scott's troops and, four days later, sailed for Jolo himself, proceeding directly to the camp at the base of Mount Dajo. The men were to have climbed the mountain the night before, but the orders were confused and only one of three groups was actually at the rim. Wood, exasperated, ordered the rest of the men up immediately. Surprise had been lost, but Wood still had overwhelming numbers and firepower. Field pieces had been hauled to the top with block and tackle, and gunners were ordered to fire as soon as they could aim directly down into the crater floor and avoid inadvertently shelling their own men on the other side of the mountain. Although one reporter who accompanied the expedition described the mountain as "the most difficult position yet taken in the Philippines,"[103] Wood lost, counting army, navy, and Philippine Constabulary troops, only eighteen killed and fifty-two wounded.[104]

Once the crater rim—defended by a few Moros with rifles, spears, knives, and stones—had been secured, the artillery and automatic guns were hoisted up and mounted and the "cleaning up" commenced. According to Wood, "All the defenders were killed as near as could be counted."[105] He estimated the dead at 600, including women and children, although other estimates ranged as high as 800 or 900. It is hard to arrive at an accurate number of survivors; an eyewitness put the number at seven although later guesses were up to 100.[106] One reporter said no one attempted to escape and added that "toward the last, Moros exposed themselves atop remaining cottas to be shot down, thus committing suicide."[107] Wood censored all telegrams from Jolo to Manila describing the slaughter.

Wood returned to Zamboanga to find a glowing telegram from the president:

> I congratulate you and the officers and men of your command upon the brilliant feat of arms wherein you and they so well upheld the honor of the American flag.[108]

Wood's day, however, ended on a sour note; he got another, less felicitous telegram from the secretary of war. Taft wired:

> It is charged there was wanton slaughter Moros, men, women, and children, in the fight Mount Dajo; wish you would send me at once all the particulars with respect to this matter, stating exact facts.[109]

The reporters, in spite of Wood's censorship, had gotten the word out. The *New York Times* sarcastically headlined:

WOMEN AND CHILDREN KILLED IN MORO BATTLE
PRESIDENT WIRES CONGRATULATIONS TO TROOPS[110]

Wood wrote his own detailed description of the action and had his subordinates do the same, emphasizing the difficulty of the assault and the danger of the rebellious Moros. He had Governor General Henry Ide file an official report calling the news accounts "extremely sensational and, in all essential details, false." Ide, in direct contradiction to every witness who had actually been at Mount Dajo, reported that "Some women and children were killed or wounded by preliminary shelling at a distance," but there had been no "wanton slaughter."[111]

Wood also thought it best to resign his ancillary position as civil governor of the Moro province in favor of Tasker Bliss and did so on March 28. He told the war department he had offered every assistance to the wounded but neglected to say how many of those there were. He also said he left the dead Moros unburied so that residents of surrounding cottas (presumably the ones whom he had just rescued from Dajo Moro "depredations") could bury their coreligionists and "succor such wounded as might be hiding." He claimed that Scott told him they would have to take Mount Dajo by force (untrue) and that he had only decided to attack after personally assessing the situation (also untrue since he dispatched troops three days after he got to Zamboanga and had his entire force mobilized before he ever went to Jolo). He concluded, "This action was unavoidable unless the government decided to give up all attempt to control in the Island of Jolo."[112] The last was an accurate statement of the general's conviction that harsh "discipline" was the only way to manage the Moro province.

To cover the last base, Wood brought a collection of cooperative datos on board his yacht *Sabah* and, using a series of transparently leading questions, pried from each agreement that the massacre rid them of "bad Moros" and was, therefore, a good thing. One chief, when asked if he was glad all his bad people had been "managed," replied with sarcasm that fairly drips off the transcript, "Yes. You killed them." So there would be no shadow of misunderstanding, Wood ended the session with a short lecture:

If you look back, over the last three years, where is Hassan, where is Pala, where is Peruka Utig, and others, and all those men on the hill, what has become of them? They are all dead. And in the future, all the men who made trouble will be dead too. We do not like it, but our orders are to keep peace, and if they make trouble we will have to do it.

What you need now is to have large families to make up for those killed on Dajo. That is the thing, let the children come and take the place of those who are gone. You want now big crops of babies, hemp, rice, and cocoanuts, and no more fighting.[113]

The datos got the message and stayed quiet. The Dajo Moros were dead and could not complain. Neither the soldiers nor the civil government wanted the issue pressed, and Washington accepted Wood's version of events. After a flurry of headlines, the papers let the matter drop, although a few reporters filed it away for future reference.

The islands were once again quiet and Wood turned back to administrative problems. He worked with Commissioner Forbes to form a local bank so Philippine farmers could get low interest loans, and he tried to get agricultural tariffs and investment taxes lowered. Disgusted with the quality of a stream of end-of-career officers relegated to the Philippines, he argued for revamping the whole promotion system to lessen the pervasive influence of the "lock step of seniority without regard to qualifications." Wood thought anyone who had not made captain by age thirty-three, field grade by forty-two, colonel by fifty-two, and general by age sixty ought to be retired. Promotions should be given out two-thirds by selection and only one-third by seniority through the rank of colonel, and "When war comes all inefficient officers must be swept aside and command given to competent men."[114] The general wanted the army's welter of small bases concentrated into large facilities where officers could have the experience of commanding division-size forces. He thought the Philippines, with their large tracts of uninhabited land, would be an ideal training ground, where armies could practice real combat skills instead of "asking a man to take a log of wood across the road, lay it down, pick it up, and bring it back, and keep it up all day.[115] The suggestions languished but foreshadowed reforms to come.

Wood's health was also an issue. Roosevelt, having heard rumors that the tropical climate had "injuriously affected" the general's head, told Wood that he could briefly replace Corbin in command of the division so he would have the post on his record, but he was then to spend some time in Europe where he could be "within striking distance of that English surgeon."[116] When Wood received the letter, he went frantic: "Your letter of January 8th received yesterday gave me a bad scare. I could not imagine who had been telling you stories about my health. I am in excellent condition, so much so that it is a matter of general comment, and so far as I can judge, everything pertaining to the wound has done all that can be expected, far better, indeed, than Horsley predicted."[117] The general admitted only to a "certain amount of cautiousness about butting my head against hard objects or standing on it."[118] For the moment, Roosevelt let the matter drop.

Without question, Wood's greatest struggle as Philippine commander was with his sister service. Shortly after Dewey defeated the Spanish Navy in Manila Bay, the navy's senior officers decided they wanted their primary Philippine base not at the capital, but thirty miles east across the Bataan Peninsula in Subic Bay. Wood and virtually every senior army officer were aghast at the prospect of fortifying and defending two bases, not least because a Subic Bay base and navy yard at Olangopo would cost $30 million, most of which would be diverted from their plans for Manila. Even worse, the land forces at Subic would probably be marines recruited at the expense of the army's already marginal manpower allotment. Typically, Wood went straight to the top; in mid-1904, he wrote the president that fortification of Subic Bay would be "a colossal mistake and one which will be a subject of serious regret and embarrassment in the future."[119] He understood that defense of the Philippines against a determined invader was next to impossible unless the United States controlled the Pacific. He predicted that the navy could not dominate the western ocean for many years since any enemy would be "either an eastern power capable of concentrating her own fleet, or a combination of two of our great European trade rivals," and the United States would have to maintain a presence in the Atlantic as well as keeping ships close to home to protect American coastal cities. The only hope was to make Manila impregnable and able to hold out until the navy could reclaim the Pacific. The problem was that Manila had no defenses to speak of.[120]

The navy, however, was fighting hard both publicly and in private for Subic Bay. Manila Bay was too shallow, a second position of strength would force an enemy to divide its fleet, Subic's narrower entrance was easier to defend against attack from the sea, and, besides, the army only wanted Manila so the officers could be closer to feather beds and Philippine mistresses. Tasker Bliss thought the whole thing was a navy plot to transfer insular defense around the world to the marines.[121] Wood understood that, unless the fleet was defeated and driven into port, there was no real difference between being based at Subic or Manila Bay. More to the point, he was sure Japan was the real risk, and the Japanese islands of southern Formosa were only forty miles north of the Philippines. His small garrison could not stop the Japanese from landing on Luzon (most likely at Lingayen Gulf) and taking Subic Bay and Olangopo from behind. If they were driven from the sea to Manila, the big ships could at least act as fixed batteries and contribute to the capital's defense. In March 1905, in spite of Wood's lobbying, Roosevelt sided with the Navy Board and authorized building a base at Subic Bay. He did, however, grasp the general's arguments and, recognizing that the Philippines were an indefensible Achilles heel, said he wished he could just make them independent.[122]

Wood was one of the few officers who predicted the Japanese would defeat Russia and, in the wake of that victory, he was more convinced than ever that America would be their next target. He urged fortification of Hawaii and fretted over the increasing population of Japanese laborers he was certain had been trained by the imperial army. He knew that, without Hawaii, resupply of the Philippines was hopeless. Japan was busily refitting captured Russian warships and was "now superior to us in the Pacific Ocean, and can take the islands (the Philippines) whenever she wants them."[123] Moreover, Japan was an emerging economic as well as military power. Wood saw the empire as "very anxious to be the New England, or England, of the east. She has unlimited cheap coal and cheap labor, and she will soon be able to manufacture finished products from crude material almost as well as we can."[124]

Even though the decision to base the navy at Subic Bay had been made, Wood refused to give up. The navy might build their base, but it was the army's job to defend it and Wood intransigently took the position that the task was an impossible waste of resources in which he would not participate. Through 1906, relations with Japan deteriorated while Wood hoarded guns, ammunition, and supplies to create a defensible fortress Manila. Laborers in California wanted the exclusion of Chinese extended to Japanese and, in October 1906, the San Francisco School Board, deciding to take its own role in the situation, segregated

Japanese students. Tokyo was outraged. Root, recently appointed secretary of state, knew the United States had no chance of winning a Pacific war until the Panama Canal was complete.[125] Roosevelt was annoyed ("I am bound to say that in the physical sense I don't see where
they [the Philippines] are of any value to us or where they are likely to
be of any value")[126] and was in no mood to be drawn into a war over
where children went to school. On his way to visit the Panama Canal
construction he told Root, "During my absence in Panama I direct you
if necessary to use the armed forces of the United States to protect the
Japanese in any portion of this country."[127] Root exercised his unique
brand of political suasion on the attorney general of California, the
United States district attorney in San Francisco, and the state supreme
court. When he got home, Roosevelt hauled the mayor of San Francisco
and the entire school board to Washington for a quick lesson in civility
and international politics. San Francisco ameliorated the school segre-
gation order and Washington and Tokyo reached a "gentlemen's agreement," whereby Japan voluntarily restricted the issuance of exit permits
for its own citizens, effectively placing a quota on the number that
could come to the United States. The crisis was over, but Wood was no
less concerned about Philippine vulnerability and no more enthusiastic
about defending Subic Bay.

The forest around Subic Bay had never been adequately mapped
and, when army cartographers finally did the job, Wood was more convinced than ever that the spot was indefensible. The area is surrounded
by a ring of hills in a thirty-mile arc that, if taken by an enemy, would
control the entire bay. The hills had no natural water supply and no
roads by which defensive positions could be supplied. Wood finally
agreed to site two 10-inch guns and a few smaller pieces on Grand Island in the bay's mouth and said, if an enemy attacked from land, the
base would just have to be surrendered (as it eventually was). On the
other side of Bataan, he was busy turning Manila into a redoubt. The
city itself would be defended in a fortified perimeter, but the real key
was Corregidor Island in the bay. Protected by two 14-inch, six 12-inch,
and one 10-inch guns; twelve 12-inch mortars; and an arsenal of smaller
ordnance and supplied with materiel originally stockpiled for the
China expedition, Corregidor was meant to withstand a six- to eight-
month siege. The island got its own water system, power plant, and
electric railway. Wood had 900 soldiers and 1,000 convicts work day
and night under gasoline searchlights building housing and fortifica-

tions. In the event of Japanese attack, which Wood predicted would come within no more than seventy-two hours of a declaration of war, the general planned to send American women and children to Mindanao and concentrate his 14,000 troops on the rock in the bay.[128] When the Japanese came, Wood predicted they would do so "in great force and with startling rapidity. . . . the force sent will undoubtedly be large enough to envelope and smother our resistance, absorb and reform the government, and occupy Manila preparatory to meeting such reinforcements as we may have to send to these waters."[129] Perhaps, but they would have a difficult time dislodging the Americans from Corregidor. Wood never really gave up the Subic Bay fight. Right up to the month he left the Philippines, he argued for devoting all available resources to Corregidor, strengthening the Pacific fleet, and defending the Hawaiian Islands.

Wood was plagued with a succession of other problems in the latter part of his tenure, especially on Samar, where the pagan Pulayans of the interior preyed on coastal Christian communities and ultimately required the exertions of 3,000 soldiers and temporary martial law to restore order. There was a brief public uproar when fourteen inmates in Bilibid prison died as a result of visiting scientists mixing vials of plague bacillus with those containing cholera anti-toxin.[130] James Smith succeeded Ide as governor general and, to Wood's acute displeasure, instituted a native Philippine assembly to participate in government. In contrast, Moro province stayed quiet, and Philippine agricultural output increased, the population grew, and the islands were generally peaceful.

The serving general-in-chief was due to retire in 1907, leaving only MacArthur senior to Wood on the promotion list. In January, it was decided that Wood should come home and take the prestigious Eastern division, but, for political reasons, Roosevelt decided his controversial friend should stay out of the country until after the elections. On February 20, 1908, Wood formally turned over command of the Philippine division and, at 3:00 P.M., sailed past his Corregidor fortress on his way home.

9

Washington, D.C., 1908–1917

IN FEBRUARY 1908, Wood and his family left Manila traveling west. Wood wanted to tour Europe, give his sons a short time in continental schools, and—most important—have a look at the British, French, and German military establishments. The general met with the Kaiser and dined with the Crown Prince, but, although he found the German organization impressive, he thought the French superior. Wood wrote, "If the French soldiers can fight as they march, they have the best army in Europe. . . . The discipline is splendid and the order excellent. The French army is in a class by itself and is decidedly ahead of anything we have seen."[1] Clearly, both armies were at a different level than anything the Americans could field. Wood also visited Spain where his old adversaries, mindful of the generous treatment their defeated soldiers had received in Cuba, greeted him as a hero. On November 10, 1908, Leonard Wood assumed command of the Department of the East at Governor's Island in New York harbor.

Wood came from the European maneuvers convinced that the richest nation in the world had to develop an army commensurate with its economic power. He told Roosevelt, "We are not ready. We have not got the necessary artillery, engineer trains, siege trains, etc., etc. 40 per cent of our colonels and 30 per cent of our field officers would be a detriment to our troops in a campaign simply because they were not promoted until their initiative was gone."[2] Worse, the undermanned, superannuated army had virtually no public support.

If the government would not furnish him new men or equipment, Wood was determined to get the most out of what he had. Based on several years spent observing Japan, he concluded that the main threat to the United States lay in its unprotected coastlines. The Japanese had moved several hundred thousand men across the straights to fight Russians in China, and Wood reckoned there were at least five nations capable of landing a force several times as large as the entire

American army in the United States. Although the idea seems quaint in retrospect, an amphibious invasion would, in fact, have been difficult to stop with 25,000 troops and a fourth-rate navy. Wood charted the harbors and beaches along the entire Atlantic coast and conducted training exercises against a hypothetical invasion of New England during the summer of 1909. He tried to organize joint maneuvers with the Massachusetts National Guard but was stopped out of fear that forced marches over sandy coastline might injure the part-time soldiers.

By June of 1909, Wood had become the army's senior general officer and, in December, Taft acceded to Roosevelt's wishes and appointed him commanding general effective the following spring. Before taking up the job, Wood needed to make one more trip abroad and one more trip to the hospital.

Wood's health had steadily deteriorated in Manila. His brain tumor had only been partially resected and, as the part left behind enlarged, it pressed on the underlying brain and caused both progressive left-sided weakness and violent seizures. Wood's limp was impossible to disguise and he lost control of his left arm, a problem especially embarrassing for a man who measured his worth by his physical prowess. Wood understood that leaders and heroes were not allowed the luxury of physical disability, so he hid his weak hand in a pocket and took care that photographs were taken only of his strong side.

The weakness was a bother, but the seizures were a potential disaster. Wood had a nightmare vision of losing consciousness without warning, falling to the ground, and jerking uncontrollably in public. Fortunately, the general's seizures had an aura, a warning before they erupted with full force. The first fits started in 1904 with localized twitching in the left foot. By the following year, they were more generalized and so frequent that Wood carried a bottle of chloroform and a handkerchief in his pocket at all times. At the first sign of twitching, he soaked the cloth with the drug, put it over his nose, and partially anesthetized himself.[3]

The seizures persisted and, by 1909, the chloroform was no longer effective. At Dr. Cabot's suggestion, Wood met Johns Hopkins' brilliant young surgeon Harvey Cushing at a New York hotel in March. Cushing, America's best brain surgeon, recommended immediate reoperation. Wood, however, consulted William Osler, Hopkins' legendary chief of medicine, and S. Weir Mitchell, the Philadelphian who fathered

American neurology. Both doubted that Wood's symptoms came from a tumor and advised against surgery. Wood waited.

But when Taft announced the chief of staff appointment, Wood feared the disability would stand between him and the promotion. In January, he went down to Baltimore under the guise of visiting General Franklin Bell who was a patient at Hopkins (and of whom Wood had never been particularly fond) and managed to "have a little talk" with Cushing while at the hospital.[4] Cushing and Wood agreed it was time for surgery, and the general arranged to come back in early February. Although the planned procedure had rarely been done (and never by Cushing) and was extraordinarily dangerous, Wood went to great lengths to conceal the risk from both his subordinates and his superiors. He wrote the president:

> I spoke to you some time ago about the advisability of having this old wound in my head overhauled before taking up the work under the new detail in Washington. As I have nothing especial to do from now on until the end of February, I have decided to go to Johns Hopkins tomorrow and have Doctor Cushing look the thing over.[5]

On February 4, 1910, Wood took a boat down to Baltimore, checked in at the hospital, and walked to Cushing's house for tea. The next morning at 9:00, the operation commenced. As expected, bleeding was copious and difficult to control. Cushing managed to get the bone over the tumor off but was forced to stop before opening the dural membrane that covered the mass and the brain.[6] Resigned to a second procedure, he closed the wound.

Wood slept through the next day and was "rather disgusted" to learn that he was not done. On February 9, the general was back for another four and a half hours of surgery. When Cushing reopened the skull and peeled back the dura, he first feared the tumor might have invaded the brain but was at last able to find a margin separating it from the normal tissue. This time the bleeding was not so severe and Cushing thought he had gotten the tumor out. Because Wood wanted to be as nearly normal as possible, Cushing replaced the disc of skull he had removed; not yet aware that meningiomas often involve the bone, he had inadvertently guaranteed that the tumor would be back.

Again Wood tolerated the surgery well. The sutures were removed two days after the operation and, by February 19, he was walking around his room. On March 5, he sailed back to New York and spent the next day working. The seizures stopped and, although Wood still limped, the dragging in his leg was noticeably less.[7] Before he left the hospital, Wood found he could once again remove coins from his pocket with his left hand. He wrote Taft, "The results of the stay at Johns Hopkins were very satisfactory, and Dr. Cushing feels that the trouble is at an end and that the leg will be good as new."[8] By mid-July, Wood was back in Washington and ready for his new assignment.

It is impossible to understand Wood's term as chief of staff without stepping back a decade to his mentor Elihu Root's experience as secretary of war. Root had been entirely serious when he told McKinley he was ignorant of military matters, but he was an able student who educated himself immediately on becoming secretary. He spent time with Adjutant General Henry Corbin and an assortment of other officers both junior and senior. The new secretary devoured Spenser Wilkinson's *The Brain of the Army* which had played a key role in British military reforms. He carefully studied the Dodge Commission report on Spanish American War failures and spent hours discussing the findings with the author who was also a personal friend.

Root's real epiphany came when Assistant Adjutant General Major William H. Carter gave him a second-hand copy of Emory Upton's *The Armies of Europe and Asia*. Root moved quickly to Peter Smith Michie's biography of the late Union officer and a frantic search for the unpublished manuscript of Upton's study of the United States Army, incomplete copies of which were circulating among the junior officer corps. Upton had been a protégé of William Tecumseh Sherman and had emerged from the Civil War convinced a great nation needed an army at least large enough both to protect its own territory and to destroy an enemy's home. He visited Germany in 1876 and marveled at the cadre system that could put 400,000 men in the field in eight days and overrun France in less than eight weeks, while it had taken the United States eleven months and $800 million to mobilize against the Confederacy in 1860–61.

For the United States to be a first-rate military power, Upton believed there had to be a corps of regular officers backed by ranks of trained, conscript reserves who could be called up in time of war—an "expansible army." Such an army should be under the direct control of a permanent general staff. Upton actually thought the army should be —as in Prussia—directly under a general-in-chief and the civilian secretary of war's job should be restricted to administration. The general staff, trained in war academies, existed to support the general-in-chief rather than civilian officials. Although Upton's volume on the American army remained unpublished after his suicide in 1881, his ideas were widely accepted among United States junior officers. Uptonianism was a source of considerable malaise since the officers of the miniscule American army were convinced the American public would not tolerate conscription, much less an autonomous standing army.[9] Perhaps the reason the public accepted Mahan's naval militarism and rejected Uptonianism was that the former wanted a navy tailored to his perceived needs of the nation, while the latter wanted a nation tailored to the needs of its army.

Regardless, Root admired Upton's organizational arguments. On Upton's death, the unpublished manuscript had been entrusted to his friend Colonel Henry Algernon Dupont, who delivered part to D. Appleton and Company and consigned the rest to his attic. Root tracked down the various parts, wrote a foreword, and had it published as an official army document under the suggestive title *The Military Policy of the United States*. Root said the book "gave me the detail in which I could base recommendations and overcame my ignorance as a civilian."[10]

Upton's idea of a large standing reserve and a powerful chief general were politically out of the question, but his proposed administrative structure formed the basis of Root's reorganization of the army. One of Root's first acts as secretary was to establish the War College under General William Ludlow, who had also admired Wilkinson's book and studied the Prussian general staff system.[11]

One of Root's primary goals was to bring the nearly autonomous bureau chiefs under a general staff and, in a signal departure from Upton's conception, replace the commanding general of the army with a chief of staff responsible directly to the secretary and, through him, to the president. That brought him directly up against Wood's old commander Nelson Miles, who haughtily contended that any good general should be able to plan his own campaign and mount it with no outside interference. Root, the logical, progressive lawyer, saw war not as an exercise in individual enterprise and heroism but rather as a business proposition to be broken down to component jobs supervised by trained specialists. Miles and opponents of the general staff argued— with an irony surely not lost on the secretary—that the experts would come to know so much that they would threaten the government.

In his annual report for 1903, the secretary wrote, "Our system makes no adequate provision for the brain which every army must have to work successfully. Common experience has shown that this cannot be furnished by any single man without assistants, and that it requires a body of officers working together under the direction of a chief of staff and entirely independent of the administrative staff of the army."[12] Root proposed replacing the commanding general with a Chief of Staff to the President arguing that "It will be perceived that we are here providing for civilian control over the military arm, but for civilian control to be exercised through a single military expert of high rank." The ranking officer would be backed by a staff of specialists and would be chosen not by seniority but rather by the secretary of war who could pick someone with whom he could work well.

Miles, however, was a formidable enemy with a long and occasionally distinguished career and an impressive collection of political supporters. He had considered running for the presidency seriously enough to approach Theodore Roosevelt as a potential running mate, an offer the New Yorker dismissed as ridiculous. Miles kept a grand office separated from Root's by the length of a hall and he was determined to maintain an even greater separation in their powers. He earned the secretary's wrath by giving reporters confidential war department plans with which he disagreed. When Roosevelt became president, Miles whispered—in a none too quiet voice—that the colonel had never actually been at San Juan Hill. When he publicly interfered in a dispute between Admirals Schley and Sampson over the naval battle at Santiago, Roosevelt had enough. He announced that "no criticism of his administration from him or any other officer of the army" would be tolerated.[13] It was time for the commanding general's relationship to the presidency to be clarified.

It was politically impossible to fire Miles, but when he reached retirement age on August 8, 1903, Root summarily transferred him to retired status without a word of congratulations or thanks. Then he abolished the office of commanding general and instituted a general staff with Wood's old commander S. B. M. Young as the first chief of staff. It took six more years before anyone actually took on the bureaus and implemented the rest of Root's reforms. Young and his successors Adna Chaffee and Franklin Bell did little to actualize the changes, but Wood was different. He had neither formal military education nor a particularly military mindset. He was (as his time in Cuba and the Philippines had proven) a better administrator than warrior. Even though he was not from the West Point–trained hierarchy and had not followed the prescribed career path, his intelligence and work ethic were generally respected. Henry Corbin grudgingly admitted:

> I have never ceased to say (Wood's promotion to general) was utterly wrong in principle, but I also say that in this lone instance the man was eminently worthy. . . . Wood was a soldier and a scholar. Then in the Philippines when I was in command, he attended to his duties all day and studied military history and science all but a few hours at night. He has made good and is becoming a scholar of the first rank.[14]

When Wood took his new office in midsummer of 1910, he found the general staff a disorganized, demoralized bureaucracy unsure of its importance and with no idea of its role. The staff was divided into three divisions whose structural inconsistency was exemplified by the fact that the War College and coastal defense were under the same office. Since the bureaus held the purse strings and issued virtually all operational orders, the line officers assumed they made the decisions. The general staff had been reduced to issuing reams of reports and memoranda most of which no one read. A typical seven-page report signed by both the chief of staff and the secretary of war concluded, "It is therefore recommended that no toilet paper be issued."[15]

If there was one talent Wood could bring to the office it was his penchant for efficiency. He replaced the old divisions with four new ones: mobile affairs, coast artillery, militia affairs, and the War College. He put an assistant chief of staff over each division and told the assistants to make routine decisions themselves and to refrain from producing lengthy studies and memoranda. In his annual report for 1911, Henry Stimson estimated Wood's reforms had saved the army $245,000 in useless paperwork alone.[16]

Unfortunately, reducing paperwork was not the most difficult of Wood's problems. The army remained scattered in "hitching post" forts around half the states and all the territories. The crippling inefficiency of that arrangement became painfully evident in March 1911 when unrest bubbled up on the Mexican border. Porfirio Díaz, the seventy-nine-year-old who had ruled Mexico as a virtual dictator for over three decades, was in trouble. His reelection to successive six-year terms as president had always been a formality, but, in recent years, he had ceded some of his power to a group of young technocrats, who had proven profoundly unpopular with both Mexico's impoverished majority and its restive professionals and land-owning elites. The latter had induced Francisco I. Madero, scion of a family of ancient Coahuilan *hacendados*, to run against Díaz, and, when Madero lost the 1910 election, they started an insurrection.

Within a month ripples from the revolution reached Wood in the form of complaints that the Maderist rebels were being armed from Presidio, Texas (a complaint that, given the historically free movement of weapons across the border, was entirely likely).[17] Wood ordered his department commanders in California and Texas to patrol the border, but the United States Army could only muster ten troops of cavalry to oversee 840 miles of frontier.[18] By June 1911, the haggard troops had marched or ridden 31,382 miles up and down the Rio Grande maintaining a blockade that was, at best, porous.[19] Wood, having soldiered in Arizona, understood.

Mexico had a growing army and a long, virtually undefended border crossed at regular intervals by bridges and rail lines that offered a worrisome potential invasion route to the Mississippi and the nation's midsection. Both Germany and Japan had, in the early years of the century, toyed with building naval bases in Baja California. As long as Díaz and his stable, tractable government were in power, the danger was minimal, but there was a deep reservoir of anti-American sentiment among the Mexican people that threatened to break free when the Porfirístas were no longer in control. Mexicans were still alive who remembered losing half their country in the 1845 war, and the spirit of revanche was alive and well. Díaz had encouraged foreign investment, and the lion's share of Mexico's productive land and resources lay in external (especially American) hands.

Wood and the administration realized that the Mexican revolution could easily involve the United States. On February 12, 1911, Wood asked the secretary to define conditions under which American troops could be allowed to cross into Mexico and specifically whether they could cross to protect American lives and property. Recognizing that American forces on the border were laughably inadequate, the secretary advised that General Tasker Bliss (now commanding general of the Department of the South) should "have his troops ready in case they should be required," but he was under no circumstances to cross the border without a direct order.[20]

The commander at Fort Bliss outside El Paso wrote Wood that the weather was unseasonably cold with mixed rain, snow, and sleet and that the arms smugglers had reopened secret trails formally used in the cross-border opium trade to supply both Mexican federal troops and the insurgents in the battle for Ciudad Juarez just across the river. The colonel wryly noted that thirty-mile forced marches at 3:00 A.M. were "good practice" that kept his men and animals from being bored.[21] When they did happen to catch a smuggler and turned him over to American authorities, sympathetic lawmen, judges, and juries almost always freed them.[22]

When the Maderistas took Ciudad Juarez in February, Díaz's days were numbered. Ambassador Henry Lane Wilson came to Washington to meet with Taft and the cabinet, and the *New York Sun* reported that the Mexicans were about to form a military alliance with Japan and invade Texas and California. The rumor had been initiated by a German military attaché and may have been intended to precipitate an American incursion into Mexico, but the reality was ominous enough without jingoistic magnification. There were more armed Mexicans south of the Rio Grande than armed Americans north of it, and if the Mexicans ever tired of killing each other, there seemed to be a real possibility they might cross the river.

On March 6, Taft called Wood away from lunch and ordered him to move "as many soldiers as possible" to the border. Therein lay a problem. Wood had been unsuccessful in getting his "hitching post" forts consolidated. He might be able to find 20,000 men to send to Texas, but they were dispersed in company-sized units without coordinated logistics or command. Getting them rounded up and moved was a gargantuan task with no hope of quick completion. After meeting with Taft and Secretary of War Jacob Dickinson, Wood instructed his department generals (Crozier, Aleshire, and Allen) to order men to Texas on "maneuvers" and to say nothing of the actual purpose. The euphemism gave rise to the unit's official title of Maneuver Division, although it hardly took a strategic genius to recognize that moving two-thirds of our regular army to Texas had more than a casual relation to Mexico's revolution.

For all the inconvenience, Wood was thrilled that his generals would actually get to command an entire division. He put the unit under Major General William H. Carter, the military intellectual who, although instrumental in helping Root reorganize the army, was woefully inexperienced in actual command. His three brigadiers were "none of them very efficient officers," but they were the best Wood had.[23] The Maneuver Division's beginnings were inauspicious and they did not get much better. The men collected at eleven different depots around the country, and it took three months to get them all to San Antonio. Even then, many of the units were only at half strength and the whole division was shot through with green recruits. European military observers who converged on Texas saw a hapless conglomeration fielded by the world's premier industrial power. Wood was frankly embarrassed.

Taft, on the other hand, was oblivious. Less than a week into the fiasco he congratulated Wood on "the success of the mobilization to date." He warned his chief of staff that Díaz was "in a volcano," and predicted his government would fall and leave forty thousand American lives and over $1 billion American dollars at risk. The president, however, promised he would never send troops across the border without specific congressional authorization, although a display of American strength might "hold up the hands of the existing government" and "have a healthy moral effect to prevent attacks upon Americans and their property in any subsequent general internecine strife." He encouraged Wood to use the opportunity to train his Maneuver Division to a high standard but only so long as he could move, house, equip, and train it without exceeding his usual budget. Wood was also to avoid conflict with the prickly Texas locals and was to see to it that "the most modern methods"—whatever those might have been—were used for "stomping out" any epidemics.[24] Wood was also instructed to "prevent the use of our borderland for the campaign of the insurrection." Taft had given the Mexican ambassador his word on the last point. The president concluded that he would be "greatly disappointed" if the mobilization "resulted in any injury or disaster to our forces from any cause." Taft allowed that he had "taken a good deal of responsibility" in mobilizing the force and he left no doubt that Wood would get the blame if everything did not come out perfectly.[25]

Wood answered that the men would get typhoid inoculations and the camps would be kept clean and disciplined, but he begged permission to continue the deployment into fiscal 1912 so he could use some of that year's money for transportation. For the rest, the president's wishes would "be carried out in letter and spirit" to the best of his ability.[26]

International reaction to the mobilization was predictably negative. On March 29, Wood dined at a table next to that occupied by Secretary

Dickinson and the British ambassador who let the general know in clear terms that putting American troops on the border was an annoyance, and he left no doubt of his government's disdain for the unilaterally declared Monroe Doctrine. For his part, Wood favored issuing a simple statement that the troops were deployed to protect both Americans and Europeans and sending a blunt message to the Mexican government and the insurrectionists that the United States was "not going to stand for any nonsense or any action which would render it necessary for foreign Governments to intervene to protect the rights of their citizens." Wood thought America should not only stand by the Monroe Doctrine but also Roosevelt's Corollary to that doctrine. Taft disagreed; Wood's mobilization was simply for "maneuvers."[27]

Wood was disgusted with the administration's waffling, but he no longer occupied the privileged position he had enjoyed with Roosevelt and was never entirely trusted by either Taft or his State Department. Military planning in 1911 was the purview of the War College, and General W. W. Wotherspoon who commanded the college, complained that, although the State Department had consuls in at least fifteen Mexican cities, he had been given no copies of their dispatches, making it "manifestly impossible to keep accurate track of the situation."[28] Wood, who had for a decade been blessed with exceptional access to presidents, got his first bitter taste of being an outsider.

Meanwhile, Díaz's situation was deteriorating. Madero had moved his headquarters and several thousand troops to Casas Grandes, a railroad town 250 miles southwest of Ciudad Juarez, and was collecting rolling stock to move his army north. The Bank of Juarez, expecting the worst, moved its records and assets across the border to El Paso.[29] Díaz was holding his own around Mexico City and in parts of Baja California and Sonora, but everywhere else the tide was running with the rebels. Díaz shuffled men from one hot spot to another knowing that he would lose control of the abandoned territory before the dust settled behind them. When he tried to enlarge his army, no one would join.[30] Anti-American action along the border was becoming increasingly bothersome. American-owned mines had been shut down, and fighting was dangerously close to the border.[31] When insurrectionists fought Federals in Aguaprietes, two Americans were killed and eleven (including several children) were wounded by stray bullets that flew across the border into Douglas, Arizona. At some points, the skirmish lines came within ten feet of the border, forcing Wood to ask that the Mexicans fire parallel to the river.[32] One local official parked a string of box cars on track running along the border as a protective barricade.[33]

Wood's old Arizona compatriot Britton Davis, who had lived and worked in northern Mexico for fifteen years, encouraged the general to intervene and promised support from citizens of Chihuahua, Sonora, and Sinaloa if the Americans would cross the border.[34] Whether such support would have actually materialized is highly uncertain, but Wood was intrigued. The whole thing was rendered moot when the insurrectionists and Federals at Juarez declared an armistice on April 22. It was just as well. The Maneuver Division remained poorly trained, undermanned, underequipped, and mired in a muddy San Antonio spring. Wood wrote, "our division was only a skeleton, our regiments were less than half strength and had to be filled up entirely with green recruits. While everybody clapped and said: 'How beautiful!' to those of us who looked behind the scenes it was clearly apparent that the real expression should have been: 'How little!'"[35] Wood wanted to divert funds from administration to operations so he could keep the army's only real division in the field for a few weeks longer, even if they only marched around in Texas, but frugality prevailed and the Maneuver Division was dispersed back to its various forts.

In the wake of the Maneuver Division debacle, Wood and Henry Stimson went to work. The forty-three-year-old Stimson had become secretary of war in May 1911, giving Wood an ally with whom he could implement Root's reforms. Wood's career had been a series of serendipitous one-on-one relationships with politically connected superiors—Lawton, Miles, Roosevelt, Root, and now Stimson. Like Root, Stimson was an eastern attorney with a wide network of illustrious friends and allies. Like Roosevelt and Wood, he loved the outdoors and found the military lifestyle admirable and attractive. He and Wood got along and the army benefited from the symbiosis.

Wood's omnivorous mind and unbounded energy extended beyond problems of organization. He read incessantly and fretted continually over problems of men and materiel. When he visited bases in California, Wood watched tests of airplanes and was impressed at their ability to fly in harsh weather over any terrain. He was convinced their usefulness had been established "beyond any doubt"[36] and pushed for an army budget of $1 million for aeronautics to include purchase of twenty airplanes.[37] Wood met with a General Electric chemist who brought a new metal "of great density, of the hardness of steel, as well as the strength of steel" and a melting point of 3,000 degrees centigrade that had been developed for lamp filaments but might also be used for small, high density, high velocity projectiles and to line cannon and rifle barrels. After the meeting, General Electric donated the technology for producing tungsten to the army.[38]

Wood's interest was not all in high technology. He harbored an anachronistic affection for cavalry and bemoaned the fact that his horsemen were only being trained in the walk and slow trot and were neglecting the rapid gaits necessary to a proper charge. On the other hand, he complained that his infantry was being taught to dig trenches too shallow to protect against artillery fired in a high arc from 6,000 yards.

Wood also had strong (and nontraditional) feelings about how the army's enlisted personnel should be treated, views that were generally resented by the West Point martinets. Although the army's pay and allowances were the world's highest, soldiers were seldom treated with respect by civilians or even by their own officers.[39] The general thought inappropriately harsh discipline originated at West Point, and he demanded that the superintendent "handle these boys as human beings."[40] Wood found the high rate of courts martial "unintelligent and pernicious" and good only for creating demoralized convicts.[41] He dispatched the judge advocate general to Leavenworth to see for himself the damage done by "military justice."[42]

On a broader level, Wood and Stimson saw two fundamental areas in which the army had to change. The service needed more men and fewer bases. It would have been hard to find two more politically charged topics. When Stimson became secretary of war, the army had 75,000 officers and men scattered in forty-nine posts over twenty-four states and territories spending "endless days of peace with tasks of carpentry and landscape gardening."[43] The largest tactical unit was the regiment, and at the rate field gun ammunition was being acquired it would be 1960 before there would be enough to actually fight a war. One brigadier general of thirty years experience commanded a brigade for the first time in his career during the hapless Maneuver Division episode. It was just as well since he marched his men to exhaustion in their first field exercise.

And that was in a world where Great Britain had sent 400,000 men to South Africa, Russia and Japan had mobilized 1 million men each, and military Cassandras were guessing that France, Germany, or Japan could each put together an amphibious force of 300,000 men to invade the United States if they wished.[44] Wood said, "If modern war emphasizes any one thing above another, it is that resources of all kinds must be promptly available and organized. Mere numbers, untrained, unorganized and under equipped, mean little; no wolf was ever frightened by the size of a flock of sheep."[45] The useless National Guard had to be replaced by a properly trained reserve force and the regular army had to be converted to well-organized large units.

Stimson and Wood first took on the issue of base consolidation by sponsoring and contributing to a series of articles in the *Independent* that unfavorably compared the military to a well-run civilian enterprise. Stimson then sent a formal study to Congress recommending immediate closure of eighteen bases and progressive elimination of seven more. Many of the targeted facilities were in the Republican West, and Taft was besieged by irate congressmen including Senator Frances Warren, who warned that Wyoming would turn Democrat if its fort was closed. Root (now a senator from New York) and Taft warned Wood and Stimson to be careful, and even Wood's old friend Hugh Scott thought the push for closures a "tactical blunder," adding that the secretary and the general were being "undiplomatic and impolitic" in promoting the plan.[46] Ultimately, the attempt failed and provided a weakness Wood's enemies later exploited. Wood told James Harbord, "we are pretty well shackled and tied down by the haphazard manner in which our posts have been built. In other words, it is hard to get rid of them."[47]

Enlarging the army proved even more difficult than consolidating it. Wood understood that the American public would not tolerate a standing army on the European scale. He agreed with the Uptonians that an untrained militia was militarily useless and publicly derided the "overweening confidence of the people in what they delight to call their undeveloped resource," but he refused to sink into the despair that permeated the officer corps.[48] He was convinced—in a typically progressive way—that being a soldier was a job like any other and that a bright high school graduate could learn that job within six months, especially if he was treated with respect and educated rather than exploited. Look at how his Rough Riders had performed with only six weeks training. Besides, Wood was himself a citizen soldier. He initially campaigned for a ten year enlistment with two years of active duty and eight years in the reserve, where a man's only obligation would be to keep the government informed of his whereabouts and to report when called.[49] He later modified that to three years active service and seven years in the reserve with three eight-day periods of training. The general reckoned that would give the nation 280,000 men ready to fight on short notice.[50] The shorter term of enlistment would also keep the army young and enthusiastic. If a brief period of military service was viewed as an obligation of citizenship and the price of suffrage, the country would have better citizens and a pool of trained soldiers. However, shortening the term of enlistment and closing bases directly encroached on the prerogatives of the most entrenched and most powerful of the army's traditional bureaucracies—the office of the adjutant general.

Major General Fred Crayton Ainsworth started his career in Arizona Territory as a contract military surgeon where he and Wood first met at Fort Whipple. It is odd that two men who started their careers at the same time and place and who shared so many of the same assets and flaws would diverge about as far as was possible in the confines of the United States Army. Neither wanted to remain in the medical corps, but, while Wood finally managed transfer to a line commission, Ainsworth took refuge in the bureaucracy. Ainsworth started his career in the bureaus when he was given charge of the Records and Pension Office, a rather more important post than the name implies. It was there that members of Congress came to take care of veterans from their home districts. The office had a well-deserved reputation for inefficiency, and powerful legislators were routinely forced to wait months to answer queries from anxious constituents. Ainsworth was a born efficiency expert. He was also power hungry and intolerably self-important, but he reorganized the pension files and turned around congressional requests in hours instead of weeks.

Ainsworth's ability to manage masses of paper earned him a web of powerful supporters and promotion to adjutant general. In his 1903 reforms, Elihu Root separated military operations from administration with the first under the general staff and the second under the bureaus at the top of which sat the adjutant general's office. Although he theoretically was subordinate to the chief of staff, Ainsworth encouraged the generally held view that his office was independent and the most powerful in the army.

In the struggle for military primacy, the bureaus had several advantages over the general staff. Perhaps the card that trumped all the others was that Root's reforms carefully defined the bureaus' powers and responsibilities but were maddeningly unclear about those of the general staff. Because they sited bases and awarded contracts, the bureau chiefs were in a unique position to make allies in Congress. Besides, they spent money in the present while the general staff only planned what would be spent in the future.[51] Almost equally important was the fact that the general staff rotated every four years while bureau positions were sinecures that some officers had occupied for thirty years.

Ainsworth intuitively understood the advantages of his position and deftly exploited them. Since 1903, there had been an ongoing battle between the adjutant general and the chief of staff as to who should have the office next to the secretary of war. When Wood came, Ainsworth had that spot and was not about to give it up. When a request came to the bureau that could be approved, the good news went out over Ainsworth's signature. Requests that were rejected were passed down to subordinates for signature. Stimson called the adjutant general "a master of paperwork and politics" who "regarded himself as the high priest of Army administration."[52]

Although Wood and Ainsworth had never been close, they had enjoyed an amicable relationship, Wood having been Ainsworth's house guest and having often used him as a source of Washington rumors. When Elting Hanna told Wood it was widely speculated that he and Ainsworth could never work together, Wood assured him he planned to get along with the bureau chief "if it was humanly possible to do so."[53] Samuel Eliot Morison said of Wood, "To his new duties and aspirations, he brought a clear, if narrow, intelligence, a toughness of spirit, and one knows not what further ambitions."[54] Those who knew and had watched Wood and Ainsworth were justifiably pessimistic.

When Wood came to the capital on January 26, 1910, he spent his first night as Ainsworth's house guest, staying up until 1:00 A.M. "talking over the situation in Washington."[55] The adjutant general was "most cordial" and promised "to cooperate in every way and to the best of his ability," although Wood felt a twinge of uneasiness when Ainsworth suggested transferring control of peacetime coastal defenses from the general staff to the bureaus.[56]

Through the spring and summer of 1910, Wood and Ainsworth surprised the doubters with their ability to work together. Wood concentrated on bringing the militia under the general staff and on lobbying Congress to remedy the sad deficiency of usable field artillery and left the bureaus to themselves. The peace broke in the fall over a paperwork issue. Ainsworth had habitually intercepted all mail to the chief of staff's office and often acted without Wood's approval and often without his knowledge. In October, Wood had "a long talk" with his adjutant general who harbored "a good many mistaken ideas about the way we are doing work," but optimistically added that he thought Ainsworth would ultimately prove tractable and seemed "anxious to be of assistance."[57]

The situation deteriorated in December when Taft—undoubtedly at the secretary of war's behest—summarily instructed that all bureau chiefs "avoid any interference in legislation," an order the meddling Ainsworth was unlikely to obey.[58] A week later Wood issued a formal directive that "all orders, instructions, and information emanating from the War Department will be issued through the Office of the Chief of Staff."[59] Later that month, Wood went personally to the secretary of war to complain about Ainsworth's interference in West Point appointments.[60] In a second memorandum, Wood wrote Ainsworth:

> The Secretary of War directs that you submit without delay recommendations looking to the simplification and reduction of official correspondence and a reduction in the number and frequency of returns, reports, etc. and to the doing away with all returns and reports which you do not consider necessary. In brief, to a radical reduction in the amount of the paperwork of the army, which it is believed is unnecessarily large, intricate and cumbersome.[61]

The "returns"—the post and service records—were the foundation of the adjutant general's power and he was not going to tolerate the chief of staff meddling with them. Worse, Wood began meetings concerning "the question of depts., their location, character, and amount of supplies to be carried, etc.,"[62] and made a formal recommendation that the army's clerical staff, most of whom worked for Ainsworth, be decreased by 15 percent. That precipitated an all out war.

On February 11, Ainsworth stormed Wood's office. A good portion of the line officers harbored no great affection for either former surgeon, and one bemused veteran suggested, "Let the two doctors fight it out. They will use more strategy and have more war than in the field."[63] Wood sniffed that Ainsworth "made a lot of foolish statements, a lot of which were undignified and unfounded in fact." He icily informed the adjutant that his bureau would be like any other part of the army—subordinate to the chief of staff.

Before week's end, Wood was patrolling the halls of Congress soliciting support from Ainsworth's own bailiwick. The contest remained in uneasy stalemate until May 1911, when Taft named Henry Stimson secretary of war. Stimson and Wood had an immediate affinity, and, within a matter of weeks, they were riding and hunting together.

Wood decided it was time to get rid of the adjutant. When Taft asked how things were going in the war department, Wood told him "it was impossible to do anything with Ainsworth" and suggested "the advisability of his being sent off, wither to inspect his recruiting stations and later assigned to a Department, or wholly retired."[64] The adjutant general, however, still had too many powerful friends to be unceremoniously shunted out of Washington. He arranged to have a bill consolidating the general staff, the adjutant general's office, and the inspector general's office introduced. That arrangement would have resulted in overall command going to the senior general in the army—Ainsworth. The attempt failed, and Wood was more convinced than ever that Ainsworth had to go.

Working with Stimson, Wood formed the Cleveland Board of Efficiency and Economy to implement his paperwork memorandum. Since Ainsworth's bureau was responsible for the lion's share of the army's paperwork, Stimson and Wood appointed him president of the commission, but gave him Elting Hanna as secretary. Hanna recommended combining Ainsworth's cherished muster rolls with command returns and payroll lists that were collected by other bureaus. The majority of the committee voted against the change, but Wood ordered further study.

Meanwhile, the chief of staff was poaching on another of the adjutant general's most prized prerogatives. Ainsworth's bureau had heretofore enjoyed free rein in appointing officers to highly prized recruiting posts. Wood could not entirely strip the adjutant general's office of that patronage plum so he gave Ainsworth a short list of potential appointees from which he was ordered to choose. When the adjutant general angrily objected, Wood wrote a private note to Stimson accusing Ainsworth of manifesting a "mental attitude entirely inconsistent with a harmonious conduct of affairs in the Department," although he later thought better of having made an accusation so direct as to require an official response and, in a handwritten postscript, added, "Please don't let my remarks disturb you. I do not mean active hostilities."[65] Perhaps not, but three days later he sent an official memorandum reminding the secretary of war that, by law, the adjutant general was his subordinate and accusing him of "gross insubordination and discourtesy" and of "lack of that high character and soldierly spirit which should be the distinguishing qualities of any officer holding the important position of the Adjutant General."[66] For the time being, Stimson chose not to respond, but the situation was coming to a head.

In December, Wood officially recommended combining all rolls into a new "descriptive list" and formally requested Ainsworth's opinion of the change. The adjutant general, recognizing a trap, kept silent. After four weeks Wood repeated his request and was again met with stony silence. Three weeks later he fired off a third, bluntly worded request, and this time Ainsworth responded. In a disastrously intemperate letter, he said the plan could only have been conceived by "incompetent amateurs" with a "complete lack of knowledge" about the army. The scheme was "unmindful," "uninformed," and was "a mere subterfuge of a kind that would be scorned by honorable men."

Wood had baited Ainsworth into a career-ending mistake. He hand delivered Ainsworth's note to Stimson who called Judge Advocate General Enoch Crowder to prepare a court martial. Stimson got Taft's and Root's support, relieved Ainsworth, and prepared to go to trial.[67] Realizing that he was beaten, Ainsworth got his friend Senator Frances Warren to ask Taft for a quiet retirement. The president agreed, and, five days later, Wood summoned the remaining bureau chiefs and informed them that, henceforth, "any correspondence with members of Congress or committees, embodying expressions of opinion concerning legislation or recommendations, or reports embodying opinions, would be transmitted only after they had been presented . . . through me."[68]

Wood won the battle, but the war was not quite over. Ainsworth's congressional supporters saw his ouster as a direct attack on their authority and, not incidentally, their access to the military pork barrel. A formal congressional investigation spearheaded by Hay concluded that Ainsworth had been the victim of a "Dreyfus-like" conspiracy. On a more practical level, the 1912 Army Appropriations Bill turned into a direct slap at Wood. It lengthened rather than shortened enlistments and effectively eliminated Wood's cherished reserve by making it an unpaid voluntary option. The bill also consolidated the quartermaster, subsistence, and pay corps under a chief from the bureaus and it insinuated thirteen officers from the adjutant general's office into Wood's general staff. The Senate introduced an amendment barring anyone who had not served ten years in the line below the rank of brigadier general from being chief of staff. Root said the provision "could not better accomplish its purpose (of removing Wood) if it read that after the 5th of March no man whose initials are LW shall be chief of staff."[69] Senator Warren sponsored those amendments. Not coincidentally, Pershing, who Wood had come to distrust and who stood to rise if Wood fell, was the senator's son-in-law. Warren offered to remove all the riders if Taft would fire Wood, and the president, heartily sick of his temperamental chief of staff, seriously considered the offer until Root and Stimson convinced him that assent would erode the power of the presidency. On June 14, 1912, the bill passed the House 162–4. Taft threatened to veto the bill after it went to conference, even though a veto would leave the government unable to meet its military payroll. Finally, under presidential pressure, the Wood rider was removed, enlistments were shortened, and the bill passed. Root called in a number of political favors to save the chief of staff and wryly observed that his job would have been easier if Wood had slightly more "ability not to make enemies."[70]

In the end, Wood beat Ainsworth on his own bureaucratic turf, but did not help his reputation with either his peers or the public. Archie Butt summed up the prevailing opinion: "Wood is never at his heart's ease as long as he holds one, not greater, but as great as himself. This is his weakness."[71]

Having lost the battle to create a large trained reserve but not the conviction that America needed a credible army, Wood decided to change tactics, but first he had to cope with the 1912 election. Trouble came when his old friend Roosevelt decided to run on the Progressive (Bullmoose) ticket against Taft. Wood went to the White House on August 11 where Stimson and the president explained the situation and, in what Wood said was "the best speech I think he has ever made," Taft denounced Roosevelt and promised a "strong stand against socialism" and a "vigorous campaign."[72] As it turned out, Roosevelt split the Republican vote and Wood was under a Democratic president for the first time since Grover Cleveland.

The chief of staff served at the pleasure of the president, and Wood reminded incoming Secretary of War Lindley Garrison on March 5,

1913, that, by law, his job was over the day after Woodrow Wilson was inaugurated. However, he did not actually resign: "Under the provision, I have the honor to request instruction."[73]

Wilson thought soldiers should be seldom seen and never heard, and Wood, besides being adamantly Republican, was both visible and vocal. The new president's plan to get the chief of staff as far from Washington as possible was delayed for two reasons. Hugh Scott's brother was an old Princeton associate and Wilson liked Scott's soft-spoken deference. He invited Wood's former aide to New Jersey to discuss military matters, and Scott told the president-elect removing Wood would be a boon to the military old guard and a blow to Stimson's reforms. Besides, Garrison and Wood had proven unexpectedly compatible and the new secretary also supported the general so Wilson let Wood stay for the time being.

Even though Wood kept his job, there was little hope that Wilson would allow either expansion of the regular army or creation of a ready reserve. The solution came to Wood from retired cavalry officer and Cornell professor Henry Bull, who suggested that college men might be persuaded to attend voluntary four- to five-week summer training camps run by regular army personnel. Wood wrote a number of college and university presidents describing the scheme and was able to get sixty-three students from twenty-nine schools to a camp in Monterey and another 159 from sixty-one schools to a second camp in Gettysburg. Wood personally chose the staff officers to be in charge and assigned a regiment of infantry, a troop of cavalry, a company of artillery, and a battery of field artillery to the camps. The students were given a crash introduction to close order drill, the manual of arms, and field problems. Wood was under no illusions about turning college students into soldiers in a month, but he was convinced he could get them interested in the military.

That fall he gave speeches at Harvard, Yale, Princeton, Lehigh, and Catholic University. The stiff, humorless general was wildly popular, perhaps because he typified the active, athletic life style that was in vogue. Whatever the reason, his popularity ensured the camp program's success and convinced Wood of his ability as a public speaker. In the summer of 1914, he attracted 600 students to four camps even though the students had to pay all their own expenses. The summer camps reinforced Wood's conviction that motivated, intelligent civilians could learn to be soldiers quickly and, when he finished his tour as chief of staff and returned to the Department of the East, he devoted the bulk of his time to expanding the program.

But before that, Mexico had again become a problem. On May 11, 1911, Díaz had agreed to leave Mexico in the hands of an interim government headed by former ambassador to the United States Francisco León de la Barra pending new elections. That November, Francisco Madero was elected president. The Coahuilan *hacendado* might have gotten past the fact that American Ambassador Henry Wilson detested him, but he could not survive the animosity of his fellow insurrectionists. Emiliano Zapata continued the revolution in the central Mexican state of Morelos while Pascual Orozco fought on with a smaller force on the Rio Grande. Revolutions are poor respecters of borders, and within a month the governor of Texas was pounding on the commanding general of Texas's desk demanding Orozco's men be kept south of the Rio Grande. When the general took the complaint to Wood, he was brusquely reminded that he worked for the federal government not the State of Texas and his instructions would come from Washington, not Austin.[74]

By February 1913, the fighting approached Juarez and the border and Wood proposed occupying a strip of land in northern Mexico to insulate Texas and Arizona from the fighting. Both the secretary of war and the secretary of state summarily refused, although nervous border state governors convinced the state department to write Madero demanding security for United States citizens and interests either in or adjacent to Mexico. Taft summoned the Mexican ambassador and told him conditions in Mexico had reached a point that he might call a special session of Congress and ask for "instructions."[75] Taft's threat of war was unrealistic since, after disbanding the Maneuver Division, Wood could not have assembled a force much larger than a cavalry troop.

In October, the chief of staff made a personal visit to the border to get an idea of what it would take to back up the president's threat. Over the winter the situation deteriorated. On February 11, Wood was awakened in the middle of the night and ordered to the White House to meet with Taft, the secretaries of war, navy, and state and with his navy counterpart Admiral Bradley Fiske. Porfirio Díaz's nephew Felix had been released from prison and had joined General Victoriano Huerta and a good part of the Mexican army in an anti-Madero uprising. Fighting in Mexico City had already cost three American lives. Wood was not told that Ambassador Wilson was actively colluding with the bullet-headed, drunken Huerta, but he was told to put a brigade of infantry on alert and to start quiet inquiries into hiring transports to move troops south. The navy was so small it could not even move the miniscule American army without civilian help. Wood snorted that no troops whatever could be mobilized in less than two months no matter how dire the situation.[76]

Huerta temporarily solved the dilemma. On February 17, he placed Madero under arrest in the National Palace and named himself interim president. Wood pressed Secretary of State Philander Knox to assure the Mexicans that America was not planning to intervene. Should Huerta attack Americans, the army would be helpless until the men could be collected from the nation's scattered posts.[77]

On February 22, while they were being moved from the National Palace to the national prison, Madero and Vice President José Maria Piro Suárez were assassinated. Wood contemptuously wrote, "The usual Mexican way of doing things. It shows the character of the people very clearly. Huerta, the President's commander, betrays and captures him, becomes president and a party to the murder of Madero. The whole situation is rotten."[78] He had no idea his own country's ambassador helped plan the coup.

Governor Oscar Colquitt was gathering the Texas militia at Brownsville and threatening to unilaterally cross the border to protect his state's interests. Under the guise of protecting American interests, Wood sent the Fourteenth Cavalry to Brownsville to control the bombastic Texans. In April, he went to Texas himself. From Brownsville ("a quiet stupid little town without much of interest")[79] he went west through Laredo and Eagle Pass promising civilians they would be safe.

Wilson's inauguration that spring left Wood completely isolated from the policymakers for the first time since 1898. Wilson possessed a Calvinist's moral clarity but only a cloudy view of how to translate those convictions into foreign policy. He led the world's richest nation and harbored visceral dislike for Huerta, but had an inexperienced army smaller than Mexico's. Wood's opinion of Huerta was no higher than Wilson's. He thought the Mexican government "thoroughly corrupt" and its leader "a pure Indian type . . . treacherous and . . . cruel."[80]

Huerta's grip on the Mexican government was proving no stronger than his predecessor's; Zapata was in rebellion in the south and Maderist Venustiano Carranza had raised a Constitutionalist banner and resumed fighting in the north. In spite of the resistance, business interests—especially European ones—saw in Huerta the possibility of a return to Porfirian stability, and sixteen countries formally recognized his regime. Although the United Kingdom was initially one of those that recognized Huerta, the United States bought a change of heart by granting British ships free Panama Canal passage. Loss of British support closed the doors of European banks, and, unable to borrow money or make debt payments, Huerta foundered. The country slipped into chaos and European creditors pressed their governments to intervene, an option the Americans and their Monroe Doctrine could not tolerate. Wood, his patience sorely tested by Wilson's waffling, wrote, "The English press, or a good deal of it, is condemning its own government. . . . One thing is quite evident, and that is that both the Germans and the English are getting ready to take some action in Mexico unless we do something."[81]

At the end of October, Wilson finally told Wood to formulate a plan for intervention. Harking back to previous invasions, the general proposed landing marines and navy "blue jackets" at Vera Cruz. While the navy secured the port, a reinforced army brigade would take the rail line to Mexico City. The initial brigade would then mount a lightning attack on the capital and hold it until a reinforcing division could be collected and landed. The alternative of a land invasion across the Rio Grande was estimated to require eight divisions of cavalry, infantry, and support, almost all of which would have to come from unreliable militias and the National Guard.[82]

In any event, troops would have to be stationed along the entire border to keep Mexicans from coming north. Wood did not believe Wilson intended to invade Mexico and had no idea what the president actually intended to do. On November 4, he read in the *Washington Post* that Wilson had demanded that Huerta leave office, but the regular army was not large enough to enforce an ultimatum, the militia was forbidden by statute from operating outside the United States, and no provision had been made to raise a volunteer army. Wood checked with George Fiske, but he had heard nothing from the president either. Senator Chamberlain of the Military Affairs Committee was similarly in the dark. Wilson was threatening war with Mexico, and neither Congress nor the military were informed, much less prepared.[83]

Wood begged Dickinson to stress "the vital importance of advanced information of the intention to intervene being furnished to the military arm of the Government at the earliest possible moment, once the policy of intervention is decided upon."[84] The general added that he had to have at least fifteen days warning before any formal notice of intention to intervene, and that would only allow him to mount the bare bones Vera Cruz plan.

Wood tried to get information from the head of the state department's Latin American division, but even he was "unable to secure expression of opinion from his chief."[85] The general was reduced to nervously perusing a history of Mexico for scraps of tactical information. Dickinson, also in the dark, proposed fortifying Panama, withdrawing from Mexico, lifting the arms embargo on the rebels, and letting the various parties "fight it out."[86] Wood objected, convinced Europe would intervene if the United States stepped aside. As an alternative he suggested enlisting the ABC Powers (Argentina, Brazil, and Chile) to mediate between Huerta and Carranza and organize elections. If the elections failed, then America could intervene.

Still the administration drifted. On November 21, Wood met with Assistant Secretary of the Navy Franklin Roosevelt and Admiral Fiske. Roosevelt had heard that Wilson was considering taking Tuxpam and Tampico (where some 16 million barrels of oil were stored) in spite of the fact that the navy had no maps of the coasts or harbors and no troops to support such an invasion.[87] Over the next three weeks, Secretary of the Navy Josephus Daniels collected a few thousand marines in Pensacola in the event Huerta was ousted and American lives were threatened. Wood was totally bypassed and fumed that the back door cooperation between the navy and the White House was underhanded, inefficient, and dangerous.[88]

The situation simmered until April 1914 when a shore party from the USS *Dolphin* landed in Tampico looking for supplies. Mexican officials, wary of American sailors, jailed the men. Although a protest secured their prompt release, Admiral Henry Mayo, demonstrating more belligerence than intelligence, demanded a formal apology and a twenty-one-gun salute. Huerta, after sardonically asking why the United States was demanding military honors from a government they did not recognize, declined. Wilson was in a corner. With a European war on the horizon, the British foreign office was nervous about oil supplies, and the English owners of Mexican oil fields were pushing for intervention. Mayo had made American intervention an affair of national honor. The domestic press was in a jingoistic mood reminiscent of 1898. The *New York World* said:

> The best way to deal with Huerta is to supplant his authority with the authority of Maj. Gen. Leonard Wood. The sooner Gen. Wood is in the City of Mexico, where he can begin the administrative work of substituting government for anarchy throughout a distracted country, the better it will be for most of the people in Mexico and for all the people in the United States.[89]

In a similar vein, the London *Spectator* said:

> A man like General Wood is a man to whom any government might commit the charge of Mexico with complete confidence and the proud knowledge that in his acts the honour of his country would be jealously saved and increased.[90]

On April 22, Wood's term as chief of staff expired and he was given "supreme command" of an army to invade Mexico as soon as such a force might be assembled (although Secretary of War Garrison declined to guess when that might be).[91] Pershing and young Douglas MacArthur begged to be included in the invasion. Wilson had not wanted to give Wood the command, but he was the only serving general with any field experience and was the army's ranking officer. After the Tampico incident, the navy had occupied Vera Cruz with the loss of nineteen American and 126 Mexican lives. They closed the port and stopped a German transport carrying arms to Huerta, although the Germans merely unloaded the cargo farther down the coast. The Americans set up shop in Vera Cruz where they would stay until the end of 1914. The occupation of the coastal city was the final blow for Huerta who, in July 1914, decamped for Spain, leaving the government to Carranza and the Constitutionalists. Unfortunately for the new regime, Zapata continued the insurrection in Morelos and Francisco "Pancho" Villa did the same on the Rio Grande while the nation as a whole drifted into starvation, disease, and chaos.

Villa and Zapata met at Aguascalientes at the end of 1914 and agreed to continue their revolution against Carranza. Unrest continued along the border through 1914, as Wilson and Secretary of State William

Jennings Bryan (whom Wood dismissed as "flabby and wabbly") waffled about extending the intervention. Wood did move Pershing and his brigade to El Paso and, on July 10, 1914, returned to Governor's Island for a second stint in command of the Division of the East.

In October 1914, with an eye toward the war that had broken out in Europe, Henry Cabot Lodge's son-in-law, Massachusetts Congressman Augustus P. Gardiner, introduced a resolution calling for formal investigation into whether the United States was ready for a war. Wilson, like the majority of Americans, had no wish to be part of the European conflict, but Wood and a coterie of eastern businessmen and intellectuals were sure war was coming and were aggressively promoting preparedness. In December, Secretary of State Bryan said, "The President knows that if this country needed a million men, and needed them in a day, the call would go out at sunrise and the sun would go down on a million men in arms."[92] Wood dismissed the secretary as "an ass of the first class."[93] As a direct response to Wood's outspokenness, Wilson instructed the war department to order that "Officers of the Army will refrain, until further orders, from giving out for publication any interview, statement, discussion, or article on the military situation in the United States or abroad, as expression of their views on this subject is prejudicial to the best interests of the service.[94] Less than two weeks later, Wood publicly quoted Revolutionary War hero Light Horse Harry Lee: "A government is the murderer of its people which sends them to the field uninformed and untaught . . . these fake humanitarians who recommend that we shall turn the youth of this country into the battlefield unprepared are the unconscious slayers of their people." Wilson demanded he be censured, but Garrison made sure the rebuke was mild and Wood stayed on the stump. Between August 1914 and August 1915, the general gave sixty major speeches—always in uniform—every one of which opposed his president's foreign policy, and he became the most visible member of the militarist American Defense Society and the National Security League.

Wood was censured a second time for using his office to promote the American Legion (not the current organization of the same name) which compiled names and addresses of veterans who would serve if needed. Roosevelt and his four sons had headed the list, and the Legion was headquartered in one of Wood's Division of the East buildings on Governor's Island.

Public opinion moved in Wood's direction with the sinking of the *Lusitania* in May 1915, and the general pressed his campaign. Pleased with the college summer camps, Wood expanded the effort at Plattsburg Barracks in upstate New York and geared it to professionals and businessmen that might become the heart of an expanded officer corps when the United States joined the war. Encouraged by Grenville Clark, a New York businessman and partner in Elihu Root's law firm, Wood organized a thirty-day camp for August that drew 1,200 volunteers.

The openly militarist Plattsburg camp was certain to irritate the pacifist president and conflict was not long in coming. Wood's invitation for Wilson to address the volunteers brought a secretary's terse response that the president "cannot come, pressure business." Roosevelt, Clark, and former ambassador to France Robert Bacon—all dedicated anglophilic or francophilic hawks—were glad to fill in. Roosevelt came, talked, and got the movement and the general in trouble. The former president, who delighted in referring to Wilson as that "infernal skunk in the White House,"[95] was unlikely to be diplomatic and he did not disappoint. He showed up on August 25 in full Rough Rider regalia and railed against anyone who wanted to "Chinafy" the country with hyphenated Americans. He sneered at "professional pacifists, poltroons, and college sissies" who advocated peace at any price. Wood tried to get Roosevelt to temper his speech, but there was no mistaking the reference when the old colonel skinned back his teeth and attacked any man who would "treat elocution as a substitute for action" and went on that "to rely on high sounding words unbacked by deeds is proof of a mind that dwells only in a realm of shadow and shame." In an impromptu interview at the Plattsburg railroad station, Roosevelt said:

> I wish to make one comment on the statement frequently made that we must stand by the president. I heartily subscribe to this on condition, only on the condition, that it is followed by the statement, "so long as the president stands by the country."[96]

Wood's assessment that he had "gone hard for the powers that be" was a monumental understatement and hardly presaged the damage the speech would ultimately do the general.[97]

Wood spent a week playing soldier with his businessmen before returning to New York. On the way he stopped in Boston to address the convention of his fellow *Mayflower* descendants and be elected the organization's national governor. When he went through Washington, he found a scathing letter from Garrison. Wood tersely responded, "Your telegram received," but Roosevelt saw no reason for contrition. He told reporters:

> If the administration had displayed one-tenth of the spirit and energy in holding Germany and Mexico to account for the murder of American men, women, and children that it is now displaying in the endeavor to prevent our people from being taught the need of preparation to prevent repetition of such murders in the future, it would be rendering a service to the people of this country.[98]

Through the summer of 1915, Wilson had actually been edging toward preparedness. He accepted the idea of gradual enlargement of the navy to parity with Great Britain by 1925 and agreed to Garrison's plan for a 140,000-man army backed by a 400,000-man reserve, but Wood was already conceptually well past those numbers. In testimony before the Senate Military Affairs Committee, he called for mandatory universal military service.[99] He told the committee, "We have never in our entire service waged single handed war with a first class country, and we have not the slightest conception of what war would mean with an organized and prepared nation."[100] In his best Social Darwinist mode, he wrote L. S. Rowe that "The suppression of war or struggles is about as difficult as to effectually neutralize the influence of gravitation or to revise the general laws which govern all things, naturally the survival of the fittest."[101] Wood proclaimed:

> The professional pacifist, the advocate of un-preparedness and non resistance, is the most dangerous of our citizens. He is essentially respectable. He is like the well-dressed and well-groomed typhoid carrier, as he goes about, poisoning the very life of the people.[102]

He called intentional failure to prepare for war "brutal . . . cowardly . . . sinister."[103]

Spurred by conviction that America would soon be in the war and energized by the unexpectedly enthusiastic response to his college and camp speeches, Wood became a whirlwind of oratorical activity through that fall and winter. He worked with Charles Schwab to ready plans for national mobilization and with Bernard Baruch (who later headed the War Industries Board) to organize the nation's transportation and supplies. He met with the president of the Delaware and Hudson Railroad to discuss coordinating America's rail traffic. From his New York base, he took every advantage of his popularity as a public speaker. In July 1916, he told Frank McCoy he reckoned he had given 156 speeches to about 137,000 people since the previous November.

Responding to Wood's and Roosevelt's popularity, public anger over German submarine warfare, and an upcoming election, Wilson embarked on a cross-country tour with the paradoxical paired message of pride in keeping the country out of war and the need for preparedness. Garrison proposed increasing the regular army to 230,000 with a reserve under federal control—the Continental Army—to bring a usable force of 500,000 backed by a third tier of National Guard. Wilson endorsed the plan after decreasing the planned regular army to 142,000 before Wood's old nemesis John Hay and House Majority Leader Claude Kitchin of North Carolina surfaced. Kitchin and the Southern Democrats did not trust a large national army and loved their state militias. Hay hated anything associated with Wood and still had Ainsworth whispering in his ear. He proposed eliminating the Continental Army and placing the National Guard under nominal federal control. Wilson sided with the two representatives and Garrison resigned in protest.

Congress went on to pass the 1916 National Defense Act, which increased the regular army to 175,000 over five years and increased the National Guard to 400,000 and paid it from the federal treasury. The bill also provided funds for more summer camps, an Officers Reserve Corps, and a college Reserve Officers Training Corps. Ainsworth got Hay to insert language stating that the general staff could serve only an administrative function and that no more than half the general staff junior officers could serve in Washington, but Garrison's successor Newton Baker summarily rejected the stipulation: "The Chief of Staff speaking in the name of the Secretary of War, will coordinate and supervise the various bureaus, officers, and departments of the War Department."[104]

The bill ignored the issue of universal service in favor of voluntary enlistment favored by Wilson and left the nation leaning on the slender reed of an ill-trained National Guard. Indeed, when Wilson tried to call up the Guard for service on the Mexican border, he was only able to muster 100,000 men, many of whom had to be physically disqualified.

Wood correctly reckoned the public would view the weak bill as a solution and told Roosevelt it was "one of the most iniquitous bits of legislation ever placed in the statute books."[105] In testimony before the
House, he called the bill "a menace to public safety" and "a raid on the
federal treasury" and "dangerous to a degree exceeding anything ever
attempted in legislation in this country."[106]

A frustrated Wood toyed with going beyond speeches and congressional testimony. In March 1916, he met with Bacon, Root, Lodge, and
Roosevelt. Roosevelt, still angry at Root for supporting Taft in 1912, rec-
onciled with his fellow New Yorker so they could deal with the upcoming Chicago Republican Convention. When Roosevelt, Lodge, and Augustus Gardiner met with a *Chicago Tribune* reporter the next day, the
former president said he was prepared to support a man

> who has indomitable courage, who believes fervently in the ideals of
> Americanism, who interprets America in forms of nationalism, and
> who believes that in a democracy every citizen owes his first duty to
> the state, and that it is necessary for the best interests and greatest hap-
> piness of the whole people that individual liberty shall at times be sub-
> servient to the greater cause of national liberty.[107]

The *Tribune* (and the general) thought Roosevelt was referring to Wood
when in fact he was describing himself.[108] The Progressives and the Republicans were to meet simultaneously in Chicago, and the plotters dispatched sculptor Gutzon Borglum (later responsible for Mount Rush-
more and the Confederate Memorial at Stone Mountain, Georgia) to
campaign for Roosevelt until the nomination looked impossible at
which point Wood's name would be offered.

The Progressives readily accepted a Roosevelt candidacy, but the
Republicans demurred. Roosevelt then proposed Wood and the party
again declined and nominated Charles Evans Hughes who went on to
lose resoundingly to Wilson. Through the spring and summer of 1916,
trouble was again brewing in Mexico and Hugh Scott, now chief of staff,
proposed putting Wood in charge of an invasion force. Wilson, in a har-
binger of things to come, opted for Pershing instead.

In the summer of 1916, there were ten more "Plattsburg" camps
with 16,000 participants, and May saw a gargantuan New York City
preparedness parade led by Mrs. Roosevelt. Wood stood next to Mayor
John Purfoy Mitchell and saluted 200 bands and 125,683 marchers in

what the *New York Times* called "the greatest civilian marching demonstration in the history of the world." Under searchlights at 9:30 at night, after Wood had stood at attention for eleven hours, the last field gun pulled in front of the general, wheeled, and fired.[109]

Wilson was now well and truly tired of his political general and decided to get him away from New York City's high profile venues. He had Baker divide Wood's Department of the East into three parts: the Department of the Northeast in Boston, the Department of the East at Governor's Island, and the Department of the Southeast at Charleston. Wood was offered the choice of Charleston, Hawaii, or Manila. Realizing that Wilson wanted him on the other side of the world, Wood took Charleston.

On April 2, while Wood was packing to leave Governor's Island, Wilson declared war on Germany. It should have been the zenith of Wood's career; he had spent three years predicting the United States would be in the war, urging the people to get ready, and castigating the government for its failure to prepare, always expecting the army would be his to command.

It is difficult to reconstruct the exact sequence of events by which John J. Pershing was chosen instead to lead the American Expeditionary Force. Wilson, not wanting to look as if he had shelved his senior general for purely political reasons, let Secretary of War Newton Baker take the responsibility. General Peyton March, who spent most of the war as Wilson's chief of staff, recalled that Wood was the only serving general with a national and international reputation when the United States came into the war and was the obvious choice for command in Europe. Pershing, although older than Wood, was, in seniority, the most junior major general. According to March, Baker based the decision on Wood's physical condition: "Wood . . . had a sham battle for my benefit and walked with me up a little mountain top to get a place to view the battle. While walking up there he panted and labored so obviously that I came to the conclusion that his health was bad, and when I later came to make the decision between Pershing and Wood, that recollection influenced the choice."[110] Baker later said that the choice came down to Wood or Pershing and, had he not taken the second, he would have sent the first. He also claimed the choice was entirely his and uninfluenced by Wilson.[111]

Baker's assumption of sole responsibility is unlikely on the face of it, and support for Wilson's having actually made the decision comes from Senator John Parker, the 1916 Progressive vice presidential candidate. At Roosevelt's behest, Parker approached Wilson in May 1917 for permission to raise a volunteer regiment with Wood in command and Roosevelt as "the most junior brigadier general." Wilson listened for thirty-five minutes before curtly informing Parker that Roosevelt was too old and Wood was not going to France in command of any kind of division under any circumstances whatever.[112]

Charleston began what an aide called one of the most trying periods of Wood's career.[113] When Pershing was given the European command, Wood choked back his anger and remained silent.[114] He still hoped Pershing would repay him for the many times he had promoted the junior general's career, even though he privately thought Pershing had been unnecessarily brutal in the Philippines, inefficient in Mexico, and unconscionable in his sexual escapades.

Wood's hopes were in vain. Before he had fully settled in Charleston, he received a telegram from the War Department asking whether he would prefer to stay in Charleston with its eleven army camps or take command of a single training camp in Kansas—a further demotion. He took the Kansas job and, a few days later, the war department stripped the department commanders of virtually all their power.[115] Had he stayed in Charleston, Wood would have been without any command at all. By August 1917, Wood, convinced he had been the target of a conspiracy, was on his way to Camp Funston.

10

Camp Funston, 1917–1920

WOOD WENT to Camp Funston on the Fort Riley Reservation convinced he had been targeted by Wilson, Baker, and the regular army hierarchy including Scott and Bliss and equally sure the British, the French, and the American people wanted him in France. The huge reservation was under a colonel and Wood asked for overall command of the base. Baker had the adjutant general inform Wood that he was in command of the Eighty-ninth training division only. When the first batch of drafted farmers arrived on September 5, Camp Funston lacked tents, barracks, blankets, and even uniforms. The 5,500 rifles stored on the base had been shipped to another training division. Wood bought 5,000 blue denim work suits so the men could dress alike, cut wooden staves to substitute for rifles, and put legs on barrels to imitate horses.

The camp was on a flood plain that turned into a black, gummy morass that swallowed cars to their axles and men and horses to their bellies when it rained. Wood called it "a death trap" of infectious disease, and, in October, meningitis swept through the camp.[1] Wood's division surgeon recommended abandoning the camp altogether, but the general quarantined the ill and the epidemic faded of its own accord. Camp Funston had, however, not seen the last of its wartime epidemics.

Kept out of France and denied what he needed to train his men, Wood railed against the administration and the general staff for mismanaging the war. As George Creel (Wilson's propaganda chief) trumpeted America's contribution to the war, Wood pointed out that the country was producing only 750 rifles a year that could fire American standard ammunition and the United States had yet to build a single military aircraft. He never understood that being right confers no license to be righteous.

In October 1917, the commanding generals of the training divisions were ordered to France for a month of front line observation. Wood left for Europe hoping to convince Pershing to let him stay, but he was in trouble from the outset. Wood stopped first in London where he met with the chief of British military intelligence, with Chief of Staff Sir William Robertson, and with Field Marshal Lord French. The British and French were desperate for American reinforcements but were convinced the underequipped American citizen army was months if not years from being able to function independently. They wanted American reserves to fill holes in the western front under experienced European officers. Wilson and Pershing wanted to wait until the doughboys could fight their own sectors. Wood told the British he thought small American units could be rotated to the front interspersed with seasoned British and French troops thereby serving as reinforcements while benefiting from on-site training. The idea might have been a good one, but it was not Pershing's. The British High Command may have appreciated Wood, but commander of the AEF decidedly did not, and rumors that the British were about to give Wood a medal precipitated a perfunctory moratorium on American soldiers accepting foreign decorations.

Wood got to Paris December 13, 1917, and again inserted himself in policy discussions. His old friend Frank McCoy, hoping to promote Wood as commander of American forces attached to the British sectors, begged the general to hold his tongue. Wood ignored his advice and assured Marshal Joffre that American troops could be mixed a brigade at a time with the French. Pershing was furious.

Wood spent two days in Paris before going to Major General A. B. E. Carter's headquarters on the East Ypres salient where he spent a week in Dugout 192, a "cozy, comfortable" billet surrounded by the constant rumble of incoming and outgoing ordnance. From Ypres, Wood visited his old friend General Sir H. W. Rawlinson who brought up the delicate subject of hired sexual relief for the troops. Wood reminded Rawlinson of the scandal engendered by Pershing's "corral" of black, white, and Mexican prostitutes during the Mexican adventure (which he assured the British officer had been "a great fizzle")[2] and huffed, "I don't think that the mother's [sic] of the soldiers of England want their sons to go to death from the arms of a prostitute."[3]

Wood met with Jules Cambon and George Clemenceau in Paris, and, as usual, he talked too much. From Paris Wood went on to visit the Sixty-first Division of the French Sixth Army and, when the French at the front complained about the slow flow of American troops, the general broadly hinted he could do it better. Colonel Charles Kilbourne said Wood was a magnet for "everyone who had a grouch against Pershing or the Administration" and that as many as seventy men gathered around him "in a great camp fire circle" of complaint wherever he went. Wood met with and liked Marshal Philippe Pétain and, once again making policy on the fly, suggested seconding half of all American artillery officers to French units for training.

On January 27, 1918, Wood and his party left Soissons for the Sixth Army School of Automatic Arms at Fere en Tardenois. The highlight of the visit was a trench mortar demonstration and, after a morning at the machine gun school and a leisurely French lunch, the party adjourned to a muddy hill a mile and a half from the village where the French had set up two 3-inch mortars. They wanted to show the Americans how they could safely increase the weapons' firing range by adding rings of cordite "accelerant" to the base of the fused projectiles. The group fell into a semicircle ten feet behind the mortars while the French artillery officer sequentially added one, then two, then three rings of explosives to the shells and watched the range gradually increase. Finally, the officer wrapped four rings, lit the fuse, and stepped back; but this time the shell stuck and the mortar exploded.

Wood was standing elbow to elbow with the school's commandant on his right and the assistant commandant on his left when pieces of the barrel exploded into shrapnel. The commandant was decapitated and gelid pieces of his brain rained onto Wood's uniform. A second piece of metal drove through the assistant's blouse, tore open his bowel, penetrated his heart, and killed him instantly. Kilbourne was struck by a piece that destroyed his right eye before lodging in the front of his brain. Four poilus and two other French officers were killed and American Major Kenyon Jones and a number of French enlisted men were injured.

Six pieces of metal ripped through Wood's coat without hitting him, but a seventh penetrated his right arm just above the elbow, severing a vessel and coming to rest against the median nerve supplying his forearm and hand. The staff stopped Wood's bleeding with a tourniquet fashioned from a handkerchief and a rock and tried to convince him to take one of the cars back to the hospital. Wood flatly refused, insisting the other wounded be carried first. He walked a mile to the nearest road where he was picked up and carried to the small hospital at Fere en Tardenois. Again Wood insisted that all the other wounded, including Kilbourne, whom he was sure would die, be cared for first. Finally, the French surgeons "chloroformed" him, cleaned the wound, took the piece of metal off the nerve, and closed the laceration.[4] The next day Wood was transferred to the American hospital at the Hotel Ritz in Paris, where he spent the next three weeks fending off a flood of visitors among whom was his old surgeon Harvey Cushing who commented on the rapidity of the general's recovery and the relative lack of disability from the nerve injury.[5]

Pershing invited Wood to complete his convalescence at Chaumont where he arrived on February 20 after a detour (at Pétain's suggestion) through the moonscape of Verdun. Wood's first night at Chaumont was a disaster. Pershing hosted a dinner at which Wood criticized his host unmercifully. Even Wood's sympathetic aide Sumner Williams said his boss "made a very bad impression." Pershing silently ignored Wood, but his response was not long in coming.

Wood had planned to return to America through London and had already arranged a meeting with British Prime Minister David Lloyd George. New York Congressman Fiorello La Guardia had visited the general at the Ritz Hospital, and with support from American Ambassador to Rome Thomas Nelson Page, broached the possibility of Wood commanding an American division on the Italian front. McCoy again brought up the possibility of command of a division attached to the British. Both McCoy and Pershing had asked whether the general would be willing to serve under his former subordinate. The Eighty-ninth Division was nearly ready to go to England. European command for Wood seemed certain until February 23 when Pershing's aide (and Wood's former aide) General James Harbord came to his room at Chaumont with crushing news. Wood was ordered to return immediately to Kansas via Bordeaux with no intermittent stops in either Paris or London. Pershing, pleading an acute case of diarrhea, did not see Wood off.

Pershing had no doubt where he wanted Wood—as far from France as geographically possible. He wrote Baker that Wood was "in his 58th year and came from the Medical Corps. . . . He has never commanded a military unit as such. . . . He is probably a good administrator, but knows very little of military tactics and little of training men."[6]

Pershing also reinforced what he must have known the secretary thought of Wood's physical disability. He called the general "seriously and permanently crippled" and totally unfit for command.[7] Then he got to the heart of the matter. Wood's attitude was "really one of disloyalty, in fact, he is simply a political general and insubordination is a pronounced trait in his character. . . . It would settle his pernicious activities if he could be retired."[8]

When Wood got back to New York he received two orders: the Senate Military Committee wanted his testimony about conditions in France and the war department ordered him to report for a physical examination to assess his fitness for continued active duty. Wood went to Washington March 25 to comply with both orders. Before the Senate, Wood was predictably critical of American preparations in France, especially the paucity of rifles and artillery and the complete lack of combat aircraft. The closed door testimony made the next day's papers and infuriated Wilson. As to the medical appointment, when Wood learned that one requirement was a demonstration of the ability to hop on each foot—a skill of dubious battlefield application but certain difficulty for one with a weak left side—he got his old friend Surgeon General William Gorgas to let him bring his own physician when he appeared before the board. Of nine generals examined, Wood was the only one who passed. Wood was also the only one who arranged to have the board's decision released to the press before it could be reconsidered or overruled.

Wood had outmaneuvered Wilson and Pershing, but it was a Pyrrhic victory. The general stayed in Washington ten more days during which the president refused repeated requests for a meeting. Wood, however, was not too worried. The Eighty-ninth was nearly ready to go and he had been found physically fit for combat command. Wood returned to Kansas and, as expected, the orders to deploy came in May. The division loaded up trains for New York and, on May 22, the general left with the first detachment to prepare for embarkation. As it turned out, he left just hours ahead of the telegram separating him from his division and sending him to command the essentially inactive Western Department in San Francisco.

The telegram, which Kilbourne personally delivered to Wood at the Waldorf, rendered the general speechless for a full quarter hour. Finally, Wood said simply, "I'm going to Washington."[9] He went directly to Pennsylvania Station and took the overnight train to the capital. From Union Station, he briefly visited Lodge and went on to the war department where Baker bluntly told him he would never go to France because Pershing did not want him there. Wilson agreed to meet him and an atypically contrite Wood reminded the president that he had organized and trained the division, that he was the army's senior general, that the board had found him physically fit, and that he deserved a chance in France. He begged for forty-five minutes but the only concession he got was assignment to train the newly formed Tenth Division rather than be exiled to San Francisco.

The public outcry was so furious that Wilson asked Baker if perhaps Wood might be sent to Italy after all, but Pershing and Bliss categorically rejected the idea. By mid-June, Wood was back in Kansas training more farmers. The Eighty-ninth went on to perform admirably at St. Mihiel and the Meuse-Argonne, but without Wood.

As the Kansas summer of 1918 set in, Wood returned to training the Tenth Division while Roosevelt counseled him to contain his bitterness and exercise patience, self-control, and, above all, silence.[10] Both men knew the war was nearing an end and Republican gains in the midterm elections boded well for their party and for the colonel and the general for 1920.

Camp Funston's sleepy tranquility was broken by an October outbreak of influenza that exploded to 800 and then to 1,000 new cases a day within a few weeks. In the first days of the epidemic, Wood noticed an unusual number of associated cases of pneumonia, but commented with wildly unjustified optimism that the death rate should not be "very high."[11] Nonetheless, knowing the disease was airborne and suspecting that it was highly contagious, he eliminated mass assemblies, dispersed the men, and separated mess tables with cotton screens. Within forty-eight hours, men began dying in hundreds and dying "very promptly."[12] Fortunately, the number of new cases spontaneously and precipitously dropped after only a week and Wood heaved a sigh of relief having no idea the disease would fly east from Camp Funston, circle the world three times, and leave over 20 million dead in its wake before disappearing as mysteriously as it had come. Wood had unknowingly presided over the beginning of the most lethal pandemic in history.

Just as the epidemic subsided, word filtered back from Europe that Germany was ready to negotiate an armistice based on the fourteen points Wilson had outlined to Congress in January and that the president planned to personally participate in any peace talks. Wood thought Wilson's insistence on freedom of the seas and elimination of colonies would drive a wedge between Britain and America, he agreed with the French that Germany should pay for a war it had fought in

France, and he thought it offensive for the leader of a country that had contributed so little blood and treasure to push himself to the forefront of negotiations. The general was not yet running for president, but he was thinking and speaking presidentially.

His ideas on the most controversial of the fourteen points—the League of Nations—were less clear. One of his mentors, Henry Cabot Lodge, led those irreconcilably opposed to the League while another, Henry Stimson, saw international involvement as an American responsibility, and a third, Elihu Root, was on the fence. Wood thought the League as proposed by Wilson was simply foolish, but he believed America had "a moral obligation . . . to do all it can to alleviate the suffering in Europe."[13] He had no wish to compromise American sovereignty, but, anticipating a later general's plan for Europe after another world war, Wood proposed sending $100,000,000 to help rebuild the continental infrastructure.

Wood was also beginning to think about domestic problems, especially those that would inevitably arise when American soldiers flooded back into civilian life. He negotiated a joint program with the Kansas State Agricultural College that allowed men from Camp Funston to take academic and vocational courses, aimed at easing their transition into the civilian workforce.[14] Before he left Camp Funston, Wood sent 27,000 men through courses in stock raising, land management, and mechanical engineering in a program that anticipated the GI Bill by a quarter century. He also established the Bureau for Soldiers, Sailors, and Marines and enlisted help from the YMCA, the Jewish Welfare Board, and the Vocational Training Board and ultimately provided direct assistance to over 100,000 veterans.[15]

With Wilson out of the country and the Democrats increasingly unpopular, Wood and Roosevelt hungrily eyed the 1920 election. It was widely believed that Roosevelt would lead the Republicans back to the White House, but he had confidentially told Kansas Governor Henry J. Allen that if, for some reason, he could not run, he wanted his friends to support Wood.[16] On Monday, January 6, 1919, the editor of the *Kansas City Star* interrupted Wood's breakfast to tell him Roosevelt had been found dead in bed.[17]

Wood released statements to the press expressing deep grief at the loss of his friend and the nation's loss at a time when Roosevelt's leadership could hardly be spared. He wired the various Roosevelt family members and prepared to go to Oyster Bay. A lone diary entry that day sighed, "Sad, sad business, all of it."[18] Wood had lost his longest and best friend.

At the funeral, Roosevelt's family urged him to step into their missing scion's shoes. The *Literary Digest* wrote, "the political mantle and moral leadership of Roosevelt have fallen, in so far as such properties may be bequeathed, on Gen. Leonard Wood."[19] Many in the Republican power structure and even more in the more liberal Progressive movement—especially Roosevelt's old Bullmoose running mate Hiram Johnson—disputed that, but Wood was ready to assume the role.

Arrangements for Wood's presidential campaign began at the funeral, and through the winter and spring of 1919, he traveled around the East accepting a series of honorary degrees (Union College, Wesleyan, George Washington University), giving speeches to wildly enthusiastic audiences, and meeting with wealthy potential supporters (Clarence Rockefeller, Henry Clay Frick, John Fortune Ryan, Augustus Gardiner, and a "Mr. W., who is head of one of the principal branches of the Tobacco Trust").[20]

Wood's oratorical successes during the preparedness campaign had convinced him he had a talent for public speaking and he liked being at the podium. In February 1919 in Kansas City, Wood addressed 20,000 cheering supporters and turned a memorial for Roosevelt into a ringing denunciation of Wilson and the League. Washington insiders called the speech "a bold and convincing bid for the Republican nomination."[21] Even Herman Hagedorn, Wood's greatest apologist, had misgivings: "Whether a memorial meeting was an appropriate occasion for an attack on the chief policy of the president, and whether an officer of the army was an appropriate person to launch it, were questions of taste."[22] Or perhaps outright insubordination.

Wood's speeches, although often bland on paper, were surprisingly effective in person. The *Chicago Daily Tribune* wrote:

> twelve minutes of detached granite . . . He tramped in, he stood up and clasped his hands behind his stocky body. He said about a columnful and then he tramped out. Grizzled, ruddy, stalwart, he stood square and talked square. No flowing periods. No gestures . . . a whimsical flicker of a smile and a burly half bow. . . . The level voice hammered out grim sentences. Not a flicker of emotion crossed the oak-hewn face. . . . He began, he said something, he finished. "Good day." He

marched out. It was like a rite, this time when the audience rose and stood until he disappeared.[23]

Wood coopted Rooseveltian political saws like "The Square Deal," "Apply the Golden Rule," and "Carry a Big Stick," but he kept his speeches general and refused to endorse pet Progressive causes such as child labor laws, a minimum wage, or old age pensions. He favored conservative Republican war horses like the protective tariff, private ownership of railroads, repeal of the excess profits tax, and small, efficient government. But he was emphatic, clear, and forceful on one issue —Americanism and those he saw as its enemies.

Wood's nativism appealed to a country bent on withdrawing into postwar isolationism. As the *Literary Digest* (no doubt with some prompting) wrote, "General Wood can trace his ancestry back, by verified records, to that fountainhead of Americanism, pure and undefiled, the *Mayflower*."[24] Besides, he had been an Indian fighter, a Rough Rider, and a life-long army officer, and an outspoken opponent of Bolsheviks and anarchists. Almost as soon as the armistice was signed, the dangers of the Red Menace became the core of Wood's speeches, and, in his black-and-white worldview, communism and Americanism were perfectly antithetical.[25]

As the brutally hot summer of 1919 progressed, returning soldiers flooded the job market at home while communists threatened to take over the governments of Germany, Austria, and Italy. Over four million American workers participated in labor actions in 1919, with the Seattle general strike and the Boston police strike put down by Governor Calvin Coolidge generating the most emotional headlines. The American Communist Party was formed in the wake of the Third International, and American Legionnaires fought radicals in the streets. Over Stimson's objection, the New York legislature expelled elected socialists. Membership in the Ku Klux Klan exploded. Even the World Series was tainted by the Black Sox scandal. Chaos was on every corner and seemed to demand a stern dose of law and order.

Wood had been given command of the Central Department, and the Midwest was the center of the maelstrom. On September 29, while on the stump in Bismarck, North Dakota, the general received a frantic call from a man he incorrectly assumed to be the acting mayor of Omaha. The man had tried to reach Wood at Central Department headquarters, but the exigencies of campaigning had left the offices entirely empty and he had called the secretary of war directly who told him where to find Wood. A local mob had lynched a young negro accused of raping a white girl and, when the city's mayor had tried to protect him, he had been assaulted as well. Wood commandeered a train and raced 160 miles to Omaha at the unheard of rate of forty miles an hour.[26] He arrived to find the city "in a state of very considerable excitement and apprehension" and already filling with 1,000 troops and a machine gun company he had ordered from Camp Funston, Fort Clark, Fort Omaha, Camp Grant, and Fort Dodge. Wood supplemented the regulars with American Legion volunteers, each supplied with a bayonet and 200 rounds of ammunition. The troops were dispersed through the city and ordered to break up any mass meeting or "large groups" with whatever force they deemed necessary.

Within a day, peace was restored, theaters and public facilities reopened, and life was well on toward being back to normal. The riots had started on a Sunday and, by the following Saturday, the troops were on their way back to their bases. Wood was convinced that the riots were purposely fomented by "the I.W.W. or some other organized element of disorder, to create very serious trouble and probably burn a good section of the city."[27] Local chamber of commerce members wrote Wood that "the action saved Omaha from a disgraceful catastrophe that undoubtedly would have been many times worse than it was had not the troops under your jurisdiction arrived at the opportune time."[28]

Barely a week after restoring order in Omaha, Indiana's governor summoned Wood to Gary to deal with 35,000 striking steel workers. When the general got to Gary on October 10, he was presented with "several hundred pounds of Red literature, mostly anarchistic and in oversea dialect . . . also quite a little alcohol and fermented drinks."[29] Wood coerced officers of the Chicago Federation of Labor into retracting charges that steel company operatives were behind the riots and even into issuing statements denouncing the rioters as Reds.[30] In Omaha and Gary, Wood found the sort of problems he was best equipped to manage, and his presidential aspirations began to take on an air of inevitability. But crises are short lived and Wood's talents in more normal situations remained questionable.

Wood was still three months from announcing his candidacy, and his new campaign manager, John T. King, recognizing the dangers inherent in the general's militaristic conservatism, desperately tried to get him to lower his profile. He wanted Wood to stay in the army, avoid actively campaigning, and merely offer his availability if the people demanded it. King thought the public would find a serving general's active pursuit of the White House unseemly. On October 25, Wood convinced William Procter, who had been enlisted to head up a campaign committee of former Plattsburgers, to become more active in the campaign. Procter had made his fortune advertising soap and was, unlike King, enthusiastic about Wood's self-promotion. The general failed to realize that the detergent magnate's ego would never allow him to be second to King, and he blithely looked past the fact that, in drafting Procter, he had put his campaign on the road to disaster.[31] When Wood phoned King to tell him he had made the Cincinnati industrialist "head of the big committee," King, pleading a bad connection, made him repeat the statement three times.

Over King's objections, Wood continued to campaign, speaking as many as three or four times a day wherever he could find a venue. At the end of November, Procter decided to oust the campaign manager. He suggested that King be required to detail all campaign expenditures to him and that Wood headquarters be moved from New York to Cincinnati, retaining only such King workers as were willing to relocate. Wood, realizing that King would be forced to quit, struggled for a month to reconcile his two advisors. He asked Stimson and Root to help him heal the rift, oblivious to the fact that Stimson despised King whom he dismissed as "raw and crude" and principally "skilled in the small and shrewd maneuver."[32] By the first week of January, King was gone and Wood's campaign was in the hands of the amateurs.

In the opening months of 1919, the campaign made a series of blunders. In February, Procter decided to enter primaries in Illinois and Ohio despite the fact that contesting favorite-son candidacies of Frank Lowden and Warren G. Harding was guaranteed to infuriate the Republican hierarchy. Putting a general on the campaign trail in uniform made him appear at best overambitious and at worst dangerous. Finally, that spring the Red Scare fell victim to the Justice Department's anti-Communist campaign, and Wood was forced to talk about issues other than Americanism and universal military service. His statements on race relations, the economy, and government efficiency proved vague, unoriginal, and uninspiring. His campaign was forced onto the unsteady ground of the general's personal reputation, support from his politically naïve friends, and the general mediocrity of his opponents.

The last might have carried him through had Procter not so efficiently alienated party regulars. As spring wore on, Wood's deficiencies as a candidate became distressingly obvious. William Allen White and Kansas Governor Henry Allen urged him to soften his anti-alien rhetoric, lest he be seen as a one-issue candidate, and Stimson pressed him to curtail his speaking schedule.

Meanwhile, Procter was trying to cobble together a coalition of American Legionnaires, old Plattsburgers, and wealthy businessmen who saw Wood as an opponent of organized labor. As Procter maneuvered, the opposition coalesced. Lowden had powerful midwestern party support. California Governor Hiram Johnson had a strong base in the West and some claim on the party's progressive wing. Harding barely limped to a win in the Ohio primary, but he had crafty old professional Harry Daugherty quietly gathering behind the scenes support. Harding entered hardly any primaries, but Johnson and Lowden worked in concert against Wood, each entering state races where they were strong and opposing one another only in New England where Wood's lead was insurmountable.[33] Republican Party leaders talked Pershing into running a symbolic campaign in Nebraska to dull the glow of Wood's military credentials. They ran Arthur Wood in Michigan and Edward Wood in Pennsylvania, both of whom attracted several thousand votes.

The high point of Wood's campaign came in the Ohio primary where he mobilized a coalition of veterans, women, Negroes, and—oddly—labor. He spent an unheard of $128,000 and came within 15,000 votes of beating favorite son Harding. Even Daugherty lost his place in the delegation, and Wood figured the Ohioan was "practically eliminated" from the campaign.[34] The general won Indiana, and a *Literary Digest* poll showed him well in the lead.

The near victory in Ohio prompted Wood's old nemesis, the *New York World*, to run a front-page story condemning the general's lavish campaign spending complete with a lengthy list of wealthy donors obligingly provided by none other than John T. King. Republican Senator William Borah called for a formal investigation, and Senate hearings in May confirmed that Wood's campaign had spent an unprecedented $1,773,303, fully one-third of which came from Procter's personal fortune. Paradoxically, it was Lowden—the loyal party man who had spent only $500,000—who suffered the most. Borah's committee discovered that Lowden's people had paid two Missouri delegates $2,500 for their votes. Wood spent more, but Lowden's campaign came away with the stain of actual corruption. By November, a poll of Republican congressmen showed that a majority still thought Wood the most likely candidate.

Running from his forty-seven independent state organizations rather than the Republican machine, Wood could only win if he came to Chicago with a commanding group of committed delegates, but there were only twenty state primaries in 1919. Johnson ran in eleven while Lowden concentrated on garnering party-designated delegates. Harding and Daugherty hovered in the wings. When the convention opened on June 8, 1920, Wood had 124 delegates, Johnson 112, Lowden 72, and Harding 39. The general had spent almost three times as much as the others combined but had not gotten the 493 votes he needed for a majority. Johnson, Lowden, Harding, and even Calvin Coolidge had enough support to make it impossible for any single candidate to collect a majority in the early ballots.

Besides coming with too few delegates, Wood came with too many enemies. Borah threatened to bolt the party if either candidate—Wood or Lowden—who had "tried to buy the election" were nominated. Confirming Stimson's suspicions, King joined Boise Penrose's effort to block Wood. Columbia Professor Nicholas Murray Butler, who had his own designs on the nomination, railed against Procter and his "insolent attempt to buy the nomination (that represented) all that is worst in American business and American political life."[35] Butler had sympathy for Wood whom he considered a foil of greedy businessmen, but he used his irresistible influence with the New York delegation to drive them away from the general. Root, who actually thought Butler would be a fine candidate, recognized that "university presidents are rather at a discount in the public mind just at present," and the New Yorker was out of the running. He dismissed Johnson's candidacy as nothing more than an "idiotic ploy" to stop Wood.[36] In the end, Root saw no way either Wood or Butler could get the nomination so he simply abandoned the whole process, endorsed no one, skipped the convention, and went to Europe to help set up the World Court.

So Wood came to Chicago as a front runner with a litany of handicaps. Procter's attempt to guarantee the nomination by winning primaries and circumventing the party hierarchy had failed. Lodge and Root had distanced themselves from his campaign; Johnson had the West and some of the party's progressives; and Lowden had the party regulars and much of the Midwest. Still, Wood had New England, part of the Midwest, and a popular public persona. None of his opponents had a broad constituency, but, as every train pulled into the Chicago station, one of Harry Daugherty's 2,000 operatives was standing on the platform urging arriving delegates to remember Warren Harding if the convention deadlocked.

On Friday, June 12, Henry Allen nominated Wood in a rambling speech that was followed by a forty-minute demonstration and a seconding speech by Roosevelt's sister Mrs. Douglas Robinson, the first woman to address a national convention. Wood lost crucial ground when his southern delegates were replaced by slates of blacks rumored to have been bought by Lowden. Years later, Republican delegate Emmett Scott claimed that Negro delegates to the convention were no more likely to have been manipulated than whites, but he did not deny that bribes had been paid.[37]

The *New York Times* claimed the anti-Wood strategy was to hold on for three or four votes followed by "a long recess, during which the 'elder statesmen' may repair to the secret council chamber and select a candidate."[38] And so it went. That first Friday, there were four ballots during which Wood's support increased from 287 1/2 to 314 1/2 votes while Lowden went from 211 1/2 to 289, Johnson went from 133 1/2 to 140 1/2, and the minor candidates—including Harding who finished the day with 61 1/2—gave up a handful of votes. Wood reckoned he needed at least 375 votes to get within striking distance, and he had a prior agreement with the Pennsylvania delegation that they would leave favorite son W. C. Sproul and lock up the nomination if he could get to 400.

Now was the time Wood really needed King, and the general knew it. In fact, some attempts at reconciliation had been made prior to the convention. One meeting had been aborted when King was detained at a Republican National Committee meeting. Wood, furious at what he took as an intentional insult, would only agree to meet King if the latter came to him. The general's pride overcame his judgment and the meeting never happened.[39] Instead, King organized Wood's opponents. After the fourth ballot, the general's men were scrambling to get ready for the next vote when Lodge unexpectedly (and over loud vocal objections from a majority of delegates), declared adjournment for the day. Wood recognized that his opponents now had the night to organize, and he never forgave Lodge for what he believed was a calculated betrayal. By early evening, rumors filtered back to Wood's headquarters that "a group of New York capitalists and certain senators" including Lodge, Frank Brandegee, and Reed Smoot were meeting with King at the Blackstone Hotel. Four months earlier, a *New York Times* reporter had chased Harry Daugherty down a hotel hallway asking if the convention would be decided by backstage manipulation among tired delegates some morning at 2:00 A.M. Exasperated, Daugherty fired back, "make it 2:11." The story got rewritten, polished, and redacted into a nomination determined by "fifteen men in a smoke-filled room."[40]

Actually, the old guard convened in a series of revolving, all-night meetings scattered around the Blackstone, the most important of which was presided over by *North American Review* editor George Harvey in Chairman Will Hays's tenth-floor suite, where Harding was proposed as a compromise untainted by large contributions and most likely to carry Ohio over presumed Democratic nominee James Cox. Indiana Senator James Watson later said Lodge was the prime mover in the decision to go with Harding.[41]

All the action that night did not occur in the "smoke-filled room"; both Wood and Lowden realized that the party hierarchy was working to circumvent them, and both offered Johnson the vice presidency in return for his delegates, but the stiff-necked Californian declined. At 10:00 P.M., Penrose and King offered Wood their support and the nomination in return for three cabinet posts. Wood's supporters were convinced those three appointments would buy the presidency, but the general brusquely refused: "Tell Senator Penrose that I have made no promises, and am making none."[42]

The most interesting offer—especially in view of the scandals that defined Harding's presidency—came from "Big Jake" Hamon whom Leonard Wood Jr. had introduced to his father during the campaign. The younger Wood spent his life in pursuit of a quick fortune and, in 1919 and 1920, he had gone to work for the Texas and Oklahoma oilman. Hamon wanted access to oil reserves in Mexico and in federally controlled lands, especially the U.S. Navy reserves at Teapot Dome. He had already spread $105,000 around the Republican hierarchy to become a national committeeman and was prepared to spend a great deal more to get at the federal reserves.[43] He told the general he would guarantee the nomination in return for the right to name the United States ambassador to Mexico and the secretary of the interior. Wood, "purple with rage," said, "I am an American soldier. I'll be damned if I betray my country. Get the hell out of here." The next day, Hamon told an associate he had just spent $1 million buying the nomination for Harding. Hamon's son claimed his father had been promised one-third of the oil in the federal reserve at Teapot Dome in return for the votes he bought.[44] Wood's son confirmed the story in testimony that was part of the congressional investigation that sent Harding's secretary of the interior to prison.[45] Hamon had wanted to be secretary himself, but he did not live long enough to press his claim. His lover (his nephew's wife) threatened to make the convention bribes public and, in the ensuing fight, she shot and killed him.[46]

Voting resumed Saturday morning and, on the seventh ballot, Wood held his last lead over Lowden 312 to 311 1/2. Harding had crept up to 105 votes. Lodge called a noon recess during which Lowden told Wood they were being victimized by a cabal of old guard senators— hardly an earth-shattering revelation. Wood and Lowden motored up and down Michigan Avenue debating an alliance, but neither would accept second place on the ticket.[47] When the convention reconvened, Lowden withdrew and the rush was on. On the ninth ballot, "things generally went to smash,"[48] and, on the tenth ballot, Harding was nominated by acclamation.

Wood was convinced that King and the "cabal of senators" had bought the nomination for Harding and was pretty sure the cost had been from $1,000 to $5,000 per delegate.[49] Stimson dismissed the whole proceeding as "notorious."[50] A variety of factors besides Hamon's bribes contributed to Wood's defeat, including his falling out with King, the naivety of Procter and the amateurs, and Wood's own weaknesses as a candidate. Perhaps the most intriguing factor, however, was the insertion of a serving general with an autocratic bent into the democratic process. Walter Lippman epitomized the fears engendered by Wood's campaign when, addressing public reaction to Wood, he wrote:

> Their frayed nerves were easily infected with the fiercest phases of war psychology, and they have boiled and fretted and fumed. The hatreds and violence which were jammed up without issue in action against the enemy, turned against all kinds of imaginary enemies—the enemy within, the enemy to the south, the enemy at Moscow, the Negro, the immigrant, the labor union—against anything that might be treated as the plausible object of unexpended feeling. . . . The sect is radical jingo with the prejudice of the junker. . . . It is a mystical sect of innovators

who propose to exalt the federal government into a state of supreme and unquestionable authority . . . they have the mood, if not the courage of the coup d'état. They have backed every attack on civil liberty.[51]

In public, Wood accepted the defeat with dignity. He stood erect in his hotel doorway, hands behind his back, smile fixed, and thanked his disappointed supporters for their efforts. Privately, he fumed at what he was certain was an election stolen. He also worried about his future. He toyed with reactivating the Progressive Party and organizing a new convention but found no support. Corrine Robinson pushed Harding to make Wood secretary of war, but that was never a possibility. Whatever happened, his military career was over. Wood considered accepting the presidency of the University of Pennsylvania and heard hints that he would be named high commissioner to Armenia.[52] Then Harding summoned him to Marion where he offered a post on an investigatory commission to the Philippines to be followed by appointment as governor general. Wood could return to Manila and Harding would be rid of an influential and demonstrably vocal potential critic.

11

Manila, 1920–1927

WITHIN WEEKS of the 1920 election, Harding was testing Wood's willingness to go to the Philippines. One of the president-elect's functionaries came to Chicago "full of the idea" of Wood going to Manila, but the general thought the Filipinos had been "pretty thoroughly demoralized" by eight years of Democratic supervision and were shot through with unreasonable ideas of independence.[1] He also knew Filipino leaders had no enthusiasm for replacing the easy-going Democratic regime with an authoritarian retired major general. More to the point, "the idea of going to the Philippines would be simply to cut oneself off from all connection with affairs here and would be entirely out of the great reorganization work which must go on."[2]

Discussions with the University of Pennsylvania continued while Harding's offer was formalized, and, by the end of February, Wood asked Louise whether she preferred Philadelphia or Manila. When word of the Philippine appointment leaked out, the general received an avalanche of mail advising against it; Stimson thought the offer was a "damned insult" that should be dismissed out of hand.[3] When incoming Secretary of War John Weeks wired an invitation to Washington, Wood knew what was coming and accepted only after telling him the governor generalship was out of the question.

Harding had chaired the Senate Committee on Territorial and Outlying Possessions, was interested in the Philippines, and, besides wanting Wood out of the way, he wanted an investigative commission that would emphasize the damage done to the possession by the Democrats. The Republicans also intended to rein in the upstart Filipinos, and Harding reckoned the hard-edged general could do that as well as anyone if they could just get him to Manila. When Harding first proposed he head the investigative commission, Wood went into a "grand fury" and told Frank McCoy he would not go under any circumstances, but, after he calmed down, he succumbed to the temptation of one last spell on the national stage.[4] He convinced the Pennsylvania trustees to hold the provost position for six months while he went on Harding's mission and rationalized, "One is never too prominent or too big to do any job that is of real importance to the nation."[5]

The Democrats had come to power in 1913 determined to reverse the years of tight Republican control over the Philippines and push the archipelago toward early independence. To that end, Wilson dispatched Francis Burton Harrison, a descendant of Virginia's Tidewater tobacco aristocracy who counted Thomas Jefferson among his forebears, to Manila. Harrison's father had been secretary to Jefferson Davis and, after the Civil War, had relocated to New York where his son became a congressman, most noted for sponsoring the bill that established federal government control over the sale of narcotics. Mostly, Harrison was monumentally lazy and expended what energy he could muster pursuing scandalously young females. He married five times and was notorious for his assignations with Filipino girls. Locals whispered to Wood that the governor general was "regarded as a pervert" and offered photographs to prove it.[6]

It is hard to say whether Wood's Puritan sensibilities were more offended by Harrison's social proclivities or his sloth. Since 1916, Harrison had taken his authority from the Jones Act which served as the Philippine organic document. William Atkinson Jones, another Virginian who had graduated from VMI and fought with the cadets at the Battle of Newmarket, had worked with Manuel Quezon through 1910 to draft the bill that was the high point of an otherwise undistinguished legislative career. The legislation, basically written by Quezon, promised an eight-year period of home rule followed by independence. It was killed by Taft and the Republican Senate, but the outlook was better in 1912, after the Democrats swept both houses of Congress and the presidency. Wilson, however, was not at all committed to Philippine independence.

Quezon, still acting as Jones's ghost writer, redrafted the bill but left out a definite date for sovereignty. In truth, he worried that a weak Philippine nation would fall victim to Japan's lust for land and resources. The bill, which called for independence when Filipinos had achieved a "stable government," passed the House in 1914 but only became law in 1916 after sixteen months of Taft-orchestrated senatorial foot dragging. The Jones Act did three things: it made Jones a Philippine hero; it became the de facto Philippine constitution for the remainder of

American rule; and it made the United States the first western power to voluntarily cede autonomy to a former colony.

Behind the scenes, a small cadre of ambitious Filipinos manipulated Harrison. The Nationalist Party won a majority in the Philippine legislature in 1907 and elected Sergio Osmeña speaker. Osmeña, a lawyer of mixed Chinese and Malay descent from the island of Cebu, had participated in the 1898 revolt and was one of the first popularly elected civil governors of his home island. With the appearance, demeanor, and work ethic of a Buddhist monk, the diminutive Osmeña proved a remarkably successful governor, and his election to head the first Philippine legislature was nearly unanimous. He was an accomplished orator in both Spanish and English and an effective compromiser able to deal with both American administrators and his fellow Filipino legislators. From 1907 to 1916, he was the acknowledged leader of island politics. One of Wood's aides called him "really first class and perfectly competent to debate and meet on equal footing with anyone, whether he be an Oriental or a Westerner."[7] Osmeña married a wealthy woman and, being of the Philippine "compadre" aristocracy, was never tempted into overt corruption.

Manuel Quezon was an altogether different matter. Son of a Spanish father and a Malay mother, he was raised in eastern Luzon. Like Osmeña, he had served in the revolution and become a lawyer. Unlike his ascetic fellow, he was famous for his contentiousness with men, his lust for women, and his susceptibility to corruption. One of Wood's aides dismissed him as "fairly honest . . . according to Malay standards,"[8] with a reputation for changing convictions as fast as quicksilver on a glass to suit his personal interest. While Osmeña stayed in Manila, Quezon went to Washington to represent Philippine interests before Congress, but, after the Jones Bill passed, he came home to fight Osmeña for control of the Nationalists.

Under the new law, the Philippines had a bicameral legislature and Osmeña remained speaker of the lower house while Quezon became president of the senate. Harrison also had a council of state composed of the two presiding officers and secretaries of the various executive departments. Above them all was a board of control—Harrison, Osmeña, and Quezon—in charge of the plethora of businesses owned by the Philippine government.

Shortly after arriving, Harrison set about replacing American administrators with Filipinos. He cut the number of Americans from 3,000 to 600 and hired 13,000 Filipinos to do the same jobs, leading local American businessmen to compare Manila to the South under reconstruction. The bureaucracy ballooned with untrained Filipinos who could not do jobs for which they had been hired, and even Quezon and Osmeña fretted that the speed of transition was damaging government efficiency. Roads deteriorated, the poor went unfed, and hospitals, which had been a notable American success, no longer cared for the sick and insane.

Wilson had finally come out for independence in his final message to Congress, but, by now, even the Filipinos were not anxious for a precipitous change. Although they had no intention of turning the Philippines loose, Harding and the Republicans knew repeal of the Jones Act was politically impossible, so they decided to use its lack of precision combined with the president's right of veto over the Philippine legislature and Wood's personality to reestablish colonial control.

The first step was to quash all the loose talk of independence, and what was now known as the Forbes-Wood Commission arrived in Manila on April 21, 1921, determined to do just that.[9] The commission spent five months visiting all but one of the forty-eight Philippine provinces, stopping in 449 municipalities, and traveling 15,000 miles by land and water. They gathered most of their information from interviews and observation and found exactly what they had intended to find. The commission concluded that, from 1907 to 1913 (under the Republicans), things had gone well. Gradual deterioration began between 1913 and 1916, and the years after 1916 constituted "the most unfortunate and darkest years in Philippine history."[10] Wood was outraged at the deterioration in public health, the explosive growth of the bureaucracy, and corruption in the judiciary.[11] He wrote Stimson that the "immoral and incompetent" Harrison administration had "left a stench in the East" which would endure for years.[12] Wherever they went, Wood and Forbes found Filipinos clamoring for independence, but they chose not to hear. Wood claimed the Nationalists he met, even though they asked for independence, really wanted supervision and protection from the United States. He remained convinced he had "not yet gotten beyond the veil which separates us from the great mass of plain people" who loved and appreciated American imperialism. Wood emerged from a meeting with Osmeña and Quezon in which he lectured them on the impossibility of Philippine self-government, convinced the two former revolutionaries finally understood "the uselessness of independence."[13] The commission's conclusion was, to understate the case, fore-gone:

> We find that the people are not organized economically nor from the standpoint of national defense to maintain an independent govern-ment. . . . It would be a betrayal of the Philippine people, a misfortune to the American people, a distinct step backward in the path of progress, and a discernable neglect of our national duty were we to withdraw from the islands and terminate our relationship there with-out giving the Filipinos the best chance possible to have an orderly and permanently stable government.[14]

Although Wood had not officially made up his mind about Hard-ing's offer, Lou must have known what was coming when he wrote:

> The situation here is so bad that I cannot go into details. It is one in which the demand for service is so strong that I cannot I fear resist it and ever again preach unselfish service for country & humanity. If you knew the details I'm sure you would feel as I do. It means the sacrifice of material advantages to inclination for the necessity to a rather stern sense of duty.[15]

On September 10, with the commission's work complete, Wood left for China and Japan. In Peking, he discussed the necessity for an Amer-ican presence in East Asia to restrain Japanese aggression although he doubted America could restrain Japanese designs on northeast China. In Tokyo, Viscount Makino, who had led the Japanese delegation at the Versailles peace talks, assured Wood that his government had "no thought of war," had no ambitions beyond an open door in Manchuria and Korea, and were optimistically anticipating the upcoming confer-ence on naval arms limitations.[16] Wood did point out to General Tanaka that, with the Russian navy destroyed and Europe exhausted by the Great War, America looked like the most likely target of Japanese naval expansion: "To be perfectly frank, General, there is a feeling in America that Japan, being a warlike and brave nation, victorious in all her recent wars, with a general staff modeled on German lines and largely Ger-man trained, that this general staff may have the same dangerous influ-ence upon Japan's general policy as the German staff did upon that of Germany. In other words, that it may push the country into war."[17]

Tanaka answered that Japan's southern islands were overpopulated, Hokkaido was too cold to live in, and Manchuria was, to be honest, land the empire needed. Wood also knew that China, Britain, and the Netherlands saw American withdrawal from the Philippines as a blank check for Japanese expansion and concluded that any agreement lessening American naval strength in the Pacific would be disastrous.

As Wood prepared to leave Kyoto, Harding wired one last plea for him to return to Manila as governor general, and this time the cagy president convinced Osmeña and Quezon to concur. Given Wood's age and ill health, the two Filipinos figured the appointment would be, at worst, a temporary inconvenience. Wood relented and sailed back to the Philippines to spend his final six years futilely trying to turn back the colonial clock.

On October 15, 1921, Leonard Wood was inaugurated governor general of the Philippines. The following day he summoned Osmeña to an impromptu council of state meeting after which he wrote, "the cabinet will not be running me, but I want them to run as I wish."[18]

In February 1922, Quezon broke from the Nationalists and formed his own Partida Nationalista Colectivista and sponsored Manuel Roxas y Acuña against Osmeña for speaker of the house. Osmeña gave in, took a seat in the senate, and fell into Quezon's shadow where he spent the rest of his career. Quezon detested Wood and resented his intention to restrict Philippine autonomy, but, assuming the arrogant general's tenure would be short, he bided his time.

Wood's first year as governor general had echoes of his finer days in Havana. He got the Rockefeller Foundation to fund rehabilitation of the Philippine medical school and renovated the disgraceful St. Lazare mental hospital. He started mosquito control programs and typhoid and smallpox vaccination campaigns, and adopted the leper colony at Culion as his special project and built proper housing for the inmates who had been sharing mud floored huts with their dogs. He heard (incorrectly as it turned out) that extract of chaulmoogra oil from India could cure 50 to 60 percent of lepers and—with thoughts of reprising his yellow fever triumph—ordered five tons of the medicine.

Wood was convinced the Filipinos understood that, without United States protection, they "could not compete successfully with the Chinese in agriculture or trade" and that "the Japanese aggressiveness would swamp them if Chinese thrift and industry did not."[19] As it turned out, although the second prediction came first, both proved true.

Within eighty years, the Japanese had come and gone, but Chinese immigrants, who accounted for 1 percent of the Philippine population, would control 60 percent of the archipelago's private economy.[20]

Direct Philippine government involvement in business was particularly galling for the new governor general. Under Harrison, the government had, with the professed intention of fostering local business, taken major ownership in businesses as varied as oil, coal, coconuts, copra, and cement, but their major investment was in sugar. The Philippine National Bank had loaned large amounts of money to sugar growers and refiners (the "sugar centrals"). When the price of sugar sank after the war, the centrals went bankrupt, and the bank— and by extension the government—was in the sugar business. In 1921, virtually all the bank's assets were tied up in the six sugar centrals and only a serendipitous rise in prices saved the government from insolvency.[21]

On December 6, 1921, Wood sent a letter to the legislature all but ordering that the government divest itself of its investments. Government business decisions under Harrison had come from the board of control through the legislature; Wood took the position that voting government stock was an executive function and henceforth would be handled by his office alone. His sale of the National Coal Company, the National Cement Company, the Manila Hotel, and the sugar holdings, was stalled by Filipino legislators who convinced Secretary of War Weeks that, since they were funding the companies, the governor general could not unilaterally sell them. Filipinos were convinced he intended to sell the businesses to Americans and suspected he planned to siphon money from the colony into his and his friends' pockets. Neither Wood nor anyone close to him ever benefited financially, but perception trumped reality.

Wood's demeanor did not help him. In his advancing age, the general, never a model of flexibility, had become overbearing, tactless, and intensely jealous of the prerogatives of office. Ernest Westerhouse said:

> I found Governor Wood to be a conceited bore, and entirely out of step with the civilian population. He has nothing in common with civil government. He has a very frigid personality, with absolutely no sense of humor, and apparently the disappointments of recent years have left him in a bunch of sour grapes.[22]

Where he had taken pride in being accessible to Cubans—at least those of the upper classes—Wood refused to meet any Filipinos without a "white man" present as a witness. Wood's aide, Colonel Edward "Peter" Bowditch thought there was more to his boss's reticence than mistrust. He said:

> the greatest handicap the General had was his physical handicap. This affected his judgment and his memory. He was one of the most inaccurate men I have ever known. It was not an uncommon thing for him to come from what he called a conference with the Filipino leaders with ideas which were diametrically opposed to what had really happened in the so-called conference, and what had been agreed upon there.[23]

Even Hagedorn, who worshipped Wood long before becoming his biographer, admitted that "the General's illness very seriously impaired his ability to get along with his fellow man."[24]

It is not easy to get a clear picture of Wood's decline. His diary remains crisp and clear-headed to the last, and both Lou Wood and Hagedorn worked mightily to minimize the illness after Wood's death. In Manila, Wood was surrounded by a coterie of dedicated subordinates led by the indefatigable Frank McCoy and including Colonel Gordon Johnston, Colonel Halstead Dorey, Wood's son Osborne, and young Lieutenant George S. Patton. The Khaki Cabinet or Cavalry Cabinet as they were variously known closed ranks around their failing leader.

Mrs. Wood claimed the general never had a seizure between his second operation and 1923 and that the spells did not become frequent until the very end.[25] But Bowditch claimed Wood had resumed carrying medicine to stop the seizures even before he went to the islands, that his paralysis made it hard for him to walk, and that his memory was defective throughout his term as governor general.[26] After visiting Wood, Judge George Malcolm said, "it was apparent that the reception had been stage managed to shield the Governor's infirmities. He was standing directly in front of a chair to shake hands with me, after which he could sink into it without too much strain. His left side was visibly not under muscular control."[27]

Wood's deficiencies became embarrassingly clear in the summer of 1922 after Quezon learned he was staying in Manila. The Philippine leader had no intention of tolerating the general over the long term, and, when Wood announced plans to expand the council of state to include non-Nationalists, Quezon raised such a ruckus that he was forced to back down, although, in a fit of pique, he vetoed the next six bills sent from the legislature.

Harrison had set up the council of state by fiat rather than statute so his successor would have some leeway in formulating relations with the body. He had, however, allowed the legislature to control the council, and Osmeña and Quezon considered the body responsible to them. Wood saw it otherwise. The council was an arm of the executive and, under the Jones Act, answerable to the governor general.

The proximate cause of the final blow-up was an unlikely fellow named Ray Conley, who headed the anti-gambling unit of the Manila secret service. Mayor Ramon Fernandez accused Conley of taking bribes based on a phone call supposedly overheard by he and Interior Secretary José Laurel (who would later earn infamy for collaborating with the Japanese). Laurel fired Conley, but Wood was convinced the man had been framed by rich Filipino gamblers and demanded investigation by a special tribunal. The tribunal acquitted Conley and Wood reinstated him, although he admitted that "We are pulling the whole government into a row over a man who, aside from the principles of justice, is not worth the trouble."[28] Quezon, allowing that he "didn't give a damn" about Conley, used the episode to challenge Wood.

On July 17, 1923, Quezon, Osmeña, and all the cabinet secretaries except the American secretary of education quit en masse. Wood announced that troops were ready to keep order if necessary and proceeded to run the government with under secretaries who proved only too happy with their unexpected promotions. Weeks reminded the Filipinos that Wood ran the executive and could veto whatever legislation he wished, and Quezon was temporarily forced to back down.

Quezon then prepared a "memorial" of grievances accusing Wood of mismanagement, of destroying the economy, of exceeding his authority, and of alienating his charges and had Roxas hand carry the document to Washington. The Philippine protest was delayed by Harding's death and Coolidge's succession but, on January 8, 1924, the document came before Congress. Coolidge curtly informed the Filipinos that they were in no way ready for independence and any further complaint could result in revocation of the concessions they already had. Wood was a perfectly good governor and they should learn to appreciate him.

A second delegation led by Quezon and Osmeña tried again in April and got as far as the Republican Party's platform committee before their demands for independence met the circular argument that their inability to get along with Wood proved their unsuitability for self-government. Wood simply ignored them: "Everytime a jackass brays, must I get up and explain what he means?"[29]

The Philippine legislature continued to send annual delegations to Washington demanding more freedom and less Wood and, although independence bills were written in every congressional session, none escaped committee and Coolidge and Weeks repeatedly assured Congress and the American people that the islands were at least two decades away from independence. When Coolidge won election in his own right in 1924, Philippine independence became a dead issue.

Defeated in Washington, the Filipinos set about making Wood's life a misery. The legislature refused to fund Wood's office expenses, refused to pay his aides' per diems, and revoked funding for the *Apo*, the governor's official yacht. Wood calmly overrode them and appropriated the money. When the legislature tried to pass bills of which he disapproved, Wood took the *Apo* into the southern islands and made himself unavailable to sign them as long as the fishing was good.[30]

Wood kept trying to get American investment, although even the American Chamber of Commerce in Manila considered Philippine politics too unstable for safe investment and the legal barriers to foreign ownership insurmountable. By statute, the extensive "friar lands" that had passed to the government in 1902 could not be sold to any single corporate or individual owner in parcels larger than 2,500 acres, effectively prohibiting commercially viable sugar and rubber plantations. Wood circumvented the law and arranged transfer of 50,000 acres to the Mindinao Sugar Company that happened to be run by former Republican Senator George Fairchild. He pushed for legislation to exempt rubber plantations from the land restriction and personally lobbied Harvey Firestone to bring his American Tire and Rubber Company to the islands. When Wood tried to change land laws to allow "any responsible person" the right to lease eight square miles for twenty-five years with an option to renew, the Filipinos feared their islands were about to become an American plantation.

In November 1926, Wood unilaterally abolished the board of control and put himself in charge of the remaining government-owned businesses. The Filipinos challenged the action, but it was upheld by the

Philippine and then the United States Supreme Court. Quezon and the legislature were beside themselves, and McCoy and the Khaki Cabinet could no longer protect the governor. Philippine newspapers "were daily filled with vituperation," and even Coolidge had to take notice.[31] By 1926, rumors of Wood's failing health gave the president an excuse to suggest a sabbatical, but Wood summarily dismissed the idea.

Meanwhile, the general's personal life was in chaos. His oldest son, Leonard Junior, had chased get rich quick schemes since he had been a young army captain. He had been principal in four small Texas oil companies, used his name in advertising, and sold shares in speculative drilling projects to enlisted men in his command. When the wells failed to produce, some of the soldiers complained to their congressmen, and there were threats of formal investigation and suggestions of mail fraud.[32] Although he narrowly escaped legal action, young Wood's personal finances were a disaster. He left the army and tried to make a living managing a traveling theater company but failed at that as well. He cancelled plans to marry one of his actresses, and, in September 1925, filed for bankruptcy, announcing that he hoped to repay his creditors out of profits from writing short stories and plays.

Osborne Wood was an even more serious problem. While serving as his father's aide in Manila, he had enjoyed suspicious success speculating in the stock market. In the fall of 1922, he began sending large sums of money to his father-in-law Henry Thompson in New York; rumor had it that the governor's son had transferred between $2.5 million and $25 million, amounts so large that the *New York Times* sent a reporter to Manila to investigate.[33] Wall Street professionals speculated that the only way Wood could have made so much so fast was by "pyramiding"—buying stock with credit backed by unrealized paper profits. Like his older brother, Osborne had a weakness for oil, making the greatest profit on short-term speculation in Standard Oil of New Jersey. As it all turned out, the profits were a more modest but still impressive $700–800,000, no small achievement on a lieutenant's salary.[34]

In February 1924, Osborne resigned his commission and left for a protracted vacation in Paris and Monte Carlo where he became something of a celebrity. By October, a combination of elaborate entertaining and injudicious wagers exhausted his fortune. In February 1925, Osborne vanished from his Paris hotel leaving a girlfriend, an angry wife, and a string of irate creditors. He surfaced in Spain a few days later having crossed the border just ahead of the French police investigating a

35,000 franc bad check. Within a month, Osborne was on his way to Tampa where he was "hopeful of making a fortune" in land speculation.[35]

He prospered briefly in Florida, but, within a few months, he was again being pursued by police for cashing bad checks. His father made the checks good and shipped him to Havana in the care of his former secretary Frank Steinhart, who had become wealthy running the Havana Street Railway. After a time in a Cuban "sanatorium," Osborne relocated to New Mexico where he worked as a $1 a day miner before becoming a labor organizer and, finally, cadging an appointment as adjutant general of the state national guard.

By 1925, the combination of friction between Wood and the Filipinos, family scandal, and the general's failing health forced Coolidge to take action. The president took the time-honored politician's way out —he appointed yet another commission, this time under Ohio businessman and well-worn Republican operative Carmi Thompson. Thompson spent five months investigating the Philippines, hardly speaking to Wood the entire time. When he made his report in December 1926, Thompson faulted both Wood and the Filipinos but was particularly critical of the Khaki Cabinet. For the most part, however, the report mirrored the findings of the Forbes-Wood Commission, finding the Philippines in need of more American investment and not ready for independence. Coolidge submitted the report to Congress, commenting only that there were parts with which he disagreed. Publicly, he continued to support Wood who remained unusually quiet.

When a disappointed Philippine legislature reconvened in 1927, they voted for a plebiscite on independence. Wood, who had doggedly insisted that the majority of Filipinos had no desire to be free but worried that the reverse might be true, was in a bind; so he vetoed the bill. The legislature overrode his veto, and the bill went to Coolidge who vetoed it once and for all reassuring Wood, "I must state my sincere conviction that the people of the Philippine Islands have not as yet achieved the capacity of full self-government."[36]

But by that time Wood was failing fast. Unable to exercise, he had grown obese and was so weak he had to be dressed and undressed by a servant. In May, he ran his car into a ditch and sustained a minor head injury which he used as the final excuse for going home. On May 28, 1927, Wood and his wife left Manila for Boston and the general's appointment with Dr. Harvey Cushing.

Epilogue

WOOD'S DEATH was followed by a predictable flurry of obituaries and—except for two biographies fifty-eight years apart—silence. Today, were it not for an army base that bears his name, we would never hear of Leonard Wood. To explain why a life so varied and so influential should have vanished from the public memory we must turn to the general's checkered career and his equally checkered personality.

Wood at his best was altruistic, intelligent, creative, supremely self-confident, and indefatigable. As the architect of American twentieth-century nation building, he brought order out of chaos, overcame epidemics, established an equitable judiciary, opened schools, funded hospitals, built roads, and eschewed personal wealth. Wood was also arrogant, intolerant, and autocratic. He did not believe the people he ruled were capable of self-government and never thought them his equal. At times his disdain descended to cruelty and even murder. As army chief of staff, he was intolerably self-righteous and, convinced he knew more about the nation's military needs than the president, he sacrificed his career to his vision. His insatiable appetite for power culminated in his run for the presidency. During his campaign, the public saw what was admirable in the general and would very likely have elected him had professional politicians not focused on his flaws and combined parliamentary manipulation and bribery to derail his candidacy. Had he won, America would have had a combination of militarism, nativism, and authoritarianism in the White House instead of Warren G. Harding.

In the end, as Elting Morison said, Wood "never quite discovered how to fulfill himself or to satisfy others in the exertion of his own remarkable powers."[1] Perhaps we have forgotten him because he was too much like ourselves.

Notes

NOTES TO CHAPTER 1

1. Harvey Cushing and Louise Eisenhardt, *Meningiomas: Their Classification, Regional Behaviour, Life History, and Surgical End Results* (Springfield, Ill.: Charles C. Thomas, 1938), 413.

2. Notes from Dr. Harvey Cushing, September 25, 1928, Hagedorn Papers.

3. Cushing note, Hagedorn Papers.

4. Harvey Cushing, "Surgery of the Head," in William Williams Keen, ed., *Surgery: Its Principles and Practice* (Philadelphia: W. B. Saunders Company, 1908), 264. Some of the details of surgical routine are missing from Cushing's report of Wood's operation in Cushing and Eisenhardt and have been taken from his general description in Keen's text of how these procedures should be performed. The descriptions of the actual operation are from Cushing's own descriptions of Wood's surgery.

5. Cushing note, Hagedorn Papers.

6. Cushing and Eisenhardt, *Meningiomas*, 413.

7. Ibid., 414.

8. John Fulton, *Harvey Cushing: A Biography* (Springfield, Ill.: Charles C. Thomas, 1946), 551.

NOTES TO CHAPTER 2

1. The material in this chapter is drawn from Herman Hagedorn, *Leonard Wood: A Biography* (New York: Harper & Brothers, 1931). Hagedorn's exhaustive research and access to Wood's family and to the people who knew him in those early years can no longer be matched.

NOTES TO CHAPTER 3

1. Charles Wood to his mother, cited in Hagedorn, *Wood*, 1:25.

2. Ibid., 31.

3. Robert E. Kohler, "Medical Reform and Biomedical Science: Biochemistry, a Case Study," in Morris Vogel, ed., *The Therapeutic Revolution: Essays in the So-*

cial History of American Medicine, (Philadelphia: University of Pennsylvania Press, 1979), 31–32.

4. One could argue that Johns Hopkins University in Baltimore was at least as important as Harvard in the American medical revolution, but that school did not open its doors until 1893.

5. Cited in Hagedorn, *Wood,* 1:31.

6. Ibid. 32.

7. Thomas Dwight in Howard A. Kelly and Walter L. Burrage, *Dictionary of American Medical Biography: Lives of Eminent Physicians of the United States and Canada, from the Earliest Times* (Boston: Milford House, 1928), 585.

8. Charles R. Bardeen in Kelly, *American Medical Biography,* 584.

9. Howard Kelly in Kelly, *American Medical Biography,* 411–13.

10. The course was taught by Charles Wood and was controversial in that Wood (no relation to Leonard) was a classically trained rather than a "medically trained" chemist. Leonard Wood's notes from this class are the only ones he preserved and are in the Library of Congress.

11. Hagedorn, *Wood,* 1:35.

12. Ibid., 36.

13. Ibid.

14. David Cheever, ed., *A History of the Boston City Hospital from its Foundation until 1904* (Boston: Municipal Printing Office, 1906), 2–11.

15. Wood to Haskell, November 6, 1883, Wood Papers.

16. George Gay in Cheever, *Boston City Hospital,* 265.

17. Wood to Haskell, February 10, 1885, Wood Papers.

18. Wood to Haskell, May 29, 1885, Wood Papers.

19. Wood to Haskell, February 10, 1885, Wood Papers.

20. Ibid.

NOTES TO CHAPTER 4

1. Wood to Jake Wood, June 29, 1885, Wood Papers.

2. Dee Brown, *Bury My Heart at Wounded Knee: An Indian History of the American West* (New York: Holt, Rinehart & Winston, 1970), 200.

3. Hagedorn, *Wood,* 1:50.

4. Brown, *Wounded Knee,* 206.

5. The reservation was large enough that, if evenly divided, it would provide almost 1,000 acres for each family. Lt. General Philip Sheridan described this as "some of the best lands," although most was not arable and much was without any water. Sheridan actually suggested cutting the allotment back to 800 acres a family and releasing the rest (no doubt the better land) for sale with the proceeds to be placed in trust and the income from that trust being used to pay expenses previously assumed by the government under treaty obligations.

The proposal was never adopted. See *Weekly Phoenix Herald*, November 26, 1885.

6. Brown, *Wounded Knee*, 392.

7. Ibid., 394.

8. Ibid., 396.

9. Ibid., 401.

10. John G. Bourke, *An Apache Campaign in the Sierra Madre: An Account of the Expedition in Pursuit of the Hostile Chiricahua Apaches in the Spring of 1883* (New York: Charles Scribner's Sons, 1958), 51.

11. Odie Faulk, *The Geronimo Campaign* (New York: Oxford University Press, 1969), 53.

12. George Crook, *Résumé of Operations against Apache Indians, 1882–1886* (1886; reprint, London: Johnson-Taunton Military Press, 1971).

13. Eugene Lawrence, "The Apaches Are Coming," *Harper's Weekly*, January 30, 1886, p. 78.

14. Crook, *Résumé*, 22.

15. *Daily Phoenix Herald*, June 4, 1886.

16. Ibid.

17. Wood to Jake Wood, June 30, 1885, Wood Papers.

18. The ride is described in a letter from Wood to Jake, in Wood's diary, and cited in Hagedorn, *Wood*, 1:52–53.

19. Wood to Jake Wood, July 6, 1885, Wood Papers.

20. Wood to Jake, cited in Hagedorn, *Wood*, 1:57.

21. This account is taken from separate descriptions in Jason Betzinez, *I Fought with Geronimo* (New York: Bonanza Books, 1959), 131–33; Britton Davis, *The Truth about Geronimo* (Chicago: The Lakeside Press, R. R. Donnelly & Sons, 1951), 279–82; S. M. Barrett, ed., *Geronimo: His Own Story* (New York: Ballantine Books, 1971), 148; and Dan L. Thrapp, *The Conquest of Apacheria* (Norman: University of Oklahoma Press, 1967), 340–42. The various descriptions, taken from both the Indian and the army points of view, are in almost complete agreement.

22. Thrapp, *Conquest*, 345.

23. Barrett, *Geronimo*, 148.

24. A very detailed, day-by-day description of the conference is found in Davis, *The Truth about Geronimo*, 279–301.

25. Ibid., 98.

26. "Our Cavalry," *Harper's Weekly*, April 24, 1886.

27. Faulk, *The Geronimo Campaign*, 107.

28. Betzinez, *I Fought with Geronimo*, 137.

29. Faulk, *The Geronimo Campaign*, 103.

30. Wood's diary, May 4, 1886, Wood Papers.

31. Description of the Geronimo Campaign by Leonard Wood from the Wood Papers.

32. Ibid.

33. Wood to Jake, May 5, 1886, Wood Papers.

34. Betzinez, *I Fought with Geronimo*, 136.

35. Most of what follows is taken from Wood's handwritten description prepared for Miles's book about the campaign. Wood's Papers and his diary also in the Wood Papers and reproduced in Jack C. Lane, ed., *Chasing Geronimo: The Journal of Leonard Wood May–September, 1886* (Albuquerque: University of New Mexico Press, 1970).

36. Thrapp, *Conquest*, 351, and Faulk, *The Geronimo Campaign*, 104.

37. Wood to Jake, June 1, 1886, Wood Papers.

38. Ibid.

39. *Weekly Phoenix Herald*, December 10, 1885.

40. Wood's diary, June 19–23, 1886, Wood Papers.

41. Wood to Jake, July 7, 1886, Wood Papers.

42. Wood's diary, July 5, 1886, Wood Papers.

43. Lawton to his wife, July 17, 1886, cited in Hagedorn, *Wood*, 1:80.

44. Barrett, *Geronimo*, 153.

45. *Arizona Journal-Miner*, July 23, 1886.

46. Davis, *The Truth about Geronimo*, 315.

47. In fact, the anticipation of his capture was so great that Gatewood was incorrectly reported to be Geronimo's prisoner almost as soon as he crossed the line into Mexico. See *Weekly Phoenix Herald*, August 19, 1886.

48. Wood's diary, August 3, 1886, Wood Papers.

49. Faulk, *The Geronimo Campaign*, 112.

50. *Weekly Phoenix Herald*, August 26, 1886.

51. Wood's diary, August 19, 1886, Wood Papers.

52. Wood's diary, August 22, 1886, Wood Papers.

53. Faulk, *The Geronimo Campaign*, 117.

54. Wood's diary, August 27, 1886, Wood Papers.

55. Ibid.

56. *Weekly Phoenix Herald*, September 9, 1886.

57. Crook, *Résumé*, 25.

58. *Weekly Phoenix Herald*, September 9, 1886.

59. Faulk, *The Geronimo Campaign*, 133.

60. Wood's diary, August 28, 1886, Wood Papers.

61. Ibid.

62. Ibid.

63. Gatewood interview cited in Faulk, *The Geronimo Campaign*, 135.

64. *Arizona Journal-Miner*, September 7, 1886.

65. Wood's diary, September 3, 1886, Wood Papers.

66. Lawton to Miles, August 30, 1886, cited in Faulk, *The Geronimo Campaign*, 140.

67. Lawton to Miles, September 2, 1886, cited in Faulk, *The Geronimo Campaign*, 142.

68. Barrett, *Geronimo*, 153–54.

69. Most of this account is from Faulk, *The Geronimo Campaign*, 152–65.

70. Wood's diary, September 8, 1886, Wood Papers.

71. Lane, *Chasing Geronimo*, 114.

72. Wood's diary, September 21–23, 1886, Wood Papers.

73. Wood to Jake, September 16, 1886, Wood Papers.

74. A copy of the citation is contained in the Wood Papers.

NOTES TO CHAPTER 5

1. Wood's diary, October 1, 1887, Wood Papers.

2. Wood's diary, July 26–August 16, 1889, Wood Papers.

3. Wood's diary, July 20, 1889, Wood Papers.

4. Wood's diary, August 1–6, 1893, Wood Papers.

5. Wood's diary, August 9–15, 1893, Wood Papers.

6. Wood's diary, September 10–October 1, 1893.

7. Personal letter, Candy Carson, Assistant Registrar, Georgia Institute of Technology, September 14, 2001.

8. *Atlanta Journal*, November 6, 1893.

9. Ibid.

10. *Atlanta Constitution*, November 5, 1893.

11. *Atlanta Journal*, November 6, 1893.

12. *Atlanta Journal*, November 30, 1894.

13. Miles to Wood, June 11, 1894, Wood Papers.

14. Hagedorn, *Wood*, 1:133.

15. Sternberg to Wood, June 20, 1895, Wood Papers.

16. Sternberg to Wood, June 24, 1895, Wood Papers.

17. Sternberg to Wood, August 5, 1895, Wood Papers.

18. Hagedorn, *Wood*, 1:136.

19. The original of the note is in the Wood Papers and was presumably returned to Wood by Roosevelt or, more likely, by the Roosevelt family who also became quite close to Wood.

20. George Bronson Rea, *Facts and Fakes about Cuba* (New York: G. Munro's Sons, 1897), 236.

21. Carlton Beals, *The Crime of Cuba* (Philadelphia: J. B. Lippincott, 1933), 95.

22. Ibid., 99.

23. Russell Fitzgibbon, *Cuba and the United States: 1900–1935* (New York: Russell & Russell, 1964), 15.

24. Ibid., 18.

25. Jack Cameron Dierks, *A Leap to Arms: The Cuban Campaign of 1898* (Philadelphia: J. B. Lippincott, 1970), 11.

26. Alfred Thayer Mahan, *The Influence of Seapower upon History: 1660–1783* (Boston: Little, Brown and Company, 1890).

27. For a discussion of Mahan, Cuba, and the canal, see David McCullough, *The Path between the Seas: The Creation of the Panama Canal, 1870–1914* (New York: Simon and Schuster, 1977).

28. Henry Cabot Lodge, "Our Blundering Foreign Policy," *Forum,* March, 1895.

29. Hagedorn, *Wood,* 1:141.

30. Walter Millis, *The Martial Spirit* (Cambridge: The Riverside Press, 1931), 153.

31. Cited in David Healy, *The United States in Cuba, 1898–1902: Generals, Politicians and the Search for Policy* (Madison: University of Wisconsin Press, 1963), 18.

32. Ibid., 19.

33. Ibid., 22.

34. Ibid., 23.

35. From *The Congressional Record,* vol. 31, cited in Healy, *The United States in Cuba,* 22, and notes 14–23.

36. Horatio Rubens, Marti's New York lawyer, subsequently claimed that he convinced Teller to offer the amendment.

37. Healy, *The United States in Cuba,* 24.

38. Hagedorn, *Wood,* 1:145.

39. Charles Herner, *The Arizona Rough Riders* (Tucson: University of Arizona Press, 1970), 9–10 and note.

40. *United States Statutes at Large,* March 1897 to March 1898, 55th Congress, vol. 30, 1898, 362.

41. Alger to various governors, April 25, 1898, Wood Papers.

42. *New York Times,* April 29, 1898.

43. *New York Times,* April 26, 1898.

44. *New York Times,* April 28, 1898.

45. *New York Times,* April 3, 1898.

46. *San Antonio Daily Express,* May 10, 1898.

47. In a May 13 letter to his wife, Wood was still urging her to press the tailor to get his "Kaikai" uniform ready. Wood Papers, Box 190.

48. *San Antonio Daily Express,* May 22, 1898.

49. Graham Cosmas, *An Army for Empire: The United States Army in the Spanish-American War* (Columbia: University of Missouri Press, 1971), 153.

50. William S. Brophy, *The Krag Rifle* (Highland Park, NJ: Gun Room Press, 1985).

51. Roosevelt to Wood, undated (about May 8, 1898), Wood Papers.

52. Herner, *Arizona Rough Riders*, 19.
53. *San Antonio Daily Express*, May 18, 1898.
54. Herner, *Arizona Rough Riders*, 32.
55. *San Antonio Daily Express*, May 2, 1898.
56. *San Antonio Daily Express*, May 6, 1898.
57. *San Antonio Daily Express*, May 7, 1898.
58. *San Antonio Daily Express*, May 3, 1898.
59. *San Antonio Daily Express*, May 7, 1898.
60. *San Antonio Daily Express*, May 12, 1898.
61. Ibid.
62. Herner, *Arizona Rough Riders*, 58.
63. *New York Times*, May 1, 1898.
64. *New York Times*, May 7, 1898.
65. *New York Times*, April 28, 1898.
66. *San Antonio Daily Express*, May 10, 1898.
67. *San Antonio Daily Express*, May 11, 1898.
68. Trooper French quoted in Hagedorn, *Wood* 1:147.
69. *San Antonio Daily Express*, May 10, 1898.
70. *San Antonio Daily Express*, May 15, 1898.
71. *New York Times*, May 7, 1898.
72. *New York Times*, May 1, 1898. The saber was discarded after Las Guási-mas when Roosevelt learned that running with the long scabbard on his waist caused the weapon to repeatedly drift between his legs and trip him. Sabers may have been good for mounted cavalry, but they were a positive hindrance to warriors on foot.
73. *New York Times*, June 3, 1898.
74. *San Antonio Daily Express*, May 19, 1898.
75. Wood to McKinley, May 22, 1898, Wood Papers.
76. *San Antonio Daily Express*, May 20, 1898.
77. *San Antonio Daily Express*, May 22, 1898.
78. *San Antonio Daily Express*, May 24, 1898.
79. *San Antonio Daily Express*, May 29, 1898.
80. *New York Times*, April 24, 1898.
81. *New York Times*, April 17, 1898.
82. *San Antonio Daily Express*, May 7, 1898.
83. Theodore Roosevelt, *The Rough Riders* (New York: Da Capo Press, 1990), 47.
84. Wood to his wife, June 9, 1898, Wood Papers.
85. Ibid.
86. Millis, *The Martial Spirit*, 213.
87. Cosmas, *Army for Empire*, 133–35.
88. It was only after the city fell that the navy learned that the cannons were,

for the most part, ancient. Some dated from the 1600s and many had been modified to allow breech loading.

89. Cosmas, *Army for Empire*, 176.

90. Ibid., 189.

91. Ibid., 181.

92. Ibid.

93. Frank Freidel, *The Splendid Little War* (New York: Dell Publishing Company, 1962), 50.

94. Cosmas, *Army for Empire*, 190.

95. Corbin to Shafter, May 31, 1898. Reproduced in Fitzhugh Lee and Joseph Wheeler, *Cuba's Struggle against Spain* (New York: The American Historical Press, 1899), 344–45.

96. Roosevelt, *Rough Riders*, 53.

97. Millis, *The Martial Spirit*, 241.

98. Wood to his wife, June 9, 1898, Wood Papers.

99. Wood to his wife, June 6, 1898, Wood Papers.

100. Roosevelt, *Rough Riders*, 55.

101. Wood to his wife, June 4, 1898, Wood Papers.

102. Millis, *The Martial Spirit*, 246.

103. Ibid.

104. Hagedorn, *Wood*, 1:159, quoting the Dodge Commission Report.

105. Roosevelt, *Rough Riders*, 60.

106. The men of the Seventy-First, after milling about the docks for several hours, commandeered a ship of their own, the rather newer and more comfortable *Vigilancia*.

107. Edmund Morris, *The Rise of Roosevelt* (New York: Modern Library, 1979), 658.

108. Dale L. Walker, *The Boys of '98: Theodore Roosevelt and the Rough Riders* (New York: A Tom Doherty Associates Book, 1998), 146.

109. Horatio Rubens, *Liberty: The Story of Cuba* (New York: AMS Press, 1970), 373. Reprinted from the 1932 edition.

110. Millis, *The Martial Spirit*, 248.

111. Roosevelt, *Rough Riders*, 63.

112. Wood to his wife, June 9, 1898, Wood Papers.

113. Roosevelt, *Rough Riders*, 64.

114. Morris, *Rise of Roosevelt*, 660.

115. Freidel, *Splendid Little War*, 54. In a typographical error, Freidel incorrectly lists 15,058 enlisted men.

116. Edward Marshall, *The Story of the Rough Riders, 1st U.S. Volunteer Cavalry: The Regiment in Camp and on the Battle Field* (New York: G. W. Dillingham Co., 1899), 57.

117. Freidel, *Splendid Little War*, 56.

118. Ibid., 57.

119. Richard Harding Davis cited by Freidel, *Splendid Little War*, 58.

120. Wood to his wife, June 15, 1898, Wood Papers.

121. Wood to his wife, June 20, 1898, Wood Papers.

122. Wood to his wife, June 15, 1898, Wood Papers.

123. Wood to his mother, June 20, 1898, Wood Papers.

124. Freidel, *Splendid Little War*, 60.

125. The mines were wired to the fort at Morro Castle and could be detonated from shore.

126. In 1741, Lord Vernon had led 5,000 British troops from Guantanamo in an effort to take Santiago. He lost 2,000 to disease and abandoned the attempt sixteen miles east of the city without ever encountering a single Spanish soldier.

127. Wood's diary, Wood Papers.

128. Herner, *Arizona Rough Riders*, 94. Millis essentially confirms this version of events although others have regular troops hoisting the American flag instead. Herner's version, confirmed by that of newsman Edward Marshall's personal recollection, is almost certainly correct. See Marshall, *Story of the Rough Riders*, 68. Still another version, in which he takes credit for the flag, is found in Joseph Wheeler's *The Santiago Campaign: 1898* (Freeport, N.Y.: Books for Libraries Press, 1970), 14.

129. Newsman Malcolm McDowell cited in Freidel, *Splendid Little War*, 69.

130. Freidel, *Splendid Little War*, 64.

131. Herner, *Arizona Rough Riders*, 96.

132. Sergeant Davis Hughes cited in Herner, *Arizona Rough Riders*, 97.

133. Freidel, *Splendid Little War*, 72.

134. G. J. A. O'Toole, *The Spanish War: An American Epic—1898* (New York: W. W. Norton, 1984), 269.

135. Edward Chrisman cited in Freidel, *Splendid Little War*, 70.

136. Wheeler, *Santiago Campaign*, 19.

137. O'Toole, *The Spanish War*, 269.

138. Marshall, *Story of the Rough Riders*, 78–79.

139. Wood "Las Guásimas" manuscript, Wood Papers. Wood handwrote a description of the Las Guásimas battle shortly after it occurred, dated only June, 1898. The manuscript is in the Wood Papers.

140. Wood "Las Guásimas" manuscript, Wood Papers.

141. Marshall, *Story of the Rough Riders*, 271.

142. Millis, *The Martial Spirit*, 271.

143. Cited in Freidel, *Splendid Little War*, 77.

144. Wood "Las Guásimas" manuscript, Wood Papers.

145. Herner, *Arizona Rough Riders*, 120.

146. From Burr McIntosh, *The Little I Saw of Cuba*, cited in Herner, *Arizona Rough Riders*, 118. McIntosh may not have gotten to Las Guásimas but he was

the first reporter ashore at Daiquirí. He bribed a sergeant to take his camera on one of the longboats going ashore while he stripped and swam in. Shafter, in an order that earned Richard Harding Davis's permanent antipathy, had refused to let reporters come ashore with the soldiers. See A. C. M. Azoy, *Charge! The Story of San Juan Hill* (New York: Longmans, Green and Co., 1961), 76.

147. Cited in Walker, *The Boys of '98*, 196–97.

148. Marshall, *Story of the Rough Riders*, 103.

149. Ibid., 103–4

150. Morris, *Rise of Roosevelt*, 673.

151. Wheeler to Adjutant-General 5th Army Corps, June 26, 1898, reprinted in Wheeler, *Santiago Campaign*, 19.

152. Marshall, *Story of the Rough Riders*, 104.

153. Ibid.

154. Ibid., 119–21.

155. Richard Harding Davis, *The Cuban and Porto Rican Campaigns* (New York: Charles Scribner's Sons, 1898), 145.

156. Marshall, *Story of the Rough Riders*, 111.

157. Ibid., 115.

158. Church was awarded the Medal of Honor on January 10, 1906 for his performance at Las Guásimas.

159. Cited in Freidel, *Splendid Little War*, 83.

160. Young to Adjutant-General, Cavalry Division, June 29, 1898, reprinted in Wheeler, *Santiago Campaign*, 28.

161. Freidel, *Splendid Little War*, 82.

162. Azoy, *Charge!* 95.

163. Hagedorn, *Wood*, 1:170–71. Hagedorn never uses Hall's name and was intensely critical of him. Herner, in *Arizona Rough Riders*, was much less critical, suggesting that Hall saw Marshall shot and mistook him for Wood but that his disciplinary responsibilities as adjutant had made him unpopular so that, in the wake of accusations of cowardice, he resigned a few days after Las Guásimas.

164. Millis, *The Martial Spirit*, 274.

165. Cosmas, *Army for Empire*, 209.

166. Wood to his wife cited in Hagedorn, *Wood*, 1:170.

167. Millis, *The Martial Spirit*, 275.

168. Wood to his wife, June 29, 1898, Wood Papers.

169. Hagedorn, *Wood*, 1:173.

170. Herner, *Arizona Rough Riders*, 115.

171. Marshall, *Story of the Rough Riders*, 138.

172. Morris, *Rise of Roosevelt*, 879.

173. Cosmas, *Army for Empire*, 209.

174. Dierks, *Leap to Arms*, 95.

175. Ibid., 97.

176. Herner, *Arizona Rough Riders,* 128.

177. Morris, *Rise of Roosevelt,* 682.

178. Roosevelt, *Rough Riders,* 118.

179. Azoy, *Charge!* 110.

180. Wood's diary, July 1, 1898, Wood Papers.

181. Azoy, *Charge!* 124.

182. Hagedorn, *Wood,* 1:175.

183. Azoy, *Charge!* 129–30.

184. Wood's diary, July 1, 1898, Wood Papers.

185. Davis, *The Cuban and Porto Rican Campaigns,* 218–20.

186. Wheeler later took some offense at the suggestion that he had missed the battle. On July 10 he wrote his superiors, "General Sumner had assumed command of the Division on the morning of the 1st, under the supposition that I was ill. I had been directed by the Adjutant General of the 5th Corps to give directions to both General Sumner and General Kent. I complied with this and gave them directions in person. I did not deem it best of kind to immediately displace General Sumner from command of the Division, or to displace Col. Carroll from command of the 1st Brigade. I therefore gave directions to the Division through General Sumner, and with the aid of my staff, also gave directions to Colonels Wood and Carroll until the afternoon after which I gave directions to General Sumner as commander of the 1st Brigade, and to Col. Wood of the 2nd Brigade." Both Sumner and Wheeler submitted reports as commanding general of the cavalry division. From Wood Papers.

187. Azoy, *Charge!* 139.

188. Wood to Adjutant General, Cav. Div., 5th Army Corps, July 6, 1898, Wood Papers.

189. Hagedorn, *Wood,* 1:178.

190. Wood's diary, July 1, 1898, Wood Papers.

191. Walker, *Boys of '98,* 229.

192. Ibid., 234.

193. Davis, *The Cuban and Porto Rican Campaigns,* 249.

194. Walker, *Boys of '98,* 238.

195. Ibid., 240.

196. Ibid., 237.

197. Cosmas, *Army for Empire,* 227, and Davis, *The Cuban and Porto Rican Campaigns,* 200.

198. Wood to his wife, July 15, 1898, Wood Papers.

199. O'Toole, *The Spanish War,* 347.

200. Cosmas, *Army for Empire,* 230.

201. Wood's diary, July 7, 1898, Wood Papers.

202. Wood to his wife, July 15, 1898, Wood Papers.

203. Davis, *The Cuban and Porto Rican Campaigns,* 250–51.

204. Wood to his wife, July 15, 1898, Wood Papers.

205. Miles to the secretary of war, July 12, 1898, reproduced in Lee, *Cuba's Struggle*, 472.

206. Shafter to Adjutant General H. C. Corbin, July 13, 1898, reproduced in Lee, *Cuba's Struggle*, 473.

207. Wood to his wife, July 15, 1898, Wood Papers.

208. *New York Times*, July 18, 1898.

NOTES TO CHAPTER 6

1. Samuel Eliot Morison, *Admiral of the Ocean Sea: A Life of Christopher Columbus* (Boston: Little, Brown and Company, 1942), 451.

2. Wood to his wife, July 21, 1898, Wood Papers, Box 190. See also George Kennan, "The Sanitary Regeneration of Santiago," *Outlook* 61 (April 15, 1899), 871–77.

3. The description and distances are derived from maps included in Wheeler, *Santiago Campaign*, and George Kennan, "Santiago de Cuba Revisited," *Outlook* 61 (March 4, 1899), 497–501.

4. Kennan, "Regeneration of Santiago."

5. George Kennan, "Destitution and Suffering in Matanzas," *Outlook* 62 (July 15, 1899), 608–14.

6. William H. McNeill, *Plagues and Peoples* (New York: Doubleday, 1977), 186–88.

7. New York lost 10 percent of its population in 1702 and Philadelphia lost 15 percent in 1793. Thomas Jefferson worried that the disease would "discourage the growth of great cities" in the new United States. See Wayne Biddle, *A Field Guide to Germs* (New York: Anchor Books, 1995), 160–65.

8. Lee and Wheeler, *Cuba's Struggle*, 468.

9. Ibid., 469.

10. Ibid.

11. *New York Times*, August 12, 1898.

12. *New York Times*, September 9, 1898.

13. Trumbull White, *Pictorial History of Our War with Spain for Cuba's Freedom* (n.p.: Freedom Publishing Company, 1898), 500.

14. Hagedorn, *Wood*, 1:200.

15. *New York Times*, November 22, 1898.

16. Clifford Westermeier, *Who Rush to Glory* (Cladwell, Idaho: Caxton Printers, 1958), 237.

17. Ibid.

18. R. A. Alger, *The Spanish American War* (New York: Harper & Brothers, 1901), 258.

19. Ibid., 261. The site for Camp Wickoff had only been selected on July 26, and the facilities were understandably far from ready.

20. Millis, *Martial Spirit*, 350.

21. Ibid.

22. Roosevelt says the meeting was July 31 (Theodore Roosevelt, *The Rough Riders* [New York: Da Capo Press, 1990], 209; originally published [New York: Charles Scribner's Sons, 1902]) but that date, given other communications from Shafter to Alger, is almost certainly wrong. See Alger, *Spanish American War*, p. 263 for Shafter's letter in which he says the meeting was August 3.

23. Jack C. Lane, *Armed Progressive: General Leonard Wood* (San Rafael, Calif.: Presidio Press, 1978), 61.

24. Roosevelt, *Rough Riders*, 209, and Walker, *Boys of '98*, 261–63.

25. Roosevelt, *Rough Riders* 210.

26. Westermeier, *Rush to Glory*, 238.

27. Hagedorn, *Wood*, 1:201.

28. The entire letter is reprinted in White, *History of Our War with Spain*, 501. Lawton, obviously concerned about the letter's effect on his career, attached an addendum that was never published. In it he stated, "I desire to express that the mandatory language used in the letter is impolitic and unnecessary. Milder expression to those high in authority generally accomplish just as much. It is also my opinion that much of the fatal illness is due to homesickness and other depressing influences." The letter is also reprinted in Alger, *Spanish American War*, 267–68.

29. Hagedorn, *Wood*, 1:201.

30. Lane, *Armed Progressive*, 61.

31. *New York Times*, August 9, 1898.

32. Walker, *Boys of '98*, 263.

33. *New York Times*, August 9, 1898.

34. Alger, *Spanish American War*, 273.

35. Letter reprinted in Alger, *Spanish American War*, 271.

36. Shafter to Corbin, August 4, 1898, Wood Papers.

37. *New York Times*, August 25, 1898.

38. *New York Times*, August 10, 1898.

39. Leonard Wood, "Santiago since the Surrender," *Scribner's Magazine* 25 (May 1899), 515–27.

40. Ibid.

41. Ibid.

42. Wood to his wife, August 4, 1898, Wood Papers.

43. Wood to his wife, August 14, 1898, Wood Papers.

44. Wood to his wife, October 11, 1898, Wood Papers.

45. Wood to his wife, July 21, 1898, Wood Papers.

46. Hagedorn, *Wood*, 1:189, and Wood, "Santiago since the Surrender."

47. Ibid., and Hagedorn, *Wood*, 1:188.

48. George Kennan, "Havana," *Outlook* 62 (June 10, 1899), 334–40.

49. George Kennan, "The Government of Santiago," *Outlook* 62 (May 13, 1899), 109–15.

50. Wood, "Santiago since the Surrender."

51. Hagedorn, *Wood*, 1:189.

52. Kennan, "Regeneration of Santiago."

53. Wood to McKinley, November 27, 1898, Wood Papers.

54. Kennan, "Regeneration of Santiago."

55. Women and children outnumbered men ten to one in the camps. See George Kennan, "The Regeneration of Cuba: General Gomez at Santa Clara," *Outlook* 63 (September 16, 1899), 151–58.

56. George Kennan, "Friction in Cuba: A Special Letter from George Kennan on General Wood's Work," *Outlook* 61 (March 25, 1899), 675–78.

57. Wood, "Santiago since the Surrender," 515–27.

58. James Purcell, Company G, 11th Infantry, cited in White, *History of Our War with Spain*, 548.

59. Kennan, "General Gomez."

60. Wood, "Santiago since the Surrender."

61. Leonard Wood, "The Existing Conditions and Needs in Cuba," *North American Review* 168 (May 1899), 593–601.

62. Kennan, "Government of Santiago."

63. Wood, "Santiago since the Surrender."

64. *New York Times*, August 15, 1898.

65. *New York Times*, September 1, 1898.

66. George Kennan, "From Santiago to Havana," *Outlook* 62 (May 27, 1899), 202–8.

67. Ibid.

68. Ibid.

69. Kennan, "Government of Santiago."

70. Ibid.

71. Wood, "Existing Conditions."

72. Ibid.

73. *New York Times*, August 22, 1898.

74. *New York Times*, July 13, 1898.

75. Rubens, *Liberty*, 349–50.

76. *New York Times*, July 13, 1898.

77. *New York Times*, March 11, 1899.

78. *New York Times*, August 17, 1898.

79. Cited in *New York Times*, November 26, 1898.

80. Kennan, "From Santiago to Havana," 201–2.

81. Wood lays out the plan in some detail in an undated memorandum that

seems to have been intended primarily for his own use and is found in the Wood Papers.

82. Wood to McKinley, November 27, 1898, Wood Papers.

83. Hagedorn, *Wood*, 1:216.

84. Rubens, *Liberty*, 379.

85. Hagedorn, *Wood*, 1:199.

86. Wood to his wife, August 14, 1898, Wood Papers.

87. Rubens, *Liberty*, 371.

88. Wood to unknown correspondent, November 1898, Wood Papers.

89. Wood, "Existing Conditions."

90. Ibid.

91. Kennan, "Regeneration of Santiago," 871–77.

92. *New York Times*, January 18, 1899.

93. *New York Times*, January 11, 1899.

94. George Kennan, "A Few Days in Guantanamo," *Outlook* 61 (April 29, 1899), 957–66.

95. Wood, "Santiago since the Surrender."

96. Wood to McKinley, November 27, 1898, Wood Papers. See Hagedorn, *Wood*, 1:213.

97. Luis Gaston to Wood, November 1, 1899, Wood Papers.

98. Wood, "Santiago since the Surrender."

99. Kennan, "Government of Santiago."

100. Wood to his wife, July 30, 1898, Wood Papers.

101. See Rubens, *Liberty*, 381.

102. Kennan, "Government of Santiago."

103. *New York Times*, January 18, 1899.

104. *New York Times*, June 14, 1899.

105. Wood, "Existing Conditions."

106. *New York Times*, January 18, 1899.

107. Wood, "Existing Conditions."

108. Kennan, "Santiago Revisited."

109. Wood, "Existing Conditions."

110. *New York Times*, January 18, 1899.

111. Wood to McKinley, November 27, 1898, Wood Papers.

112. Theodore Roosevelt, "General Leonard Wood: A Model American Military Administrator," *Outlook* 61 (January 7, 1899).

113. Wood, "Santiago since the Surrender."

114. Wood, "Existing Conditions."

115. Wood to Roosevelt, August 3, 1899, Wood Papers.

116. Wood in a 1902 speech at Williams College, cited by Hagedorn, *Wood*, 1:217.

117. Wood to his wife, November 27, 1898, Wood Papers. See also Wood,

"Existing Conditions," and Leonard Wood, "The Present Situation in Cuba," *The Century* 58 (August 1899), 639–40.

118. Charlton Lewis to Elihu Root, December 20, 1899, Wood Papers.

119. Hagedorn, *Wood*, 1:217.

120. Ibid.

121. Wood to McKinley November 27, 1898, Wood Papers.

122. Osborne Wood was born in 1897.

123. Wood to his wife, August 21, 1898, Wood Papers.

124. Wood to his wife, August 20, 1898, Wood Papers.

125. Wood to his wife, August 8, 1898, Wood Papers.

126. Wood to his mother, September 8, 1898, Wood Papers.

127. Wood to his wife, September 18, 1898, Wood Papers.

128. Wood to McKinley, November 27, 1898, Wood Papers.

129. *New York Times*, January 18, 1899.

130. G. D. Meiklejohn to Wood, November 21, 1898, Wood Papers.

131. Roosevelt to Hay, July 1, 1899, Wood Papers.

132. Roosevelt to Griggs, July 1, 1899, Wood Papers.

133. Emiliano Bacardi to Wood, June 13, 1899, Wood Papers.

134. Healy, *The United States in Cuba*, 55.

135. Robert Bacon and James Brown Scott, ed., *Military and Colonial Policy of the United States: Addresses and Reports by Elihu Root* (Cambridge, Mass.: Harvard University Press, 1916), 161.

136. Root later reorganized the division as the Division of Insular Affairs which rose to bureau status in 1902.

137. Hagedorn, *Wood*, 1:235. See also Kennan, "Friction in Cuba."

138. Hagedorn, *Wood*, 1:232.

139. Ibid., 226.

140. On April 19 and July 1, 1899, revisions were made to combine two provinces in each subdepartment with Havana remaining separate. This left a total of four commands under Brigadier General James Wilson (Matanzas and Santa Clara), Brigadier General Fitzhugh Lee (Havana Province and Pinar del Rio), Brigadier General William Ludlow (Havana City), and Wood (Santiago and Puerto Principe).

141. Hagedorn, *Wood*, 1:235.

142. Rubens, *Liberty*, 382–83.

143. Chaffee to Wood, January 10, 1899, Wood Papers.

144. Roosevelt, "General Leonard Wood."

145. Ibid.

146. *New York Times*, January 18, 1899.

147. Lodge to Wood, March 16, 1899, Wood Papers.

148. Wood to his wife, May 3, 1899, Wood Papers.

149. Pearson to Wood, May 24, 1899, Wood Papers.

150. Roosevelt to Griggs, July 1, 1899, Wood Papers.

151. Roosevelt to Hay, July 1, 1899, Wood Papers.

152. *New York Times,* June 24, 1899.

153. *New York Times,* June 29, 1899.

154. *New York Times,* June 23, 1899.

155. *New York Times,* June 25, 1899.

156. *New York Times,* July 24, 1899.

157. Wood to his wife, July 19, 1899, Wood Papers.

158. *New York Times,* July 13, 1899.

159. *New York Times,* July 14, 1899.

160. *New York Times,* July 15, 1899.

161. Wood to Roosevelt, July 12, 1899, Wood Papers.

162. Roosevelt to Wood, August 9, 1899, Wood Papers.

163. José M. Hernandez, *Cuba and the United States: Intervention and Militarism, 1868–1933* (Austin: University of Texas Press, 1993), 60.

164. Ibid., 74.

165. Brooke had some justification for his fears. The city had just come through three days of anti-Spanish riots in which a number of civilians had been killed.

166. Hernandez, *Cuba and the United States,* 52–54.

167. *New York Times,* August 28, 1899.

168. Lewis to Root, December 20, 1899, Wood Papers.

169. Albert G. Robinson, *Cuba and the Intervention* (London: Longmans, Green and Co., 1905), 129.

170. Havard to Wood, September 21, 1899, Wood Papers.

171. Robinson, *Cuba and the Intervention,* 136.

172. Bacon, *Military and Colonial Policy,* 171.

173. Ibid.

174. *New York Times,* May 12, 1899.

175. *New York Times,* January 18, 1899.

176. Robert Porter, "The Future of Cuba," *North American Review* 168 (April 1899), 418–23.

177. *New York Times,* June 24, 1899.

178. *New York Times,* September 5, 1899.

179. Mrs. Wood to Wood, October 3, 1899, Wood Papers.

180. Wood to Mrs. Wood, October 18, 1899, Wood Papers.

181. Mrs. Wood to Wood, October 23, 1899, Wood Papers.

182. Wood to McKinley, October 27, 1899, Wood Papers.

183. Roosevelt to Root, October 9, 1899, Wood Papers.

184. Mrs. Wood to Wood, October 31, 1899, Wood Papers.

185. *New York Times,* November 10, 1899.

186. *New York Times,* December 1, 1899.

NOTES TO CHAPTER 7

1. Wood to Root, December 22, 1899, Wood Papers.
2. *New York Times,* December 21, 1899.
3. *Boston Advertiser,* December 21, 1899.
4. Healy, *The United States in Cuba,* 120.
5. Rubens, *Liberty,* 397.
6. Ibid., 236.
7. Ibid., 255–56.
8. Ibid., 265.
9. Ibid., 266.
10. *New York Times,* December 22, 1899.
11. Hagedorn, *Wood,* 1:264.
12. Gómez to Wood, December 30, 1899, Wood Papers.
13. Wood to Root, December 21, 1899, Elihu Root Papers.
14. Wood to Root, December 30, 1899, Wood Papers.
15. Ibid.
16. Wood to Root, February 6, 1900, Wood Papers.
17. *New York Times,* December 29, 1899.
18. Ibid., December 31, 1899.
19. Wood learned on the day he landed in Havana that Lawton had been killed shortly after arriving at his new assignment in the Philippines. Although Lawton had a plethora of personal problems and his relationship with Wood had not always been smooth, the two had known each other for years and had spent many hard months in Mexico, and the senior general's death was a real blow to the younger man.
20. When it became obvious that he would not get the governorship, Ludlow had even suggested dividing Cuba in two to be shared by he and Wood, or, failing that, to make Wood governor of the Philippines.
21. Healy, *The United States in Cuba,* 129.
22. Wood to Root, December 22, 1899, Root Papers.
23. Wood to Root, January 13, 1900, Wood Papers.
24. Wood to Root, February 8, 1900, Wood Papers.
25. Root to Wood, February 13, 1900, Wood Papers.
26. Root to Wood, January 27, 1900, Wood Papers.
27. Wood to Root, February 8, 1900, Wood Papers.
28. Charlton Lewis to Root, December 20, 1899, Wood Papers.
29. Wood to Root, February 6, 1900, Wood Papers.
30. Leonard Wood, "The Military Government of Cuba," *The Annals of the American Academy of Political and Social Sciences* 21 (March 1903), 5–7.
31. Ibid., 7–8.

32. Fitzgibbon, *Cuba and the United States,* 34.

33. Hagedorn, *Wood,* 1:270.

34. Wood, "The Military Government of Cuba," 22.

35. Philip C. Jessup, *Elihu Root* (New York: Dodd, Mead and Company, 1938), 1:305.

36. Root to Paul Dana, editor of the *New York Sun,* cited in Jessup, *Root,* 1:305.

37. Healy, *The United States in Cuba,* 180.

38. Fitzgibbon, *Cuba and the United States,* 3, and Wood, "The Military Government of Cuba," 11.

39. Wood, "The Military Government of Cuba," 11.

40. H. W. Brands, *Bound to Empire: The United States and the Philippines* (New York: Oxford University Press, 1992), 69.

41. Wood to Henry Cabot Lodge, August 8, 1900, Wood Papers.

42. Robinson, *Cuba and the Intervention,* 147.

43. Ibid., 50.

44. Ibid.

45. Wood to McKinley, August 31, 1900, Wood Papers.

46. Jessup, *Root,* 1:290.

47. Wood to Root, May 5, 1900, Wood Papers.

48. Wood to Root, February 8, 1900, Wood Papers.

49. Morris, *Rise of Theodore Roosevelt,* 566.

50. Root to Wood, March 24, 1900, Wood Papers.

51. Wood to Root, May 5, 1900, Wood Papers. Also Hagedorn, *Wood,* 1:294.

52. Wood to Root, May 6, 1900, Wood Papers.

53. Root to Wood, May 9, 1900, Wood Papers.

54. Roosevelt to Wood, August 9, 1900, Wood Papers.

55. Frank McCoy to Philip Jessup, May 29, 1937, cited in Jessup, *Root,* 1:290.

56. *Washington Post,* May 16, 1900.

57. Wood to Root, May 23, 1900, Wood Papers.

58. Ibid.

59. Platt to Wood, June 1, 1900, Wood Papers.

60. Root to Wood, June 2, 1900, Wood Papers.

61. Wood to Root, June 12, 1900, Wood Papers.

62. Jessup, *Root,* 1:292.

63. Leland Jenks, *Our Cuban Colony* (New York: Vanguard Press, 1928), 59–60.

64. Hernandez, *Cuba and the United States,* 54.

65. Louis A. Pérez, *Cuba between Empires, 1878–1902* (Pittsburgh: University of Pittsburgh Press, 1983), 346–47.

66. Ibid., 348–49.

67. Healy, *The United States in Cuba,* 189–90.

68. Wood to Root, April 12, 1900, Root Papers. Wood to McKinley, April 12, 1900, Wood Papers.

69. Wood to Root, January 13, 1900, Wood Papers.

70. Platt to Wood, January 1, 1900, Wood Papers, discusses the futility of seeking repeal of the Foraker Amendment.

71. Healy, *The United States in Cuba*, 130–31.

72. Wood to Root, February 8, 1900, Wood Papers.

73. Perez, *Cuba between Empires*, 311, and Root to Wood, February 1, 1900, Wood Papers.

74. Wood to Root, February 23, 1900, Root Papers.

75. Wood to Root, June 3, 1900, Wood Papers.

76. Wood to Root, June 18, 1900, Wood Papers.

77. Albert Truby, *Memoir of Walter Reed: The Yellow Fever Episode* (New York: Paul B. Hoeber, 1943), 43–44.

78. Ibid., 50.

79. Wood to Root, June 27, 1900, Wood Papers.

80. Hagedorn, *Wood*, 1:281, and Wood to Ludlow, October 25, 1900, Wood Papers.

81. Truby, *Walter Reed*, 85.

82. Ibid., 112.

83. Hagedorn, *Wood*, 1:300.

84. *New York Evening Post*, October 23, 1900.

85. Ludlow to Wood, October 24, 1900, Wood Papers.

86. Wood to Ludlow, October 25, 1900, Wood Papers.

87. Ludlow to Wood, October 27, 1900, Wood Papers.

88. Wood to Villard, November 3, 1900, Wood Papers.

89. Wood to *Outlook* and Wood to *New York Sun*, November 3, 1900, Wood Papers.

90. Wood to Ludlow, November 3, 1900, Wood Papers.

91. Wood to Adjutant General, November 3, 1900, Wood Papers.

92. Fitzgibbon, *Cuba and the United States*, 37.

93. Forest monkeys were later found to harbor the virus but they do not develop yellow fever.

94. Lawrence K. Altman, *Who Goes First? The Story of Self-Experimentation in Medicine* (New York: Random House, 1986), 142.

95. Ibid., 148.

96. Ibid.

97. Fitzgibbon, *Cuba and the United States*, 41.

98. Hagedorn, *Wood*, 1:325–26.

99. Kean from a speech at the dedication of Walter Reed's birthplace, printed in *Military Surgeon*, March 1928, and cited in Hagedorn, *Wood*, 1:327.

100. *La Discusion,* November 21, 1900. Translation from the Philip S. Hench Yellow Fever Collection, University of Virginia.

101. Truby, *Walter Reed,* 132.

102. John Gibson, *Physician to the World: The Life of General William C. Gorgas* (Tuscaloosa: University of Alabama Press, 1989), 70.

103. Ibid.

104. Altman, *Who Goes First?* 157.

105. Ibid., 152–54.

106. Truby, *Walter Reed,* 69.

107. Kean to Adjutant General, Department of Western Cuba, October 13, 1900, cited in Truby, *Walter Reed,* 222.

108. Gibson, *Physician to the World,* 76.

109. Truby, *Walter Reed,* 225–28.

110. Hugh Scott to Albert Truby, Commanding Officer, Roswell Barracks, Paso Caballos, Cuba, April 17, 1901, cited in Truby, *Walter Reed,* 229–30.

111. Truby, *Walter Reed,* 82–83.

112. Gibson, *Physician to the World,* 90.

113. Fitzgibbon, *Cuba and the United States,* 43.

114. Wood, "The Military Government of Cuba," 20.

115. Fitzgibbon, *Cuba and the United States,* 59.

116. *Civil Report of General Leonard Wood, Military Governor of Cuba* (Washington, D.C.: Government Printing Office, 1902), 5.

117. Wood to Root, February 6, 1900, Wood Papers.

118. Ibid.

119. Wood to Root, August 13, 1900, Wood Papers.

120. Wood to Root, June 8, 1900, Wood Papers.

121. Wood to Senator Nelson Aldrich, June 21, 1900, Wood Papers.

122. Ibid.

123. Wood to Root, July 6, 1900, Wood Papers.

124. Wood to Root, June 3, 1900, Wood Papers.

125. Wood to Root, June 8, 1900, Wood Papers.

126. Wood to Root, June 3, 1900, Wood Papers.

127. Wood to Root, June 8, 1900, Wood Papers.

128. Robinson, *Cuba and the Intervention,* 190.

129. Wood to Root, April 4, 1901, Wood Papers.

130. Ibid.

131. Wood to Lodge, May 12, 1900, Wood Papers.

132. Wood to Roosevelt, July 7, 1900, Wood Papers.

133. Cited in Hagedorn, *Wood,* 1:336.

134. Wood to Root, February 6, 1900, Wood Papers.

135. Wood to McKinley, February 6, 1900, Wood Papers.

136. Wood to Root, January 13, 1900, Wood Papers.
137. Wood to Root, June 18, 1900, Wood Papers.
138. Donatus, Bishop of Havana to Wood, August 10, 1900, Wood Papers.
139. Wood to Root, June 8, 1901, and June 10, 1901, Wood Papers.
140. Jenks, *Our Cuban Colony*, 63.
141. Healy, *The United States in Cuba*, 191.
142. Wood to Root, February 16, 1900, Wood Papers.
143. Wood to McKinley, August 31, 1900, Wood Papers.
144. Wood to McKinley, October 28, 1901, Wood Papers.
145. Ibid.
146. The last of three railroad laws was actually published only three weeks before the Americans left Cuba.
147. Fitzgibbon, *Cuba and the United States*, 55.
148. Wood to Root, June 3, 1900, Wood Papers.
149. Wood to Aldrich, June 21, 1900, Wood Papers.
150. Healy, *The United States in Cuba*, 152, and Wood to Root, August 6, 1900, Wood Papers.
151. Wood to Root, August 13, 1900, Wood Papers.
152. Wood to McKinley, August 31, 1900, Wood Papers.
153. Wood to Root, September 8, 1900, Wood Papers.
154. Hagedorn, *Wood*, 1:328.
155. Root to Wood, January 9, 1901, Wood Papers.
156. Ibid.
157. Wood to Root, February 25, 1901, Root Papers.
158. Robinson, *Cuba and the Intervention*, 227–28.
159. Ibid.
160. Jenks, *Our Cuban Colony*, 75.
161. Root interview, January 19, 1929, cited in Jessup, *Root*, 1:313–14.
162. Wood to Root, January 19, 1900, Wood Papers.
163. Wood to Root, February 8, 1901, Wood Papers.
164. Wood wrote this stipulation with the intent of preventing the return of yellow fever and other insect-borne diseases that might threaten United States cities.
165. Much of the Isle of Pines was owned and farmed by Americans who hoped the island would pass directly to American control.
166. Root to Wood, May 31, 1901, Wood Papers.
167. Robinson, *Cuba and the Intervention*, 236.
168. Root to Wood, February 25, 1901, Wood Papers.
169. Wood to Root, February 27, 1901, Root Papers.
170. Ibid.
171. Robinson, *Cuba and the Intervention*, 244.
172. Ibid., 238–40.

173. Healy, *The United States in Cuba*, 168.

174. Wood to Root, March 4, 1901, Root Papers.

175. Root to Wood, March 2, 1901, Wood Papers.

176. Wood to Root, March 4, 1901, Wood Papers.

177. Wood to Root, March 23, 1901, Wood Papers.

178. Root to Wood, cited in Perez, *Cuba between Empires*, 325.

179. Root to Wood, March 29, 1901, Wood Papers.

180. Root to Wood, April 15, 1901, Wood Papers.

181. Root to Wood, March 28, 1901, Wood Papers.

182. Wood to Root, June 9, 1901, Root Papers.

183. Wood to Roosevelt, October 28, 1901, cited by Healy in *United States in Cuba*, 178.

184. Wood to Root, June 16, 1901, Wood Papers.

185. Wood to Root, September 12, 1901, Wood Papers.

186. Wood to Root, January 4, 1902, Wood Papers.

187. Root, *Annual Report for 1900*, cited in Robinson, *Cuba and the Intervention*, 222.

188. Ewing Wilson, "The Anti-Imperialist Position," *North American Review* 171 (October 1900), 460–68.

189. B. R. Tilman, "Causes of Southern Opposition to Imperialism," *North American Review* 171 (October 1900), 439–46.

190. Ibid.

191. Walter Zimmerman, *The First Great Triumph: How Five Americans Made Their Country a World Power* (New York: Farrar, Straus and Giroux, 2002), 292.

192. Ibid., 339.

193. Ibid., 340.

194. W. A. Peffer, "Imperialism, America's Historic Policy," *North American Review* 171 (August 1900), 246–59.

195. "Concerning Self Government," *Outlook* 62 (May 27, 1899), 196–98.

196. Wood to Root, March 23, 1901, Wood Papers.

197. Wood to Root, April 15, 1901, Wood Papers.

198. Wood to Root, October 12, 1910, Wood Papers.

199. Wood to Root October 17, 1901, Wood Papers.

200. Wood to Lodge, May 12, 1900, Wood Papers.

201. Wood to Platt, December 19, 1900, Wood Papers.

202. Wood to Root, January 8, 1901, Wood Papers.

203. Wood to Roosevelt, October 7, 1901, Wood Papers.

204. Root to Wood, January 9, 1901, Root Papers.

205. Ibid.

206. United States Department of Commerce, *Customs and Tariff Regulations* (Washington, D.C.: Government Printing Office, 1898).

207. Perez, *Cuba between Empires*, 363.

208. Wood to Root, February 8, 1902, Root Papers.

209. Perez, *Cuba between Empires*, 363.

210. Leonard Wood, William H. Taft, Charles H. Allen, Perfecto Lacoste, and M. E. Beall, *Opportunities in the Colonies and Cuba* (New York: Lewis, Scribner & Co., 1902), 140.

211. The description is from Wood's diary in Wood Papers. Wood later took both Cuban flags and the last American flag as well as the old Spanish governor general's chair and kept them in his private collection.

212. The records became a source of discord when Estrada Palma unsuccessfully tried to commandeer them over Wood's strenuous objection.

213. Robinson, *Cuba and the Intervention*, 201.

NOTES TO CHAPTER 8

1. Wood's diary, May 20, 1902, Wood Papers.

2. Wood's diary, undated, Wood Papers.

3. Wood's diary, August 16, 1902, Wood Papers.

4. Wood's diary, September 10, 1902, Wood Papers.

5. Ibid.

6. Wood to Root, October 13, 1902, Root Papers.

7. Ibid.

8. Wood's diary, October 25, 1902, Wood Papers.

9. McCoy to Hagedorn, 1930, cited in Hagedorn, *Wood*, 1:404.

10. Wood to Roosevelt, January 4, 1902, Wood Papers.

11. Brands, *Bound to Empire*, 45.

12. Garel A. Grunder and William Livezey, *The Philippines and the United States* (Norman: University of Oklahoma Press, 1951), 71.

13. Ibid., 36.

14. Ibid., 55.

15. Brands, *Bound to Empire*, 56.

16. Grunder and Livezey, *The Philippines and the United States*, 60.

17. From Cameron Forbes's report cited in Grunder, *The Philippines and the United States*, 139.

18. James H. Blount, *American Occupation of the Philippines: 1898–1912* (New York: Knickerbocker Press, 1913), 230.

19. Jessup, *Root*, 1:364.

20. Bacon, *Military and Colonial Policy*, 320.

21. Ibid., 321.

22. Hagedorn, *Wood*, 1:406. In his memoirs, General Hugh Scott says Wood had been sent to take over the Philippine division and volunteered to let Wade (who was junior in rank but not in time of service) "serve out his term." Wood's

reaction when Roosevelt appointed Corbin to succeed Wade makes that version unlikely. See Hugh Lenox Scott, *Some Memories of a Soldier* (New York: The Century Company, 1928), 275.

23. Adjutant General's document, December 28, 1903, Wood Papers.

24. Alger to Lou Wood, November 19, 1903, cited in Hagedorn, *Wood,* 2:31.

25. Roosevelt speech, May 14, 1903, cited in Hagedorn, *Wood,* 1:412.

26. Roosevelt to Wood, June 16, 1903, Wood Papers.

27. Roosevelt to Wood, June 13, 1903, Wood Papers.

28. Wood to Roosevelt, July 23, 1903, Wood Papers.

29. Ibid.

30. Chauncey Baker to Wood, December 19, 1903, Wood Papers.

31. Roosevelt to Root, December 12, 1903, Wood Papers.

32. Roosevelt to Lou Wood, December 12, 1903, Wood Papers.

33. Roosevelt to Root, December 12, 1903, Wood Papers.

34. Taft to Foraker, March 14, 1904, Wood Papers.

35. Baker to Wood, December 19, 1903, Wood Papers.

36. Garfield to Wood, March 30, 1904, Wood Papers.

37. Wood to Roosevelt, January 7, 1904, Wood Papers.

38. Roosevelt to Wood, March 19, 1904, Wood Papers.

39. Hagedorn, *Wood,* 1:416.

40. Wood to Roosevelt, September 20, 1903, Wood Papers.

41. Wood to Roosevelt, September 22, 1903, Wood Papers.

42. Roosevelt to Wood, December 1, 1903, Wood Papers.

43. Roosevelt to Wood, March 19, 1904, Wood Papers.

44. Wood to Roosevelt, July 28, 1903, Wood Papers.

45. Wood to Steinhart, October 11, 1903, Wood Papers.

46. Scott, *Memories of a Soldier,* 276.

47. Wood to Hadji Butu, Jolo Island, August 24, 1903, transcript in Wood Papers.

48. Scott, *Memories of a Soldier,* 316.

49. Ibid., 399.

50. Ibid., 279.

51. Wood to Taft, September 5, 1903, Wood Papers.

52. Wood to Roosevelt, September 20, 1903, Wood Papers.

53. Wood to Cockrell, September 11, 1903, Wood Papers.

54. Wood to Roosevelt, September 20, 1903, Wood Papers.

55. Wood's diary, October 1–2, 1903, Wood Papers.

56. Wood to Taft, October 7, 1903, Wood Papers.

57. Wood to Roosevelt, October 10, 1903, Wood Papers.

58. Wood's diary, November 9, 1903, Wood Papers.

59. Ibid., November 16, 1903.

60. Ibid., November 21, 1903.

61. Roosevelt to Wood citing a letter home from an American soldier, August 12, 1904, Wood Papers.

62. Wood's diary, November 18, 1903, Wood Papers.

63. Wood to Roosevelt, December 7, 1903, Wood Papers.

64. Wood to Dodge, December 26, 1903, Wood Papers.

65. Wood to Verela Jado, February 3, 1904, Wood Papers.

66. Wood to Steinhart, December 26, 1903, Wood Papers.

67. See Root's comments to Jessup, September 20, 1930, cited in Jessup, *Root*, 1:345.

68. Wood's diary, March 9, 1904, Wood Papers.

69. Ibid., March 11, 1904.

70. Ibid., March 15, 1904.

71. Wood to Adjutant General Simpson, March 16, 1904, Wood Papers.

72. Wood's diary, April 7, 1904, Wood Papers.

73. Ibid.

74. Ibid., April 29, 1904.

75. Ibid., May 15, 1904.

76. Ibid., May 11, 1904.

77. Folger to Wood, June 3, 1904, Wood Papers.

78. Wood's diary, July 28, 1904, Wood Papers.

79. Quoted in Roosevelt to Wood, August 12, 1904, Wood Papers.

80. Wood's diary, October 26, 1904, Wood Papers.

81. Wood's diary, May 3–4, 1905, Wood Papers.

82. Ibid., May 5, 1905.

83. Brengt Lunggren, "The Case of General Wood," *Journal of Neurosurgery* 56 (1982), 471–74.

84. Ainsworth to Wood, August 26, 1905, Wood Papers.

85. Ibid., October 9, 1905.

86. Ibid., October 30, 1905.

87. Wood to Corbin, November 6, 1905, Wood Papers.

88. Corbin actually got that job.

89. Ainsworth to Wood, December 12, 1905, Wood Papers.

90. Wood to Roosevelt, December 13, 1905, Wood Papers. Wood, however, was specifically opposed to bringing in Chinese or "any race with which we cannot intermarry."

91. Notes from Wood's conference with the Sultan of Sulu, April 3, 1906, Wood Papers.

92. Wood's diary, February 1, 1905, Wood Papers.

93. Wood to Roosevelt, January 7, 1904, Wood Papers.

94. Ibid.

95. Ibid.

96. Wood to Chief of Staff, February 15, 1906, Wood Papers.

97. Wood to commanding generals Luzon, Viscaya, Mindanao, February 12, 1906, and Wood to Chief of Staff, February 21, 1906, Wood Papers.

98. Transcript Sawajaan to Reeve, December 4, 1905, Wood Papers.

99. Reeve to Captain George Langhorne, Secretary, Moro Province, March 31, 1906, Wood Papers.

100. Wood to Captain George Langhorne, February 17, 1906, Wood Papers.

101. Transcript from translator Charles Schuck, March 29, 1906, Wood Papers.

102. Wood's diary, February 28, 1906, Wood Papers.

103. Telegram from Thomas Kinghorne to *Manila Commercial Pacific,* March 10, 1906, Wood Papers.

104. Wood to Andrews, March 9, 1906, Wood Papers.

105. Ibid.

106. The higher estimate came from datos that Wood interviewed aboard his yacht *Sabah* on April 13, 1906. A transcript of the meeting is in the Wood Papers.

107. Kinghorne telegram, March 10, 1906, Wood Papers.

108. Roosevelt to Wood, March 10, 1906, Wood Papers.

109. Taft to Wood, March 12, 1906, Wood Papers.

110. *New York Times,* March 9, 1906.

111. Ide to Taft, March 20, 1906, Wood Papers.

112. Wood to Military Secretary, Washington, D.C., March 13, 1906, and April 22, 1906, Wood Papers.

113. From transcript of meeting on *Sabah,* April 13, 1906, Wood Papers.

114. Wood to General William Crozier, April 6, 1905, Wood Papers.

115. Wood to Roosevelt, February 25, 1906, Wood Papers.

116. Roosevelt to Wood, January 8, 1906, Wood Papers.

117. Wood to Roosevelt, February 21, 1906, Wood Papers.

118. Ibid.

119. Wood to Roosevelt, June 1, 1904, Wood Papers.

120. Ibid.

121. Bliss to Wood, October 25, 1904, Wood Papers.

122. Brands, *Bound to Empire,* 84.

123. Wood to Roosevelt, December 13, 1905, Wood Papers.

124. Ibid.

125. Jessup, *Root,* 2:10.

126. Roosevelt Papers, August 21, 1907, Library of Congress, cited in Jessup, *Root,* 2:11.

127. Jessup, *Root,* 2:11.

128. Wood to Roosevelt, December 13, 1907, Wood Papers.

129. Wood to Adjutant General, December 23, 1907, Wood Papers.

130. Wood's diary, December 5, 1906, Wood Papers.

NOTES TO CHAPTER 9

1. Wood's diary, September 18, 1908, Wood Papers.

2. Wood to Roosevelt, cited in Hagedorn, *Wood*, 2:87.

3. Cushing and Eisenhardt, *Meningiomas*, 409.

4. Wood's diary, January 27, 1910, Wood Papers.

5. Wood to Taft, February 3, 1910, Wood Papers.

6. Cushing and Eisenhardt, *Meningiomas*, 410.

7. Archie Butt, *Taft and Roosevelt: The Intimate Letters of Archie Butt, Military Aide* (Garden City, N.Y.: Doubleday, Doran & Company, 1930), 465.

8. Wood to Taft, March 8, 1910, Wood Papers.

9. See discussion in Russell Weigley, *Towards an American Army: Military Thought from Washington to Marshall* (New York: Columbia University Press, 1962), 100–123.

10. Jessup, *Root*, 1:243.

11. See Brigadier General James D. Hittle, *The Military Staff: Its History and Development* (Harrisburg, Pa.: The Military Service Publishing Company, 1944), 197. Ludlow later gave Root his personal, autographed copy of Wilkinson's book.

12. United States War Department, *Five Years of the War Department Following the War with Spain, 1899–1903 as Shown in the Annual Reports of the Secretary of War* (Washington, D.C.: Government Printing Office, 1904), 293.

13. Edmund Morris, *Theodore Rex* (New York: Random House, 2001), 79.

14. *New York Times*, October 24, 1909.

15. Cited in Lane, *Armed Progressive*, 168.

16. United States War Department, *Annual Report of the Secretary of War, 1911* (Washington, D.C.: Government Printing Office, 1911), 16.

17. Wood's diary, December 19, 1910, Wood Papers.

18. Wood's diary, November 29, 1911, Wood Papers.

19. W. H. Carter to Wood, June 13, 1911, Wood Papers.

20. Wood's diary, February 12, 1911, Wood Papers.

21. Colonel A. C. Sharpe to Wood, February 21, 1911, Wood Papers.

22. Ibid., and Colonel E. Z. Steeves to the Adjutant General of the Department of Texas, March 19, 1911, Wood Papers.

23. Wood's diary, March 7, 1911, Wood Papers.

24. In fact, Wood mobilized 23,000 troops on the border, many in towns where typhoid was endemic, and had only two cases of the fever, one in a civilian teamster and one in a soldier who was not vaccinated because he claimed to have already had the disease. By contrast, a single division in the Spanish War suffered 1,700 definite and 400 possible cases. Wood to Dr. Frederick Shattuck, August 3, 1911, Wood Papers.

25. Taft to Wood, March 12, 1911, Wood Papers.

26. Wood to Taft, March 15, 1911, Wood Papers.

27. Wood's diary, March 29, 1911, Wood Papers.

28. Wotherspoon to Wood, April 12, 1911, Wood Papers.

29. Colonel E. Z. Steeves to Wood, April 12, 1911, Wood Papers.

30. Wotherspoon to Wood, April 13, 1911, Wood Papers.

31. Britton Davis to Wood, April 21, 1911, Wood Papers.

32. E. P. Grinnell to Taft, April 14, 1911, Wood Papers.

33. Wood to Commanding Officer, Douglas, Arizona, undated but probably April 15, 1911, Wood Papers.

34. Davis to Wood, April 21, 1911, Wood Papers.

35. Wood to Halbord, April 26, 1911, Wood Papers.

36. Wood to M. Y. Bunyan Varillas, August 17, 1910, Wood Papers.

37. Wood's diary, June 25, 1913, Wood Papers.

38. Wood's diary, August 22, 1911, Wood Papers.

39. See Wood to Nicholas A. Vyne, August 9, 1911, Wood Papers.

40. Wood's diary, August 30, 1912, Wood Papers

41. Wood to Roosevelt, February 18, 1911, Wood Papers.

42. Wood's diary, November 8, 1911, Wood Papers.

43. Elting Morison, *Turmoil and Tradition: A Study of the Life and Times of Henry L. Stimson* (Boston: Houghton Mifflin, 1960), 146.

44. Weigley, *Towards an American Army,* 152.

45. Leonard Wood, *Our Military History: Its Facts and Fallacies* (Chicago: The Reilly & Britton Co., 1916), 85.

46. Scott to Hagedorn, April 13, 1930, cited in Lane, *Armed Progressive,* 172.

47. Wood to Harbord, December 12, 1911, Wood Papers.

48. See Wood's diary, December 11, 1911, Wood Papers.

49. Wood to Representative Wayne Parker, January 17, 1911, Wood Papers.

50. Wood to James McClintock, June 26, 1911, Wood Papers.

51. See discussion in Morison, *Turmoil and Tradition,* 150–51.

52. Henry L. Stimson and McGeorge Bundy, *On Active Service in Peace and War* (New York: Harper & Brothers, 1947), 33.

53. Hanna to Lawrence Abbott, November 8, 1928, Hagedorn Papers.

54. Morison, *Turmoil and Tradition,* 153.

55. Wood's diary, January 26, 1910, Wood Papers.

56. Ibid.

57. Wood's diary, October 12, 1910, Wood Papers.

58. Wood's diary, December 9, 1910, Wood Papers.

59. Memorandum, Chief of Staff to Adjutant General, December 16, 1910, cited in Lane, *Armed Progressive,* 160.

60. Wood's diary, December 27, 1910, Wood Papers.

61. Wood's diary, December 29, 1910, Wood Papers.

62. Ibid.

63. Morison, *Turmoil and Tradition*, 154.

64. Wood's diary, May 17, 1911, Wood Papers.

65. Wood's diary, September 5, 1911, Wood Papers.

66. Wood to Stimson, September 8, 1911, Wood Papers.

67. Stimson and Bundy, *On Active Service*, 35.

68. Wood's diary, February 20, 1912, Wood Papers.

69. Hagedorn, *Wood*, 2:123.

70. Morison, *Turmoil and Tradition*, 166–67.

71. Butt, *Taft and Roosevelt*, 781.

72. Wood's diary, August 11, 1912, Wood Papers.

73. Wood to Garrison, March 5, 1913, Wood Papers.

74. Wood's diary, November 21, 1911, Wood Papers.

75. Wood's diary, September 6, 1912, Wood Papers.

76. Wood's diary, February 12, 1913, Wood Papers.

77. Wood's diary, February 17, 1913, Wood Papers.

78. Wood's diary, February 24, 1913, Wood Papers.

79. Ibid.

80. Wood's diary, September 18, 1913, Wood Papers.

81. Wood's diary, October 22, 1913, Wood Papers.

82. Wood to General Hunter Liggett, October 30, 1913, and memorandum, Wood to Liggett, November 6, 1913, Wood Papers.

83. Wood's diary, November 4, 1913, Wood Papers.

84. Wood to Dickinson, November 7, 1913, Wood Papers.

85. Wood's diary, November 8, 1913, Wood Papers.

86. Wood's diary, November 11, 1913, Wood Papers.

87. Wood's diary, November 21, 1913, Wood Papers.

88. Wood's diary, December 17, 1913, Wood Papers.

89. *New York World*, April 24, 1914.

90. *Spectator*, April 25, 1914.

91. *New York Sun*, April 21, 1914.

92. Cited by Merle Curtis in "Bryan and World Peace," *Smith College Studies in History* 16 (1931), 233.

93. Wood's diary, November 19, 1914, Wood Papers, Box 8.

94. *New York Times*, December 3, 1914.

95. Theodore Roosevelt to Kermit Roosevelt, cited in Elting Morison, *The Letters of Theodore Roosevelt* (Cambridge, Mass.: Harvard University Press, 1951–54), 8:965.

96. *New York Times*, August 25, 1915.

97. Wood's diary, August 27, 1915, Wood Papers, Box 8.

98. *New York Times*, August 28, 1915.

99. 64th Congress, 2nd session, 1916, cited in Lane, *Armed Progressive*, 197.

100. Senate Military Affairs Committee, January 18, 1916, cited in Hagedorn, *Wood*, 2:171.

101. Wood to L. S. Rowe, September 30, 1915, cited in Hagedorn, *Wood*, 2:173.

102. Wood, *Our Military History*, 183.

103. Ibid., 184–85.

104. Hagedorn, *Wood*, 2:209.

105. Wood to Roosevelt, cited in Lane, *Armed Progressive*, 199.

106. Ibid., 200.

107. *Chicago Daily Tribune*, April 13, 1916.

108. Wood subsequently said Roosevelt told him "in case he did not run I could fill the bill." Wood's diary, April 7, 1916, Wood Papers.

109. Hagedorn, *Wood*, 2:190.

110. *Washington Sunday Star*, December 14, 1930.

111. Baker to Hagedorn, November 2, 1929, Hagedorn Papers.

112. Parker to Hagedorn, undated but probably March 1929, Hagedorn Papers. Also Parker to Abbot, undated, Hagedorn Papers.

113. S. M. Williams to Hagedorn, December 7, 1928, Hagedorn Papers.

114. Newton Baker later said the choice of American Expeditionary Force commander was between Wood and Pershing and insisted that he, not Wilson, had chosen the latter. Baker to Hagedorn, November 2, 1929, cited in Hagedorn, *Wood*, 2:222.

115. Kilbourne to Hagedorn, November 26, 1928, Hagedorn Papers.

NOTES TO CHAPTER 10

1. Hagedorn, *Wood*, 2:243.

2. Wood's diary, January 11, 1918, Wood Papers.

3. Wood's diary, January 4, 1918, Wood Papers.

4. The description of the episode is from eyewitness Sumner Williams to Hagedorn, April 18, 1929, Hagedorn Papers.

5. Cushing to Hagedorn, December 23, 1930, Hagedorn Papers.

6. Pershing to Baker, February 18, 1918, Pershing Papers.

7. Ibid.

8. Pershing to Baker, February 24, 1918, Pershing Papers.

9. Kilbourne to Hagedorn, November 26, 1928, Hagedorn Papers.

10. Wood's diary, June 18, 1918, Wood Papers.

11. Wood's diary, October 5, 1918, Wood Papers.

12. Wood's diary, October 10, 1918, Wood Papers. Also, Wood to R. C. Stout (editor of the *Kansas City Star*), October 22, 1918, Wood Papers.

13. From debate with Miles Poindexter, March 20, 1920, cited in Hagedorn, *Wood*, 2:349.

14. Wood's diary, January 2, 1919, Wood Papers.

15. Hagedorn, *Wood*, 2:329.

16. Allen to Hagedorn, February 18, 1929, Hagedorn Papers. Also W. A. White to Hagedorn, November 24, 1928, Hagedorn Papers.

17. Wood's diary, January 6, 1919, Wood Papers.

18. Ibid.

19. "The Americanism of General Leonard Wood," *Literary Digest* 64 (March 6, 1920), 47–52.

20. Wood's diary, May 3, 1919, Wood papers.

21. *Philadelphia Public Ledger,* February 11, 1919.

22. Hagedorn, *Wood*, 2:327.

23. *Chicago Daily Tribune,* March 14, 1919.

24. "Americanism of General Wood," 47.

25. *New York Times,* June 10, 1919, describing Wood's Union College commencement address.

26. Wood's diary, September 19, 1919, Wood Papers.

27. Ibid.

28. Wood's diary, October 16, 1919, Wood Papers.

29. Wood's diary, October 10, 1919, Wood Papers.

30. Wood's diary, October 15, 1919, Wood Papers.

31. Wood's diary, October 25, 1919, Wood Papers.

32. Morison, *Turmoil and Tradition,* 250.

33. *New York Times,* May 5, 1920.

34. Wood's diary, April 30, 1920, Wood Papers.

35. *New York Times,* June 15, 1920.

36. Root to Colonel Archibald Hopkins, May 31, 1920, cited in Jessup, *Root,* 2:411.

37. Scott to Hagedorn, February 19, 1931, Hagedorn Papers.

38. *New York Times,* July 3, 1920.

39. See S. M. Williams to Hagedorn, December 7, 1928, and March 20, 1929, Hagedorn Papers.

40. Paul F. Boller, *Presidential Campaigns* (New York: Oxford University Press, 1984), 215.

41. Wesley Bagby, *The Road to Normalcy: The Presidential Campaign and Election of 1920* (Baltimore: The Johns Hopkins Press, 1962).

42. Ibid., 87.

43. *New York Times,* April 16, 1924.

44. Ibid.

45. *New York Times,* March 20, 1924.

46. An Oklahoma jury subsequently acquitted her after a lurid trial. The murder and trial are described in detail in the *New York Times,* December 2, 1920;

December 3, 1920; December 5, 1920; December 6, 1920; March 11, 1921; May 13, 1921; and May 18, 1921.

47. Wood's diary, June 20, 1920, Wood Papers.

48. Ibid.

49. Ibid.

50. Stimson and Bundy, *On Active Service*, 105.

51. Walter Lippman, "Truth about Leonard Wood," *The Nation* 110 (May 29, 1920), 714.

52. Wood's diary, December 1, 1920, Wood Papers.

NOTES TO CHAPTER 11

1. Wood's diary, January 23, 1921, Wood Papers.

2. Ibid.

3. Wood to Stimson, January 28, 1921, and Stimson to Wood, January 31, 1921, Wood Papers.

4. Note from Frank McCoy, March 1, 1929, McCoy Papers.

5. Wood's diary, March 10, 1921, Wood Papers.

6. Wood's diary, May 10, 1921, Wood Papers.

7. Edward Bowditch to Hagedorn, November 26, 1930, Hagedorn Papers.

8. Ibid.

9. Named for Wood and his cochairman, former Governor General Cameron Forbes.

10. Brands, *Bound to Empire*, 121.

11. Regarding the San Lazaro insane asylum where men were kept naked and women nearly so and violent inmates wandered the halls shrieking and yelling, the general said "That such conditions should have obtained during twenty years of American occupation is an indictment not only of the Philippine medical authorities but even more of our own authorities." Wood's diary, June 4, 1921, Wood Papers. Care in tuberculosis sanitaria and leper colonies was little better.

12. Wood to Stimson, July 21, 1921, Wood Papers.

13. Wood's diary, May 10, 1921, Wood Papers.

14. *Report of the Special Mission on Investigation to the Philippines to the Secretary of War*, in House Document no. 398, 67th Congress, 2nd session, 1921, pp. 42–43.

15. Wood to his wife, undated but probably August 1921, Wood Papers.

16. Wood's diary, October 2, 1921, Wood Papers.

17. Hagedorn, *Wood*, 2:399.

18. Wood's diary, October 16, 1921, Wood Papers.

19. Hagedorn, *Wood*, 2:413.

20. *New York Times,* January 31, 2004.

21. Lewis Gleeck, *The American Governors-General and High Commissioners in the Philippines: Proconsuls, Nation-Builders, and Politicians* (Quezon City: New Day Publishers, 1986), 180.

22. Ibid., 183.

23. Bowditch to Hagedorn, December 18, 1930, Hagedorn Papers.

24. Hagedorn to Bowditch, January 14, 1931, Hagedorn Papers.

25. Dr. Alexander Lambert to Hagedorn, January 10, 1931, Hagedorn Papers.

26. Bowditch to Hagedorn, January 12, 1931, Hagedorn Papers.

27. Gleeck, *American Governors-General,* 190.

28. McCoy memorandum, July 12, 1923, McCoy Papers.

29. Hagedorn, *Wood,* 2:446.

30. Lambert to Hagedorn, January 10, 1931, Hagedorn Papers.

31. Christian Hildebrand to Hagedorn, March 1, 1929, Hagedorn Papers.

32. *New York Times,* December 29, 1923, December 30, 1923, January 4, 1924.

33. *New York Times,* December 26, 1923.

34. *New York Times,* December 27, 1923.

35. *New York Times,* March 30, 1925.

36. Coolidge to Wood, April 6, 1927, in Appendix C, *Report of the Governor General, 1927,* 64–69.

NOTES TO EPILOGUE

1. Morison, *Turmoil and Tradition,* 183.

Bibliography

BOOKS

Alger, R. A. *The Spanish American War.* New York: Harper & Brothers, 1901.

Altman, Lawrence K. *Who Goes First? The Story of Self-Experimentation in Medicine.* New York: Random House, 1986.

Ambrose, Stephen. *Upton and the Army.* Baton Rouge: Louisiana State University Press, 1964.

Araneta, Salvador. *America's Double-Cross of the Philippines, A Democratic Ally in 1899 and 1946.* Manila: Bayanikasan Research Foundation, 1978.

Azoy, A. C. M. *Charge! The Story of San Juan Hill.* New York: Longmans, Green and Co., 1961.

Bacon, Robert, and James Brown Scott, eds. *Military and Colonial Policy of the United States: Addresses and Reports by Elihu Root.* Cambridge: Harvard University Press, 1916.

Bagby, Wesley. *The Road to Normalcy: The Presidential Campaign and Election of 1920.* Baltimore: The Johns Hopkins Press, 1962.

Barrett, S. M., ed. *Geronimo: His Own Story.* New York: Ballantine Books, 1971.

Beals, Carlton. *The Crime of Cuba.* Philadelphia: J. B. Lippincott, 1933.

Betzinez, Jason. *I Fought with Geronimo.* New York: Bonanza Books, 1959.

Biddle, Wayne. *A Field Guide to Germs.* New York: Anchor Books, 1995.

Blount, James H. *American Occupation of the Philippines: 1898–1912.* New York: Knickerbocker Press, 1913.

Boller, Paul F. *Presidential Campaigns.* New York: Oxford University Press, 1984.

Bourke, John G. *An Apache Campaign in the Sierra Madre: An Account of the Expedition in Pursuit of the Hostile Chiricahua Apaches in the Spring of 1883.* New York: Charles Scribner's Sons, 1958.

Brands, H. W. *Bound to Empire: The United States and the Philippines.* New York: Oxford University Press, 1992.

Brophy, William S. *The Krag Rifle.* Highland Park, N.J.: Gun Room Press, 1985.

Brown, Dee. *Bury My Heart at Wounded Knee: An Indian History of the American West.* New York: Holt, Rinehart & Winston, 1970.

Browne, G. Waldo, ed. *The New America and the Far East.* Boston: Marshall Jones Company, 1901.

Butt, Archie. *Taft and Roosevelt: The Intimate Letters of Archie Butt, Military Aide.* Garden City, N.Y.: Doubleday, Doran & Company, 1930.

Cheever, David, ed. *A History of the Boston City Hospital from Its Foundation until 1904.* Boston: Municipal Printing Office, 1906.

Clifford, John Garry. *The Citizen Soldiers: The Plattsburg Training Camp Movement, 1913–1920.* Lexington: University Press of Kentucky, 1972.

Cosmas, Graham. *An Army for Empire: The United States Army in the Spanish American War.* Columbia: University of Missouri Press, 1971.

Crook, George. *Résumé of Operations against Apache Indians, 1882 to 1886.* Reprint. London: Johnson-Taunton Military Press, 1971.

Cushing, Harvey. "Surgery of the Head," in *Surgery: Its Principles and Practice,* ed. William Williams Keen, 17–276. Philadelphia: W. B. Saunders Company, 1908.

———. *The Life of Sir William Osler.* Oxford: Clarendon Press, 1926.

Cushing, Harvey, and Louise Eisenhardt. *Meningiomas: Their Classification, Regional Behaviour, Life History, and Surgical End Results.* Springfield, Ill.: Charles C. Thomas, 1938.

David, Evan J., ed. *Leonard Wood on National Issues: The Many-Sided Mind of a Great Executive Shown by His Public Utterances.* Garden City, N.Y.: Doubleday, Page & Co., 1920.

Davis, Britton. *The Truth about Geronimo.* Chicago: Lakeside Press, R. R. Donnelly & Sons, 1951.

Davis, Burke. *The Long Surrender.* New York: Random House, 1985.

Davis, Richard Harding. *The Cuban and Porto Rican Campaigns.* New York: Charles Scribner's Sons, 1898.

Dean, John. *Warren G. Harding.* New York: Times Books, Henry Holt and Company, 2004.

Dierks, Jack Cameron. *A Leap to Arms: The Cuban Campaign of 1898.* Philadelphia, J. B. Lippincott, 1970.

Faulk, Odie B. *The Geronimo Campaign.* New York: Oxford University Press, 1969.

Fitzgibbon, Russell. *Cuba and the United States: 1900–1935.* New York: Russell & Russell, 1964.

Foner, Philip. "Causes of the War. Why the United States went to War with Spain in 1898," in *American Expansionism: The Critical Issues,* ed. Marilyn Blatt Young. Boston: Little, Brown and Company, 1973.

Freidel, Frank. *The Splendid Little War.* New York: Dell Publishing Company, 1962.

Fulton, John F. *Harvey Cushing: A Biography.* Springfield, Ill.: Charles C. Thomas, 1946.

Gardner, Lloyd C. *Imperial America: American Foreign Policy since 1898.* New York: Harcourt Brace Jovanovich, 1976.

Gibson, John. *Physician to the World: The Life of General William C. Gorgas.* Tuscaloosa: University of Alabama Press, 1989.

Gleeck, Lewis. *The American Governors-General and High Commissioners in the Philippines: Proconsuls, Nation-Builders, and Politicians.* Quezon City: New Day Publishers, 1986.

Grunder, Garel, and William Livezey. *The Philippines and the United States.* Norman: University of Oklahoma Press, 1951.

Hagedorn, Herman. *That Human Being Leonard Wood.* New York: Harcourt, Brace & Howe, 1920.

———. *Leonard Wood: A Biography.* 2 vols. New York: Harper & Brothers, 1931.

Halstead, Murat. *Life and Distinguished Services of William McKinley, Our Martyr President.* Washington, D.C.: Memorial Association, 1901.

Harries, Meirion, and Susie Harries. *The Last Days of Innocence: America at War, 1917–1918.* New York: Random House, 1997.

Hatcher, Edward. *Gayoso Bayou: A Narrative of the Plague of 1878.* Memphis: St. Luke's Press, 1982.

Healy, David. *The United States in Cuba, 1898–1902: Generals, Politicians and the Search for Policy.* Madison: University of Wisconsin Press, 1963.

Hernandez, José. *Cuba and the United States: Intervention and Militarism, 1868–1933.* Austin: University of Texas Press, 1993.

Herner, Charles. *The Arizona Rough Riders.* Tucson: University of Arizona Press, 1970.

Hittle, Brigadier General James D. *The Military Staff: Its History and Development.* Harrisburg, Pa.: Military Service Publishing Company, 1944.

Hobbs, William Herbert. *Leonard Wood: Administrator, Soldier, and Citizen.* New York: G. P. Putnam's Sons, 1920.

Holme, John G. *The Life of Leonard Wood.* Garden City, N.Y.: Doubleday, Page & Co., 1920.

Jenks, Leland. *Our Cuban Colony: A Study in Sugar.* New York: Vanguard Press, 1928.

Jensen, Larry. *Children of Colonial Despotism: Press, Politics, and Culture in Cuba, 1790–1840.* Tampa: University of South Florida Press, 1988.

Jessup, Philip C. *Elihu Root.* 2 vols. New York: Dodd, Mead and Company, 1938.

Judson, Clara Ingram. *Soldier Doctor: The Story of William Gorgas.* New York: Charles Scribner's Sons, 1942.

Karnow, Stanley. *In Our Image: America's Empire in the Philippines.* New York: Random House, 1989.

Keesing, Felix. *The Philippines: A Nation in the Making.* Shanghai: Kelly & Walsh, 1937.

Kelly, Howard A., and Walter L. Burrage. *Dictionary of American Medical Biography: Lives of Eminent Physicians of the United States and Canada, from the Earliest Times.* Boston: Milford House, 1928.

Kohler, Robert E. "Medical Reform and Biomedical Science: Biochemistry, a Case Study," in *The Therapeutic Revolution: Essays in the Social History of American Medicine,* ed. Morris Vogel, 31–32. Philadelphia: University of Pennsylvania Press, 1979.

Lane, Jack C., ed. *Chasing Geronimo: The Journal of Leonard Wood, May–September, 1886.* Albuquerque: University of New Mexico Press, 1970.

———. *Armed Progressive: General Leonard Wood.* San Rafael, Calif.: Presidio Press, 1978.

Latané, John Holladay. *America as a World Power, 1897–1907.* New York: Harper & Brothers, 1907.

Lea, Homer. *The Day of the Saxon.* Harper & Brothers, 1912.

———. *The Valor of Ignorance.* New York: Harper & Brothers, 1942.

Leckie, Robert. *The Wars of America.* New York: Harper Collins, 1968.

Lee, Fitzhugh, and Joseph Wheeler. *Cuba's Struggle against Spain: Causes for American Intervention and a Full Account of the Spanish-American War, including the Final Peace Negotiations.* New York: American Historical Press, 1899.

Linn, Brian McAllister. *The Philippine War: 1899–1902.* Lawrence: University Press of Kansas, 2000.

Mahan, Alfred Thayer. *The Influence of Seapower upon History: 1600–1783.* Boston: Little, Brown and Company, 1890.

Marcosson, Isaac F. *Leonard Wood: Prophet of Preparedness.* New York: John Lane Company, 1917.

Marshall, Edward. *The Story of the Rough Riders, 1st U.S. Volunteer Cavalry: The Regiment in Camp and on the Battle Field.* New York: G. W. Dillingham Co., 1899.

McCullough, David. *The Path between the Seas: The Creation of the Panama Canal, 1870–1914.* New York: Simon and Schuster, 1977.

McNeill, William H. *Plagues and Peoples.* New York: Doubleday, 1977.

Melencio, Jose P. *Arguments against Philippine Independence and Their Answers.* Washington, D.C.: Philippine Press Bureau, 1919.

Millis, Walter. *The Martial Spirit.* Cambridge: Riverside Press, 1931.

———. *Road to War: America, 1914–1917.* Boston: Houghton Mifflin, 1935.

Morison, Elting. *The Letters of Theodore Roosevelt.* 8 vols. Cambridge, Mass.: Harvard University Press, 1951–54.

———. *Turmoil and Tradition: A Study of the Life and Times of Henry L. Stimson.* Boston: Houghton Mifflin, 1960.

Morison, Samuel Eliot. *Admiral of the Ocean Sea: A Life of Christopher Columbus.* Boston: Little, Brown and Company, 1942.

Morris, Edmund. *The Rise of Theodore Roosevelt.* New York: Modern Library, 1979.

———. *Theodore Rex.* New York: Random House, 2001.

Musicant, Ivan. *Empire by Default: The Spanish-American War and the Dawn of the American Century.* New York: Henry Holt and Company, 1998.

Ortiz, Rafael Martinez. *Cuba: Los Primeros Años de Independencia.* Paris: Editorial "Le Livre Libre," 1929.

O'Toole, G. J. A. *The Spanish War: An American Epic—1898.* New York: W. W. Norton & Company, 1984.

Pérez, Louis A. *Cuba between Empires, 1878–1902.* Pittsburgh: University of Pittsburgh Press, 1983.

Pomeroy, William J. *American Neo-Colonialism: Its Emergence in the Philippines and Asia.* New York: International Publishers, 1970.

Porter, Robert. *Report on the Commercial and Industrial Condition of Cuba.* Washington, D.C.: Government Printing Office, 1899.

Pringle, Henry R. *The Life and Times of William Howard Taft: A Biography.* New York: Farrar & Rinehart, 1939.

Rea, George Bronson. *Facts and Fakes about Cuba.* New York: G. Munro's Sons, 1897.

Robinson, Albert G. *Cuba and the Intervention.* London: Longmans, Green and Co., 1905.

Roosevelt, Theodore. *The Rough Riders.* New York: Da Capo Press, 1990. First published 1902.

Root, Elihu. *Five Years of the War Department Following the War with Spain, 1899–1903, as Shown in the Annual Reports of the Secretary of War.* Washington, D.C.: Government Printing Office, 1904.

Rubens, Horatio. *Liberty: The Story of Cuba.* New York: AMS Press, 1970.

Sattin, Anthony. *Lifting the Veil: British Society in Egypt, 1768–1956.* London: J. M. Dent & Sons, 1988.

Schirmer, Daniel, and Stephen Rosskamm Shalom, eds. *The Philippines Reader: A History of Colonialism, Neocolonialism, Dictatorship, and Resistance.* Boston: South End Press, 1987.

Schlesinger, Arthur M., and Fred Israel, eds. *History of American Presidential Elections, 1789–1968.* New York: McGraw-Hill, 1971.

Scott, Hugh Lenox. *Some Memories of a Soldier.* New York: The Century Company, 1928.

Scott, James Brown. *Robert Bacon: Life and Letters.* Garden City, N.Y.: Doubleday, Page & Company, 1923.

Sears, Joseph Hamblin. *The Career of Leonard Wood.* New York: D. Appleton and Company, 1919.

Smith, Page. *America Enters the World: A People's History of the Progressive Era and World War I.* New York: McGraw-Hill, 1985.

Stanley, Peter W. *A Nation in the Making: The Philippines and the United States, 1899–1921.* Cambridge: Harvard University Press, 1974.

Starr, Paul. *The Social Transformation of American Medicine.* New York: Basic Books, 1982.

Stimson, Henry L., and McGeorge Bundy. *On Active Service in Peace and War.* New York: Harper & Brothers, 1947.

Storey, Moorfield, and Marcial Lichauco. *The Conquest of the Philippines by the United States: 1898–1923.* New York: G. P. Putnam's Sons, 1926.

Thrapp, Dan L. *The Conquest of Apacheria.* Norman: University of Oklahoma Press, 1967.

Truby, Albert. *Memoir of Walter Reed: The Yellow Fever Episode.* New York: Paul B. Hoeber, 1943.

United States Department of Commerce. *Customs and Tariff Regulations.* Washington, D.C.: Government Printing Office, 1898.

United States War Department. *Five Years of the War Department Following the War with Spain, 1899–1903, as Shown in the Annual Reports of the Secretary of War.* Washington, D.C.: Government Printing Office, 1904.

———. *Annual Report of the Secretary of War, 1911.* Washington, D.C.: Government Printing Office, 1911.

Vogel, Morris J., ed. *The Therapeutic Revolution: Essays in the Social History of American Medicine.* Philadelphia: University of Pennsylvania Press, 1979.

Walker, Dale L. *The Boys of '98: Theodore Roosevelt and the Rough Riders.* New York: A Tom Doherty Associates Book, 1998.

Weigley, Russell. *Towards an American Army: Military Thought from Washington to Marshall.* New York: Columbia University Press, 1962.

———. *History of the United States Army.* Bloomington: Indiana University Press, 1967.

Westermeier, Clifford. *Who Rush to Glory.* Cladwell, Idaho: Caxton Printers, 1958.

Wheeler, Joseph. *The Santiago Campaign: 1898.* Freeport, N.Y.: Books for Libraries Press, 1970. First published 1898.

White, Trumbull. *A Pictorial History of Our War with Spain.* N.p.: Freedom Publishing Company, 1898.

Williams, William Appleton. *The Tragedy of American Diplomacy.* New York: Dell Publishing Co., 1959.

Wood, Eric Fisher. *Leonard Wood, Conservator of Americanism.* New York: George H. Doran Company, 1920.

Wood, Leonard. *Civil Report of Brigadier General Leonard Wood, Military Governor of Cuba.* Washington, D.C.: Government Printing Office, 1902.

———. *The Military Obligation of Citizenship.* Princeton: Princeton University Press, 1915.

———. *Our Military History: Its Facts and Fallacies.* Chicago: The Reilly & Britton Co., 1916.

———, and Cameron Forbes. *Report of the Special Mission on Investigation to the*

Philippine Islands to the Secretary of War. Washington, D.C.: Government Printing Office, 1921.

———, et al. *The History of the First World War.* New York: Grolier, 1965. Published in part as *The World War* in 1919.

———. *Annual Report of the Civil Governor, Philippine Islands.* Washington, D.C.: Government Printing Office, 1921–27.

———, et al. *Opportunities in the Colonies and Cuba.* New York: Lewis, Scribner, & Co., 1902.

Wood, L. N. *Walter Reed: Doctor in Uniform.* New York: Julian Messner, 1943.

Young, Marilyn Blatt, ed. *American Expansionism: The Critical Issues.* Boston: Little, Brown and Company, 1973.

Zimmerman, Walter. *The First Great Triumph: How Five Americans Made Their Country a World Power.* New York: Farrar, Straus and Giroux, 2002.

JOURNALS

Curtis, Merle. "Bryan and World Peace." *Smith College Studies in History* 16 (1931), 233.

Harper's Weekly. "Heliography in the Army." August 14, 1886.

———. "Our Cavalry." April 24, 1886.

Kennan, George. "Santiago de Cuba Revisited." *Outlook* 61 (March 4, 1899), 497–501.

———. "Friction in Cuba: A Special Letter from George Kennan on General Wood's Work." *Outlook* 61 (March 25, 1899), 675–78.

———. "The Sanitary Regeneration of Santiago." *Outlook* 61 (April 15, 1899), 871–77.

———. "A Few Days in Guantanamo." *Outlook* 61 (April 29, 1899), 957–66.

———. "The Government of Santiago." *Outlook* 62 (May 13, 1899), 109–15.

———. "From Santiago to Havana." *Outlook* 62 (May 27, 1899), 202–8.

———. "Destitution and Suffering in Matanzas." *Outlook* 62 (July 15, 1899), 608–14.

———. "The Regeneration of Cuba: General Gomez at Santa Clara," *Outlook* 63 (September 16, 1899), 151–58.

Lawrence, Eugene. "The Apaches Are Coming." *Harper's Weekly,* January 30, 1886, 78.

Lippman, Walter. "The Truth about Leonard Wood." *The Nation* 110 (May 29, 1920), 714.

Literary Digest. "The Americanism of General Leonard Wood." *Literary Digest* 64 (March 6, 1920), 47–52.

Lodge, Henry Cabot. "Our Blundering Foreign Policy." *Forum,* March 1895.

Lunggren, Brengt. "The Case of General Wood." *Journal of Neurosurgery* 56 (1982), 474.

Peffer, W. A. "Imperialism, America's Historic Policy." *North American Review* 171 (August 1900), 246–59.

Porter, Robert. "The Future of Cuba." *North American Review* 168 (April 1899), 418–23.

Remington, Frederic. "A Scout with the Buffalo-Soldiers." *Century Magazine* 37 (April 1889), 903–13.

Roosevelt, Theodore. "General Leonard Wood: A Model American Military Administrator." *Outlook* 61 (January 7, 1899), 19–23.

Runcie, James. "American Misgovernment of Cuba." *North American Review* 170 (February 1900), 284–95.

Sternberg, G. M. "The bacillus icteroides (Sanarelli) and bacillus X (Sternberg)." *Transactions of the Association of American Physicians* 13 (1898), 71.

Tilman, B. R. "Causes of Southern Opposition to Imperialism." *North American Review* 171 (October 1900), 439–46.

Time Magazine. "Island Checkup." April 19, 1926.

Wilson, Ewing. "The Anti-Imperialist Position." *North American Review* 171 (October 1900), 460–68.

Wood, Leonard. "Santiago since the Surrender." *Scribner's Magazine* 25 (May 1899), 515–27.

———. "The Existing Conditions and Needs in Cuba." *North American Review* 168 (May 1899), 593–601.

———. "The Present Situation in Cuba." *The Century* 58 (August 1899), 639–40.

———. "The Military Government of Cuba." *The Annals of the American Academy of Political and Social Sciences* 21 (March 1903), 5–7.

NEWSPAPERS AND MAGAZINES

Arizona Journal Miner
Atlanta Constitution
Atlanta Journal
Boston Advertiser
Chicago Daily Tribune
La Discusion
New York Evening Post
New York Sun
New York Times
New York Tribune
New York World
Philadelphia Public Ledger
Phoenix Herald
San Antonio Daily Express
San Antonio Light

The Spectator
Tucson Arizona Star
Washington Post
Washington Sunday Star

UNPUBLISHED MATERIAL

Herman Hagedorn Papers, Library of Congress, Washington, D.C.
Frank McCoy Papers, Library of Congress, Washington, D.C.
John J. Pershing Papers, Library of Congress, Washington, D.C.
Post Returns, Fort Huachuca, Arizona. National Archives M617, Roll 490.
Theodore Roosevelt Papers, Library of Congress, Washington, D.C.
Theodore Roosevelt Papers, Houghton Reading Room, Harvard University, Cambridge, Mass.
Elihu Root Papers, Library of Congress, Washington, D.C.
Leonard Wood Papers, Library of Congress, Washington, D.C.
Philip S. Hench Walter Read Yellow Fever Collection, University of Virginia, Charlottesville.

Index

343

About the Author

JACK McCALLUM holds an M.D./Ph.D. and is Medical Director of Neuroscience at Baylor Medical Center in Fort Worth, Texas. He also teaches history at Texas Christian University.